Corporate Governance Lessons from Transition Economy Reforms

Corporate Governance Lessons from Transition Economy Reforms

Merritt B. Fox and
Michael A. Heller, Editors

William Davidson Institute, University of Michigan

PRINCETON UNIVERSITY PRESS
PRINCETON AND OXFORD

Published by Princeton University Press, 41 William Street, Princeton, New Jersey 08540

In the United Kingdom: Princeton University Press, 3 Market Place, Woodstock, Oxfordshire OX20 1SY

Library of Congress Cataloging-in-Publication Data

Corporate governance lessons from transition economy reforms / edited by Merritt B. Fox and Michael A. Heller.
p. cm.
Includes bibliographical references and index.
ISBN-13: 978-0-691-12561-9 (hardcover : alk. paper)
ISBN-10: 0-691-12561-9 (hardcover : alk. paper)
1. Corporate governance—Case studies. 2. Corporate governance—Law and legislation—Case studies. I. Fox, Merritt B. II. Heller, Michael, 1962–
HD2741.C77645 2006
338.6—dc22 2005035712

British Library Cataloging-in-Publication Data is available

This book has been composed in Janson

Printed on acid-free paper. ∞

pup.princeton.edu

Printed in the United States of America

10 9 8 7 6 5 4 3 2 1

Contents

Introduction

To DATE, most sophisticated theoretical work on corporate governance has focused on advanced market economies. Faced with the daunting problems of corporate governance in the post-socialist transition economies, scholars have had little more to offer policymakers than this received advanced-economy wisdom. In this volume, we bring together the world's leading corporate governance theorists to focus, for the first time, on the reverse concern: what, if anything, do the reform experiences of transition countries teach about corporate governance more generally? In answering this question, this volume shows that existing corporate governance theory represents a special case derived from the limited experience of advanced market economies, and not necessarily applicable more generally in the world. Conversely, the transition experience points the way toward a broader conception of corporate governance, one with timely implications even for wealthier countries.

This volume returns to the basics of corporate governance: how we define the term, what effect the key elements of governance have on economic performance, and how our understanding of these questions is refined by the greater richness and diversity of corporate experience as revealed by the study of transition countries.

Defining Good Corporate Governance

The first lesson from transition this book offers is to show how the existing definitions can be usefully updated. Scholars have not, to date, given sufficient attention to providing a precise and policy-oriented definition of what constitutes "good corporate governance." Part I defines the term by developing a framework that allows one to pinpoint deviant behavior and trace its links to the real economy. The existing literature has so far focused primarily on marginal changes within developed market economies, with debate breaking down between "Anglo-American" and "Continental" perspectives. But this debate misses insights that can be gained from examining the much greater deviations in corporate behavior from the welfare-maximizing norm that exist in transition countries.

We suggest that *good corporate governance* is best defined by looking to the economic functions of the firm, rather than to any particular set of national corporate laws. From this perspective, firms exhibit good corporate governance when they maximize residuals and, in the case of investor-owned firms, make pro rata distributions to shareholders. A framework built on this narrow definition allows for the most policy-sensitive measurements and focused prescriptions. Our framework disentangles corporate governance from related, but analytically distinct, discussions of microeconomic policy such as how to account for government subsidies or the role of labor and community "stakeholder" interests.

The Elements of Good Corporate Governance

A recurring challenge for policy-oriented research in the corporate governance area is how to pin down the channels through which institutional practices relating to corporate behavior aid or hinder the performance of the real economy. Part II explores the key institutional elements that make up good corporate governance: the intersecting role of law, owners and managers, and capital market entities. In this connection, we invited the world's leading corporate governance scholars to address these issues at a conference cosponsored by the William Davidson Institute and the University of Michigan Law School. The resulting chapters showcase a range of cutting-edge methodologies and paint a rich portrait of the state of corporate governance thinking, tools, and approaches and demonstrate the significant lessons that can be learned from transition experiences.

The Role and Limits of Law

The two chapters of part II sweep the most broadly, measuring and locating the role of law in corporate governance performance. Katharina Pistor's chapter, "Patterns of Legal Change: Shareholder and Creditor Rights in Transition Economies," is a particularly sophisticated entrant in the growing literature that uses cross-country formalized legal indicators to investigate statistically the interaction between legal and economic change. She assembles a database of twenty-four countries covering the period 1990 to 1998, which allows her to show the strong tendency toward convergence of formal legal systems, driven in part by particular groups of American and European Union advisors. But formal convergence is only part of a more complex story, since Pistor finds a wide divergence in enforcement institutions, the quality of which tends to be correlated with economic performance. As to the primary direction of causation underlying this correlation, Pistor writes that "law reform has been primarily responsive to economic change rather than initiating or leading it."

Paul Mahoney presents "The Common Law and Economic Growth: Hayek Might Be Right." Along with Pistor, he leads a second wave of scholars attempting to tease out quantitatively the role and limits of law's effect on economic growth. Mahoney digs into the reported difference in corporate performance between common-law versus civil-law countries. His results suggest that the better performance of common-law countries is not an artifact of different rules of investor protection. Rather, it stems from a more fundamental divergence between the security of property and contract rights in the two systems, with common-law systems providing the greater security.

Constraining Owners and Managers

The two chapters in part III take up the role of the frontline players in corporate governance, the owners and managers. These authors recognize that formal law creates for owners and managers only a loose structure of constraints and incentives. Bernard Black, Reinier Kraakman, and Anna Tarassova contribute "Russian Privatization and Corporate Governance: What Went Wrong?" They explore the intersection of law and owner behavior and note that even the most carefully thought-out formal corporate law cannot by itself prevent massive self-dealing by owners, where owners and managers loot rather than restructure firms, and that this can happen even when the owners and managers have substantial ownership stakes. The authors tell a story of a type of formal law that is highly ineffective at aligning the interests of managers and harmonizing majority shareholder interests with those of minority shareholders. As a result, the owners and managers behave in a far from even a residual-maximizing fashion, let alone providing the minority with pro rata distributions of the gains from corporate activity. The authors draw from the Russian experience the lesson that the background institutions of good corporate governance—a well-trained honest judiciary and requisite enforcement officials, a capable corporate bar and corporate managers with skills at producing rather than looting and an understanding of the long-run value of their reputation—take time to build. Rapid privatization before these institutions are built and having assets end up in the hands of unqualified, looting-oriented owners can represent a step backward from state ownership rather than a step forward.

Roman Frydman, Marek Hessel, and Andrzej Rapaczynski dig further into the role of managers in their chapter, "Why Ownership Matters: Entrepreneurship and Restructuring in Central Europe." They note the widespread findings that enterprise performance depends not just on the switch from state to private ownership, but also on the type of private owners, such as whether they are outside owners or corporate insiders. But why does ownership matter? The key appears to be how corporate governance affects owners' accountability and incentives for risk-taking. All firms in the authors' sample engaged in more or less the same types of restructuring; but outsider-owned firms did better and showed greater variance in performance.

The Role of Market-Supporting Institutions

The three chapters in part IV consider the financial institutional setting within which firms operate. The corporate governance literature has often debated the relative merit of dispersed versus concentrated ownership, and the role of stock markets versus banks in promoting value-maximizing behavior. To explore these issues, Yoshiro Miwa and Mark Ramseyer examine an intriguing example in "Lessons from Japanese Transition, 1870–1910." A hundred years ago Japan faced similar institutional problems as do transition economies today: courts did not work, markets were not developed, statutes were unwritten. Modern corporate governance theory would predict that under such circumstances firms that raised equity from concentrated sources would be more likely to succeed. However, in Japan, the more successful firms raised funds from dispersed investors. For Ramseyer and Miwa the transition experience suggests the surprising lesson that there are only limited conditions under which investors with relatively large stakes can indeed provide a firm value.

The remaining two chapters consider the crucial collateral institutions that affect corporate governance, securities markets, and their regulatory regimes. John Coffee, in "The Lessons of Securities Market Failure: Privatization, Minority Protection, and Investor Confidence," suggests that the corporate governance benefits of good securities regulation have been underappreciated in studies of the relationship between law and economic performance. He reaches this conclusion in part on the basis of a comparison of Czech and Polish privatization. The Czech Republic privatized very rapidly, using vouchers that were broadly distributed among the population. Poland privatized more slowly. Rapid privatization with initially broad distribution of shares is precisely where there is the greatest need for good-quality securities regulation (namely, ownership transparency, high disclosure standards, restrictions on "creeping control" acquisitions, and so on). Yet of the two countries' securities regulation, that of the Czechs was the weaker. The result was distinctly inferior economic performance.

Offering a quite contrasting methodology, Randall Morck, Bernard Yeung, and Wayne Yu contribute "The Information Content of Stock Markets: Why Do Emerging Markets Have Synchronous Stock Price

Movements?" They examine the extent to which share prices in an economy move synchronously, as measured by a factor they call R^2. They show that R^2 varies considerably across the economies of the world. In particular, it is high in emerging economies relative to developed economies. And among developed economies, it is higher in countries that indexes suggest provide less protection to outside investors. All these results are independent of the size of the market, the number of issuers trading, and the extent to which issuer earnings are correlated. Rather, synchronicity in stock returns appears to be best explained by the lack of property rights protection, which discourages informed risk arbitrage. This suggests that differences in R^2 across countries are the result of differences in the extent to which information is impounded in individual share prices and hence the accuracy of share prices as a predictor of future cash flows to shareholders. This is an important conclusion, since theory suggests that outside securities markets can only promote efficient capital allocation and good corporate governance when share prices are relatively well informed.

The Role of Initial Conditions

In part V, we highlight the role of initial conditions in shaping postsocialist transition. Here we use the Russian experience again, this time to highlight the importance of firm boundaries and the initial allocation of shares. With radical transition—the creation of corporate law from scratch—countries have engaged in a grand natural experiment that shows how important initial conditions are to development. Who initially receives shares of newly privatized firms and the boundaries of these firms prove to be just as essential a determinant of the quality of corporate governance as the efficacy of laws, managers, and institutions.

Linking corporate governance theory to policymaking is a dicey project. Early in postsocialist transition, consultants parachuted in ready-made recommendations derived from existing corporate governance theory. With little time to tinker, Western advisors jumped into the fray and adapted policy on the fly. They assumed that whatever the initial share allocation and firm boundaries, markets would work in the way they did in developed countries and guarantee that assets would fairly quickly find their way into the hands of those who would put them to highest-value use. But many transition economies remain stuck in difficult circumstances, in part because of the origins of existing theory. Transition economies are not a simple subset of Western ones; rather, they expand the universe of corporate governance experience and thereby force theorists to ask anew, What makes corporate governance work?

PART I

Framework

CHAPTER ONE

What Is Good Corporate Governance?

Merritt B. Fox and Michael A. Heller

This book draws on a rich array of deviant corporate behavior from economies in transition to craft lessons for corporate governance theory. The very first lesson from transition is that standard corporate law theory needs a better definition of good corporate governance. Theorists have long used the term freely, but rarely explained just what they mean. We define corporate governance by looking to the economic functions of the firm. On the basis of this definition, we develop a typology that comprehensively shows all the channels through which bad corporate governance can inflict damage on a country's real economy. Many of these channels are far more visible when approached from the transition angle, but they are present in rich economies, just harder to spot. This definition helps unify such seemingly diverse experiences as Miwa and Ramseyer's nineteenth-century Japanese case in chapter 6 and Coffee's modern Czech example in chapter 7.

In developing our definition, we use the Russian experience in the first post-Soviet decade for our primary case, in part because it exhibits such a rich array of deviant corporate behavior. Overall, Russian industry performed poorly after privatization. The voluminous literature on transition economies explains this poor performance primarily in terms of continued bureaucratic meddling, poor macroeconomic and tax policy, and low human capital; problems in corporate governance often are mentioned as well but little analyzed.[1]

After the fall of Russian communism, state enterprises were privatized rapidly, stock markets created, and a corporate legal code adopted. However, even at its peak, before the 1998 collapse, the total stock market capitalization of Russia's two hundred largest companies only reached about $130 billion[2]—less than that of Intel Corporation. In early 1999 the numbers were "phenomenally abysmal; if they could sink any further, shares would literally have a value of zero. As it is, the entire market is made up of penny stocks."[3] These numbers represent a trivial fraction of the apparent value of the underlying corporate assets controlled by Russian corporations.[4] The low prices reflect severe corporate governance problems, including the high probability that the firms' underlying assets will be mismanaged grossly and that whatever cash flow is produced will be diverted to benefit insiders or reinvested in unproductive projects, as Black, Kraakman, and Tarassova discuss in chapter 4.[5] What were the consequences of these corporate governance problems for the real economy in Russia?

To answer this question, we define corporate governance in a way that looks to the economic functions of the firm rather than to any particular set of national corporate laws. Firms exhibit good corporate governance when they both maximize the firm's residuals[6]—the wealth generated by real operations of the firm—and, in the case of investor-owned firms, distribute the wealth so generated to shareholders in a pro rata fashion. Bad corporate governance is just the failure of a firm to meet one or both of these conditions. Whether managers operate their firms in ways that meet these conditions depends on the structure of constraints and incentives in which they operate, a structure that depends in part, but only in part, on the prevailing legal system—a point that Rapaczynski develops further in chapter 5. In this chapter, we give more precision to the idea of "bad" corporate governance by developing a novel typology of the kinds of damage to the real economy that loosely constrained and poorly incentivized managers can inflict. By canvassing a rich array of deviant behavior, we identify why this damage has been particularly severe in Russia.

Our analysis is not confined to the Russian experience alone; rather, it provokes rethinking of corporate governance theory more generally. For the first time and in a comprehensive way, we link poor corporate governance to real economy effects. We create an analytic tool that identifies the complete set of vulnerabilities to corporate governance problems that may arise in any economy and that helps to generate more tailored policy responses than previously possible. To skip ahead, the chapter works toward table 1.1, which summarizes the complete framework of corporate governance pathologies. We will arrive there by defining what counts as good corporate governance, and then by drilling down to each of the ways that governance can go wrong.

A Typology of Corporate Governance Failures

A. A Simple Definition

Commentators on transition economies invariably discuss the consequences of "poor corporate governance" but without specifying what that means. What little commentary does exist tends to focus on some idealized set of corporate law rules.[7] In contrast, we measure the quality of corporate governance in terms of the social welfare impact of firm

Table 1.1
Framework of Corporate Governance Pathologies

I. Nonmaximization of residuals	
Pathology 1: Unreformable value-destroying firms fail to close	Arises when an unreformable value-destroying firm can dissipate cash reserves or salvageable assets. Corporate governance is not the key issue when firm has no reserves or salvageable assets, or when subsidies or unsuitable credits are present.
Pathology 2: Viable firms fail to use existing capacity efficiently	Arises when continued firm operation, if undertaken as efficiently as possible and without new investment, would be a positive net present value (NPV) decision, but costs are not minimized, the best price is not obtained for given output, or a non-profit-maximizing output level is chosen.
Pathology 3: Firms misinvest internally generated cash flows	Arises when a firm uses internally generated cash flow to invest in new negative NPV projects instead of paying out this cash flow to shareholders who could invest the funds better elsewhere in the economy.
Pathology 4: Firms fail to implement positive NPV projects	Arises when a firm identifies but then fails to act on positive NPV projects. Managers tend to be risk averse because they can't diversify away unsystematic risk of a firm's project. If others do not pick up the opportunity, the firm's failure also reduces social welfare.
Pathology 5: Firms fail to identify positive NPV projects	Arises when a firm's managers fail to identify positive NPV projects that the firm is particularly well positioned to find. The possibility of venture financing and spinoffs can reduce the prevalence and social costs of this pathology.
II. Non–pro rata distributions	
Pathology 6: Firms fail to prevent diversion of claims	Arises when some residual owners of a firm manipulate corporate, bankruptcy, and other laws to shift ownership away from other residual owners—often by diluting shares held by outside minority shareholders.
Pathology 7: Firms fail to prevent diversion of assets	Arises when some residual owners privately appropriate assets and opportunities belonging to the firm, but leave the firm's formal ownership structure intact.

decision making. We make no prejudgments about which institutional arrangements work best in any particular country. Indeed, Pistor's and Mahoney's work, in chapters 2 and 3, suggests the challenges of such an enterprise. Under our definition, good corporate governance requires two things: (1) managers must maximize their firm's residuals; and (2) firms, at least investor-owned firms, must distribute those residuals on a pro rata basis to shareholders. Let us consider each element in turn.

The first key feature of a well-governed firm is that its managers make decisions that seek to maximize the residuals that the firm generates over time, discounted to present value. Residuals are defined as the difference between what a firm pays at contractually predetermined prices to obtain its inputs and what it receives for its output.[8] We define this criterion in terms of residual maximization rather than share value maximization to avoid foreclosing the possibility that labor- or consumer-owned firms may be optimal in certain situations.[9] In an ordinary investor-owned corporation, however, the residuals go to shareholders who provide the firm's equity-based capital, which is the only input not obtained at contractually predetermined prices. Thus, for such a firm, maximizing share value is equivalent to maximizing residuals.[10]

The conclusion that it is socially desirable for a firm to maximize its residuals flows from two assumptions, both of which are standard in simple models of the corporation: (1) that the firm purchases its inputs and sells its outputs in competitive markets, and (2) that there are no important externalities or subsidies. Thus, the contractually predetermined prices the firm pays for its inputs (other than its equity-based capital) are equal to the value of what the firm takes from society; similarly, the firm's selling prices for its output equals the value of what it gives to society. Maximizing the difference in value between inputs and outputs maximizes the firm's contribution to society and hence constitutes efficient behavior.[11]

In the case of an ordinary investor-owned firm, the second feature of good governance is that the residuals are distributed to shareholders and in a pro rata fashion.[12] Meeting this second condition is not strictly necessary for one-period, static efficiency. For a single period, all that is necessary is that the residuals be maximized, regardless of who receives them. The pro rata distribution condition is helpful, however, in achieving the efficient allocation of resources over time because pro rata distribution greatly increases the ability of firms to raise capital by issuing new equity.

For a firm to raise capital by selling equity at a price worthwhile to its owners, a firm needs credibly to promise to abide by both principles of good corporate governance—striving to maximize its future residuals and guaranteeing shareholders some determinable proportion of these residuals as dividends or other distributions. The expectation of eventually receiving such distributions is what makes worthwhile holding a share as a financial instrument and what induces outsiders to provide cash in return for shares. A firm gains credibility in several ways: by developing a record of abiding by its promises, by being subject to a binding legal system, and by structuring incentives so that managers gain if they fulfill their promises and suffer if they do not. If a firm acts contrary to its promises, it undermines its own record and becomes less able to acquire new equity financing.[13] Note, also, that when a legal system fails to punish such a firm, an individual firm's decision to break its promises imposes externalities: investors become generally less willing to buy equity of other firms governed by the same legal system. In other words, weak corporate governance in existing firms poisons the well for new firms that hope to use equity markets.[14]

Defective corporate governance means that a firm does not meet one or both elements of our definition. Most attention in reports on transition economies has focused on problems relating to non–pro rata distributions: for example, when insiders dilute shares of outsiders, loot companies, fail to pay dividends, or engage in other tactics that deprive outside shareholders of their pro rata share of the wealth generated by the firm.[15] Black, Kraakman, and Tarassova, later in this volume, develop a rich portrait of such non–pro rata behaviors. Non–pro rata distributions indeed do help explain low stock prices and the poor performance of the corporate sector. But failure to maximize residuals has the same effect, indeed even more directly. The vast transition economy literature never makes clear which failure dominates in any particular enterprise fiasco. Instead, bad corporate governance becomes a catchall explanation for problems that should be understood as being quite distinct.[16] Pinning down and separating out these distinctions should prove helpful when it comes time to prescribe policy cures.

A cautionary methodological note is in order at the outset, however. The study of corporate governance in Russia is hampered by two problems. First, serious firm-level econometric study of corporate governance changes in Russia is difficult, if not impossible, because meaningful hard data on enterprise behavior are hard to come by. Firms did not publish credible accounts of their own performance, because managers hid their ongoing thefts of firm assets from outside shareholders and from others, including labor and the mafia, who likewise sought to steal those assets themselves.[17] Back-tax debts, which pervaded the corporate sector, meant that any reported income might be seized, making the effective tax rate 100 percent.[18] Thus, most income statements and balance sheets were fictional. Perhaps surprisingly, Miwa and Ramseyer, in chapter 6, are able to collect more robust corporate data on nineteenth-century Japan than seems available for twenty-first-century Russia. Second, econometric work testing propositions about corporate governance based on country-level comparisons of economic performance is similarly difficult, as evidenced by Pistor's and Mahoney's work. Good corporate governance is neither a necessary nor a sufficient condition for achieving a developed capitalist economy—it simply helps. Italy, for example, has a vibrant economy even though the governance of its corporations generally would fall far short of the standards set out here.[19] Russia, in contrast, likely would have continued to languish economically absent a solution for some of its other pressing problems even if its firms all fully met these standards. The sample size of countries is small relative to all the other factors that affect national economic performance.

These two problems mean that we are left with anecdotal accounts and surveys as our main sources of empirical information. These sources involve their own biases; nevertheless, they present a reasonably coherent picture of the landscape of corporate governance failures. Imposing a theoretical framework on this picture yields a plausible and informative account of the relationship between corporate governance and national economic performance.

B. The Failure to Maximize Residuals

In this section, we identify five distinct pathologies that loosely constrained and poorly incentivized managers may inflict on firms and that may result in the firms' failure to maximize residuals.[20] We focus first on this prong of bad corporate governance because it is crucial to explaining why insiders sometimes do not operate their firm even to maximize their own joint benefit, a puzzle we take up in part III. As we shall see, the initial structure of ownership makes Russian firms particularly vulnerable to these five corporate governance pathologies. When the initial ownership structures intersect with untenable firm boundaries, the pathologies we identify here become self-reinforcing and even more intractable.

1. PATHOLOGY 1: CONTINUED OPERATION OF VALUE-DESTROYING FIRMS

Any economy has some unreformable value-destroying firms that should be shut down immediately.[21] Continued operation of these firms, even if undertaken as efficiently as possible, represents a negative net present value decision from a social point of view: The cost of operation in the current period results in a social loss too great to be offset by social gains, if there are any, from continued operation in subsequent periods.[22] Despite the social harm, institutional arrangements in an economy nevertheless may permit such a firm to continue operating. For example, in Russia the Tutayev Engine Factory continued to operate despite the plant manager's estimate that "it costs the plant about 1.33 rubles to produce about 1 ruble in output."[23] In the case of many unreformable value-destroying firms, poor corporate governance is the main cause of their continued operation, and hence the reason for identifying this problem as the first type of potential corporate governance pathology. Firm managers wish to continue operations in order to hold on to their jobs and the associated perquisites.[24] Because they are not constrained by effective corporate governance mechanisms, the managers get their way. In other cases, however, good corporate governance is not necessary to shut down a firm that in fact should be closed. And in yet other cases, good corporate governance is a necessary but not a sufficient condition to close the firm. Making these distinctions is important for identifying effective policy responses.

a. When Is Corporate Governance Relevant? Retain the assumption for a moment that an unreformable value-destroying firm purchases inputs and sells outputs in competitive markets; that there are no important externalities; and that credit and other finance is extended to firms only on a reasonably informed, rational basis. Even with no new investment, such a firm's ordinary operations result, in the current period, in a negative cash flow (one that is sufficiently negative that expected future cash flow, discounted to present value, would, even if positive, be unable to offset it). The firm thus would lack enough current cash flow to purchase the inputs it needs to continue production and would lack cash flows in the future to use as a basis to obtain credit or other finance sufficient to cover this deficit.

The importance of corporate governance here depends entirely on whether the firm has any cash reserves or assets with significant salvage value. Without reserves or salvageable assets, the firm would be forced to close immediately, regardless of how much its managers wanted to continue operations, and regardless of how ineffective existing corporate governance mechanisms were in restraining the managers. Russia's generally outmoded factories suggest that many firms lacked assets with any significant salvage value.[25] There was also a general cash shortage.[26] Thus, absent subsidies and problems in the way credit is extended, many firms whose continued operation was value destroying would have shut down promptly even though the corporate governance regime was highly ineffective. Neither improved corporate governance nor an effective bankruptcy regime would have been necessary to eliminate such firms.[27]

For firms with reserves or salvageable assets, however, effective corporate governance is necessary to shut down the firm immediately. Even if the legal regime reflects a sound model, there is still the problem of enforcement, as Pistor shows in chapter 2. With weak enforcement, managers can indulge their desires to continue operation. Where cash reserves are available, the cash can be used directly to buy the needed inputs. Where the firm has salvageable assets, cash can be raised by selling the assets or using them as a basis for gaining credit. Many value-destroying Russian firms did have assets with significant salvage value.[28] Manufacturing businesses, for example, often were located inside large cities on real estate with far more value in other uses. If a firm has a negative cash flow, its managers nevertheless may be able to keep operating by cashing out the salvage value of these assets to acquire needed inputs. Even with a positive cash flow, closing the firm may be socially desirable once the rental value of the land is counted properly as an opportunity cost.[29]

b. The Role of Subsidies and Inappropriate Credit and Finance. Now, drop the assumptions made above concerning subsidies, credit, and finance. Where there is a subsidy, or where credit or finance is extended on other than a reasonably informed and rational basis, a firm can have a positive cash flow even though the social benefit from the firm's output might be less than the social cost of its inputs. Under such circumstances, the firm's continued operation, even though involving a social loss, can be perfectly consistent with maximizing residuals. Corporate governance mechanisms that push a firm's managers to maximize residuals will not lead by themselves to the socially desirable result of closing down these firms. Indeed, for firms without reserves or salvageable assets, the quality of corporate governance is not even relevant. Such firms will be shut down, regardless of the quality of corporate governance, only if the subsidies or inappropriate credit provision is ended.[30]

Russia continued to provide many subsidies, particularly in the energy area.[31] The system by which input suppliers were paid, often involving barter, was highly chaotic, implying that credit was not extended in a rational, well-informed fashion.[32] Workers often became involuntary creditors when firms did not pay them.[33] All this suggests that, while many Russian firms that were continuing to operate should have been shut down immediately, improved corporate governance would not, or would not by itself, have solved the problem. Instead, elimination of subsidies and improvement of the credit process were necessary reforms.

In sum, Russian firms that should have been shut down immediately fall into three groups. The first consists of firms with no cash reserves or assets with significant salvage value that did not benefit from subsidies or unsuitable credit extensions. These firms were presumably closing on their own, no matter how bad their corporate governance mechanisms. In the second group are firms with no cash reserves or assets with significant salvage value but that did benefit from subsidies or unsuitable credit extensions. Given the pervasiveness of the problems that existed in the economy, particularly the provision of energy at below world market prices, this second group may well be much larger than the first.[34] Effectively addressing the subsidy and credit problems will cause these firms to close, but they will not close otherwise. Improvements in corporate governance will have no effect on this second group. The third group, which is also large, includes firms with cash reserves or assets with significant salvage value that also benefited from subsidies or unsuitable credit extensions. These firms will not close unless there is both an improvement in corporate governance and an end to the subsidies and unsuitable credit extensions.

c. The ZiL Example. Moscow's ailing ZiL truck company is a useful example of a firm in the third group. The company was a "dinosaur"[35] that continued to produce many of the same poor-quality trucks that it did under the Soviet regime, despite the trucks' terrible reputation and scant market.[36] As two reporters note:

> The total amount of [postprivatization] state assistance to ZiL through various channels is estimated at approximately $100 million. . . .
>
> . . . "The plant never regarded the money it received as credits that had to be paid back." . . .
>
> While receiving money for the production of trucks that customers were unwilling to pay for, ZiL continued to ship them out. . . .
>
> . . . From force of old Soviet habit, it kept pushing to fulfill a plan that was long gone, at a time when it should have been cutting production and thinking about structural reorganization.[37]

As the company continued to fall apart, Moscow mayor Yuri Luzhkov acquired a controlling stake for the city in the firm but kept incumbent management in place.[38] Consistent with Rapaczynski's findings in chapter 5, these corporate insiders performed poorly, despite privatization. Rather than closing the firm and liquidating its main assets, the mayor reportedly began ordering city services to buy ZiL vehicles only.[39] He also secured a large new line of credit on the basis of the firm's main asset, "tens of hectares of prime land in south Moscow with a potential market value of hundreds of millions of dollars."[40] The mayor's plans were to relocate the firm's production facilities, raise about $35 million by selling forty-nine-year leases to some of the land, and then transfer the new funds to the company rather than to shareholders or to more viable firms.[41] But, as one commentator suggested, "it is not clear that even Luzhkov can create a market for ZiL trucks."[42]

Shutting down the firm at the outset likely would have been the residual-maximizing decision. The government could have targeted its limited subsidies to providing a social safety net for workers,[43] and the land could have been sold to its highest-value users at a price that would have substantially benefited shareholders.[44] As it was, outside shareowners "realized that, despite the municipal and federal authorities' special treatment of this flagship of the automotive industry, the enterprise was a hopeless failure, and [when] they tried to exert some direct influence on the situation . . . [it] proved to be not such an easy thing to do."[45]

2. PATHOLOGY 2: FAILURE TO USE EXISTING CAPACITY EFFICIENTLY

The second type of pathology arises when continued operation, if undertaken as efficiently as possible and without new investment, would be a positive net present value decision, but operation is not done as efficiently as possible. Costs are not minimized, the best price is not obtained for a given level of output, or a non-profit-maximizing output level is chosen—again, all common problems in Russia.[46] Thus, residuals are not maximized. Such firms should not shut down, but they should deploy existing facilities more efficiently.[47] Their residuals shortfall represents a social welfare–diminishing corporate governance failure.

Consider, for example, the Baltic Shipping Company (BSC), "Russia's oldest and best known shipping enterprise."[48] Under the Soviets, the firm already had wide experience working on world markets, but they relied on inexpensive Russian fuel to cover for management deficiencies, and these deficiencies, unlike the low fuel prices, persisted into the postprivatization period:

> Nearly everyone admits that the management at BSC has simply not been up to the challenges of a new economy. . . .
>
> In his parting words, former president Filimonov, who retains a place on the board, pretty much admitted the management could not adapt. "Those titles we've become accustomed to hearing, such as deputy chief of finances, are simply not those functions that these people have become used to fulfilling."[49]

Although the firm could have been profitable, BSC faced a "spiral of decline" that could "lead to the company's fleet disappearing completely."[50] According to one official, "'It's difficult to say how many ships we have in operation, because at any moment, we could get another call saying another ship has been seized [by creditors].'"[51]

The widespread existence of Pathology 2 may mask the potential extent of Pathology 1. If firms generally are not using their inputs efficiently, the marginal products of these inputs are likely to be lower, and thus, in a competitive economy, the price that needs to be paid for them and the opportunity cost of their use will be lower as well. A wholesale reduction in Pathology 2 will increase the price and social opportunity cost of at least some, and quite possibly all, major classes of inputs.[52] Input price adjustments may sharply increase the number of firms displaying Pathology 1 as the increased opportunity cost of their inputs makes their continued operation socially undesirable.

3. PATHOLOGY 3: MISINVESTMENT OF INTERNALLY GENERATED CASH FLOW

The third type of pathology arises when a firm uses its internally generated cash flow to invest in new negative net present value projects. Instead of making bad investments, such a firm should pay out this cash flow to shareholders. Shareholders could invest these funds better elsewhere in the economy.[53] An example of Pathology 3 includes the seemingly responsible act of using funds labeled by accountants as depreciation to replace worn-out plant and equipment, if doing so is a negative net present value project. Pathology 3 can arise in conjunction with, or independently of, Pathology 2. Significant indirect evidence from two sources suggests that Pathology 3 is widespread in Russia.

First, consider the paucity of interfirm cash flows in Russia. In any economy, good investment opportunities are unlikely to be spread so evenly among existing enterprises that interfirm transfers of cash flows through capital markets are not called for. Nor is the quality of existing firms' opportunities likely to be consistently superior to the opportunities that could be found by new firms. Thus, some existing firms (capital-surplus firms) will have cash flows greater than what is needed to fund all their positive net present value projects; other existing firms (capital-deficit firms) will have insufficient cash flows to fund all such projects. In addition, there will exist new firms that have positive net present value projects but that, by definition, have no cash flows at all. Thus, interfirm cash flow transfers are called for from surplus firms to deficit firms and new firms. In a market economy with clearly distinct firms, these transfers are accomplished when surplus firms pay dividends and deficit firms and new firms enter the capital markets, through, for example, the offering of new equity. In Russia, firms paid little or nothing in the way of dividends[54] and equity finance was negligible.[55] The lack of interfirm transfers strongly suggests that the surplus firms were instead displaying Pathology 3 and likely investing in negative net present value projects.[56]

The second source of indirect evidence for Pathology 3 relates to firms' failure to make pro rata distributions of residuals. One way that controlling shareholders can divert a disproportionate share of residuals to themselves is to have the firm invest in projects personally benefiting these shareholders. On balance, controlling shareholders may prefer to fund such projects, even if they have a negative net present value—their personal benefits more than outweigh the reduction in share value from implementing the project. Controlling shareholders will be able to indulge these preferences if the mechanisms to constrain non–pro rata distribution of dividends are weak. The abundant evidence of non–pro rata distributions in Russia also strongly suggests that Pathology 3 is still likely to be prevalent.

4. PATHOLOGY 4: FAILURE TO IMPLEMENT POSITIVE NET PRESENT VALUE PROJECTS

The fourth pathology of residual nonmaximization arises directly or indirectly when a firm identifies, but then fails to act on, positive net present value projects. If others do not pick up the opportunity, the firm's failure reduces social welfare, because of the forgone chance to deploy funds to produce a return greater than the cost.

Pathology 4 is a direct result of corporate governance failures in cases in which managers, because of weak control mechanisms, reject a positive net present value project because they wish to avoid personal risk. Managers tend to be risk averse because they cannot diversify away the unsystematic risk associated with any individual firm project. If managers can get away with it, they may reject projects with high expected returns if the projects have high unsystematic risk as well, even though such rejections are not in the interests of shareholders or society as a whole. By contrast, portfolio shareholders, who can diversify their holdings, are risk neutral with respect to unsystematic project-level risk. Management risk aversion causes problems everywhere, but the problems were likely accentuated in established Russian firms because incumbent managers typically internalized a high degree of risk aversion through Soviet-era careers in which punishment for major mistakes far exceeded gains from major successes.[57] Rapaczynski's work in chapter 5, this volume, reinforces this view that the type of private owner matters, with firms controlled by the prior incumbent managers typically undergoing less successful restructuring.

Corporate governance failures also can lead firms indirectly to forgo positive net present value projects. Consider a firm with willing managers and with the prospect of a value-creating project that is nevertheless unable to proceed because financing is unavailable at a price equal to the capital's social opportunity cost.[58] The lack of financing may be an externality imposed by corporate governance failures in other firms. When firms generally fail to make pro rata distributions and to maximize residuals, they may severely undermine the ability of firms with good projects to acquire financing through new equity offerings. Banks are the usual alternative sources for outside finance, but in Russia, banks are still providing little long-term corporate lending. The lack of a vibrant new equity market or of bank financing proves fatal for good projects in firms that do not generate sufficient internal funds to self-finance the project.[59]

In Russia, failures by established firms to take advantage of what appear to be positive net present value projects have been spectacularly large. Consider, for example, the saga at Segezhabumprom, one of Russia's biggest pulp and paper mills.[60] Swedish owners acquired a 57 percent stake in the firm, while a major pulp distributor and the Karelian regional government controlled most of the rest of the shares. Early in the relationship, when the town of Segezha had run out of fuel oil, the Swedes were sufficiently enthusiastic that they agreed to "burn expensive wood chips, normally used in paper production, to prevent the town from freezing."[61] Later, the Swedes identified, and committed to make, more than $100 million in new investments. However, the modernization plans provoked local suspicion that there would be job losses, prompting a campaign to force the Swedes out, in a drive that included judicial findings that the Swedes' initial share purchases had been illegal.[62] A breakpoint occurred when the Russian co-owners—the regional government and the major distributor—refused to cofund the working capital to keep the plant open.[63] By the end of this episode, the Swedes had abandoned the investment and written off their ownership stake, but only after the existing managers and local government officials had driven them off, using "mafia-style threats against [their] staff."[64] A story of this sort is likely to scare off even a determined large-scale investor, which in most countries could protect itself using the control powers that come with large shareownership. The story is even more discouraging for individual noncontrol portfolio investors. As discussed further in part V, events such as those at Segezhabumprom also suggest that Russian corporate law enforcement may be so weak that the results of the ordinary processes of corporate decision making are not respected by officials charged with enforcing property rights. Incumbent managers still appear to have de facto property rights in assets whose title is nominally in the hands of the corporation.

5. PATHOLOGY 5: FAILURE TO IDENTIFY POSITIVE NET PRESENT VALUE PROJECTS

The fifth type of pathology arises when a firm's managers fail even to identify positive net present value projects that the firm, through its specialization and the resulting accumulation of knowledge, is particularly well positioned to find.[65] Organizational capacity to identify these opportunities is related to the incentives available to firm employees for identifying such projects as well as the incentives for them to help one another in a joint endeavor to do so.[66]

In the United States, venture capital significantly reduces the social costs of Pathology 5 by making available funds for promising projects that employees identify, but managers misassess. Venture capital also significantly lessens the effects of Pathology 4 on the U.S. economy by making spinoffs possible whereby employees suggesting promising projects can implement the proposal by creating a new firm, despite the employer's rejection. The possibility of getting rich in a spinoff gives employees substantial incentives to identify positive net present value projects even if they work for firms that ultimately may not implement the ideas.[67] Furthermore, when spinoffs occur, Pathologies 4 and 5 do not harm the economy, because the project is implemented anyway.[68]

In Russia, venture capital has not been readily available.[69] Therefore, Pathology 5 is likely to be more prevalent in Russia than in the United States, and Pathology 4 is likely to be more damaging. Ronald Gilson and Bernard Black have argued persuasively that a necessary condition for developing venture capital is a vibrant equity market.[70] Miwa and Ramseyer's Japanese textile example in chapter 6 in this volume reinforces the view that even a developing economy can create a significant public equity market under certain conditions. But Russia will not be able to develop such a market until most of its firms begin to try to maximize residuals and give pro rata distributions.[71] Again, we see the cumulative, self-reinforcing tendency of multiple corporate governance pathologies.

C. The Failure to Make Pro Rata Distributions

The second feature of good corporate governance is that a firm makes the residuals it generates available on a pro rata basis to the residual claimants, that is, to the common shareholders in an investor-owned company. Much of modern corporate law has been built around this principle, not only in rules requiring that dividends and distributions be made pro rata, but also in the basic fiduciary rules policing non-arm's-length transactions involving insiders and the corporation.[72] In post-privatization Russia, violation of this second feature has been the most visible and widely reported symptom of bad corporate governance. Just as nonmaximization comes in different flavors, Russian firms have exhibited a wide range of non–pro rata distributions, which we simplify into two main groups, each with many variations, explored in more depth by Black, Kraakman, and Tarassova in chapter 4. Loosely, one type is what we call "diversion of claims" and the other, "diversion of assets." We explore each in turn.

1. PATHOLOGY 6: DIVERSION OF CLAIMS

To give just a few illustrations, ranging from blatant to subtle, managers divert claims of the corporation when they refuse to register share purchases by outsiders,[73] refuse to recognize board directors properly elected by outside shareholders,[74] dilute stock in ways that freeze out outsiders by issuing shares to insiders for inadequate consideration,[75] or engage in fake bankruptcies that wipe out shareowners' interests.[76] The key feature of these non–pro rata distributions is that the people perpetrating them, usually insider owner-managers, are keeping the firm, including its assets and opportunities, intact. They gain instead by manipulating the corporate legal system and the bankruptcy law and other laws in an effort to reduce or eliminate the claims of some or all of the firm's shareholders on the firm's residuals—usually wiping out the outside minority shareholders.[77] As one investor put it, "'A 51% shareholding interest in a Russian company conveys to the owner a license to steal from the remaining 49%.'"[78]

In one notorious case that dragged on for years, the incumbent manager at Kuban Gypsum-Knauf refused to vacate even though he had been fired by the majority owner, a German company.[79] Supported by the local government, the manager installed Cossack guards, held his own shareholder meetings, locked out the owners, diluted the owners' stock, and ignored dozens of court rulings against him over the years.[80] Finally, and for the first time in Russia, the German owners were able to wrestle their way back in, following intervention by a commission headed by the prime minister.[81] According to one Knauf lawyer, "'It's a sort of legal nihilism. . . . The farther from Moscow, the less attention they pay to the legal side of things. There is no understanding of a final court decision.'"[82]

And managers were not the only ones diverting control. Reports suggest that local and regional governments with minority-share interests began engaging in the same game, forcing firms into bankruptcy over unpaid taxes and then asserting control, in essentially a form of renationalization in cases where tax rates are absurdly high, exceeding 100 percent marginal rates.[83] Also, outside shareholders such as those associated with financial-industrial groups (FIGs) have taken over firms, replaced managers, and then also froze out minority shareholders, including employees.[84]

Many of these tactics are familiar to students of the history of Western corporate law, as Mahoney explores in chapter 3, but in Russia this game seems limited only by the creativity of those controlling the firm: the Russian regulatory apparatus has been notoriously ineffective in controlling such diversions. To give one example, in late 1997, insider shareholders had the Sidanko oil company offer exclusively to themselves, for nominal consideration, a form of bonds that were convertible into Sidanko shares.[85] Once the conversion occurred, the remaining shareholders would see their ownership stake diluted down to one-third of their original claim, yet the company gained no significant new assets.[86] The only unusual aspect of this share dilution was that for the first time in its history, the Russian Securities and Exchange Commission, in the glare of particularly intense negative press about the scheme, intervened, in early 1998, and blocked the issuance of the convertible bonds. As a result, the majority insiders agreed to negotiate with minority shareholders.[87] Such regulatory oversight has been extremely rare in Russia. But even this victory was Pyrrhic. Since then, Sidanko insiders apparently have forced the company into a fake bankruptcy, effectively freezing out another major shareholder, British Petroleum, which had invested $500 million in the firm for 10 percent ownership, a stake now apparently worthless despite the valuable assets that the reorganized firm will control.[88]

Professor Coffee, in his comparison in part IV of the relatively successful Polish privatization experience and relatively unsuccessful Czech experience, gives considerable credit to well-enforced securities law rules requiring ownership transparency and prohibiting any person or group from crossing a certain percentage of ownership threshold without making a tender offer for all the firm's shares. In countries with relatively weak corporate laws, such securities law rules may be necessary conditions to prevent widespread diversion of claims. The Russian experience, however, suggests that so many things were wrong that they would not constitute sufficient conditions.[89]

2. PATHOLOGY 7: DIVERSION OF ASSETS

The second major class of non–pro rata distributions, and the last pathology in our framework, involves direct diversion of assets and opportunities belonging to the firm. The key feature of this type of corporate governance failure is that insiders leave the ownership structure intact as they hollow out the firm.[90] For managers, diversion of assets may be accomplished by outright looting of the firm—taking cash or assets belonging to the firm and effectively giving title to themselves.[91] Or it may take the form of sweetheart business deals with firms controlled by insiders or their families,[92] using, for example, transfer-pricing agreements that move profits to subsidiaries or parents in which the insiders have a larger interest.[93] According to one report, "Protecting sweetheart financial deals is behind much of the hostility to outside investors. Virtually every Russian enterprise, big or small, is surrounded by "independent" companies set up by managers or their families. In many cases, sales and purchasing contracts are structured to go through these firms, raking off profits from the main enterprise."[94]

Russian firms also engage in non–pro rata distribution of residuals when they continue to pay for redundant shareholder employees or when they provide public services without compensation or relief from reasonably and equitably imposed tax obligations. The experience of Tatneft shows a simple but creative form of non–pro rata distribution in favor of a local-government shareholder. According to one report,

> Tatneft is the victim of parasitism, pure and simple. . . . [Regional] bureaucrats who control the company essentially were under orders to borrow as much money as possible on international capital markets to support the region's economy and the government's pet programs. . . .
>
> . . . The company piled on almost $800 million in debt in 1997 alone, and now has over $1 billion of the stuff on its balance sheet. Tatneft was forced to make sizeable loans to the regional government (now broke).[95]

Neither the diversion of assets nor the diversion of claims noted in the previous section necessarily decreases social welfare in a static analysis—the diversions merely redistribute wealth from one group of owners to another. But moving to a dynamic analysis changes the story. If outsiders do not believe that they will receive pro rata distributions, then they will be unwilling generally to treat shares as financial assets, and they will be unwilling to provide equity finance in exchange for anything less than total control.[96] So the prevalence of diversion imposes a substantial externality on the Russian enterprise sector. Because potential outside investors cannot protect against ex post diversions of their investments in firms that turn out to be successful, they have little ex ante incentive to invest on terms that would be appealing to firms with positive net present value projects.[97]

D. A Simple Framework Meets Complex Failures

Table 1.1 above summarizes our framework of Russia's corporate governance pathologies. Real-world cases do not fit neatly into one or another of the boxes we describe, but rather represent complex mixtures of several failures. To start, if managers are neither sufficiently constrained nor given incentives to prevent the diverting of claims, they similarly will be able to divert assets—both types of diversion may be undertaken at once, often in ways that are hard to tease apart.[98] Next, there is a potential interaction between the failure to make pro rata distributions and the failure to maximize residuals.

Some tactics used to effect a non–pro rata distribution of a firm's wealth have no direct effect on residual maximization. This generally would be true of diversion of claims and of brazen, outright theft of assets. Other tactics, however, do reduce a firm's residuals; for example, when owner-managers grant themselves unjustifiably large perquisites,[99] make non-arm's-length sweetheart deals involving the company and its insiders,[100] or engage in direct thefts of assets that require considerable efforts to cover up.

Finally, a management intently focused on, and especially skilled in, diversions may have neither the time nor the ability to give adequate attention to maximizing residuals as well. Consider AvtoVAZ, Russia's largest automaker coming out of the Soviet era. The company evidenced several of the pathologies of nonmaximization of residuals: it continued to employ 114,000 workers and essentially constituted the town of Togliatti; production took 450 worker-hours per car, compared with 15 worker-hours for Toyota; seven of ten current production models were designed in the 1970s; the firm lacked working capital; and the size of the plant made changeover to new production extremely expensive.[101] Poor management undermined the company in many ways: working capital disappeared, "insider deals and criminal groups sap would-be profits, and attempts at reform have been half-baked at best."[102] According to one analyst, "The company is going to die a death by a thousand cuts. It's just going to sit there . . . until someone sees the potential value in some of its assets, strips them out and creates a different franchise or does a complete management overhaul."[103] With its mix of management failures, the company became the country's largest tax laggard.[104] To get an extension on tax arrears, the firm guaranteed that it would dilute its stock enough to give 51 percent of voting shares to the government if the firm missed two tax payments.[105] But then the firm proved unable to finish cars, because "almost the entire amount of income [was] used to pay taxes."[106] After missing several tax payments, AvtoVAZ agreed to what amounted to renationalization.[107]

And so, with AvtoVAZ in mind, we turn to part II and examine in more detail how firm performance is linked to the key elements of good corporate governance. That is, how do the mediating effects of law, owners and managers, and stock markets affect firm behavior and its impact on the real economy?

Notes

Reprinted from N.Y.U. Law Review, vol. 75 no. 6, Merritt Fox and Michael Heller, *Corporate Governance Lessons from Russian Enterprise Fiascoes*, p. 1720, copyright 2000, with permission from New York University.

1. *See, e.g., Organisation for Econ. Co-operation and Dev.* (OECD), OECD Economic Surveys 1997–1998: Russian Federation 129–35 (1997) (listing "barriers to restructuring and investment: corporate governance, capital markets, the tax system, and regional protectionism"); Anders Aslund, *A Crisis of Confidence*, Moscow Times, June 3, 1998, at 8, 1998 WL 11690335 (noting that "the fundamental issue is . . . not primarily macroeconomic. All along, Russia has suffered from serious

problems in corporate governance"). *See also* ch. 4, this volume, in which Black, Kraakman, and Tarassova offer a comprehensive account of Russian privatization failures.

2. *See* Gary Peach, *1997 an Outstanding Year Despite Market Narrowness*, Moscow Times, Jan. 13, 1998, Lexis, World Library, Mostms file. This peak represented an elevenfold improvement over 1994, when total stock market capitalization, based on voucher auctions prices, was less than $12 billion. *See* Maxim Boycko et al., Privatizing Russia 117 (1995). By the summer of 1998, "the Moscow Times index of 50 leading shares hit an all-time bottom, lower than its starting level four years ago." Katy Daigle, *Bill Improves Shareholder Rights in Russia*, Moscow Times, July 14, 1998, Lexis, World Library, Mostms file; *see also, e.g.*, Patricia Kranz, *Fall of an Oligarch*, Bus. Wk., Mar. 1, 1999, at 44, 44 ("From its peak in October, 1997, the market capitalization of [these] three big industrial holdings—Sidanko Oil, Svyazinvest Telecommunications, and Norilsk Nickel—has dropped from about $31 billion to $3.8 billion").

3. Gary Peach, *Poor Management Destroys Sberbank, Tatneft, MGTS*, Moscow Times, Dec. 15, 1998, at 14, 1998 WL 11691867.

4. Put another way, as measured by stock prices, a barrel of proven oil reserves owned by a Russian oil company was worth about one-twentieth of a similar barrel owned by a Western oil company. *See* Boycko et al., *supra* note 2, at 120; *Das Kapital Revisited*, Economist, Apr. 8, 1995, Survey, at 15, 16 ("[A] barrel of oil in the ground owned by a Russian company is worth 10 cents. A barrel owned by a Western company is worth $5.50"). This disparity is striking because oil is a quintessential export product with a uniform and well-recognized global value. Of course, poor corporate governance is just one important factor in the low stock price equation; other factors include political instability and expropriation risk.

5. *See also* Floyd Norris, *The Russian Way of Corporate Governance*, N.Y. Times, Apr. 5, 1999, at A20 (noting that Russia's second-largest oil company stock value declined 98 percent in part because of poor corporate governance).

6. A firm's residuals are defined as the difference between what a firm pays at contractually predetermined prices for its inputs and what it receives for its outputs. *See* ch. 1, sec. I.A for a more precise statement of this definition.

7. *See, e.g.*, OECD, OECD Principles of Corporate Governance (1999) (outlining principles of corporate governance recommended for OECD countries).

8. Note that cost of inputs includes expenditures for real investment. Thus, in any given period, a firm's cash flow from operations—its cost of inputs other than real investment minus its revenues from sale of output—either can be distributed to the firm's residual claimants during that period, in which case they become residuals in that period, or can be expended to purchase real investment assets. The rationale for such reinvestment is to create a larger firm cash flow in some subsequent period that then would be available for distribution as residuals to residual claimants.

9. *See* generally Henry Hansmann, The Ownership of Enterprise (1996) (discussing circumstances in which labor-owned, customer-owned, and other types of firms may succeed).

10. *See* Oliver Williamson, *Corporate Governance*, 93 Yale L.J. 1197, 1198–1200 (1984) (discussing problems created by multiple classes of corporate constituencies).

11. We make the standard assumptions that the firm purchases its inputs and sells

its outputs in competitive markets and that there are no important externalities or subsidies, but not because we believe they are consistently true in Russia or any other country—clearly they are not. Instead, we make these assumptions because they allow us to focus on the social welfare effects of activities that take place within the firm in reaction to the constraints imposed directly by the legal system and by the firm's markets for inputs, outputs, and capital. Such a focus allows us to separate out more precisely the different problems in the Russian economy. Thus, these assumptions allow for more precise policy analysis. Their standard nature also makes it easier to draw larger corporate governance lessons from the Russian experience because most analyses of corporate governance problems in other countries make the same assumptions.

12. *See* Richard A. Brealey & Stewart C. Myers, Principles of Corporate Finance 5, 63 (6th ed. 2000). Fast-growing firms, such as Microsoft, frequently reinvest all operational cash flow rather than pay dividends. Nevertheless, the only reason to hold shares in such a company is the prospect that, at some point, it will make pro rata dividends or other distributions to its shareholders. *See supra* note 8 (discussing reinvestment of cash flows from operations).

13. *See* Bernard S. Black, *The Legal and Institutional Preconditions for Strong Securities Markets*, 48 UCLA L. Rev. 781 (2001).

14. *See id.*; *see also* Andrew Jack, *Pouring Oil on Troubled Waters*, Fin. Times (London), Jan. 19, 2000, at 21 (noting that, because of poor corporate governance, "foreigners were also far less keen on the Russian stock market last year. . . . There was a net outflow of $400 million in portfolio investment during the first nine months of 1999, compared with an inflow of $8 billion for all of 1998").

15. *See, e.g.*, Black, Kraakman, and Tarassova *supra* note 1, at 1765 (focusing on self-dealing explanations for poor Russian corporate performance).

16. The mixed corporate governance problems may be difficult to tease apart. For example, one commentator notes that "problems range from murder to bad market trends, but all boil down to basic corporate governance: Directors and their cohorts appear to have milked or outright plundered the companies to the detriment of any outside shareholders, real or potential." Mark Whitehouse, *The Other Side of the Boom*, Moscow Times, Sept. 16, 1997, Lexis, World Library, Mostms file. When insiders gut a firm, they could be failing to maximize residuals according to several of the pathologies we identify as well as making non–pro rata distributions.

17. *See* World Bank, World Development Report 1996: From Plan to Market 55 (1996); Dmitru Vasilyev, *Remarks at the Luncheon of the American Chamber of Commerce in Russia* (Dec. 4, 1998), *in* Lexis, News Library, Sovnws file (stating that "at present . . . the board of directors and the excessive power of the director make theft of company assets possible").

18. *See* Anna Meyendorff, Barter in Russia 17 (Dec. 1998) (unpublished manuscript, on file with the authors).

19. *See* Luigi Zingales, *The Value of a Voting Right: A Study of the Milan Stock Exchange Experience*, 7 Rev. Fin. Stud. 125, 146 (1994) (suggesting that huge control premium for shares of Italian firms shows poor corporate governance regime).

20. Note that we continue to assume that the firm purchases its inputs and sells its outputs in competitive markets and that there are no important externalities or subsidies. Therefore, the firm's input costs should reflect the social opportunity

costs of continued operation and its output prices should reflect the social benefits of production.

21. For some American examples, *see* James Surowiecki, *Why Won't Anyone Pull the Plug on UPN?* New Yorker, Apr. 3, 2000, at 32, 32 (puzzling over question why "companies and divisions are kept afloat long after they've stopped creating value and started destroying it. Plenty of businesses exist only—well, because they exist").

22. More precisely, for a firm to fall into this category, two requirements must be met. First, the social benefit from the firm's output in the current period must be less than the social cost of its inputs. Second, after comparing the social benefits and costs for each subsequent period, and discounting the difference to present value, the aggregate of these discounted differences must be either negative or, if positive, less than the deficit in the current period. In terms of current operations, this assumes that the firm operates at lowest possible cost for the level of output chosen and that it chooses the level of output that will maximize its cash flow from operations. In terms of decisions made in the current period that affect future periods, this assumes that the firm follows an optimal investment policy, which commonly would mean undertaking no investment at all.

23. Maura Reynolds, *A Russian Company Town's Miracle*, L.A. Times, Mar. 5, 1999, at A1.

24. *See* European Bank for Reconstruction & Devevelopment (EBRD), Transition Report 1998, at 32 (1998) (noting lack of effective checks on insider managers in transition economies); *id.* at 142 (describing conflict of interest between "private objectives of managers" and investors in bank privatizations); Roman Frydman et al., *Investing in Insider-Dominated Firms: A Study of Russian Voucher Privatization Funds, in* 1 Corporate Governance in Central Europe and Russia 187, 219–20 (Roman Frydman et al. eds., 1996); Cheryl W. Gray & Kathryn Hendley, *Developing Commercial Law in Transitional Economies: Examples from Hungary and Russia, in* The Rule of Law and Economic Reform in Russia 139, 154 (Jeffrey D. Sachs & Katharina Pistor eds., 1997); Meyendorff, *supra* note 18, at 15. For an analysis of the same phenomenon in the American context, *see* Surowiecki, *supra* note 21, at 32 (noting that "the value that the [firm] is destroying can seem distant; the rewards it brings to those on [the] payroll are immediate").

25. *See* Maura Reynolds, *Yeltsin Legacy Impressive but Clouded*, L.A. Times, Jan. 1, 2000, at A1 (stating that "shareholders have no guarantee that their stock certificates have real value").

26. *See* Meyendorff, *supra* note 18, at 16.

27. *See* World Bank, *supra* note 17, at 45 (noting that government policies such as macroeconomic stabilization and credible commitment to reform play largest role in whether enterprises in transition economies actually adjust).

28. *See* EBRD, *supra* note 24, at 33 (describing how loss-making Russian firms use various devices to solve cash flow problems); World Bank, *supra* note 17, at 55 (describing how Russian corporate insiders divert assets to other firms they also control).

29. *See* Brealey & Myers, *supra* note 12, at 123 (describing alternate use of land as opportunity cost).

30. *See* EBRD, *supra* note 24, at 33 (showing how subsidies and credit extension support failing Russian firms); World Bank, *supra* note 17, at 45.

31. *See* World Bank, *supra* note 17, at 45 (noting drop in direct subsidies but significant increase in tax arrears and ad hoc tax exemptions); *IEA Urges the Elimination of Subsidies in Developing Nations*, Petroleum Economist, Dec. 1999, at 59, 59 (noting that sizable subsidies remain in Russia's energy sector); *Coal Sector to Develop Without State Subsidies*, BBC Summary of World Broadcasts, Feb. 11, 2000, Lexis, News Library, Non-U.S. file (relaying ITAR-TASS report of February 1, 2000, that Ministry of Fuel and Energy set goal of subsidy-free energy industry for 2000).

32. *See* Clifford Gaddy & Barry W. Ickes, To Restructure or Not to Restructure: Informal Activities and Enterprise Behavior in Transition 6–7 (William Davidson Inst. Working Paper No. 134, 1998), available at ⟨http://eres.bus.umich.edu/docs/workpap-dav/wp134.pdf⟩ (discussing causes of pervasive barter in Russian economy); Meyendorff, *supra* note 18, at 3 (indicating that Russian firms increasingly are using barter trade, which is inefficient means of transacting business).

33. For purposes of this analysis, workers can be considered involuntary creditors, but only for the wage arrears that have accumulated during the period before sporadic wage payment became their firm's ordinary and usual behavior. Once the pattern of sporadic payment becomes expected and there is no reasonable prospect that the arrears are going to be paid, the practice is more appropriately viewed as a de facto wage reduction. At that point, the decision of workers to stay in the firm's employment suggests that the alternatives available to them were no more desirable. Thus, the de facto lower level of wages is presumably a reasonable measure of the social opportunity cost of their labor.

34. The Soviet Union built its whole manufacturing sector on a base of deep energy resource subsidization. These subsidies continued to a considerable extent through provision of these resources at prices below the world level, a problem that was somewhat disguised by the prevalence of barter transactions. Most of the firms that resulted from the privatization of this sector would have been unprofitable in an open economy. *See* Gaddy & Ickes, *supra* note 32, at 7–8.

35. Peter Galuszka & Patricia Kranz, *Look Who's Making a Revolution: Shareholders*, Bus. Wk., Feb. 20, 1995, at 60, 60 (noting that ZiL has been "turning out the same basic truck for 30 years").

36. *See* Michail Berger & Dmitry Dokuchayev, *Divided Authority at ZiL: The Giant Can No Longer Live in the Old Way but Doesn't Yet Want to Live in the New Way*, Current Dig. Post-Soviet Press, May 15, 1996, at 10, 10–11 (quoting Aleksandr Yefanov, head of Mikrodin Company).

37. *Id.* (quoting Aleksandr Yefanov); *see also* James Rupert, *Post-poll Jitters for Russian Industry*, Int'l Herald Trib., July 6–7, 1996, at 9 ("If Mr. Yeltsin now gets serious about ending state support for dying industries, ZiL faces desperate times. Despite having been privatized, the plant seems to be having trouble weaning itself from Soviet-style subsidies").

38. Moscow increased its stake to 60 percent by buying the 30 percent stake previously owned by Mikrodin, the main outside shareholders, who had, for a short period, brought in new management before the city government, labor, and the old managers intervened. *See* Sergey Lukianov, *Mayor Pulls Out Stops to Rescue ZiL*, Moscow Times, Sept. 27, 1996, at 12 ("Luzhkov blamed Mikrodin for failing to boost production. He said lack of proper management was the main reason"); Elizabeth Sullivan, *Reforms Sour for Disenfranchised*, Plain Dealer (Cleveland), June 9, 1996, at

1–A (outside managers were "forcibly escorted off the premises by the security forces of the old" managers).

39. *See* Lukianov, *supra* note 38, at 12; *ZiL Takes Alternative Road to Capitalism*, Russia Express Briefing, Jan. 13, 1997, 1997 WL 9450577.

40. Poul Funder Larsen, *Buying Land Is Next Hurdle for Private Firms*, Moscow Times, Nov. 26, 1996, at III (stating, "Most of Russia's 120,000 privatized firms do not own the land they stand on. They do not even have a clear lease agreement. Instead, they occupy the land under a Soviet-era concept of temporary management which gives city officials a big say in how the land is used and gives companies few rights to sublet, sell or redevelop").

See also Lukianov, *supra* note 38, at 12 (noting that rescue plan includes local and federal tax breaks, direct subsidies, guaranteed purchases of ZiL output by city, and auctioning some ZiL real estate, "with 70 percent of the proceeds going to the company and 30 percent to the city government").

41. *See* Larsen, *supra* note 40, at III.

42. David Hoffman, *The Man Who Rebuilt Moscow: Capitalist Style Could Propel Mayor to National Power*, Wash. Post, Feb. 24, 1997, at A1.

43. *See Moscow Truck Maker Mulls Upgrade Plans*, BBC Summary of World Broadcasts, Jan. 22, 1999, Lexis, News Library, Non-U.S. file. As it was, "the plant stopped housing construction long ago, and the plant workers, dissatisfied that they have not received the apartments once promised to them, intend to petition the International Court of Justice in the Hague." *Id.*

44. Cf. Michael A. Heller, *The Tragedy of the Anticommons: Property in the Transition from Marx to Markets*, 111 Harv. L. Rev. 621, 639 (1998) (suggesting difficulties in selling land because of fragmented ownership in Russian enterprise assets).

45. Berger & Dokuchayev, *supra* note 36, at 10–11.

46. As one account notes: "Eyeing [outside investors] warily are entrenched company directors, many of whom enjoy virtually unchecked command of the production lines they've presided over for decades. Outside investors allege these "Red Directors" are used to running enterprises according to Soviet tenets: overpricing supplies, underpricing output and pocketing the rest." Natasha Mileusnic, *The Great Boardroom Revolution*, Moscow Times, July 16, 1996, at I.

47. One investment banker looking over the Volga Paper Company "noticed huge, dust-covered crates packed away in the corner of the factory. They contained $100 million worth of brand-new Austrian-made equipment. The Russians hadn't bothered unpacking the stuff." Paul Klebnikov & Caroline Waxler, *The Wild East*, Forbes, Dec. 16, 1996, at 348, 349.

48. Rachel Katz, *The Strange Case of the Disappearing Ships*, Moscow Times, May 14, 1996, at VII.

49. *Id.*

50. *Id.*

51. *Id.* (quoting Yury Sukhorukov, foreign affairs chief, Baltic Regional Organization of the Seafarers Union of Russia).

52. If the efficiency gains are spread evenly around all classes of inputs, the effect on the marginal product of each would be positive. If the gains were concentrated primarily with respect to one class of inputs, for example, labor, the effect on marginal productivity is, as a theoretical matter, ambiguous. On the one hand, the gains

increase the number of effective units of labor represented by each actual unit. On the other hand, the increase in effective units of labor relative to other inputs decreases the marginal product of each effective unit of labor. If the first effect outweighs the second, then the marginal product of labor will increase even if the more effective use of labor is the primary efficiency gain from restructuring. Whether this is the case depends on the elasticity of substitution of labor for other inputs. Empirical studies of the United States and other developed economies suggest that the elasticity is large enough that the marginal product of labor would increase even under these circumstances. For a more detailed discussion of these points, see Merritt B. Fox, *Securities Disclosure in a Globalizing Market: Who Should Regulate Whom*, 95 Mich. L. Rev. 2498, 2562–69, 2630–31 (1997).

53. *See* Brealey & Myers, *supra* note 12, at 178.

54. *See* Merton J. Peck, *Russian Privatization: What Basis Does It Provide for a Market Economy?* 5 Transnat'l L. & Contemp. Problems 21, 32 (1995); John Thornhill, *"World's Last Greatest Emerging Market" Back in Favor*, Fin. Post (Toronto), July 18, 1997, at 49, 1997 WL 4100028.

55. *See* Vladimir Popov, *The Financial System in Russia Compared to Other Transition Economies: The Anglo-American versus the German-Japanese Model*, 49 Comp. Econ. Stud. 1, 26 (1999) (finding that equity financing accounts for less than one percent of capital investment in Russia).

56. The lack of interfirm transfers undoubtedly is also in part caused by various techniques that managers use to make non–pro rata distributions that result in cash flow diversions to accounts that they control overseas. Because of these diversions, the firms involved have less cash, if any, available to pay dividends. To the extent that a foreign destination was chosen for these diversions because of a desire to protect what at home would have been considered stolen money or because it assists an attempt at tax evasion, the expected returns of the foreign investment funds by these diversions are likely to be lower than those of some of the unfunded projects of Russian firms. The idea here is that absent any distortions on transnational capital flows, the risk-adjusted expected return on investment opportunities in Russia should equal those abroad even if there are fewer good investment projects in Russia because of the Russian economy's serious problems. The diversions cited here represent a diversion that creates a capital shortage in Russia relative to the quality of its investment opportunities. The reductions in residuals resulting from such diversions are examples of the complex mixture of corporate governance failures in which the method by which a non–pro rata distribution is undertaken leads to a failure to maximize residuals as well, a point discussed in more detail *infra* sec. I.D.

57. The average age of enterprise directors was still more than fifty years. *See* Joseph R. Blasi et al., Kremlin Capitalism: The Privatization of the Russian Economy 203 table 10 (1997). The OECD notes that "these directors were trained under the Soviet system. Although management skills were often important for promotion (as were political ties) during Soviet power, entrepreneurial ingenuity for successful restructuring or reorganization involving risk was usually not rewarded." OECD, *supra* note 1, at 158 n.171.

58. It is hard to get a sense of the extent of this problem for established (as opposed to new) Russian firms. Many firms face one of three choices: continued operation in its current form, massive investment to build an entirely new factory, or

dissolution. Often, continued operation in the firm's current form would be a highly inefficient choice because there is no market for its product at prices sufficient to pay for the inputs and for any opportunity costs associated with its fixed assets. And funds for a massive investment in a new factory are often not available. As a result, "[t]he conflict between production-oriented Soviet-era management and aggressive new owners has been played out at hundreds of factories across the country. The fledgling entrepreneurs have lacked the massive capital required to make the ageing red giants profitable and their attempts to make money by shutting them down and selling off their assets have proven politically explosive. As a result, privatisation has often failed to deliver effective restructuring." *ZiL Takes Alternative Road to Capitalism*, *supra* note 39. It is not clear whether the lack of funds is solely the result of capital market defects that arise from economy-wide corporate governance problems or whether, even without these problems, the new factory would be an insufficiently promising investment project to get funded. In general, entrepreneurs seem likely to claim the former reason.

59. Non–pro rata distributions that result in cash flow diversions to accounts that managers control overseas also may result in firms without sufficient internal resources having to forgo projects that have a positive net present value when discounted at a rate reflecting capital's true social opportunity cost. *See supra* note 56 (discussing diversions).

60. *See* Greg McIvor, *Risk and Reward in Equal Measure*, Fin. Times (London), Mar. 3, 1998, at 17.

61. *Swedish-Owned Paper Mill in Karelia Paralyzed by Fuel Shortage*, BBC Summary of World Broadcasts, Jan. 3, 1997, *available in* Lexis, News Library, Non-U.S. file.

62. *See* McIvor, *supra* note 60, at 17.

63. *See* Greg McIvor, *Assi Hurt by Russian Plant Write-Off*, Fin. Times (London), Feb. 13, 1998, at 29.

64. McIvor, *supra* note 60, at 17; see also *infra* notes 85–87 and accompanying text (discussing Sidanko story).

65. *See* Whitehouse, *supra* note 16 (describing paper and pulp company that failed to produce more paper in face of declining pulp prices and suffered financially).

66. *See* Joseph Bankman & Ronald Gilson, *Why Start-Ups*? 51 Stan. L. Rev. 289, 301–4 (1999) (arguing that providing incentives to individual employees to develop innovations may hamper overall research and development efforts of firms, as individuals may hoard information that is useful to other research and development personnel in effort to protect their proprietary claim over information).

67. *See id.* at 306.

68. A record of successful spinoffs demonstrates a failure in the finance processes of established firms and hence shows some mix of Pathologies 4 and 5. One study of the semiconductor industry shows the reason that proponents of successful spinoffs took their ideas elsewhere is that top management of employer firms simply did not perceive the ideas to be worth substantial investment. *See* Merritt B. Fox, Finance and Industrial Performance in a Dynamic Economy: Theory, Practice, and Policy 305 (1987).

69. *See* World Bank, *supra* note 17, at 64 fig. 3.2 (showing that direct foreign investment inflows as percentage of 1994 GDP is lower for Russia than for several other transition economies).

70. *See* Bernard S. Black & Ronald J. Gilson, *Venture Capital and the Structure of Capital Markets: Banks versus Stock Markets*, 47 J. Fin. Econ. 243, 245 (1998) (explaining that vibrant venture capital market is dependent on ability of venture capitalists to exit from start-ups through initial public offerings, because venture capital providers desire exit mechanism that will allow them to enter into implicit contracts with entrepreneurs concerning future control of firms).

71. *See*, e.g., Norris, *supra* note 5, at A20 (concluding, "If Russia is ever to become an economic success story, its oil will play an important role. But before that happens, a Russian Morgan—someone who understands Russian capitalism and earns the trust of overseas investors—will have to come along to assure that a dollar invested is not sure to become a dollar stolen. The Yukos affair shows Russia is a long way from that goal").

72. Frank Easterbrook and Daniel Fischel argue that this statement of basic norms in corporate law needs refinement. Unequal divisions of gains from corporate activity will be tolerated, they suggest, provided that the transaction makes no shareholder worse off. *See* Frank H. Easterbrook & Daniel R. Fischel, The Economic Structure of Corporate Law 143–44 (1991). Their refinement is valid to an extent, but whether the refinement should be stated so broadly is irrelevant to our discussion of the Russian situation. Few of the many blatant violations of the principle against non–pro rata distributions that we see in Russia possibly could be justified as necessary to permit transactions that leave no shareholder worse off.

73. *See*, e.g., David Fairlamb, *Moscow Madness*, Institutional Investor, July 1995, at 132, 134 ("Some companies think nothing of striking shareholders' names off registers if they look like they're becoming a nuisance"); Mileusnic, *supra* note 46, at I ("One notorious incident involved Krasnoyarsk Aluminum, which deleted from its share register—the only legal proof of ownership—a 20 percent stake held by the British Trans World Group, effectively wiping out its holding").

74. One long-running case involves the Novolipetsk Metal Factory, one of Russia's largest metal producers. Western investment funds were unable, over the course of several years, to place anybody on the board of directors, despite controlling more than 40 percent of the firm's shares and despite cumulative voting rules that should have guaranteed them some voice. *See* Mark Whitehouse, *Novolipetsk Slams Foreign Investors*, Moscow Times, Mar. 15, 1997, at 10. According to Novolipetsk's chairman, Vladimir Skorokhodov, "'In Russia's special situation, the master is, after all, not the shareholder.'" *Id.; see also* Mileusnic, *supra* note 46, at I (describing Western investors' unsuccessful attempt to gain board seats); John Thornhill, *Risks of Russian Market Exposed*, Fin. Times (London), Mar. 25, 1997, at 2 (same). Finally, in 1998, the outside investors were able to win seats on the board after the general director switched sides in this "marquee shareholders' rights case." *Shareholders Win Two-Year Case, Can Appoint Board Members to Firm*, Int'l Sec. Reg. Rep., Jan. 29, 1998, at 10, 10.

75. *See* Geoff Winestock, *Ship Firm Managers, Shareholders Face Off in Russia*, J. Com., Apr. 24, 1995, at 10A (reporting,

> Managers have seen their position change dramatically over the last year with the public sale of their stock to outside investors. Shareholders, for one, have started to ask for higher profits and a voice in the company.

Investors charge that management decided on a simple solution to the problem. They unilaterally issued themselves enough shares to take back control of their companies).

See also Gary Peach, *Financial Ethics Crackdown Bodes Well for Shareholders*, Moscow Times, Feb. 24, 1998, *available in* Lexis, World Library, Mostms file ("Dalmoreprodukt, Russia's largest seafood exporter, is in the process of watering down outsiders' interest by means of an insider share issuance for select major stakeholders, managers, and employees").

76. *See, e.g.*, Andrew Higgins, *As One Bank Shows, Bankruptcy in Russia Is a Real Cat Fight*, Wall St. J., Apr. 5, 1999, at A1 (reporting, "Just as Russia's earlier drive to put state property in private hands often yielded cozy inside deals instead of a spur to efficiency, bankruptcy has mutated into a cat fight often involving shadowy cabals and allegations of asset stripping. 'Many enterprises are being artificially bankrupted, to be taken over by some groups,' Prime Minister Yevgeny Primakov [said]").

See also Kranz, *supra* note 2, at 45 ("In regions across Russia, both local governments and creditors have filed bankruptcy suits against subsidiaries of Potanin's Sidanko Oil. The suits ostensibly seek payment of back taxes and delinquent energy bills. But the real prize could be Sidanko's oil assets").

77. *See* Norris, *supra* note 5, at A20 (citing Yukos example, in which minority shareholders were barred from voting:

> A judge had ruled that since the minority holders all planned to vote the same way, they must be in league with one another and therefore in violation of antitrust laws because they had not registered as such. The minority shareholders were not invited to the hearing that led to the ruling.
>
> The shareholders managed to get another judge to rule that they could vote at one of the meetings. But his ruling was simply ignored).

78. *Investor Hell*, J. Com., June 15, 1998, at 6A (editorial) (quoting E. Michael Hunter, president of Dart Management).

79. *See* Lyudmila Leontyeva, *Red Director's Stronghold in Kuban*, Moscow News, Oct. 30, 1997, *in* Lexis, World Library, Mosnws file.

80. *See* Mark Whitehouse, *Germans Cry Foul in Gypsum Plant Feud*, Moscow Times, Nov. 29, 1997, *in* Lexis, World Library, Mostms file; Mark Whitehouse, *Under Siege*, Moscow Times, Dec. 9, 1997, *in* Lexis, World Library, Mostms file.

81. *See* Katy Daigle, *Nemstov Hails Win for Investors' Rights*, Moscow Times, Mar. 10, 1998, at 13, 1998 WL 11690493.

82. Mark Whitehouse, *Take 'Em to Court*, Moscow Times, Feb. 10, 1998, *in* Lexis, World Library, Mostms file (quoting Innokenti Ivanov).

83. *See* Elizabeth V. Mooney, *Russia Must Implement Tax, Corporate Governance Reforms*, RCR Radio Comm. Rep., Feb. 28, 2000, at 26, 2000 WL 9540310 ("'The tax burden is arbitrary and capricious, frequently more than net earnings because companies are taxed on gross income,' [Professor Richard E.] Ericson said. 'This amounts to confiscation of the capital available for investment'").

84. *See* EBRD, *supra* note 24, at 143 box 8.1 (discussing financial-industrial groups (FIGs) and need to limit their powers); *see also infra* notes 214–27 and accompanying text (discussing FIGs).

85. *See* Jeanne Whalen, *FSC Cracks Down on Yukos, Sidanko*, Moscow Times, Feb. 19, 1998, *in* Lexis, World Library, Mostms file (noting that Russian Federal Securities Commission action to cancel offering perhaps marks "'turning point'" (quoting attorney Walter Rieman)); Jeanne Whalen, *Shareholders Rights: Round 2*, Moscow Times, Feb. 17, 1998, *available in* Lexis, World Library, Mostms file (reporting subsequent developments). In the interest of full disclosure, the authors of this chapter state that they served as consultants to some minority shareholders in this matter.

86. *See* Whalen, *Shareholders Rights*, *supra* note 85 (stating that convertible bond issue excluding minority shareholders would have tripled Sidanko's charter capital).

87. *See Sidanko Offers Settlement to Minority Shareholders*, Russia & Commonwealth Bus. L. Rep., Mar. 25, 1998, *in* Lexis, News Library, Rcblr file.

88. *See Dilemma over BP Role in Oil, Gas Industry*, BBC Summary of World Broadcasts, Nov. 12, 1999, *available in* Lexis, News Library, Non-U.S. file; Vitaly Makarchev, *British Petroleum—Amoco Intends to Secede from Sidanko*, TASS, Nov. 22, 1999, *available in* Lexis, Europe Library, Tass file.

89. *See* ch. 7, sec. III.A.

90. *See*, e.g., Mooney, *supra* note 83 ("Asset stripping and its companion, transfer pricing, are two other commonplace occurrences that victimize investors. [According to one analyst], 'asset stripping involves transactions with affiliates on non-market terms, and it siphons assets from minority shareholders. . . . Transfer pricing involves the sale of goods and services at below-market prices.'" (quoting Lee Wolosky)).

91. *See, e.g.*, Edwin Dolan, *Resisting Shock of New*, Moscow Times, Apr. 8, 1997, at 10 (calling some insider managers "simply bandits").

92. *See* Daigle, *supra* note 2 ("In Russia, company directors and managers are routinely accused of insider dealing, which includes everything from accepting bribes to act against their company's interests to selling assets or shares to relatives or friends").

93. *See, e.g.*, Jeanne Whalen, *Navigating the Russian Subsidiaries Minefield*, Moscow Times, Mar. 10, 1998, at III, 1998 WL 11690632 ("Share swaps aside, transfer pricing is the practice most feared by subsidiary shareholders. Holding companies force subsidiaries to sell their oil at below-market prices, and then resell it for a profit that is kept by the holding company"); Whalen, *Shareholders Rights*, *supra* note 85 (discussing transfer pricing at Tomskneft, about which one minority shareholder protested, "tax debts and the cost of production are left with the subsidiaries, while profits are illegally upstreamed to the parent" (internal quotation marks omitted)).

94. Patricia Kranz, *Shareholders at the Gate*, Bus. Wk. (int'l ed.), June 2, 1997, at 60, 1997 WL 8270209.

95. Peach, *supra* note 3.

96. *See, e.g.*, Blasi et al., *supra* note 57, at 165.

97. *See id.*

98. Consider the recent looting of Moscow City Telephone Network (MGTS). Even though it is the largest telecommunications company in Russia, its share price dropped 95 percent from its high. According to one report, majority ownership was transferred from a public body "to a secretive outfit that has links both political and economic to Moscow Mayor Yury Luzhkov. Any growth potential for the stock has thus been eliminated. . . . It is safe to say that [the new owners] have no concern for

shareholders of MGTS. What [they] care about, though, is getting Luzhkov elected to the presidency, so MGTS' available cash will be utilized accordingly." Peach, *supra* note 3; *see also* Gary Peach, *Mayor's Industrial Policy Carries Big Costs*, Moscow Times, Dec. 8, 1998, at 16, 1998 WL 11691775 (noting that diverting control of "prize municipal assets" ensures that these firms' "bountiful cash flow" will be available to help Luzhkov "meet the presidential challenge in 2000").

For another complex diversion example, *see* Alan S. Cullison, *Russian Share Shuffle Maddens Investors*, Wall St. J., July 23, 1999, at A12 (discussing Yukos Oil company's quiet transfer of bulk of its two most valuable petroleum-producing assets to offshore entities); *see also* Alan S. Cullison, *Yukos Transfers Two Oil Units to Offshore Firms*, Wall St. J., June 4, 1999, at A12 (noting earlier part of saga in which the tycoon who controls Yukos had "barred minority investors from shareholder meetings at three Yukos subsidiaries and pushed through permission for massive share issues that will dilute investors' holdings").

99. *See, e.g.*, Blasi et al., *supra* note 57, at 87.

100. The perquisites are unlikely to give the insiders as much utility as the cash that they would cost. *See* Michael C. Jensen & William H. Meckling, *Theory of the Firm: Managerial Behavior, Agency Costs, and Ownership Structure*, 3 J. Fin. Econ. 305, 312–13 (1976) (outlining increase in appropriation as owner-managers' percentage of equity decreases). The sweetheart deals are unlikely to be with the least cost provider of the service or good needed.

101. *See* Alexander M. Jenkyn, *Russian Auto Manufacturers, Hobbled by Inefficient Management, Look to Foreign Investors*, East/West Executive Guide, May 1997, *available in* Dow Jones Interactive ⟨http://djinteractive.com⟩.

102. Mark Whitehouse, *Slow Death*, Moscow Times, June 16, 1998, *in* Lexis, World Library, Mostms file (recounting at length AvtoVAZ's management difficulties and slow decline).

103. *Id.* (quoting automobile analyst Victor Frumkin).

104. *See Russia's Nemtsov Threatens Asset Seizures, Bankruptcies over Huge Tax Arrears*, AFX News, Sept. 23, 1997, *available in* Dow Jones Interactive ⟨http://djinteractive.com⟩.

105. *See Avtovaz to Issue New Shares*, Russian Bus. News Update, Sept. 1, 1997, 1997 WL 9832802.

106. *Auto Giant Labours under Tax Burden*, BBC Summary of World Broadcasts, June 5, 1998, *in* Lexis, News Library, Non-U.S. file (quoting AvtoVAZ chairman Vladimir Kadannikov).

107. *See* Kirill Koriukin, *Debt-Laden AvtoVAZ Hands State 50% Stake*, Moscow Times, Dec. 31, 1998, 1998 WL 11692046.

PART II

The Elements of Good Corporate Governance: Law

CHAPTER TWO

Patterns of Legal Change: Shareholder and Creditor Rights in Transition Economies

Katharina Pistor

TRANSITION ECONOMIES have introduced remarkable changes in the laws that govern shareholder and creditor rights, with more changes being exhibited in countries with lower levels of protection at the outset of reforms. Most countries went beyond the average level of legal protection found in the legal families to which they once belonged, which suggests a strong trend toward convergence of statutory law across transition economies. The high level of convergence is largely the result of an external supply of legal solutions. Strong similarities between laws that were influenced by identifiable groups of foreign advisors suggest that the contents of enacted legal rules were strongly influenced by the group of advisors that dominated in a given country. Nonetheless—the external supply of legal rules notwithstanding—patterns of legal reform have been primarily responsive to economic change rather than initiating or leading it.

I. INTRODUCTION

The reform of the enterprise sector in the former socialist countries has been at the core of the economic-reform programs, which were launched ten years ago, beginning in Poland and followed by other governments throughout the region. A key element of the enterprise-reform package was privatization. Depending on the country and the specific area of the law in question, this reform measure was preceded, accompanied, or followed by legal reforms. Legal reforms in the region have been comprehensive and have affected not only areas immediately relevant for the enterprise sector, but the entire legal system, ranging from constitutional, administrative, criminal, and civil law to the organization and procedural rules of the court system.[1] This chapter focuses on laws that are immediately relevant for the restructuring and financing of enterprises, in particular, the rights of shareholders as stipulated in company laws, securities regulations, and the right of creditors as holders of collateral and in bankruptcy. I investigate the patterns of legal change in these areas of the law and identify key determinants of legal change. The method employed is a formalized comparison of legal change based on predefined legal indicators. A database was constructed, one that codes the development of shareholder and creditor rights from 1990 through 1998 for twenty-four transition economies (excluding only Serbia, Tajikistan, and Turkmenistan). The chapter joins a growing literature that uses cross-country formalized legal indicators to investigate the interaction between legal and economic change using statistical tools.[2] It introduces the data used and descriptively analyzes the patterns of legal change that can be observed. A statistical analysis of the interaction between legal and economic change is addressed elsewhere.[3]

The results presented in this chapter can be summarized as follows: differences in the law on the books were less pronounced at the outset of reform than one may have expected. Moreover, there is a strong tendency toward convergence of formal legal rules as the result of extensive legal reforms. Convergence seems to be primarily the result of foreign technical-assistance programs as well as of harmonization requirements for countries wishing to join the European Union. The external supply of legal rules notwithstanding, the pattern of legal reforms suggests that law reform has been primarily responsive to economic change rather than initiating or leading it. In comparison, the presocialist heritage of transition economies has little explanatory power for the observed patterns of legal change. Partial exceptions are countries with German legal heritage, which favor creditor over shareholder protection and displayed substantially better creditor protection at the outset of reforms than did other transition economies.

II. Convergence and Divergence in Legal Development

The literature of the new institutional economics (NIE) defines institutions as "any form of constraint that human beings devise to shape human interaction,"[4] which includes both the formal law and informal constraints, or social norms. A question raised in this literature, which shall also be addressed in this chapter, is how institutions change over time. Two competing hypotheses address the dynamics of institutional change. The first suggests that competition will over time self-select the most effective institutions, and different social systems will converge on these.[5] The second hypothesis proposes that institutions develop along path-dependent trajectories. Institutional change is incremental and shaped by preexisting conditions. Thus, systems will continue to diverge rather than converge, even in the presence of competition.[6] In light of the increasing integration of markets, some authors suggest that while specific institutions may remain different, the globalization of the economy will lead to functional convergence through substitution effects.[7] Thus, a third hypothesis could be added, namely, that different institutional arrangements may be used for similar functions. The variance in institutions may be the result of different initial conditions, but the tasks they perform are largely the same.

There is a lively debate in the corporate governance literature about these alternative patterns of institutional development and, in particular, about the role of law for convergence or divergence of corporate governance systems. Proponents of the divergence, or path-dependence, hypothesis argue that even if corporate law was harmonized across countries, other legal rules (tax laws, codetermination legislation, etc.) and institutional constraints (financial structure, existing ownership structure of firms) or simply political considerations would stand in the way of convergence.[8] The opposite view holds that convergence is likely to take place, once the main regulatory obstacles are removed.[9] The economic forces toward success, they suggest, are the same all over the world. Both views regard legal institutions as important for promoting or hindering convergence, but they differ in their assessment of the propensity of a particular body of law, such as corporate law, to achieve this goal.

The literature up to now has used qualitative analysis as a method to investigate these questions. In this chapter, by contrast, I propose a way to test the competing hypotheses this literature has developed in a more rigorous way by systematically coding legal rules in time series. In this regard, the chapter also deviates from La Porta and coauthors, who code legal rules at a single point in time—the early 1990s—and boldly assume that law does not change dramatically over time.[10]

I focus here on the development of legal change in transition economies (TEs), documenting change in the law on the books. There are several reasons for mapping out the details of change in the law on the books. First, some authors have argued that even though corporate law may be trivial in developed market economies,[11] it is likely to play a much greater role in transition economies, where it not only redefines the allocation of rights and responsibilities of various stakeholders, but also serves an educational function.[12] Second, new research results stress the importance of legal rules as determinants for corporate finance and corporate governance. In a survey of corporate governance around the world, Shleifer and Vishny argue that the structure of companies and the level of stock market development is determined by the quality of shareholder protection.[13] In countries with strong shareholder protection, investors can afford to take minority positions rather than controlling stakes. As a result, companies tend to have dispersed shareholders as owners, and capital markets are rather liquid. By contrast, where shareholder rights are not well protected, investors will compensate for this deficiency by taking controlling stakes. This leads to high levels of ownership concentration. Regression analyses using indicators for the quality of the law on the books in forty-nine countries around the world (excluding transition economies) on the one hand, and ownership concentration of the largest listed companies as well as key indicators for stock market development on the other, confirm that high-quality law on the books—as measured by the legal indicators used in this study—is positively correlated with (relatively) dispersed ownership and liquid capital markets.[14] Similarly, Levine shows that high-quality creditor-protection law is important for bank performance as measured by the volume of credit to the private sector.[15]

Third, a detailed analysis of change in the law on the books will enhance our understanding of the interaction between legal and economic change. Law is frequently treated as exogenous to socioeconomic change, because many countries received their formal legal order from other countries by way of transplantation.[16] In the most simplistic scenario of the convergence theory, identical legal rules should lead to largely similar outcomes. However, even when law is transplanted, the law does not necessarily precede the development of a country's enterprise or financial sector. Structural differences in the ownership concentration of firms, the existence or absence of stock markets, the quality of the banking sector, and the extent to which the state controls the real sector, the financial sector, or both, either directly as an owner or indirectly through regulation and case-by-case interventions, may have created conditions that put countries on different development paths, which are not easily broken by changing the laws on the books.[17]

The problem of preexisting conditions is of particular relevance in transition economies. From the socialist regime, they inherited an enterprise sector that was in need of restructuring. Although the development of a new enterprise sector is important, the main challenge at least in the initial stages of economic transition was to devise a legal system that would help meet the financial needs of the *existing* enterprises and facilitate their restructuring. Privatization strategies may have created another path dependence, as they determined the initial ownership structure of firms. Mass-privatization programs tended to promote relatively more dispersed ownership structures, large fractions of insider ownership, or both, whereas direct-sales methods led to block holdings by strategic investors.[18] In addition, the legacy of the socialist system meant that most countries were saddled with banks that carried bad-loan portfolios and lacked the capacity to assess and monitor the viability of investment projects they were financing.[19] Whether these initial conditions or the quality of laws can explain the outcomes we observe today, such as the extent of enterprise restructuring, the level of development of the financial sector, or the effectiveness of corporate governance, can only be assessed once we know the pattern of legal change.

Path dependence is relevant not only for economic development, but also for the development of the legal system. An important finding of La Porta and coauthors is that countries that became part of the same legal family in the nineteenth century display remarkably similar features in the quality of investor protection today.[20] Transition economies were not barren countries, either, with respect to their legal development. Many of the Central and Eastern European countries still had their prewar codes on the books. They were often riddled with socialist principles, but still contained key provisions on shareholder and creditor rights. Most of these countries can trace their formal legal systems back to either the German or the French civil-law family.[21] Following the logic of the path-dependence hypothesis, one might expect that they will now borrow again from countries that belong to the same legal family, rather than looking for more effective rules elsewhere.[22]

In addition, the socialist system itself, including the early transition to a market economy, may have created new path dependencies. Many transition economies had started to introduce legal change prior to the collapse of the socialist system.[23] Hungary was the first country to introduce a bankruptcy code, in 1986, and to promulgate a law on business associations, in 1988. The Soviet Union also engaged in extensive legal reforms during the period of perestroika, which has shaped the postsocialist legal system.[24] A law on enterprises was adopted in 1987, and decrees on joint stock companies were issued at the Soviet level as well as in Russia in 1990. Many of these laws had serious gaps. Moreover, because the laws were adopted when the socialist doctrine still shaped the basic understanding and design of law, they frequently introduced hybrid legal constructions, which created obstacles for market-based legal reforms in the postsocialist era. This is true in particular in the area of property rights. A good example is the concept of operative management, which allocates full control over assets to a company without transferring ownership. The separation between ownership and control leaves management unaccountable to the owner and fails to allocate liabilities of the enterprise.[25]

Thus, prewar history, late socialist reforms, and the policy choices at the outset of the transition process may have constrained policymakers and legislators in designing a new legal system. And yet the change of the political and economic regime, which they initiated, could have given them the opportunity to design the law on the books in a way they deemed most appropriate for future development. Because of the relative ease with which laws can be enacted in comparison to the difficulties of restructuring the enterprise or financial sectors (prolonged political struggles in parliament notwithstanding) this is the area where policy design should be most apparent. This scenario assumes that policymakers are fully aware of the possible implications of alternative institutional design and are free to choose among them. The actual experience of transition shows that this is a rather bold assumption. Case study analyses of institutional reform in transition economies show that the selection and implementation of reform measures was more erratic, with frequently several reform avenues pursued simultaneously.[26]

In order to analyze the determinants of legal change in transition economies, we have constructed a database that codes shareholder and creditor rights in twenty-four transition economies from 1990 through 1998. We capture annual change, with the year-end status being used for coding purposes. The coding includes, but extends, the indicators selected by La Porta and coauthors.[27] The primary purpose of this extension is to capture possible functional substitutions that different legal systems offer for shareholder or creditor protection. I will discuss the additional variables as well as the cumulative indexes we constructed using these variables in sections 3 and 4 below.[28] The original indicators are, however, sufficient for a first test of the convergence or divergence hypothesis in legal development. They also enable us to compare emerging patterns in transition economies with those found in other countries.

We refer to the cumulative shareholder rights index[29] as LLSVsh, and to the cumulative creditors rights index as LLSVcr. LLSVsh is composed of six variables, which reflect the position of minority shareholders in firms and code provisions that protect them on the one hand, as well as the absence of provisions that weaken their position, on the other. The index includes (1) proxy voting by mail; (2) shareholders not required by law to deposit their shares prior to the general shareholders' meeting; (3) cumulative voting, or proportional representation of minorities on the board of directors ensured by other means; (4) an oppressed-minorities mechanism, defined as the ability of shareholders to sue directors or to challenge the decisions of shareholder meetings in court; (5) the minimum percentage of share capital that entitles a shareholder to call an extraordinary shareholders' meeting, being less than or equal to 10 percent; and (6) shareholders having preemptive rights when new shares are issued that can be waived only by a shareholder vote.

LLSVcr includes four variables, all of which address the role of creditors, and in particular secured creditors, in bankruptcy procedure: (1)

restrictions such as creditor consent exist for going into reorganization as opposed to liquidation; (2) secured creditors are not stayed in bankruptcy; (3) secured assets are satisfied first when assets are distributed; and (4) management does not stay in bankruptcy, but is replaced with a court or creditor-appointed receiver.

The convergence hypothesis as applied to legal change predicts that countries select the legal rules that have been shown to be most effective in other countries, and regulatory competition leads to the harmonization of legal rules. By contrast, the divergence hypothesis proposes that the choices lawmakers face are constrained by preexisting institutions and political and social forces. Transition economies may have been caught in this pattern of path-dependent development, or they may have taken the opportunity of a regime change to fundamentally alter their inherited legal systems by choosing legal rules that have been shown to be most effective in competitive institutional evolution. To test these two propositions, we determine the level of shareholder and creditor protection in transition economies at the outset of the transition period. Rather than 1990, we chose 1992, because of variations in the onset of the regime change, and because we lack early data for some countries.

Using the presocialist legal heritage as a basis, we can distinguish three groups of countries, moving from west to east. The first are the countries with a German legal heritage. They either received their formal legal systems from Austria, because they belonged to the Austrio-Hungarian Empire prior to its dissolution, or copied the law from Germany in the interwar period. The countries that belong to this family include most of the nations of Central and Eastern Europe and the Baltics, namely, Croatia, the Czech Republic, Estonia, Hungary, Latvia, Lithuania, Poland, the Slovak Republic, and Slovenia (hereinafter CEE/Baltics).[30] The second group are countries that used to belong to the Ottoman Empire and received French law, from when the French legal system underwent modernization in the mid-nineteenth century.[31] These countries include Albania, Bosnia, Bulgaria, the Federal Yugoslav Republic (FYR) of Macedonia, and Romania (i.e., the countries of southeastern Europe, hereinafter SEE). The final group is composed of the former Soviet Socialist Republics, with the exception of the Baltic states. Their legal history is quite diverse. Russia was influenced by Roman/Byzantine law; reforms in the late nineteenth and early twentieth century were modeled on primarily German law.[32] The central Asian republics were governed by Islamic law and various customary rules. What they have in common is the absence of a firmly established modern formal legal order prior to the emergence of the socialist system. Table 2.1 lists the level of shareholder and creditor rights in the

TABLE 2.1
Shareholder and Creditor Rights in Comparison with Legal Families and World Average

	Shareholder rights		*Creditor rights*	
	1992	1998	1992	1998
CEE/Baltics	2	3.05	2.55	3.55
SEE	2	2.6	0	3
Eurasia	2.35	3.45	1.05	3.05
All transition economies	2.17	3.13	1.40	3.23
Common law	4.0		3.11	
French civil law	2.33		1.58	
German civil law	2.33		2.33	
Scandinavian civil law	3.0		2.0	
World average (49 countries)	3.0		2.30	

Source: La Porta et al. (1998; *see* note 2) and compilation by author.

three regions in 1992 and 1998 and compares it with the level of protection in the four major legal families reported on.[33]

At the outset of legal reforms, the level of shareholder and creditor protection in all transition economies was well below world average. In the breakdown by legal families, the only exception is the level of creditor rights protection in transition economies of German legal origin. They are above world average, and even higher than the Germany-family average. By 1998, legal changes had been introduced that raised the level of investor protection in most transition economies above the level of the civil-law systems and brought them within close range of the average for common-law countries, which offer the best protection for investors, according to La Porta and coauthors.[34]

The fact that transition economies of French origin continue to lag behind most other transition economies in 1998 can be attributed largely to the late onset of reforms in the countries that used to be part of Yugoslavia, where war and civil unrest delayed economic as well as legal reforms.[35] Still, changes in creditor rights have been remarkable in these countries. An interesting feature of the Eurasian countries is that their performance as of 1992 is less bad than one might have expected of countries that did not have a presocialist history of a developed civil and commercial law. This is primarily the result of the late perestroika reforms, which introduced some basic rules on the organization of enterprises, including shareholder-protection rules.[36] Not only have the Eurasian transition economies caught up with other transition economies by 1998, but their laws now offer better protection on average than the laws of other transition economies. In contrast, creditor rights are only very weakly protected in this region as of 1992, and in 1998 they continue to lag behind the CEE/Baltics. The latter group of countries displays the least dramatic change between 1992 and 1998. Yet legal change during the transition period has improved the level of investor protection to above that of other German legal systems. The results suggest that overall the law on the books in transition economies is converging toward legal rules of the highest level irrespective of the presocialist legal heritage.

Convergence of legal rules can have different causes. It may be the result of top-down harmonization, which in turn may be induced by international standardization of selected areas of the law, the influence of a common pool of advisors, or the conscious selection by domestic policymakers in the law-receiving country of the best-quality laws based on comparative research. Alternatively, convergence of legal rules may be the result of a response to similar problems, which call for similar solutions. For example, widespread violation of minority-shareholder rights may have triggered similar efforts to strengthen the protection of these rights across the region.

There is strong evidence that much of the legal change in shareholder and creditor rights we can observe in transition economies is the result of foreign technical assistance. Various countries have offered extensive aid to transition economies for reforming their legal systems. The United States Agency for International Development (USAID) has been particularly active in many countries of the former Soviet Union, including Armenia, Georgia, Kyrgyzstan, Kazakhstan, Moldova, Russia, Uzbekistan, and Ukraine, but also in Bosnia-Herzegovina and FYR Macedonia and, with regard to creditor rights, also in Poland.[37] Countries wishing to join the European Union (EU) are required to harmonize extensive parts of their laws with European standards. This includes key areas of the law that affect shareholder rights, as well as creditor rights. The 1998 corporate law amendments in the Czech Republic, and Hungary, for example, can be attributed to an effort to comply with harmonization requirements. To illustrate the supply-induced convergence, table 2.2 reports the value for LLSVsh and LLSVcr in 1998 for, on the one hand, countries that received substantial aid from USAID for reforming their legal system and, on the other, those that have completed accession arrangements with the EU. We drop Bosnia-Herzegovina and FYR Macedonia for the comparison, as the late onset of reforms may skew the results.

The most striking result is the high level of minority-shareholder protection in the countries that received aid from the United States. The average for the six countries listed in table 2.2 is close to the aver-

TABLE 2.2
Supply-Led Convergence of Legal Rules

	LLSVsh (1998)	*LLSVcr (1998)*
Recipients of USAID		
Armenia	5.5	NA
Georgia	3.0	2.75
Kazakhstan	5.25	2.75
Kyrgyzstan	2.25	3
Latvia	NA	4
Moldova	3.5	4
Poland	NA	2.25
Romania	3	4
Russia	5.5	2.5
Ukraine	3.5	2.5
Uzbekistan	3.5	2.5
Mean	3.85	3.03
First-tier EU-accession countries		
Czech Republic	3	3
Estonia	3.75	4
Hungary	3	3.75
Poland	3	2.25
Slovenia	2.5	4
First-tier EU-accession countries	3.05	3.4
Sample mean all TEs	3.13	3.23

Source: Author's compilation.
Note: NA = not applicable, meaning that for this area of the law, there was no substantial involvement of USAID.

age of the common-law family. The countries that belong to the first tier of future EU-accession countries offer lower levels of minority-shareholder protection, but are still well above the average of German or French civil-law systems. The reason could be that several EU guidelines that were used for reforming the corporate laws of prospective member states are influenced by U.K. law and thus are leading to an influx of common-law principles into the core countries of the civil-law systems.[38] Differences in creditor protection are more difficult to attribute to different donors than are differences in shareholder rights, at least if we confine ourselves to the few indicators constructed by La Porta and coauthors.[39]

The evidence of convergence of legal rules across the region notwithstanding, the basis for comparison when using only LLSVsh and

LLSVcr is rather limited. For a more comprehensive assessment of the patterns of legal change in transition economies, a more extensive taxonomy of shareholder and creditor rights will be developed in the following two sections.

III. Taxonomy of Shareholder Rights

The indicators we used for a first test of the convergence and divergence hypotheses focus only on particular aspects of the law. For shareholders (LLSVsh), minority-shareholder rights are coded, and for creditor rights (LLSVcr), the rights of creditors, in particular of secured creditors, in bankruptcy. Neither corporate law statutes nor legal rules aimed at protecting creditors, however, are necessarily limited to these functions, nor is there necessarily only one set of rules to achieve a particular outcome. A broader analysis of the dynamics of legal change in transition economies therefore requires the inclusion of variables that capture other goals of the law or offer functional substitutes.[40] In this section a taxonomy of shareholder rights is developed, while the following section is devoted to creditor rights. Although the inclusion of some variables was motivated by legal developments in transition economies, in principle this taxonomy may also be used to analyze the patterns of legal change in other countries in more detail.

For shareholder rights there are five cumulative indexes in addition to LLSVsh: VOICE, EXIT, ANTIMANAGE, ANTIBLOCK, and SMINTEGR. The corporate governance literature commonly distinguishes between *voice* and *exit* as the two alternative strategies that shareholders may invoke to assert their control over company management.[41] *Voice* refers to control through voting rights, including hiring and dismissing managers, shareholder suits, and the like. *Exit* is used to indicate that shareholders may liquidate their holdings by selling their shares in case they are not satisfied with the way a company is managed. Both mechanisms shall protect shareholders, but they provide different avenues for that purpose and are secured by different legal rules. Most of the LLSVsh indicators are legal rules that protect voice. The fact that these variables appear to be important determinants for stock market development may seem puzzling. A naive application of the voice versus exit concepts to the law would suggest that for equity market development, exit rules should be more important than voice rules. The strong correlation between minority-voice rights and capital market development,[42] however, suggests that even though minority shareholders may be passive and prefer exit, they are likely to acquire minority stakes only if this position gives them the potential to exert control through voice, despite the fact that (because of cost considerations) voice may never be exercised. Yet, since LLSVsh does not include indicators for shareholder exit rights, we cannot test whether they indeed substitute for weak voice rights.

The VOICE index includes all the LLSVsh variables, as well as other control variables, which may, but do not have to, be specifically targeted at minority shareholders. In particular, VOICE includes the right of minority shareholders to call an audit commission, a minimum-quorum requirement for a shareholder meeting to take binding decisions, supermajority requirements for adopting decisions that affect the existence of the corporation in its current form (including amendments to the charter, the liquidation of the company, and mergers and reorganizations), the possibility to fire directors and managers at any time without cause, and the absence of provisions that mandate employee or state representation on the board. The last provision may strengthen the position of other stakeholders in the company, but it does so at the expense of shareholder control. Finally, we have included a provision that reflects a special feature of many corporate statutes in transition economies: the allocation of the right to hire and fire top management (chief executives) of the company. In most developed market economies today this right is vested in the board of directors (supervisory board), which in turn is elected by the shareholder meeting. This "representative democracy" model is widely believed to be more effective in controlling management than the "direct democracy" model,[43] in which shareholders themselves hold this key control right. The reason is that shareholders may lack the information necessary to respond, and even if they have access to adequate information, they will be slow to act. Yet several transition economies still favor the direct-democracy model, although different arrangements in the corporate charter are often optional.

The EXIT index includes legal rules that facilitate shareholders' leaving the corporation. This includes a legal provision that protects the right to sell shares without prior approval by other shareholders or the company's directors (without exceptions to this rule, i.e., for bearer shares, which are quite common in civil-law countries) and the absence of extensive formal requirements for selling one's shares. EXIT also includes rules that facilitate exit by shareholders in the case of takeovers and other major transactions that may endanger their position in the company. In particular we include put options and mandatory-takeover rules. While the latter may prevent takeovers (which in the context of transition economies may in fact be desirable), the protection of minority shareholders is still an important objective.

With ANTIMANAGE and ANTIBLOCK we try to assess the relative weight given by a legal system to the conflict between shareholders and management, on the one hand, and minority shareholders and blockholders, on the other. Comparative corporate governance analysis has shown that the conflict that is widely assumed to be at the heart of the governance problem, the principal-agent conflict between shareholders and managers, is not the relevant conflict in many countries.[44] Companies with highly concentrated ownership typically have a shareholder whose stake is large enough to effectively control management. The strong position of a blockholder may, however, endanger the position of minority shareholders. ANTIMANAGE includes legal rules aimed at protecting shareholders against management, and ANTIBLOCK rules are designed to protect minority shareholders against blockholders. The relevance of either set of rules will be determined by the ownership structure of firms. In firms with a high concentration of ownership, minority shareholders will require effective ANTIBLOCK provisions. By contrast, in firms with dispersed shareholdings, ANTIMANAGE provisions are warranted.

ANTIMANAGE is not identical to LLSVsh, discussed above. In the oppressed-minority variable, for example, LLSVsh lumps together the right of shareholders to sue directors with the right to challenge in court decisions that were taken at the general shareholder meeting. Management is the target of the first right, while other shareholders, in particular, controlling ones, are the target of the latter. We therefore split this variable into two separate ones and use the right to sue management for ANTIMANAGE, and the right to challenge decisions of the shareholder meeting for ANTIBLOCK. ANTIMANAGE also includes self-dealing rules, which require management to abstain from or disclose transactions that compromise their loyalty to the company, while ANTIBLOCK combines some of the voice and exit variables, including quorem requirements and put options, that protect minority shareholders, especially against controlling shareholders.

Finally, we create a stock market integrity index (SMINTEGR), which codes rules of which the primary purpose is the protection not of individual shareholder rights, but of the integrity of the capital market. This is a classic example of a functional substitute. The ultimate goal of individual shareholder rights is to effectively control the use of capital by the firm, which should influence the market value of shares and thus their liquidity on the market. However, market liquidity could be equally well, or in some circumstances even better, protected with rules that are designed to protect the functioning of the market and enforced by the state.[45] To capture this function, we use self-dealing, insider-trading rules, provisions on the independence of a shareholder registry, and regulations on the supervision of the stock market by a state agency.[46] Appendix 1 includes the definitions of the variables used to

TABLE 2.3
Shareholder Rights, 1992 and 1998

	All 24 TEs		*CEE/Baltics*		*SEE*		*Eurasia*	
Indicators	*1992*	*1998*	*1992*	*1998*	*1992*	*1998*	*1992*	*1998*
LLSVSH (0–6)								
Mean	2.17	3.13	2	3.06	2	2.6	2.4	3.45
% of index	36.1	52.1	33.3	50.9	33.3	43.3	40.0	57.5
SMINTEGR (0–6)								
Mean	0.96	2.86	1.44	3.44	0.6	2.4	0.7	2.58
% of index	13.7	40.9	20.6	49.2	8.0	34.3	10.0	36.8
VOICE (0–13)								
Mean	5.89	7.86	4.69	6.72	4.85	6.7	7.4	9.5
% of index	45.3	60.6	36.1	51.7	32.8	51.5	57.7	73.1
EXIT (0–4)								
Mean	1.06	1.76	1.06	1.67	0.45	0.9	1.4	2.26
% of index	26.6	44.0	26.4	41.6	10.0	22.5	35	56.9
ANTIMANAGE (0–6)								
Mean	2.58	3.60	2	3.33	2.8	3.6	2.3	3.85
% of index	38.2	60.1	33.3	55.6	46.6	60.0	38.3	64.2
ANTIBLOCK (0–8)								
Mean	1.85	3.49	1.72	3.53	2	3.3	1.9	3.55
% of index	23.2	43.6	21.5	44.1	25.0	41.3	23.8	44.4

Source: Database compiled by author.

construct the various indexes and explains how they were coded. Appendix 2 reports the level of shareholder protection for these six indices for all 24 transition economies from 1992 through 1998. Table 2.3 gives the mean score as well as the percentage of each index for all transition economies and for the three legal families.

The data in column 1 clearly demonstrate the extent of legal reforms since 1992. The average score increased substantially across all indexes. Change was particularly great for SMINTEGR and ANTIMANAGE. Interestingly, the focus of corporate law reform as captured by our shareholder indexes has not changed over time, at least not for transition economies taken as a group. Shareholder rights that are reflected in the VOICE index were and still are the most developed rights. As noted above, VOICE reflects internal-control rights of shareholders, including, but not limited to, minority shareholders. Second in importance is ANTIMANAGE (i.e., those legal provisions that are specifically targeted at management). This reflects the classic corporate governance paradigm with its focus on the conflict between shareholders as principals and management as their agent. Third in order is LLSVsh (i.e., the protection of minority-shareholder rights). EXIT, that is, legal rules that protect the right to sell shares and, in exceptional situations, give shareholders the right to redeem their investments, is fourth and thus ranks before ANTIBLOCK. This fourth index, which captures legal rules that protect minority shareholders against blockholders rather than management, are only relatively weakly developed. Finally, last in order are legal rules that ensure the integrity of the capital market, as captured by SMINTEGR.

For 1992 the weakness of SMINTEGR is not surprising. After all, only a few stock exchanges had already been established (Warsaw and Budapest) and many transition economies lacked prewar experiences with stock exchanges. More interesting is that SMINTEGR still ranks lowest on average in 1998. Whether or not state regulations of securities markets are desirable is highly disputed in developed market economies.[47] In transition economies and emerging markets, the situation may, however, be quite different. Many of the assumptions on which the quest for deregulation rests in developed market economies—such as transparent information, market intermediaries with superior knowledge of the market that may signal investors' choice, and so on—do not hold true in these environments. Case studies of the experience of different transition economies suggest that more stringent regulation of these markets positively correlates with better market development.[48] Moreover, given that courts in the region lack expertise in dealing with shareholder rights, reliance on internal-control mechanisms alone may not be sufficient.

The breakdown of transition economies into those with different legal histories does not fundamentally alter the picture presented above. For the Eurasian group, the order is virtually the same with the exception that in 1998 ANTIMANAGE ranks before LLSVsh. A closer look at the transition economies with German and French legacies gives a more refined picture. In the countries with German legal influence, ANTIMANAGE takes the lead in 1998 and pushes VOICE into second place and LLSVsh into third place. This suggests that legal reforms have been primarily aimed at strengthening shareholder rights vis-à-vis management. More important, SMINTEGR takes the fourth place in this group, and thus ranks higher than in the other two legal families. To be sure, the reform of securities legislation has been quite uneven in these countries. While Poland and Hungary, for example, established an independent securities and exchange commission (SEC) at the outset of reforms, the Czech Republic followed suit only in 1998.[49] Yet by 1998, most of these countries had established an SEC, although insider trading and self-dealing rules are still uneven. Finally, ANTIBLOCK in these countries is more important than are EXIT rules. The weak performance of "exit" can in part be attributed to the fact that many countries with German legal heritage include rules that allow the issuance of bearer as well as registered shares and permit corporate statutes to restrict the right to sell shares. Our definition of registered free exit, which does not permit such exemptions, lowers the EXIT score for these countries.

For the countries with French legal heritage, the strong emphasis on ANTIMANAGE is visible already in 1992 and is retained through 1998. But ANTIBLOCK also received more attention than in other transition economies. By contrast, EXIT is only weakly developed (for similar reasons as those of the German transition economies). Finally, SMINTEGR has been improved substantially by 1998, but still lags behind the German-family scores.

Comparing the level of protection for each index across the three families, the most surprising result is the strong performance of the Eurasian countries, not only in 1998, but also in 1992. In 1992 they rank first on three indexes (LLSVsh, VOICE, and EXIT), and in 1998 on five of six, excluding only SMINTEGR. The countries of French origin take the lead in two indexes in 1992 (ANTIMANAGE and ANTIBLOCK), but perform worst than the German transition economies on VOICE and EXIT, and on SMINTEGR also worse than the Eurasian transition economies. The fact that these countries do not have any top ranking in 1998 is most likely the result of the slower pace of reforms in southeastern Europe for the reasons noted above. The strong performance of the Eurasian countries in 1998 appears to be the result of primarily the strong U.S. influence in reforming the corporate laws in these countries. This is apparent especially in the elaborate provisions on judicial recourse for shareholders (included in LLSVsh, VOICE, ANTIMANAGE, and ANTIBLOCK). However, some provisions go beyond legal protections that are common in the United States. An example is the (mandatory) requirement to transfer the administration of the shareholder register to an independent agency (an indicator included in EXIT).[50] This provision was included in several Eurasian countries in response to the misuse of control over shareholder registers by company insiders.[51] Similar provisions do not exist in other transition economies, where this was less of a problem. Thus, more stringent regulation does not necessarily imply a generally superior law, but may simply reflect a response to problems not known elsewhere. This also suggests that existing problems are not simply a response to weak regulation or could be easily solved through regulatory intervention. The said provision, for example, has remained rather ineffective.

Although rules with identical contents were introduced in Russian privatization regulations, only a fraction of Russian companies implemented them. Moreover, the independence of the depositaries was often doubtful, and control over the depositary by company management has proved to be an easy vehicle for circumventing those rules.[52]

With respect to other provisions, it may be said that the countries with a German legal tradition in fact have inferior rules. Most of these countries, for example, include provisions that allow company statutes to restrict the sale of registered shares. Similarly, quorum requirements and supermajority requirements for major transactions, which are captured by VOICE and ANTIBLOCK, are also weakly developed in several of these countries. Note, for example, that in the Czech Republic, the presence of 30 percent of shares suffices for a shareholder meeting to take binding decisions, while in most other countries the quorum requirement is 50 percent.[53]

The further analysis of patterns of legal change, using six shareholder indexes that capture different functions and mechanisms to improve the governance of companies, refines rather than refutes our earlier finding that formal legal change in transition economies is converging irrespective of presocialist legal heritage. As table 2.3 shows, all three legal families have implemented comprehensive legal reforms across the board. The refined analysis has, however, shown that different legal families display similar priorities in the focus of legal change. Still, the improvement of the internal-control structure, including minority and antimanagement rights, has been foremost on the agenda in all countries. By contrast, antiblockholder and exit rights, as well as rules aimed at ensuring the integrity of the securities market, were also improved, but in 1998 still rank behind our indexes that capture primarily internal-control rights. Several reasons may account for this. First, the classic conflict between shareholders and management rather than between minority shareholders and blockholders was used as the paradigm for reforming corporate law in transition economies. Second, outside advice came primarily from two sources, the United States and Europe (i.e., legal systems that are recently displaying increasing signs of convergence or at least functional substitution).[54] Third, the lack of attention paid to securities market regulation can be attributed to a combination of ideological bias against regulation—as has clearly been the case in the Czech Republic—and domestic political obstacles. An example of the latter is Russia, where conflicts between the new SEC and the Central Bank as well as the Ministry of Finance prevented the strengthening of this institution and the regulatory framework for its operation.

IV. Taxonomy of Creditor Rights

For creditor rights, we constructed three cumulative indexes in addition to LLSVcr, which we call CREDCON, REMEDY, and COLLAT. CREDCON captures the extent to which creditors can control the bankruptcy process. It modifies LLSVcr to account for the difficulties in adapting the first variable to local circumstances, and also includes additional control variables. Recall that LLSVcr includes a variable called restriction on reorganization. This variable reflects concerns about the U.S. Bankruptcy Code. Under this law, a debtor who files for bankruptcy has the option to file under Chapter 11 (reorganization) or Chapter 7 (liquidation). No creditor consent or court review is required for either decision. This implies that even though the winding up of the company may be the economically most efficient outcome, a protracted reorganization procedure can first be initiated, and only after that fails may a firm be forced into liquidation procedures.[55]

The problem with this variable is that in many countries outside the United States the law does not know a clear separation between reorganization and liquidation procedures. Instead it may offer only a liquidation procedure, or it may establish a unified bankruptcy procedure during the course of which liquidation as well as reorganization are options that might be considered. In these countries, the problem La Porta and coauthors want to address does not exist[56] or is less severe. CREDCON therefore excludes this variable, but employs the other three variables of LLSVcr and adds two more variables: automatic trigger to go into bankruptcy, and creditor consent for adopting a liquidation or reorganization plan. An automatic trigger is a provision that mandates a debtor to file for bankruptcy, in case legally specified conditions have occurred. Several transition economies have experimented with automatic triggers. Hungary came to fame when it introduced a provision in 1992 mandating companies to file for bankruptcy, in case they were unable to meet their payment obligations for more than three months. This resulted in a flood of bankruptcy cases.[57] Since courts were unable to deal with these numbers, the legislature was forced to backtrack and relaxed the provision in 1997.

Coding an automatic trigger is somewhat tricky. Most countries use rather forceful language (*shall*, *must*) indicating that a debtor who is insolvent is obligated to file for bankruptcy. However, the conditions that trigger bankruptcy, in particular the definition of insolvency, often remain ambiguous. Our coding requires that the law specify a time period of illiquidity along the lines of the Hungarian example. The last variable captures whether creditor consent is required for adopting a reorganization or liquidation plan. Since most countries in our sample have unified bankruptcy, or include only liquidation procedures, creditor consent at this later stage appears to be more relevant than when bankruptcy is initiated.

The relevance of LLSVcr as well as CREDCON depends on the existence and scope of collateral rules in a legal system. The two indexes assume that creditors can secure their claims and that information about security interests is readily available. This is not necessarily the case. To capture the existence of legal provisions on security interests, we included the COLLAT index. It does not capture the entire range of possible security interests,[58] but focuses on securing tangible assets, including movable assets (personal property) and immovable assets (real estate). First, we code whether land can be used as a collateral. The privatization of land is still a contentious issue in many transition economies.[59] Where land cannot be freely transferred, its economic value as a collateral is also in question. The appropriate coding of land as a collateral has proved to be difficult, because many countries have enacted legal provisions for mortgaging land, but restrict the enforcement of these rights directly or indirectly. It was not possible to include appropriate variables capturing legal restrictions on the use of land as a collateral, wherefore our index may overstate the extent to which land is actually available and used to secure credits. Second, we code the legal framework for security interests in movable assets. As is well known, civil-law jurisdictions for the most part require that a movable asset must be transferred to the creditor in order to establish a legally valid security interest. This not only is cumbersome, but also deprives the debtor of the possibility of using the asset for productive use and of repaying the credit. Legal practice in many civil law countries has found ways to circumvent these rigid rules. An example is Germany, where the transfer of full ownership with the contractual obligation to retransfer ownership after the credit has been repaid has become a substitute for collateral. Obviously, this practice lacks precisely the publicity and transparency that initially gave rise to the legal rule that secured assets should be transferred to the creditor. Most of the former socialist countries followed the civil-law model and required transfer of the asset for establishing a legally valid security interest.[60] Some countries relaxed this provision early on in the reform process, without, however, creating an alternative for publicity and transparency. The 1992 Russian law on pledge, for example, requires that debtors keep a book of the secured interests in their assets.[61]

The European Bank for Reconstruction and Development (EBRD) developed a model law for secured transactions with the purpose of improving the legal framework for security interests in transition economies, in particular the possibility to use movable assets as a security.[62] Numerous transition economies have used this law to reform their civil codes or related statutes, even though they may not have copied all the provisions of the model law.[63] Others, Poland in particular, used U.S. law (Section 11 of the Uniform Commercial Code) rather than the EBRD model law.[64] The key element of this reform effort was to establish a registry for security interests in movable assets. Our index COLLAT captures whether security interests can be created without transferring assets to the creditor and whether a law that regulates the establishment and functioning of a register has been enacted.

Finally, we include an index called REMEDY. The position of creditors can be strengthened by creating a legal framework that allows them to secure their loans and to enforce their rights in an insolvency procedure. These rules, which are captured in the CREDCON and COLLAT indexes, give creditor ex ante control rights, which they can enforce in a bankruptcy procedure. Alternatively, or as a supplement to these rules, the law may allow creditors to impose sanctions on management ex post, sanctions that go beyond management's original contractual rights or claims based on security interests. For instance, creditors may hold management liable for violating bankruptcy rules, or they may challenge the validity of transactions between the debtor and other parties that were carried out in the time immediately preceding bankruptcy. REMEDY addresses these ex post sanctions. For liability, we require that creditors be able to invoke civil liability. Criminal sanctions in extreme cases only are not sufficient. As far as invalidating transactions that precede bankruptcy is concerned, legal systems differ in the type of transactions that may be invalidated and the time period prior to bankruptcy that is defined as sufficiently sensitive to permit an invalidation claim. To keep matters simple, we only code for the time period and ignore the type of transaction. In particular, we note whether transactions that were carried out three months, six months, one year, or more than one year before bankruptcy was filed can be invalidated.

Managers may not be the only targets of ex post creditor sanctions. REMEDY therefore also includes a variable that asks whether creditors also have recourse against shareholders of the corporation. In principle, shareholders of a company with limited liability are not liable for the debt the company incurred. Yet several countries have developed doctrines that allow creditors in exceptional cases to "pierce the corporate veil." In most countries, this right is limited to extreme cases in which shareholders purposely misuse creditor rights. However, some countries have codified piercing-the-corporate-veil provisions in parent-subsidiary relations.[65] Including this variable in our REMEDY index was motivated by a provision in the Russian civil code, which stipulates

TABLE 2.4
Creditor Rights, 1992 and 1998

	All 24 TEs		*TEs of German origin*		*TEs of French origin*		*Eurasian TEs*	
Indicators	*1992*	*1998*	*1992*	*1998*	*1992*	*1998*	*1992*	*1998*
LLSVcr (0–4)								
Mean	1.40	3.23	2.56	3.56	0	3	1.05	3.05
% of index	34.9	80.7	63.9	88.9	0	75	26.3	76.3
CREDCON (0–5)								
Mean	1.65	3.69	3.11	4.33	0	3	1.15	3.45
% of index	32.9	73.8	62.2	86.7	0	60	23	69
COLLAT (0–3)								
Mean	0.58	2.04	0.67	1.89	0.4	1.6	0.6	2.4
% of index	19.4	68.1	22.2	63.0	13.3	53.3	20	80
REMEDY (0–3)								
Mean	0.42	1.38	0.83	1.25	0.2	1.35	0.15	1.5
% of index	13.9	45.8	27.8	41.7	7	45	5	50

Source: Compilation by author from database of creditor rights. See appendixes 2 and 3 for details.

that a parent company that controls the actions of its subsidiary may be held liable for the obligations of that subsidiary. The drafters of the 1996 Joint Stock Company Act sought to limit the extent to which this provision extends the liability of the parent company by including a provision that requires an explicit contract or a stipulation in the statutes of the subsidiary regarding the parent company's control rights.[66]

Appendix 3 gives the scores for each country from 1992 through 1998 on the four creditor rights indexes. Table 2.4 reports the mean and percentage changes in 1992 and 1998 for all countries included in the sample, as well as for the breakdown by legal family.

According to these data, creditor rights were improved substantially in transition economies since the inception of economic reforms. As with shareholder rights, the ranking of the four indexes does not change over time for the entire sample. LLSVcr comes first, followed by CREDCON, then COLLAT, and finally REMEDY. However, there are a number of regional variations. In the transition economies of German legal heritage, REMEDY is better developed in 1992 than COLLAT. In these countries, bankruptcy codes with some ex post creditor controls were in place at that time already; however, the law on secured transactions, in particular for securing movable assets, was only weakly developed. Obviously, the absence of a well-developed collateral regime renders ineffective those provisions in bankruptcy codes that deal with the rights of secured creditors. This demonstrates that for an adequate assessment of the quality of the law, limiting creditor rights, for example, only to rights of creditors in bankruptcy, without analyzing the conditions for establishing these rights, gives a distorted picture. In comparison to the Central and Eastern European countries (CEEs), the southeastern European countries (SEEs) took longer to put bankruptcy codes in place.[67] For the Eurasian countries, the most dramatic change has been the development of a collateral law. In 1998 it ranks first of the four indexes. REMEDY also changed substantially, but it still ranks behind LLSVcr and CREDCON.

Looking at the level of creditor rights across regions, the most notable fact is that countries with German legal heritage offered substantially better creditor protection as of 1992 than did all other transition economies on the four creditor rights indexes. By 1998, Eurasian countries have taken the lead in COLLAT and REMEDY. Indeed, for the latter, the CEEs rank only third in 1998 despite the fact that they also show improvements in this index since 1992. A possible explanation is that the Eurasian and SEEs compensated for the initially weak protection of ex ante creditor rights with very strong ex post rights in response to the problems creditors experienced when trying to enforce their claims.

As far as COLLAT is concerned, the Eurasian countries have not only caught up with, but have superseded the CEEs in reforming the legal framework for security interests in movables. However, many of the registers that have been established recently are not yet in operation.[68] The high ranking of the Eurasian countries also disguises the fact that land is often not usable for securing loans, because of continuing legal uncertainties about the eviction of present users of the land and subsequent sales.[69] As noted above, legal provisions that in principle permit using land for mortgages (hypothec) therefore overstate the relevance of these laws for commercial practice.

The analysis of changes in different types of creditor rights does not fundamentally challenge our earlier convergence proposition, but sheds light on the dynamics of change. Most important, the patterns that are emerging suggest not that legal change happened at the outset of reforms, but that the law was amended in response to apparent problems. In other words, it was primarily reactive rather than proactive. In fact, there is evidence that countries shopped around for solutions to particular problems, even though they may have been inconsistent with the initial choice of a particular legal system as their model. An example is the rather broad piercing-the-corporate-veil provision found in Russia today. It was copied from continental European civil-law systems,[70] whereas the 1996 Russian corporate statute was largely modeled after U.S. law. Interestingly, most of the CEEs and SEEs have not included similar provisions in their corporate statutes. An explanation, which would be consistent with the retroactive story, is that they have not (yet) encountered similar problems of parent-subsidiary relations.

A second pattern we find is compensatory (or over-) protection in countries with initially weak transition economies laws. The strong emphasis on ex post creditor protection in Eurasian and SEE transition economies, in particular, show that weak initial protection has led to a strengthening not only of overall creditor rights, but in particular also of ex post control rights (REMEDY). These rights, which allow creditors to invalidate transactions that were carried out in the period preceding the opening of bankruptcy procedure, and to increase the pool of debtors by holding shareholders (in particular parent companies) liable for debt incurred by the company, may indeed increase the pool of assets available for distribution. However, the extended liability of shareholders changes the relative rights and obligations of shareholders versus creditors in the corporation in favor of creditors. Unless the enforcement of such provisions is limited to extreme cases that are typically captured by piercing-the-corporate-veil provisions,[71] they may cause concern among equity investors about the reliability of the limited-liability provisions that are an essential part of corporate statutes. Thus, differences in initial legal conditions may shape the path of subsequent law reforms. They will not only take into account the initial weaknesses, but also respond to the problems that have occurred in the meantime and that may, at least in part, be attributed to these weaknesses. This may result in overreactions, which are understandable but may have longer-term implications for the balance of rights of different stakeholders in the company.

V. Corporate Governance by Design?

The above analysis of the development of shareholder and creditor rights in transition economies shows that lawmakers have not been seriously constrained by the historical ties of their country to a particular legal family. If history was not a major determinant of legal change, other factors may be more relevant. In particular, legal change may have been influenced by the choice between alternative corporate governance models. The corporate governance literature typically distinguishes two major corporate governance models, one based on equity finance and control primarily by capital markets, the other on debt finance and control by banks in the dual role of shareholders and major creditors.[72] The former is typically associated with the United States and the United Kingdom, the latter with Germany and Japan.

At the beginning of the transition process there was a lively debate about which of these two models would be most appropriate for transition economies. Given the state of the banking sector, many cautioned against giving banks control rights over enterprises.[73] Others warned against relying on equity market control, in light of the underdeveloped state of stock markets in the region.[74]

The actual development of financial markets in transition economies diverge from both models. The overall trend seems to be toward a control model (i.e., relatively concentrated ownership).[75] However, control does not necessarily imply debt financing or control by creditors rather than equity holders, as both equity and debt financing remain highly underdeveloped, and many companies rely on retained earnings or capital investments by strategic owners. As far as banks, as potential agents of corporate governance, are concerned, short-term rather than long-term lending is still the norm,[76] with only modest progress in expanding the maturity of lending activities over time. With respect to the Czech Republic, some authors had earlier asserted that firms controlled by voucher funds, which in turn are controlled by banks, outperform other firms,[77] suggesting that a bank-based corporate governance model similar to the German one may be emerging in this country. Meanwhile, this has given way to a more sober assessment, namely, that the better performance of these companies' shares reflects the fact that investment funds controlled by major banks tend to loot less than funds not controlled by major banks.[78] However, this does not imply that the banks or their funds finance or control these firms effectively.

It may still be too early to expect the emergence of clearly distinguishable governance models in the region. Still, our data on the patterns of change in shareholder and creditor rights may offer some insight into the preferences of policymakers in different countries for either model. We therefore compare the level of shareholder versus creditor rights protection at the beginning of the transition process and as of today, and analyze the scope of change in different regions. For this analysis, we use the sum of all shareholder rights (SUMsh) and creditor rights (SUMcr) indicators rather than the various indexes we have constructed.[79] As before, we use the percentage of the total indexes for comparison. Table 2.5 reports the results.

The data show that at the outset of reforms, shareholder rights on average were better protected than were creditor rights. Legal reforms introduced since have not changed this ranking, although the difference

Table 2.5
Shareholder vs. Creditor Rights

	All 24 TEs		*German TEs*		*French TEs*		*Eurasian TEs*	
	1992	*1998*	*1992*	*1998*	*1992*	*1998*	*1992*	*1998*
SUMsh								
Mean	8.1	13.99	8.31	13.19	6.65	10.9	10.58	16.25
% of index	38.72	60.82	36.1	57.34	28.91	47.4	46.0	70.65
SUMcr								
Mean	3.40	9.28	5.75	9.72	0.8	8.35	2.6	9.35
% of index	24.3	66.3	41.1	69.4	5.71	59.64	18.6	66.8

Source: Compilation by author using shareholder and creditor rights database.

has declined from 14.42 to only 5.48 percentage points (column 1). In the CEEs, creditor rights are better protected in both time periods. In SEE, creditor rights were only weakly protected at the outset of reforms, but in 1998 were better protected than were shareholder rights. Finally, in the countries of Eurasia, shareholder rights are better protected in both periods, although the gap between shareholder and creditor rights protection has decreased substantially between 1992 and 1998 from 27.4 to only 3.85 percentage points.

The clearest indication of a preference for one group of stakeholders over the other can be found in transition economies of German origin. Given the relatively high level of creditor protection at the outset of reform, this may be the result of path-dependent legal development rather than an independent policy choice at the time economic reforms were introduced. It is interesting to note that the only countries that have, according to the EBRD, "experienced growth in both deposit taking and lending to the private sector beyond that of nominal GDP" since 1993[80]—namely, Croatia, the Czech Republic, Estonia, Poland, the Slovak Republic, and Slovenia—can all trace their legal origin back to the German civil-law family. This certainly requires further research.

Another indication for policy choices that may have determined a particular governance model is the privatization strategy pursued in different countries. Mass-privatization programs were expected to lead to relatively dispersed shareholder ownership (i.e., to a governance model that would rely heavily on market control rather than on control by blockholders).[81] Following the logic of La Porta and coauthors,[82] the success of this strategy was highly dependent on the existence of well-defined minority-shareholder rights. Absent effective legal protection of minority stakes, investors holding small stakes were unlikely to hold

TABLE 2.6
Mass Privatization and Minority Shareholder Protection

Country	Start of privatization	LLSVsh			
		1992	1994	1996	1998
Armenia	1994	2.5	2.5	5.5	5.5
Azerbaijan	1997	2.5	2	2	2
Czech Republic	1992	2	2	3	3
Georgia	1995	2.5	2.5	3	3
Kazakhstan	1994	2.5	2.5	2.25	5.25
Kyrgyzstan	1994	2.5	2.5	2.25	2.25
Latvia	1994	3.5	3.5	3.5	3.5
Lithuania	1991	2.5	3.75	3.75	3.75
Moldova	1993	3	3	3	3.5
Russia	1992	2	2.5	5.5	5.5
Ukraine	1994	2.5	2.5	2.5	2.5
Mean mass-priv. TEs	—	2.55	2.66	3.3	3.61
Mean other TEs	—	1.85	2.23	2.67	2.71
Mean (24 TEs)	—	2.17	2.43	2.95	3.13

Source: EBRD (1998; *see* note 19) and compilation by author from shareholder and creditor rights database.

on to their shares for long. The predictable result was the concentration of ownership in privatized firms. This suggests that only a combination of a privatization strategy and a compatible legal framework could have resulted in a more dispersed ownership structure.

To allow for analysis of whether those countries that chose mass-privatization programs made reasonable efforts to develop complementary protection for minority shareholders, table 2.6 reports the scores of LLSVsh from 1992 through 1998 for all countries that used voucher privatization as the primary privatization method according to the EBRD transition report.[83] We also indicate the beginning of privatization to see whether improvements in minority-shareholder rights preceded or followed privatization.

For the eleven countries that used vouchers as the primary privatization method, the mean of LLSVsh is somewhat above the mean for the entire sample in all years since 1992, and substantially higher than in countries that did not pursue mass-privatization strategies. In fact, the difference between the sample means has increased over time from .7 (1992) to .9 (1998). Yet even in countries that pursued mass-privatization strategies, the level of minority-shareholder protection was quite low in 1992 when compared to the average of the common-law family, which is associated with relatively dispersed share ownership and liquid capital markets (see table 2.1).[84] Moreover, with respect to this index, improvements were made in most countries only after mass privatization began, and in several only after it ended. In the Czech Republic, for example, mass privatization ended in 1995, but the revision of the commercial code, which improved the position of minority shareholders, had to wait until 1996. Similarly, in Russia, mass privatization ended in July 1994, but it took until 1996 for the new Joint Stock Companies Act to come into force. This suggests that legal reform was to a significant degree response driven. The fact that improvements in the level of LLSVsh were less pronounced in countries that did not follow mass-privatization strategies lends further support to this proposition. Note that in those countries that did not implement mass-privatization programs, the mean of LLSVsh in 1998 was only slightly higher than in 1992. In other words, the importance of effective minority-shareholder protection was realized to a much greater extent in countries that had pursued mass-privatization strategies than in countries that used either management-employee buyouts (MEBs) or direct sales as the primary privatization method.

This response pattern of law-making is not uncommon. Much of the historical development of corporate law in Europe and the United States seems to follow this pattern.[85] The differences between these countries and transition economies that experimented with mass privatization, however, is that the latter attempted to implement a fundamental change in the ownership structure and governance of companies. The failure to provide effective minority-shareholder protection ex ante has seriously limited, if not undermined, this attempt.[86] Perhaps the response pattern of legal change suggests that a change of regime of the scale attempted by some transition economies is simply not feasible, precisely because policy makers and lawmakers tend to react to rather than lead economic change. This would call for a more gradual policy approach that took into account the lag-effect of legal and institutional response.

It remains an open question whether the strengthening of minority-shareholder rights ex post will substantially alter the trend toward concentrated ownership that is prevalent in the region, including in countries that used mass-privatization programs. There are several reasons to be cautious about this. First, the absence of effective minority-shareholder protection has caused a loss of confidence by many small investors, which will take time to recover from. Second, securities market protection remains weak in most transition economies. To the extent that the emergence of viable securities markets in the region is dependent on effective market oversight,[87] improvements in the level of minority-shareholder protection alone will not be sufficient. As the data in table 2.7 reveal, improvements in the level of SMINTEGR also tended to respond to rather than precede mass privatization. More important, the

TABLE 2.7
Mass Privatization and Securities Market Regulation

Country	*Start of priv.*	*SMINTEGR 92*	*SMINTEGR 94*	*SMINTEGR 96*	*SMINTEGR 98*
Armenia	1994	0	3	5	5
Azerbaijan	1997	1	1	1	1
Czech Republic	1992	3	3	4	5
Georgia	1995	0	0	0	0
Kazakhstan	1994	1	1	5	6
Kyrgyzstan	1994	0	0	2	2
Latvia	1994	1	1	1	1
Lithuania	1991	2	1	1	1
Moldova	1993	1	2	2	4.75
Russia	1992	2	3	3	3
Ukraine	1994	1	1	1	1
Mean mass-priv. TEs	—	1.09	1.45	2.27	2.27
Mean other TEs	—	0.84	1.46	2.53	3
Mean (24 TEs)	—	0.95	1.45	2.41	2.86

Source: EBRD (1998; see note 19) and author's compilation.

mean of the subsample of countries that implemented mass-privatization programs in 1992 was only marginally higher than that of the countries that pursued other privatization strategies, and was equal to or even lower than that of the control group in the subsequent years.

Third, the environment in which companies operate may make dispersed, or noncontrol ownership structures (NCS), unsustainable.[88] Explaining the prevalence of concentrated ownership structures around the world,[89] Bebchuk argues that in the presence of private benefits of control those holding control rights are unlikely to relinquish them.[90] Should NCS be established in such an environment, they are unlikely to be sustained. Bebchuk suggests that the law may increase the level of private benefits by not preventing self-dealing transactions or insider trading.[91] The weakness of legal rules precisely in this area of the law as displayed by transition economies that pursued mass-privatization strategies (see table 2.6) can therefore help explain why control structures (CS) have come to dominate in these countries despite the theoretical bias of mass-privatization strategies for NCS. This may have compounded other private benefits, including the desire by incumbent management and employees to ensure the survival of, and to retain their position in, the company.[92]

To conclude, there is little evidence in our data that countries chose particular legal rules with a certain governance structure in mind. The initial level of shareholder and creditor rights protection was the result of historical accident rather than clear policy choice. Subsequent change was made primarily in response to emerging problems, the scope of which were determined by the choice of economic reform strategies. Countries that experimented with radical economic reform without having adequate legal protection in place (in particular SMINTEGR), were at greater risk of experiencing strong negative reactions in the development of financial markets. This has given way to legal reforms aimed at remedying the shortcomings. The new laws, however, typically came too late to prevent certain market developments in response to the earlier weaknesses, including a development toward concentrated ownership of companies or the formation of company groups, and the loss of confidence by small investors in the market. The pattern of reform, where economic reforms (privatization, price liberalization, etc.) typically preceded legal reforms, has meant that incumbents who held de facto control rights had an advantage over new title holders with weak rights to protect them. This has increased the private benefits of control for incumbents and decreased the likelihood that they would voluntarily relinquish their control rights. Improvements of the law typically came too late to further the intended reallocation of rights. Rather, it secured control rights gained by whatever methods and thus has undermined, rather than built, a broader constituency for legal reform. The new laws are therefore likely to be less effective now than if they had been enacted at the outset of reforms.

Countries that pursued less radical economic reforms were often not slower in reforming their legal systems. While they may have foregone the opportunity of radically altering the structure of their economies, they also did not confront the negative results that the more radical reformers had to face in light of the weak institutional infrastructure. A proposition that follows from this analysis is that countries that implemented economic reforms more gradually and tied them in with legal and other institutional reforms have developed more effective institutions than have those that pursued a radical reform agenda.

VI. Conclusion

Over the past years, transition economies have introduced remarkable changes in the laws that govern shareholder and creditor rights. Change has been more extensive in countries that exhibited lower levels of protection at the outset of reforms. Presocialist legacies have not impeded or shaped the scope of reforms to a significant degree. Most countries went beyond the average level of legal protection found in legal families to which they once belonged. This suggests a strong trend toward convergence of statutory law across transition economies.

Yet there are notable differences in the pattern of legal change in different countries, suggesting that a simple convergence story does not do justice to the complexity of legal change. In particular, initial preferences for shareholder versus creditor rights have not been leveled out completely, as the still comparatively strong level of creditor protection in countries of German legal heritage suggests. Policy choices mattered for the scope of legal reform in particular areas of the law, such as minority-shareholder protection. Countries that pursued mass-privatization strategies improved this set of rules considerably more than did others. Curiously, however, they neglected the related area of securities market regulation, where improvements lagged behind in comparison to those in countries that relied on more conventional methods of privatization. Weaknesses in this area of the law can explain why the potential for a more dispersed ownership structure and relatively liquid stock markets created by mass-privatization programs was not sustained after privatization.

The high level of statutory legal convergence is largely the result of an external supply of legal solutions. We cannot quantify the influence of domestic versus external forces in shaping legal reform. However, the strong similarities between laws that were influenced by identifiable groups of foreign advisors (United States versus European Union) suggests that the contents of legal rules that were enacted in response to certain problems were strongly influenced by the group of advisors that dominated in a given country. How these externally supplied rules have been received in the different countries, and whether they are followed and enforced by domestic legal institutions, are questions that cannot be captured by a simple analysis of changes in the law on the books and require further analysis.[93]

These features of the past reform process influence not only the evolving legal system, but also the emerging governance structure of firms. Weaknesses in the governance structure that are noted today are often attributed to weaknesses in the law, which in turn leads to new proposals for improving statutory law. The evidence of the quality of the law on the books, however, suggests that this is at best a partial story. The level of shareholder and creditor rights protection in transition economies today is higher than in many other countries. Other factors, including the dynamic of the reform process and its impact on the development of effective institutions to enforce the new law, need to be analyzed more closely in order for us to understand the remarkable difference in the governance of firms despite the trend toward convergence of the law on the books.

Appendix 1: Coding of Shareholder and Creditor Rights Indexes

Table A1.1
Shareholder rights

No.	*Indicator*	*Value*	*LLSVsb**	*SMINTEGER*	*VOICE*	*EXIT*	*ANTIMANAGE*	*ANTIBLOCK*
1	Mandatory one-share-one-vote rule	1/0	(X)		X			
2	Proxy by mail (not sufficient: authorization of proxy statement)	1/0	X		X			
3a	Shares not blocked before the meeting	1/0	X		X			
3b	No registration cutoff date before the meeting	1/0	X		X			
4a	Cumulative voting for election of members of board (supervisory board)	1/0	X	X		X		
4b	Other rules to ensure proportional board representation	1/0	X		X			X
5a	Shareholder may take judicial recourse against decisions by executives, (supervisory) board	1 = direct and/or derivative suit by individual shareholder or minority group (not more than 10%)	X	X		X		

(*continued*)

Table A1.1 (*continued*)

No.	*Indicator*	*Value*	*LLSVsb**	*SMINTEGER*	*VOICE*	*EXIT*	*ANTIMANAGE*	*ANTIBLOCK*
		0.5 if legal claim is limited to nullifying decisions of the board and does not include liability of management 0 if shareholders cannot sue or have to request supervisory board to sue						
5b	Shareholders may take judicial recourse against decisions taken at the shareholder meeting (SHM)	1 = judicial recourse provided 0 = no such provision	X		X			X
6	Current shareholders have a preemptive right in case new shares are issued by company	1 = preemptive right mandated by law, which may be changed only by decision of shareholders 0 = no preemptive right, or only optional	X		X			X
7	Shareholders representing not more than 10% of total shares may demand convocation of extraordinary shareholder meeting	10% = 1 20% = 0.5 0 = more than 20% of shares required for calling extraordinary shareholder meeting	X		X		X	

8	Corporate statutes specify the amount of dividends to be paid out to shareholders	1 = proportion of profits set aside for paying dividends 0 = no such provision	(X)	X	X	
9	Executives (incl. general directors) are appointed/dismissed by the board (supervisory board) rather than the shareholder meeting	1 0.5 if board appoints, but general meeting dismisses 0 if shareholder meeting appoints and dismisses				
10	Members of the management/supervisory board may be dismissed at any time without cause	1 = if law does not specify conditions for dismissal 0 = if law requires specific cause (including violation of contract)		X	X	
11	At least 50% of total voting shares must be represented at a SHM for it to take binding decisions	1 = 50% or more of total shares required for quorum 0 = less than 50% required		X		X
12	Audit commission may be called by minority shareholder representing not more than 10% of shares	1 = if 10% of shares required 0.5 = if 20% of shares required 0 = if more than 20% required or not regulated		X	X	
13	Fundamental decisions, including charter changes,	0.5 for charter changes and liquidation only		X		

(continued)

Table A1.1 (*continued*)

No.	*Indicator*	*Value*	*LLSVsh**	*SMINTEGER*	*VOICE*	*EXIT*	*ANTIMANAGE*	*ANTIBLOCK*
	liquidation of companies, sale of major assets, require qualified majority (at least 3/4)	0.75 the above plus changes in charter capital, and/or company reorganization (incl. mergers, takeovers) 1 for the above and sale of major assets						
14	Board (supervisory) board members are elected by shareholders (no mandatory representation of employees or the public)	1/0			X			
15	Right to transfer shares is not restricted by law and may not be limited by charter	1 = if the right to freely transfer shares cannot be restricted by statute 0 = if this right can be restricted, even only for bearer shares				X		
16	Formal requirements for the transfer of shares are limited to endorsement (bearer shares) and registration (registered shares)	1 = no additional formal requirements 0 = notarial certification, documentation of contracts, etc., required for valid transfer			X			
17	Minority shareholders have a put option (may de-	1 = put option by law 0 = not regulated			X		X	

	mand that their shares are bought by the company at fair value) in case they have voted against major transactions, including mergers, reorganization, sale of major assets, charter changes, etc.					
18	Mandatory takeover bid (threshold)	1 for 25% or less 0.75 for >30% 0.5 for > 50%		X		X
19	Conflict of interest rules, including rules on disclosing conflict and abstaining from voting, are included in the law	1 = transaction specific conflict of interest rules 0 = no such rules, even if some competition rules (i.e., members of the board may not serve on boards of other firms) are included	X		X	
20	Shareholder register must be conducted by independent firm (*not* the issuing company)	1 = mandatory rule for publicly traded companies, including companies exceeding a legally specified number of shareholders 0 = if register is administered by the company	X			

(*continued*)

Table A1.1 (*continued*)

No.	*Indicator*	*Value*	*LLSVsh**	*SMINTEGER*	*VOICE*	*EXIT*	*ANTIMANAGE*	*ANTIBLOCK*
21	Insider trading prohibited by law	1 = rules against insider trading exist		X				
		0 = no insider-trading rules		X				X
22	Acquisition of larger blocks of shares triggers mandatory disclosure (thres hold)	1 for 10% 0.75 for 25% 0.5 for 50% 0.25 for more than 50% 0 if no mandatory disclosure						
23	A state agency conducts capital market supervision	1 = if the task of supervising the securities market is assigned to a designated state agency		X				
24	Capital market supervision is formally independent	1 = if the agency is independent and neither part of or directly subordinate to a government ministry (i.e., Ministry of Finance)			X			

*LLSVsh includes 7 separate indicators. I have decomposed some of their indicators into two separate ones. Note, for example, that indicators 4a and 4b as well as 5a and 5b are each one indicator in their database. To achieve comparable results with LLSV, they should therefore be computed as (4a + 4b)/2, and (5a + 5b)/2, respectively. With respect to indicators 3a and 3b, LLSV use only 3a. I have added 3b, because registration of shares prior to the shareholder meeting has effects similar to those of blocking shares. Although trading remains possible in the first case, trading shares after the registration date will have not influence on voting at the shareholder meeting. Again, the two indicators could be computed as (3a + 3b)/2. Indicators that were originally coded by La Porta et al. but were not included in their cumulative index are in parentheses.

Table A1.2
Creditor Rights

	Indicators	*Value*	*LLSVcr*	*CREDCON*	*COLLAT*	*REMEDY*
1	Restrictions for going into reorganization (i.e., creditor consent)	1/0	X			
2	*No* automatic stay on secured assets	1/0	X	X		
3	Secured assets first	1 = first or after costs of bankruptcy procedure are met 0.75 = second after costs and other creditor category 0.5 = third after costs and other two creditor categories 0.25 = fourth after costs and other creditor categories 0 = priority not different from unsecured creditors	X	X		
4	Management does not stay (receiver)	1/0	X	X		
5	Legal reserve minimum percentage of total shares required to avoid voluntary dissolution 0 for no restriction	0.5 for simple majority 1 for qualified majority	(X)			
6	Automatic trigger to file bankruptcy (i.e., if debtor unable to meet	1/0		X		
	obligations for more than 90 days)	1/0		X		

(continued)

Table A1.2 (*continued*)

Creditor rights

	Indicators	*Value*	*LLSVcr*	*CREDCON*	*COLLAT*	*REMEDY*
7	The adoption of a reorganization or liquidation plan requires creditor consent					
8	Establishing a security interest in movable assets does *not* require transfer of asset	1/0			X	
9	Law requires establishment of register for security interests in movables	1/0			X	
10	An (enforceable) security interest in land may be established	1/0		X		
11	Legal provision that allows creditors to pierce the corporate veil	1/0				X
12	Management can be held liable for violating provisions of insolvency law (lower threshold than criminal activities required)	1/0				X
13	Transactions preceeding the opening of bankruptcy procedures may be declared null and void	0.25 = 3 months prior to bankruptcy 0.5 = 6 months prior to bankruptcy 0.75 = 1 year prior to bankruptcy 1 = more than 1 year				X

Note: La Porta et al. (198) code 1/0 and do not use the scaled coding proposed for variable 3. Indicators that were originally coded by La Porta et al. but were not included in their cumulative index are in parentheses.

Appendix 2: Scores for Shareholder Rights Indexes (1992–98)

Table A2.1

	LLSVsh				*SMINTEGR*			
Country	*1992*	*1994*	*1996*	*1998*	*1992*	*1994*	*1996*	*1998*
Albania	3	3	3	3	1	1	1	1
Armenia	2.5	2.5	5.5	5.5	0	3	5	5
Azerbaijan	2.5	2	2	2	1	1	1	1
Belarus	1.5	1.5	1.5	1.5	1	1	1	1
Bosnia	0	0	0.5	0.5	0	0	0	0
Bulgaria	4	4	4	4	1	1	5	5
Croatia	0	2.5	2.5	2.5	0	1	6	6
Czech Rep	2	2	3	3	3	3	4	5
Estonia	2	2	3.75	3.75	0	2	4	4
FYR Macedonia	0	0	2.5	2.5	0	0	1	5
Georgia	2.5	2.5	3	3	0	0	0	0
Hungary	2.5	2.5	2.5	3	3	3	3	5
Kazakhstan	2.5	2.5	2.25	5.25	1	1	5	6
Kyrgyzstan	2.5	2.5	2.25	2.25	0	0	2	2
Latvia	3.5	3.5	3.5	3.5	1	1	1	1
Lithuania	2.5	3.75	3.75	3.75	2	1	1	1
Moldova	3	3	3	3.5	1	2	2	4.75
Poland	3	3	3	3	4	4	4	4
Romania	3	3	3	3	1	1	1	1
Russia	2	2.5	5.5	5.5	2	3	3	3
Slovak Rep	2.5	2.5	2.5	2.5	0	2	2	2
Slovenia	0	2.5	2.5	2.5	0	3	3	3
Ukraine	2.5	2.5	2.5	2.5	1	1	1	1
Uzbekistan	2.5	2.5	3.5	3.5	0	0	2	2

	VOICE				*EXIT*			
Country	*1992*	*1994*	*1996*	*1998*	*1992*	*1994*	*1996*	*1998*
Albania	7.75	7.75	7.75	7.75	1	1	1	1
Armenia	8	8	12	12	1	1	3	3
Azerbaijan	8	7.5	7.5	7.5	1	1	1	1
Belarus	6	6	6	6	1	1	1	1
Bosnia	0	0	3.5	3.5	0	0	0	0
Bulgaria	10.75	10.75	10.75	10.75	0	0	2	2
Croatia	0	5.25	5.25	5.25	0	1	1	1
Czech Rep	3.5	3.5	4.5	4.5	1	1	2.5	2.5
Estonia	6.75	6.75	9.5	9.5	2	1	2	2
FYR Macedonia	0	0	5.75	5.75	0	0	0.5	0.5
Georgia	8	8	9	9	1	1	0	0

(*continued*)

TABLE A2.1 (*continued*)

	LLSVsh				*SMINTEGR*			
Country	*1992*	*1994*	*1996*	*1998*	*1992*	*1994*	*1996*	*1998*
Hungary	6.25	6.25	6.25	6.75	1.5	1.5	1.5	0.5
Kazakhstan	8	8	7.25	12.5	1	1	3	3
Kyrgyzstan	7	7	9.25	9	1	1	2	2
Latvia	7.25	7.25	7.25	7.25	1	1	1	1
Lithuania	8.25	9.75	9.75	9.75	1	1	1	1
Moldova	7.75	7.75	7.75	9	2	2	2	4
Poland	6.25	6.25	6.25	6.25	3	3	3	3
Romania	5.75	5.75	5.75	5.75	1	1	1	1
Russia	6	7	12	12	3	3	3.75	3.75
Slovak Rep	4	4	4	4	0	1	1	1
Slovenia	0	6.25	6.25	7.25	0	3	3	3
Ukraine	8	8	8	8	2	2	2	2
Uzbekistan	8	8.25	10	10	1	2	3	3

	ANTIMANAGE				*ANTIBLOCK*			
Country	*1992*	*1994*	*1996*	*1998*	*1992*	*1994*	*1996*	*1998*
Albania	5	5	5	5	3	3	3	3
Armenia	2.5	2.5	5	5	2	2	4.5	4.5
Azerbaijan	2.5	3	3	3	2	1	1	1
Belarus	1.5	1.5	1.5	1.5	1	1	1	1
Bosnia	0	0	1.5	1.5	0	0	0	0
Bulgaria	5	5	5	5	3	3	5	5
Croatia	0	4	4	4	0	2	3	3
Czech Rep	2	2	2	2	1	1	4.5	4.5
Estonia	2	2	4.5	4.5	1	1	4	4
FYR Macedonia	0	0	2.5	2.5	0	0	3.5	4.5
Georgia	2.5	2.5	4	4	2	2	2	2
Hungary	2	2	2	4	2.5	2.5	2.5	4.5
Kazakhstan	2.5	2.5	3.5	5.5	2	2	3	6.25
Kyrgyzstan	1.5	1.5	3.5	4	2	2	3	3
Latvia	3	3	3	3	3	3	3	3
Lithuania	4	3.5	3.5	3.5	2.5	3.5	3.5	3.5
Moldova	2	2	2	3	2	2	2	6.25
Poland	3	3	3	3	4.5	4.5	4.5	4.5
Romania	4	4	4	4	4	4	4	4
Russia	3	3	5	5	2	2.5	6	6
Slovak Rep	2	2	2	2	1	1	1	1
Slovenia	0	3	3	4	0	3.75	3.75	3.75
Ukraine	2.5	2.5	2.5	2.5	2	2	2	2
Uzbekistan	2.5	2.5	5	5	2	2	3.5	3.5

Appendix 3: Scores for Creditor Rights Indices (1992–98)

	LLSVcr				*CREDCON*			
Country	*1992*	*1994*	*1996*	*1998*	*1992*	*1994*	*1996*	*1998*
Albania	0	0	3	3	0	3	3	3
Armenia	0	0	0	3	0	0	0	4
Azerbaijan	0	3	3	4	0	4	4	3
Belarus	2	2	2	2	3	3	3	3
Bosnia	0	0	0	4	0	0	0	4
Bulgaria	0	3	3	3	0	4	4	4
Croatia	0	0	4	4	0	0	5	5
Czech Rep	3	3	3	3	4	4	4	4
Estonia	3	3	3	4	4	4	4	4
FYR Macedonia	0	0	1	1	0	0	0	0
Georgia	0	0	2.75	2.75	0	0	2.75	2.75
Hungary	3.75	3.75	3.75	3.75	4.75	4.75	4.75	3.75
Kazakhstan	1.5	1.5	1.5	2.75	1.5	1.5	1.5	2.75
Kyrgyzstan	0	0	0	3	0	0	0	3
Latvia	4	4	4	4	4	4	5	5
Lithuania	4	4	4	3	3	3	3	3
Moldova	3	3	3	4	3	3	3	4
Poland	2.25	2.25	2.25	2.25	4.25	4.25	4.25	4.25
Romania	0	0	4	4	0	0	4	4
Russia	0	3	3	2.5	0	3	3	3.5
Slovak Rep	3	3	3	4	4	4	4	5
Slovenia	0	4	4	4	0	5	5	5
Ukraine	4	4	4	4	4	4	4	4
Uzbekistan	0	2.5	2.5	2.5	0	4.5	4.5	4.5

	COLLAT				*REMEDY*			
Country	*1992*	*1994*	*1996*	*1998*	*1992*	*1994*	*1996*	*1998*
Albania	0	1	1	1	1	1	2	2
Armenia	0	0	2	2	0	0	0	1
Azerbaijan	0	0	1	3	0	0.5	0.5	1.75
Belarus	1	1	1	1	0.75	0.75	0.75	0.75
Bosnia	0	0	0	0	0	0	0	0.75
Bulgaria	1	1	3	3	0	2	2	2
Croatia	0	0	1	1	0	0	2	2
Czech Rep	1	1	1	1	1	1	1	1
Estonia	0	3	3	3	1	1	1	1
FYR Macedonia	1	1	1	3	0	0	0	0
Georgia	0	2	2	3	0	0	0	0

(*continued*)

Appendix 3: (*continued*)

	COLLAT				*REMEDY*			
Country	*1992*	*1994*	*1996*	*1998*	*1992*	*1994*	*1996*	*1998*
Hungary	1	1	3	3	1	1	1	1
Kazakhstan	2	2	2	3	0	0	1	2.75
Kyrgyzstan	0	0	1	3	0	0	0	2.75
Latvia	0	0	0	1	0.75	0.75	0.75	1
Lithuania	1	1	1	3	0.75	0.75	0.75	0
Moldova	0	1	2	3	0	0	1	1
Poland	1	1	1	3	1.5	1.5	1.5	1.5
Romania	0	0	0	1	0	0	2	2
Russia	1	1	1	2	0	0.5	1.5	2.5
Slovak Rep	1	1	1	1	1.5	1.5	1.5	2
Slovenia	1	1	1	1	0	1.75	1.75	1.75
Ukraine	2	2	2	2	0.75	0.75	0.75	0.75
Uzbekistan	0	0	0	2	0	1.75	1.75	1.75

Notes

Reprinted with permission by European Business Organizational Law Review (vol. 1, 2000). T.M.C. Asser Press.

This chapter was completed during my stay at the Max Planck Institute for Foreign and International Private Law in Hamburg, which generously contributed its resources, without which this study would not have been feasible. Financial support from the European Bank for Reconstruction and Development (EBRD) is gratefully acknowledged. Violetta Bessenich, Sorniza Dimitrova, and Dmitri Gavriline provided excellent research assistance. I would like to thank Klaus J. Hopt for helpful comments and suggestions in developing the framework for this analysis. Helpful comments were also received from participants at seminars at the Max Planck Institute, the Stockholm Institute for Transition Economies (SITE), and the Institute for East European Law at the University of Vienna.

1. Katharina Pistor, Law Meets the Market: Matches and Mismatches in Transition Economies, mimeo, World Bank (1995). Cheryl Gray, Evolving Legal Framework for Private Sector Development in Central and Eastern Europe (1993). Jeffrey Sachs & Katharina Pistor, Rule of Law and Economic Reform in Russia (1997).

2. Rafael La Porta, Florencio Lopez-de-Silanes, Andrei Shleifer, & Robert W. Vishny, *Law and Finance*, 106 J. Pol. Econ. 1113–55 (1998). Rafael La Porta, Florencio Lopez-de-Silanes, Andrei Shleifer, & Robert W. Vishny, *Legal Determinants of External Finance*, 52 J. Fin. 1131–50 (1997). Ross Levine, *The Legal Environment, Banks, and Long-Run Economic Growth*, 30 J. Money, Credit, & Banking 596–613 (1998).

3. Katharina Pistor, Martin Raiser, & Stanislaw Gelfer, *Law and Finance in Transition Economies*, 8 Econ. Transition 325–68 (2000).

4. Douglass C. North, Institutions, Institutional Change, and Economic Performance 4 (1st ed. 1981).

5. Frank H. Easterbrook & Daniel R. Fischel, The Economic Structure of Corporate Law (1991). The convergence hypothesis has been most prevalent among macroeconomists. They show strong trends toward convergence in levels of GDP per capita among regions within the United States. See strong convergence of OECD countries, Steve Dorwick and Duc-Tho Nguyen, *OECD Comparative Economic Growth, 1950–1985*, 79 Am. Econ. Rev. 1010–30 (1989); however, only conditional convergence for developing countries, Robert J. Barro & Xavier Sala-i-Martin, *Convergence*, 100 J. Pol. Econ. 223–51 (1992).

6. North, (1981), *supra* note 4; Mark J. Roe, *Chaos and Evolution in Law and Economics*, 109 Harv. L. Rev. 641–68 (1996).

7. John C. Coffee, Jr., *The Future as History: The Prospects for Global Convergence in Corporate Governance and Its Implications*, 93 Nw. Univ. L. Rev. 631–707 (1999). For a similar point based on a case study of recent trends in German corporate governance, see Jeffrey Gordon, *Corporate Governance: Pathways to Corporate Convergence? Two Steps on the Road to Shareholder Capitalism in Germany*, 3 Colum. J. Eur. L. 219 (1999). However, he correctly points out that political constraints, as well as long-term practices of insider governance, may limit the scope of convergence. See id., at 241.

8. Roe, *supra* note 6; Lucian Arye Bebchuk and Mark J. Roe, *A Theory of Path Dependence in Corporate Governance and Ownership*, 52 Stanf. L. Rev. 127 (1999). *See also* Gordon, *supra* note 7.

9. Easterbrook & Fischel, *supra* note 5 (1991). J. Mark Ramseyer, *The A-Contextual Logic to the Japanese Keiretsu*, *in* Corporate Governance Today, 527–63 (Roe ed., New York City, offset 1998).

10. *See* La Porta et al. (1998), *supra* note 2, at 1126.

11. Bernard S. Black, *Is Corporate Law Trivial? A Political and Economic Analysis*, 84 Nw. Univ. L. Rev. 542–97 (1990). The argument holds that efficient capital markets and well-functioning and competitive managerial labor and product markets are more effective constraints on managerial power than are formal legal constraints.

12. Bernard S. Black & Reinier H. Kraakman, *A Self-Enforcing Model of Corporate Law*, 109 Harv. L. Rev. 1911–82 (1996). Hay, Shleifer, & Vishny, *Toward a Theory of Legal Reform*, 40 Eur. Econ. Rev. 559–67 (1996).

13. Andrei Shleifer & Robert W. Vishny, *A Survey of Corporate Governance*, 52 J. Fin. 737–83 (1997).

14. La Porta et al. (1998), *supra* note 2; La Porta et al. (1997), *id.* The authors of these studies also mention the importance of effective enforcement institutions. Yet even if these variables are controlled, the contents of legal rules and their origin seems to matter.

15. Levine, *supra* note 2.

16. La Porta et al. (1998), *supra* note 2.

17. Bebchuk and Roe, *supra* note 8; Lucian Arye Bebchuk, *A Rent-Protection*

Theory of Corporate Ownership and Control, Nat'l Bureau of Econ. Research Working Paper No. 7203 (1999). Katharina Pistor, *Law as a Determinant for Stockmarket Development in Eastern Europe*, *in* Assessing the Value of Law in Transition Economies (Peter Murrell ed., 2001).

18. Despite these differences in initial conditions, commentators agree that transition economies are increasingly converging on a control structure with concentrated ownership rather than sustaining dispersed ownership. *See* Erik Berglöf, *Corporate Governance in Transition Economies: The Theory and Its Policy Implications*, *in* Corporate Governance in Transitional Economies, 59–98 (Masahiko Aoki & Hyung-Ki Kim eds., 1995) with data for the largest companies in three transition economies. For a theoretical explanation of the instability of noncontrol structures, see Bebchuk, *supra* note 17.

19. Lawrence J. Brainard, *Reform in Eastern Europe: Creating a Capital Market*, Econ. Rev. 49–58 (1991). EBRD, Transition Report: Financial Sector in Transition (1998).

20. La Porta et al. (1998), *supra* note 2.

21. Many of the countries in Central and Eastern Europe modeled their legal systems in the interwar period on the German system. In the countries of southeastern Europe that used to be part of the Ottoman Empire, French law had stronger influence, mostly because of the reception of French law in the nineteenth century when the Ottoman Empire reformed its legal system. Nevertherless, the borrowing does not suggest that the model was followed closely or that other legal systems were not consulted in the process. A brief summary of the history of formal private law in different countries can be found in International Encyclopedia of Comparative Law, National Reports (1972). For a summary of the socialist legal system, *see* Konrad Zweigert & Hein Kötz, Einführung in die Rechtsvergleichung auf dem Gebiet des Privatrechts, 332–403 (1984). This legal family has now been discarded from this book. *See* Zweigert & Kötz, Introduction to Comparative Law (3d ed. 1998).

22. There is, of course, a lively debate about the relevance of legal families. The area of the law for which the legal families have been developed is the core of the civil law (i.e., contract law, property rights, and torts). Constitutional and administrative law development usually do not follow the same pattern. Even for other areas of private law, including corporate law and capital market development, it is doubtful whether a consistent set of criteria exists that makes the distinction of different legal families meaningful.

23. Pistor, *supra* note 1.

24. William E. Butler, Soviet Law (2d ed. 1988). Ferdinand Feldbrugge, Russian Law: The End of the Soviet System and the Role of Law (1993).

25. See Feldbrugge, *supra* note 24, at 236–39.

26. See Jon Elster, Claus Offe, and Ulrich K. Preuss, Institutional Design in Post-communist Societies: Rebuilding the Ship at Sea (1998), for the pattern of institutional change in Bulgaria, the Czech Republic, Hungary, and Slovakia.

27. La Porta et al. (1998), *supra* note 2.

28. Details for the definition of variables and their coding are given in Appendix 1.

29. Called antidirectors index by La Porta et al. (1998), *supra* note 2.

30. Part of Poland, of course, received French law during the Napoleonic Wars. However, subsequent German law has been stronger.

31. Note that periodically Bosnia belonged to the Austro-Hungarian Empire, but this has not strongly affected its legal development during the nineteenth century.

32. Thomas C. Owen, The Corporation under Russian Law, 1800–1917 (1991); International Encyclopedia *supra* note 21, at 1.

33. La Porta et al. (1998), *supra* note 2.

34. *Id.*

35. Compare also the indicators for economic reforms in EBRD, *supra* note 19.

36. Feldbrugge, *supra* note 24; Katharina Pistor, *Company Law and Corporate Governance in Russia*, *in* Sachs & Pistor, *supra* note 1, at 165–87. Cheryl W. Gray & Kathryn Hendley, *Developing Commercial Law in Transition Economies: Examples from Hungary and Russia*, *in* Sachs & Pistor, *supra* note 1, at 139–64.

37. This information was given by Alexander Shapleigh of USAID. According to USAID, the results have not been equally strong in all countries. Good results were achieved in shareholder rights reforms in Armenia, Kazakhstan, Kyrgyzstan, and Romania. For creditor rights, good results were reported for Kazakhstan, Kyrgryzstan, Latvia, Poland, Romania, and Ukraine. Since this assessment is highly subjective, in our analysis we include all countries that have received USAID for legal reforms of shareholder and creditor rights.

38. For a discussion of the effects of the takeover guideline in Poland, *see* Stanislaw Soltysinski, *Transfer of Legal Systems as Seen by the "Import Countries": A View from Warsaw*, *in* Systemtransformation in Mittel- und Osteuropa und ihre Folgen für Banken, Börsen und Kreditsicherheiten, 69–82 (Drobnig et al. ed., 1998). Compare this with the positive evaluation of the City Takeover Code for transition economies by John C. Coffee, Jr., The Lessons From Securities Market Failure: Privatization, Minority Protection, and Investor Confidence (Sept. 1999) (unpublished manuscript on file with author).

39. La Porta et al. (1998), *supra* note 2.

40. In comparative law methodology, analyzing the function of legal rules rather than trying to find identical legal rules in different systems has long been recognized. *See* Zweigert & Kötz (1984), *supra* note 21, who call this approach a functional approach to comparative law. Critical, however, is Günter Frankenberg, *Critical Comparisons: Re-thinking Comparative Law*, 26 Harv. Int. L.J. 411–55 (1985). On the importance of functional substitutes in corporate governance and securities market regulation, see Coffee, *supra* note 7.

41. Albert O. Hirschman, Exit, Voice, and Loyalty: Responses to Decline in Firms, Organizations, and States (1970). John C. Coffee, Jr., *Liquidity Versus Control: The Institutional Investor as Corporate Monitor*, 91 Colum. L. Rev. 1277–368 (1991).

42. La Porta et al. (1997), *supra* note 2.

43. Black and Kraakman, *supra* note 12, at 1911–82.

44. Berglöf, *supra* note 18; Erik Berglöf & Ernst-Ludwig von Thadden, *The Changing Corporate Governance Paradigm: Implications for Transition and Developing Countries*, *in* Proceedings of the Annual Bank Conference on Develop-

ment Economics (1999). Rafael La Porta, Florencio Lopez-de-Silanes, & Andrei Shleifer, *Corporate Ownership around the World*, 54 J. Fin. 471–517 (1999).

45. Coffee, *supra* note 38.

46. Unfortunately, it was not possible to obtain reliable data on changes in disclosure requirements for all countries. Most laws have provisions mandating the annual disclosure of company information to their shareholders. We did not include this variable, because of the lack of variance, and because it does not reflect the extent of disclosure requirements for publicly traded companies.

47. George J. Stigler, *Public Regulation of the Securities Markets*, 27 J. Bus. 117–42 (1964). Gregg A. Jarrell, *The Economic Effects of Federal Regulation of the Market for New Security Issues*, 24 J.L. & Econ. 613–75 (1981). John C. Coffee, Jr., *Market Failure and the Economic Case for a Mandatory Disclosure System*, 70 Virg. L Rev. 717–53 (1984). Joel Seligman, *The Historical Need for a Mandatory Corporate Disclosure System*, 9 J. Corp. L. 1–61 (1983). Klaus J. Hopt & Harald Baum, *Börsenrechtsreform in Deutschland*, *in* Börsenreform—Eine ökonomische, rechtsvergleichende und rechtspolitische Untersuchung, 287–467 (Hopt, Bernd Rudolph, & Baum eds., 1997). The debate is now taking a new turn, where the importance of (some) regulation is acknowledged in principle, but the need for federal versus state (or decentral) regulation debated. See Roberta Romano, *Empowering Investors: A Market Approach to Securities Regulation*, 107 Yale L.J. 2359–430 (1998).

48. Pistor, *supra* note 17; Coffee, *supra* note 7. For experiences in other parts of the world, *see also* Robert C. Rosen, *The Myth of Self-Regulation or the Dangers of Securities Regulation without Administration: The Indian Experience*, 2 J. Comp. Corp. L. & Sec. Reg. 261–302 (1979) *as well as* Katharina Pistor & Philip Wellons, The Role of Law and Legal Institutions in Asian Economic Development, ch. 6 (1999).

49. Pistor, *supra* note 17.

50. This requirement typically does not apply to all joint stock companies, but only those that exceed the stipulated number of shareholders (i.e., five hundred in the case of Russia and Kazakhstan).

51. Pistor, *supra* note 36.

52. Pistor, *supra* note 36.

53. In fact, in the early period many of the former Soviet Union republics required 60 percent. This may, however, be counterproductive, because it decreases the likelihood for a shareholder meeting to reach the quorum.

54. Erik Berglöf, *Reforming Corporate Governance: Redirecting the European Agenda*, 24 Econ. Pol'y 93–119 (1997); Coffee, *supra* note 7.

55. On the pros and cons of the U.S. Bankruptcy Code, *see* Douglas G. Baird, The Elements of Bankruptcy 283 (1993).

56. La Porta et al. (1998), *supra* note 2.

57. Gray and Hendley, *supra* note 36.

58. Philip R. Wood, Comparative Law of Security and Guarantees, Law and Practice of International Finance (1995).

59. Hiroshi Oda, *Law on Secured Transaction in Russia*, *in* The Russian Civil Code (Simons ed., 2000).

60. Pistor (1995), *supra* note 1. Elizabeth A. Summers, *Recent Secured Trans-*

action Law Reform in the Newly Independent States and Central and Eastern Europe, 23 Rev. Cent. and E. Eur. L. 177–203 (1997).

61. For a detailed analysis of Russian law on security interests, *see* Oda, *supra* note 59.

62. EBRD, Model Law on Secured Transactions (1994).

63. According to information obtained from the EBRD, the following countries have established registers for security interests that used the EBRD model law or U.S. law: Azerbiajan (1998); Belarus (1999); Bulgaria (1996); Estonia (1996); FYR Macedonia (1998); Georgia (1997); Hungary (1997); Kazakhstan (1998); Kyrgyzstan (1997); Latvia (1999); Lithuania (1998); Moldova (1996—simplified version now under revision); Poland (1998); Romania (1999); Ukraine (1997/99); Uzbekistan (1998). The enactment of these laws, however, is only the first step. Functioning registries for security interests in movables apparently exist as of now only in Bulgaria; Hungary; Latvia; Lithuania; Poland, with some reservations; and, apparently since March 1999, Ukraine.

64. Summers, *supra* note 60.

65. An example is the German law on concerns. Art. 317 of the German corporate law on marketable share companies (AktG), for example, states that a company that controls another one, *without* having concluded a control contract, may be held liable for damages incurred by that company or its shareholders, if it made that company conclude detrimental transactions without compensation.

66. Compare Art. 106 of the Russian Civil Code with Art. 6, Section 3 of the Joint Stock Companies Act.

67. Note: since we do not code for law in the former Yugoslav republics, our coding is likely to overstate the absence of law in this region.

68. Information obtained from the EBRD.

69. Oda *supra* note 59.

70. Note that they were first included in the Civil Code, which borrowed heavily from the Dutch Civil Code.

71. Gainan Avilov, Bernard S. Black, Dominique Carreau, Oksana Kozyr, Stilpon Nestor, & Sarah Reynolds, General Principles of Company Law for Transition Economies, OECD (1999) strongly advocate that such provisions should be strictly limited to these cases.

72. Mark J. Roe, *Some Differences in Corporate Structure in Germany, Japan, and the United States*, 102 Yale L.J. 1927–2003 (1993); Berglöf, *supra* note 18; Masahiko Aoki, *Controlling Insider Control: Issues of Corporate Governance in Transition Economies, in* Corporate Governance in Transitional Economies, 3–32 (Aoki and Hyung-Ki Kim eds., 1995).

73. Jacek Rostowski, *The Banking System, Credit, and the Real Sector in Transition Economies*, in Banking Reform in Central Europe and the Former Soviet Union, 16–41 (Rostowski ed., 1995). Peter Dittus & Stephen Prowse, *Corporate Control in Central Europe and Russia: Should Banks Own Shares? in* Corporate Governance in Central Europe and Russia, 20–67 (Roman Frydman, Cheryl William Gray, & Andrzej Rapaczynski eds., 1996).

74. Jenny Corbett & Colin Mayer, *Financial Reform in Eastern Europe: Progress with the Wrong Model*, 7 Oxf. Rev. Econ. Pol. 57–75 (1992).

75. Berglöf, *supra* note 18.

76. Claudia M. Buch, *Creating Efficient Banking Systems*, *in* Kieler Studien (Paul Siebeck ed., 1996); Herbert L. Baer & Cheryl W. Gray, *Debt as a Control Device in Transitional Economies: The Experience of Hungary and Poland*, *in* Frydman et al. eds., *supra* note 73, at 68–110; EBRD, *supra* note 19.

77. Stijn Claessens, Simeon Djankov, & Gerhard Pohl, Ownership and Corporate Governance: Evidence from the Czech Republic, International Symposium on Capital Markets and Enterprise Reform (1996).

78. John C. Coffee, Jr., *Inventing a Corporate Monitor for Transitional Economies: The Uncertain Lessons from the Czech and Polish Experiences*, *in* Comparative Corporate Governance: The State of the Art and Emerging Research, 67–138 (Klaus J. Hopt, Hideki Kanda, Mark J. Roe, Eddy Wymeersch, & Stefan Prigge eds., 1998).

79. Obviously, this can be only a rough estimate of the relative importance of shareholder and creditor rights, as the variables included are not encompassing, and not all variables may have equal weight.

80. EBRD, *supra* note 19, at 118.

81. Maxim Boycko, Andrei Shleifer, & Robert W. Vishny, *Voucher Privatization*, 35 J. Fin. Econ. 249 (1993). Roman Frydman & Andrzej Rapaczynski, *Markets and Institutions in Large Scale Privatization: An Approach to Economic and Social Transformation in Eastern Europe*, *in* Reforming Central and Eastern European Economies: Initial Results and Challenges, 253–74 (Vittorio Corbo, Fabrizio Coricelli, & Jan Bossak eds., 1992); Classens et al. (1996), *supra* note 77.

82. La Porta et al. (1998), *supra* note 2.

83. EBRD, *supra* note 19.

84. La Porta et al. (1997), *supra* note 2.

85. Philip I. Blumberg, The Multinational Challenge to Corporation Law 316 (1993). Colleen A. Dunlavy, *Corporate Governance in the Late 19th-Century Europe and the USA: The Case of Shareholder Voting Rights*, *in* Klaus J. Hopt & Eddy Wymeersch eds., *supra* note 78, at 5–39. Accounts of the development of corporate law in the United States and Germany since the nineteenth century show a close interaction between legal and economic development. See Heinz-Dieter Assmann, *Introduction* to vol. 1 for Germany, *in* Aktiengesetz: Großkommentar (Klaus J. Hopt & Herbert Wiedemann eds., 1992). For a summary of the development in the United States, cf. John C. Coffee, Jr., *The Mandatory/Enabling Balance in Corporate Law: An Essay on the Judicial Role*, 89 Colum. L. Rev. 1618–91 (1989) and Black & Kraakman (1996), *supra* note 12. Note also that the enactment of extensive minority-shareholder protection in the United States in 1933–34 follows on the heels of the publication of the famous book by Adolf A. Berle & Gardiner C. Means, The Modern Corporation and Private Property (1932), in which they point out the weakness of dispersed small shareholders vis-à-vis company management. Response-driven legal evolution has also been observed for the development of corporate law and securities regulations in emerging markets in Asia. See Pistor & Wellons, *supra* note 48.

86. Katharina Pistor, *Privatization and Corporate Governance in Russia: An Empirical Study*, *in* Privatization, Conversion and Enterprise Reform in Russia 69–

84 (Michael A. McFaul and Tova Perlmutter eds., 1995); Pistor *supra* note 36; John C. Coffee, Jr., *Institutional Investors in Transitional Economies: Lessons from the Czech Experience*, *in* Frydman et al. *supra* note 73; Bernard S. Black, Reinier Kraakman, and Anna Tarassova, Russian Privatization and Corporate Governance: What Went Wrong? chaper 4, *infra*. Among economists, there was little interest in the extent and effectiveness of the law at the outset of reform. In their
attempt to explain the extremely low valuation of Russian companies in privatization, Boycko and coauthors do not even discuss the possible role of the weak legal environment. Maxim Boycko, Andrei Shleifer, & Robert W. Vishny, *Privatizing Russia*, Brookings Papers for Economic Activity 139–80 (1993). *But see* Jeff Sachs in his comments on that paper, *id.* at 181, with reference to Pistor (1995, *id.*).

87. Pistor, *supra* note 17.

88. Bebchuk, *supra* note 17.

89. La Porta et al., *supra* note 44.

90. Bebchuk, *supra* note 17.

91. *Id.*

92. Roman Frydman, Katharina Pistor, & Andrzej Rapaczynski, *Investing in Insider-Dominated Firms: A Study of Russian Voucher Privatization Funds*, *in* Frydman et al. (1996), *supra* note 73, at 187–241. Igor Filatov, Mike Wright, & Michael Bleaney, Insider Control and Managerial Entrenchment in Privatised Firms in Russia: Analysis and Policy Implications (1999) (manuscript on file with the University of Nottingham Business School).

93. A first attempt is made in Pistor et al., *supra* note 3. Using data on the effectiveness of legal institutions (legality) they show that countries differ remarkably in this respect and that these differences can explain differences in financial-market development in transition economies. Using a large sample set (which excludes transition economies), Berkowitz and coauthors show that domestic demand for a transplanted legal order is an important determinant for the long-term development of legality. Daniel Berkowitz, Katharina Pistor, & Jean-François Richard, Economic Development, Legality, and the Transplant Effect, (1999) (EBRD mimeo).

CHAPTER THREE

The Common Law and Economic Growth: Hayek Might Be Right

Paul G. Mahoney

> [T]he ideal of individual liberty seems to have flourished chiefly among people where, at least for long periods, judge-made law predominated.
>
> —Friedrich A. Hayek, *Law, Legislation, and Liberty: A New Statement of the Liberal Principles of Justice and Political Economy*

Recent finance scholarship finds that countries with legal systems based on the common law have more developed financial markets than do civil-law countries. In the present chapter I argue that finance is not the sole, or principal, channel through which legal origin affects growth. Instead, following Hayek, I focus on the common law's association with limited government. I present evidence that common-law countries experienced faster economic growth than did civil-law countries during the period 1960–92 and then present instrumental variables results that suggest that the common law produces faster growth through greater security of property and contract rights.

I. Introduction

Recently, financial economists have produced evidence that financial markets contribute to economic growth and legal institutions contribute to the growth of financial markets. Robert King and Ross Levine demonstrate that the average rate of increase in per capita gross domestic product (GDP) is greater in countries with more developed financial markets.[1] Rafael La Porta and coauthors show that legal rules protecting creditors and minority shareholders are an important determinant of the cost of external capital.[2] What is also interesting is that they find that countries whose legal systems are derived from the common-law tradition provide superior investor protections on average, particularly in comparison to the French civil-law tradition.

Building on these results, Levine, Norman Loayza, and Thorsten Beck treat legal origin as an instrumental variable for financial development.[3] Legal origin is well suited to the purpose. It is largely exogenous, as most countries obtained their legal systems through colonization or conquest. It also correlates strongly with policies (such as creditor and minority shareholder protections) that on the basis of theory and empirical results should lead to greater financial market development. The principal drawback of the analysis is the lack of a theoretical reason to expect legal origin to be especially relevant to investor protection. Indeed, because corporate and bankruptcy law are generally codified in both common- and civil-law countries, differences in those areas should be small compared to differences in other commercial law fields.

In the present chapter, by contrast, I argue that legal origin does not affect economic growth solely, or even principally, through its effect on financial markets. The major families of legal systems were created as a consequence of debates about government structure, not merely about the rules that should govern particular transactions. A country's legal system accordingly reflects, albeit remotely and indirectly, a set of prior choices about the role of the state and the private sector in responding to change.

Friedrich Hayek provides the most prominent discussion in the economics literature of differences between legal families.[4] He argues vigorously that the English legal tradition (the common law) is superior to the French (the civil law), not because of substantive differences in legal rules, but because of differing assumptions about the roles of the individual and the state. In general, Hayek believed that the common law was associated with fewer government restrictions on economic and other liberties. More recently, La Porta and coauthors revived this argument, positing that "[a] civil legal tradition . . . can be taken as a proxy for an intent to build institutions to further the power of the State. . . . A common law tradition . . . can be taken as a proxy for the intent to limit rather than strengthen the State."[5]

These views are correct as a matter of legal history. Although legal systems are most often acquired involuntarily, they were an object of conscious choice in England and France. English common law developed as it did because landed aristocrats and merchants wanted a system of law that would provide strong protections for property and contract rights and limit the Crown's ability to interfere in markets. French civil law, by contrast, developed as it did because the revolutionary generation, and Napoleon after it, wished to use state power to alter property rights and attempted to ensure that judges could not interfere. Thus, quite apart from the substance of legal rules, there is a sharp difference between the ideologies underlying common and civil law, with the latter notably more comfortable with a centralized and activist government.[6]

The more complex question is whether these differences in origin and ideology translate into institutional differences that could affect economic outcomes today. We are far removed from seventeenth-century England and eighteenth-century France, and most countries did not choose a legal family. Moreover, civil law has not hindered much of continental Europe from developing highly successful economies, and the common law has not guaranteed economic growth and the security of property rights in every former English colony.

Nevertheless, there is evidence that legal origin explains part of the cross-sectional variation in various measures of government intervention, government size, and public-sector efficiency.[7] I attempt to tie that observation in with the law and finance results in two ways. First, I discuss in detail the historical origins of the common and civil law and show that they reflect different views about the relative role of the private sector and the state. Second, I note that there are structural differences between common- and civil-law systems, most notably in the greater degree of judicial independence in the former and the lower level of scrutiny of executive action in the latter, that provide governments more scope to alter property and contract rights in civil-law countries. Thus, while the explanation does not turn narrowly on the substance of specific investor protection rules, neither does it rely solely on different "cultural" features of common and civil law.

I then report results of cross-country regression analyses for a large set of nonsocialist countries showing an association between the common law and higher rates of real per capita GDP growth. I eliminate socialist countries from the sample in order to focus specifically on differences between common and civil law. Finally, I test the idea that the institutional features of the common law I have identified are an important avenue through which legal origin affects growth. I use legal origin as an instrument for variables measuring the quality of the judiciary and the security of property and contract rights.

Section II provides theoretical background by drawing a link between the role of the judiciary and economic growth. Section III draws on the history of the common- and civil-law traditions to show that the two differ sharply in attitudes toward the judicial role and notes ongoing institutional effects. Section IV reports the results of cross-country growth regressions. Section V provides additional evidence that the association between the common law and growth is a consequence of greater judicial protection of property and contract rights from executive interference, and Section VI concludes.

II. Theoretical Background

Why should legal origin affect economic growth? One possibility is that the average quality of legal rules varies by origin. The finance literature focuses on the association between the common law and superior rules of investor protection. Nevertheless, it is difficult to make out a strong case for the superiority of the rules produced by the common law or the civil law across the board. Although there are substantive differences, each performs well on the most important measures, providing for enforcement of property and contract rights and requiring compensation for certain wrongful (tortious) acts. The creation of a system of enforceable property rights is one of the most important institutional prerequisites to economic growth.[8] The substantive rules of common and civil law provide redress for private actors' interference in property or contracts. One might therefore think that the results obtained by La Porta and coauthors tell us nothing systematic about legal origin—the common law happened, by chance, to produce good corporate governance rules, and good corporate governance rules are especially important for growth.

Some scholars argue that the common law's adversarial adjudication process tends to result in the survival of efficient and the demise of inefficient rules.[9] The unspoken implication is that statutory law is generally less efficient than judge-made law. More recently, however, these claims have come under sustained attack. Legislatures have incentives to create efficient and not merely redistributive rules.[10] Courts, moreover, can and do promote wealth-destroying, rent-seeking litigation, a fact that prompts Gordon Tullock to argue in favor of civil-law codification.[11]

Another possibility is that the average quality of rules is similar, but the common law provides greater stability and predictability. The common-law tradition includes two features—respect for precedent and the power of an appellate court to reverse the legal conclusions of a lower court—that should result in more predictable outcomes.[12] These features are nominally lacking in the civil law. Only the code itself—not prior judicial decisions or the pronouncement of a superior tribunal—counts as binding law in the civil-law tradition. Legislatures, unlike common-law courts, are not bound by precedent. The differences are not, however, as sharp in practice as in theory. Civil-law courts in fact consult precedents and the decisions of higher courts.

A final possibility is that the economic significance of the distinction between the common and civil law derives principally from their distinct ideological and constitutional content, not in their substantive rules. As I show below, the common law is historically connected to strong protection for property rights against state action, whereas the civil law is connected to a strong and less constrained central government. The distinction not only is ideological, however, but also leads to an important structural difference—the role of the judiciary. In the common-law system, the judge is an independent policymaker occupying a high-status office, whereas in the civil-law system, the judge is a (relatively) low-status civil servant without independent authority to create legal rules.

This difference in the judicial role fragments power more in a common-law system than in a civil-law system. A recent literature focuses on self-enforcing limits on governmental power as a critical feature of a stable and prosperous state.[13] One important form of self-enforcing limitations consists of the fragmentation of governmental power. Fragmentation limits the ability of government actors to grant, and therefore of interest groups to obtain, rents because it is more difficult to coordinate the decisions and actions of multiple government actors.[14] Federalism, or the vertical dispersion of governmental authority among different levels, is an example. Another is the horizontal separation of legislative, executive, and judicial powers. Recent theoretical and empirical scholarship shows that the horizontal dispersion of power produces less redistribution.[15] The fundamental structural distinction between the common law and civil law lies in the judiciary's greater power to act as a check on executive and legislative action in a common-law system. Thus, although both the common and civil law provide strong protections for property and contract rights against other private actors, those rights may be more secure against the government itself in a common-law system.

III. Ideological and Constitutional Distinctions

A. Individual versus Collective Liberty

The substantive rules of most common- and civil-law jurisdictions evolved from a combination of Roman-law concepts and local practices and share many substantive traits. The common law and civil law also played important roles in the creation of the modern English and French constitutional arrangements. Those roles were sharply divergent, however, and as a consequence each system has an ideological content distinct from the substance of particular legal rules.

England's constitutional structure, including the role of the judiciary, took its modern shape as a result of conflicts between Parliament and the Crown in the seventeenth century. During that period, the common law became strongly associated with the idea of economic freedom and, more generally, the subject's liberty from arbitrary action by the Crown. While that association came about partly by chance—because judges opposed the Crown and sided with Parliament—it had substantial consequences for the future role of the judiciary.

Over the course of several centuries, England's large landowners had pried their land loose from the feudal system and became in practice owners rather than tenants of the king. Because landowners served as local justices of the peace and the landowning nobility as judges of last resort, the judges unsurprisingly developed legal rules that treated them as owners with substantial rights. The common law they created was principally a law of property. Thus the first of Sir Edward Coke's *Institutes of the Laws of England* is an extensive treatise on the law of real property, structured as a commentary on Thomas Littleton's earlier treatise, which itself is devoted entirely to property law.[16] William Blackstone describes the Court of Common Pleas, which resolved disputes between subjects, as "the grand tribunal for disputes of property."[17]

During the seventeenth century, however, the Stuart kings attempted to reassert feudal prerogatives, as a means of raising revenue.[18] The Crown responded to a budgetary crisis by coercing merchants to grant it loans, using claims of feudal rights to appropriate land and goods, and selling monopoly rights. Disputes over the security of property and executive intervention in the economy played a central role in both the English Civil War and the Glorious Revolution.

Indeed, as Richard Pipes argues, the equation of good government with secure property rights reached a high-water mark in English seventeenth-century political thought.[19] Commentators such as James Harrington, Henry Neville, and John Locke described the foremost function of government as the protection of property.[20] They also championed the concept of the rule of law as a superior organizational principle to royal absolutism.

In the dispute between property owners and the Crown, the common-law courts and Parliament took the side of economic freedom and opposed the Crown. For example, in the *Case of Monopolies*, the Court of King's Bench decided that the king's sale of monopoly rights violated the common law.[21] This decision and others challenging the king's right to alter property rights drew the courts, led by Chief Justice Coke, into a confrontation with James I, who insisted that unconstrained royal power trumped the common law. Coke's insistence that the common law bound even the king led James I to dismiss him and like-minded judges. Thus Coke, his successor Matthew Hale, and other common-law judges came to stand for the protection of the rule of law and economic rights against royal power.

Unable to control the ordinary courts, the Stuarts brought politically sensitive cases in a separate body of prerogative courts, such as the Star Chamber, that were under the Crown's direct control and could be counted on to uphold royal authority. After Parliament prevailed in the Civil War, it abolished the prerogative courts. It also rewarded common-law judges with tenure during good behavior and a salary sufficient to make the potential loss of office a substantial disincentive to corruption.[22]

The French experience was very different. Judges were villains, not heroes, in French constitutional development. While security of economic rights was the motivating force in the development of English common law, security of executive power from judicial interference was the motivating force in the postrevolution legal developments that culminated in the Code Napoléon.

The highest courts in prerevolutionary France, the parlements, were very different from the common-law courts in England. They were part court, part legislature, and part administrative agency. They decided cases, promulgated regulations, and had partial veto power over royal legislation. As a practical matter, judicial offices were salable and inheritable. The purchase of a judgeship or other royal office automatically conveyed noble status and qualified the purchaser and his descendants for entry into the parlements.[23] The return on the investment was straightforward; in addition to obtaining prestige and various exemptions from taxation that accompanied noble status, judges enforced the rigidly controlled system of guilds and monopolies that characterized Bourbon France.[24]

Like the Stuarts in seventeenth-century England, the Bourbons faced a fiscal crisis in eighteenth-century France. Since monopoly rights had been sold over nearly every trade possible and taxes had been raised on the peasantry to levels that could not easily be sustained, continuance of royal consumption and war making required new sources of revenue. Louis XV's and Louis XVI's ministers attempted to address the situation by increasing the role of royal administrators, the *intendents*, in the profitable business of enforcing guild and monopoly rights at the expense of the parlements. This was partly successful, judging from the fact that the prices of judicial offices declined on average throughout most of the century.[25] The Crown also attempted to increase the tax base by eliminating some aristocratic privileges. The parlements, not surprisingly, strongly resisted these strategies, and the resulting conflict between king and parlements helped ignite the revolution.

A central goal of postrevolution legal reform, then, was to prevent a return of "government by judges."[26] A law of 1790 forbade the judiciary to review any act of the executive.[27] The parlements themselves were shortly thereafter abolished and replaced with courts of drastically reduced authority. The Civil Code was accordingly much more than a simplification and codification of legal rules. As the code's principal drafter explained, it was also the expression of an "overriding desire to sacrifice all rights to political ends and no longer consider anything but the mysterious and variable interests of the State."[28] This assertion of the primacy of politics over law later dovetailed nicely with Napoleon's goal of centralizing power in the executive.

The English experience was that dispersion of authority to judges helped to secure desirable political and economic outcomes. The French experience was just the opposite. The authority of the parlements stalled needed reforms in ancien régime taxation, and the lesson drawn was that economic and political progress required the centralization of power. The civil law and common law, then, are closely connected to the more centralizing tendency of French political thought and the decentralized, individualistic tradition of English political thought, respectively. Hayek argued that English and French concepts of law stemmed from English and French models of liberty, the first (derived from Locke and Hume) emphasizing the individual's freedom to pursue individual ends and the second (derived from Hobbes and Rousseau) emphasizing the government's freedom to pursue collective ends.[29]

In this, Hayek echoed many nineteenth- and early twentieth-century writers. Francis Lieber argued that "Gallican liberty is sought in the *government*, and according to an Anglican point of view, it is looked for in a wrong place, where it cannot be found. Necessary consequences of the Gallican view are, that the French look for the highest degree of political civilization in *organization*, that is, in the highest degree of interference by public power. The question whether this interference be despotism or liberty is decided solely by the fact *who* interferes, and for the benefit of which class the interference takes place, while according to the Anglican view this interference would always be either absolutism or aristocracy."[30]

More recently, Pipes described the French eighteenth century as a period of intellectual "assault" on property.[31] A part of the French intellectual heritage is a concept of law that is more congenial to economic intervention and redistribution as acts of the "general will."

B. Structural Consequences

The common law and civil law continue to reflect their intellectual heritage, and as a consequence, legal origin is relevant both to the ideological background and the structural design of government. At an ideological or cultural level, the civil-law tradition assumes a larger role for the state, defers more to bureaucratic decisions, and elevates collective over individual rights. It casts the judiciary into an explicitly subordinate role. In the common-law tradition, by contrast, judicial independence is viewed as essential to the protection of individual liberty.[32] These ideological distinctions may be particularly important given the prevalence of lawyers in government in many countries.

At a structural level, the two systems' different attitudes about the judicial role have produced distinct institutional arrangements, including a difference in the authority of judges to review executive action. A central feature of the civil law is a sharp distinction between "private" law (the law that governs relations between citizens) and "public" law (the law that governs relations between the citizen and the state). The ways in which private and public rights are protected differ both procedurally and substantively, and in general, public law in a civil-law system puts light restraints on public officials compared to public law in a common-law system.[33]

Procedurally, the ordinary courts in a civil-law jurisdiction typically have no authority to review government action. In France, the relevant statute remains unchanged from 1790: "It shall be a criminal offence for the judges of the ordinary courts to interfere in any manner whatsoever with the operation of the administration, nor shall they call administrators to account before them in respect of the exercise of their official functions."[34] France eventually developed a system of specialized administrative courts authorized to review administrative decisions. These courts, however, are under the direct supervision of the executive. Its judges are trained at the administrative schools alongside the future civil servants whose decisions they will oversee.[35]

Substantive administrative law in a civil-law system insists that the courts intrude as little as possible in the administration's pursuit of the public interest.[36] The strong emphasis on property and contract that characterizes private law gives way in public law to a concern for preserving the government's freedom to pursue collective ends.[37]

Under the common law, by contrast, there is no sharp distinction between private and public law. As described by the United Kingdom's highest court, the House of Lords, the same principles apply to deprivations of property by private and public actors.[38] The same judges who enforce private rights, moreover, review administrative action. Although some common-law jurisdictions (such as the United States) have administrative courts, their decisions are subject to review by the ordinary courts.

Long after the English and French revolutions, commentators have described these differences in judicial review of administrative action as a proxy for restrictions on the executive's freedom of action. A recent comparative law text argues that the common law's hostility to specialized courts stems from the controversy over prerogative courts in the seventeenth century.[39] A. V. Dicey notoriously argued that France did not possess the "rule of law" because ordinary courts are not permitted to review administrative action, touching off a debate among comparative law scholars that continues to the present day.[40]

C. The Problem of Germany and Scandinavia

German and Scandinavian civil law are distinct traditions that developed separately from French civil law. This complicates the task of drawing general distinctions between common- and civil-law systems. On several dimensions, German and Scandinavian civil law can be grouped together with French civil law without difficulty. All rely on legislative rather than judge-made rules, and, in all, the judiciary occupies a lower status than in a common-law system. Both the French and German civil codes are associated with the development of a powerful central government.

There are also important differences. Codification was not part of a general upheaval but, rather, was a gradual process, in the various German states and in Scandinavia from the time of rediscovery of Roman law in the Middle Ages. More important, the development of separate administrative courts in Germany did not, as in France, stem from a fear of judicial interference with the bureaucracy—rather, Germany's administrative court system proceeded from a desire to subject administrators to external control.[41] In order to prevent executive or legislative interference, Germany's constitution provides for the independence of judges, who cannot be reassigned without their consent.[42] For these reasons, Hayek found the German civil-law system more conducive to individual liberty than its French counterpart.[43] Much of the prior law and finance literature treats German and Scandinavian civil law as separate categories.[44]

Drawing a sharp distinction between the civil-law subfamilies, however, might appear to a skeptical observer to be post hoc rationalization. The handful of countries outside Western Europe that have adopted German civil law include Japan and South Korea, which have had extremely successful economies in the postwar period.[45] Most of the remaining German, and all Scandinavian, civil-law countries are in economically advanced Western Europe. In order to avoid this concern, I treat all civil-law countries as a single category except as otherwise noted. Any bias, then, would be in the direction of making the civil law look better.

IV. Law and Growth: Cross-Country Evidence

In the tradition of cross-country growth studies, I examine differences in average annual growth in real per capita GDP. The sample consists of 102 countries (see appendix A) covered by the Penn World Tables, Mark 5.6.[46] Growth rates are averaged over the period 1960–92, and I eliminate any country for which real per capita GDP data are missing for more than three years of that period. Following the prior literature, I take the description of legal systems from Thomas Reynolds and Arturo Flores.[47] For all but a handful of countries, assignment to a legal family is straightforward.[48] There are a few countries in east Asia and Africa that have had both English and French influence. However, for several of these, the Privy Council in England remains the highest court of appeal. Given my focus on the common law as a constitutional arrangement, I assign these to the common-law family.[49] I eliminate only Cameroon from the sample, on the basis that French and English influences are too mixed to make a choice. I also exclude some Middle Eastern countries whose legal systems are almost entirely based on Islamic law (such as Saudi Arabia and Oman) and a few countries whose legal systems have been largely free of European influence (such as Ethiopia and Iceland). Finally, all socialist countries are eliminated in order to focus strictly on differences between the common and civil law.

I test the effect of the common law using ordinary least squares regressions with the average annual rate of real per capita GDP growth (GROW) as the dependent variable (see appendix B). The independent variable of interest is a dummy (COMMONLAW) that takes on the value one for common-law countries and zero otherwise. I begin with a "base" regression that includes prevalent conditioning variables from the cross-country growth literature.[50] The variables are initial real per capita GDP (PCG60), the initial rate of enrollment in primary education (PRI60), the average annual rate of population growth during the sample period (GPO), and the average investment share of GDP over the sample period (INV). Table 3.1 provides descriptive statistics for each variable in the base regression for the full sample and the common- and civil-law subsamples.

The first column of table 3.2 reports results for the base regression (Model 1). All the conditioning variables enter with the signs we would predict from theory and prior empirical studies. Initial per capita GDP and the rate of population growth are both negatively related to growth, and initial enrollment in primary education and average investment share of GDP are positively related to growth. The coefficient on the common-law dummy variable is both economically and statistically sig-

TABLE 3.1
Descriptive Statistics, Common- and Civil-Law Countries

A. Full sample (n = 102)				
Variable	*Mean*	*Standard deviation*	*Minimum*	*Maximum*
GROW	2.06	1.71	−2.00	7.03
PCG60	2421.98	2309.97	313.00	9895.00
PRI60	.75	.34	.05	1.44
GPO	2.11	1.00	.17	4.08
INV	16.34	7.94	1.40	34.43
B. Common-law countries (n = 38)				
Variable	*Mean*	*Standard deviation*	*Minimum*	*Maximum*
GROW	2.44	1.81	−.83	6.67
PCG60	2274.89	2504.96	313.00	9895.00
PRI60	.72	.33	.09	1.26
GPO	2.18	.96	.17	3.71
INV	15.83	7.66	1.47	31.18
C. Civil-law countries (n = 64)				
Variable	*Mean*	*Standard deviation*	*Minimum*	*Maximum*
GROW	1.83	1.61	−2.00	7.03
PCG60	2509.31	2201.92	367.00	9409.00
PRI60	.76	.35	.05	1.44
GPO	2.07	1.03	.24	4.08
INV	16.64	8.14	1.40	34.43

Note: The variables are the average annual rate of real per capita GDP growth (GROW), the initial real per capita GDP (PCG60), the initial rate of enrollment in primary education (PRI60), the average annual rate of population growth during the sample period (GPO), and the average investment share of GDP over the sample period (INV).

nificant. Controlling for the other variables, the common-law countries grew, on average, .71 percent per year faster than the civil-law countries ($p = .007$).

I also estimate an extended model that includes other variables that have been found to be significantly related to growth but that should not be related to legal origin. The additional variables are the initial rate of secondary school enrollment (SEC60), William Easterly and Levine's ethnoliguistic fractionalization index (ETHNIC),[51] the average annual rate of change in the GDP deflator (INFLATION), and the average export share of GDP over the sample period (EXPORT).

TABLE 3.2
Common Law and Growth, 1960–92

Variable	*Model 1*	*Model 2*
COMMONLAW	.714**	.768**
	(.261)	(.258)
PGC60	−.0004**	−.0005**
	(.000)	(.000)
PRI60	1.790**	1.546**
	(.531)	(.527)
GPO	−.300*	−.092
	(.145)	(.134)
INV	.121**	.113**
	(.028)	(.029)
ETHNIC		−1.405**
		(.504)
SEC60		.719
		(.944)
INFLATION		−.002+
		(.001)
EXPORT		1.074+
		(.599)
R^2	.54	.59
N	102	97

Note: The dependent variable for all regressions is GROW. For variable definitions, see appendix B. White-corrected standard errors are in parentheses.
+Significant at the 10 percent level.
*Significant at the 5 percent level.
**Significant at the 1 percent level.

Results for the extended model are reported as Model 2 in table 3.2. Each of the new variables enters with the expected sign. The estimated coefficient on the common-law dummy is little changed from Model 1 and remains significant at the 1 percent level. As found in other studies, initial per capita GDP and the investment share of GDP are the most robust predictors. The common-law dummy, however, performs quite well.

Table 3.3 reports the results of regressions that attempt to meet two possible objections to the analysis thus far. Sub-Saharan Africa and Latin America were notably poor performers during the period of interest. Latin America consists almost entirely of civil-law countries. Any omitted variable causing low growth in Latin America could, therefore, lead to a mistaken conclusion that the civil law is to blame. Africa is un-

TABLE 3.3
Sensitivity: Region and Religion

Variable	*Model 3*	*Model 4*
COMMONLAW	.561*	.557*
	(.266)	(.241)
PCG60	−.0005**	−.0004**
	(.000)	(.000)
PRI60	1.967**	2.064**
	(.617)	(.680)
GPO	−.155	−.234
	(.141)	(.145)
INV	.086**	.085**
	(.029)	(.028)
AFRICA	−1.293**	
	(.375)	
LATINAM	−1.321**	
	(.352)	
PROTESTANT		−.197*
		(.099)
CATHOLIC		−.0001
		(.004)
MUSLIM		1.432**
		(.448)
CONFUCIAN		7.646**
		(1.42)
BUDDHIST		1.289+
		(.759)
R^2	.64	.70

Note: The dependent variable for all regressions is GROW. For variable definitions, see appendix B. White-corrected standard errors are in parentheses.

+Significant at the 10 percent level.

*Significant at the 5 percent level.

**Significant at the 1 percent level.

usual on many accounts during the period of interest.[52] I accordingly estimate the base regression after adding in dummy variables for sub-Saharan Africa and Latin America. The results are reported as Model 3 in table 3.3. The common-law dummy is still associated with higher growth, although the magnitude is lower and the significance level is 5 percent.

One might also wonder whether common-law versus civil-law origin, for part of the world, is merely a proxy for Protestant versus Catholic religious heritage. The package of endowments received by many former colonies includes, along with the common or civil law, the English, French, Spanish, or Portuguese language and Protestantism or Catholicism. Max Weber famously argued that Protestant (particularly Calvinist) doctrine encouraged vigorous worldly pursuits as a means of demonstrating one's faith and thereby unleashed a "heroic age" of capitalism.[53] I therefore estimate the base regression together with a set of religion variables previously used by Robert Barro.[54] These variables measure the percentage of the population that practices some form of Protestantism, Roman Catholicism, Islam, Buddhism, or Confucianism.[55] The results are reported as Model 4 in table 3.3. Estimated coefficients on all religion variables other than the percentage of Catholics are significant, and those on the Confucianism, Buddhism, and Islam variables are large. The estimated coefficient and significance level for the common-law dummy, however, is almost unchanged from that of Model 3.

The variables I have used to this point are drawn principally from Levine and David Renelt's study of variables whose estimated coefficients are highly robust to different specifications of the growth equation.[56] In regressions not reported here, I added to the base regression groups of variables from Xavier Sala-i-Martin's 1997 survey of empirical growth research.[57] Using a less restrictive approach than Levine and Renelt, Sala-i-Martin found twenty-two variables from the prior literature that are robust. In addition to those already reported herein, these include equipment investment,[58] the number of years an economy was open between 1950 and 1992,[59] the capital city's distance from the equator,[60] the average number of revolutions and coups per unit time,[61] the fraction of GDP in mining,[62] and several policy-related variables. Although I did not use every possible specification, I employed each of the additional "robust" Sala-i-Martin variables in small groups in additional regressions and found that the estimated coefficient on the common-law dummy remains in the range of .5–.7 and is statistically significant in all specifications. The estimated coefficient becomes unstable when using large numbers of variables and regional dummies. However, the coefficients on all of the variables (including the investment variable) are unstable in these specifications.

As discussed above, the German and Scandinavian civil-law families can be viewed as distinct from the French law tradition. There are not enough German and Scandinavian civil-law countries to include separate dummies for each and expect significant results. I did, however, estimate all of the regressions using a dummy for French civil law in place of the common-law dummy, in effect grouping German and Scandinavian origin countries with the common-law countries. The absolute values of the coefficients were slightly higher on average compared to those in the regressions estimated with a common-law dummy. The result, although far from conclusive, is consistent with the notion that German and Scandinavian law fit somewhere between French law and common law.

V. Testing the Intervention Hypothesis

The results so far confirm directly what Levine finds using legal origin as an instrument for financial market development.[63] The existing literature focuses on variation in minority shareholder and creditor rights and their effects on financial markets as the causal link between legal origin and growth.

I suggest a different and broader link from legal origin to more dispersed governmental power and from there to superior protections for property and contract rights. I therefore examine measures of judicial power, security of property rights, and contract enforcement and use legal origin as an instrument for those variables.

The economic growth literature provides measures, albeit imperfect, for each of these phenomena. Paolo Mauro uses Business International Corporation's (BIC's) index of judicial quality, a survey-based assessment of the "efficiency and integrity" of the judiciary.[64] I expect judges in common-law countries, who occupy a higher-prestige office (and therefore have more to lose) relative to their civil-law counterparts, and who have more authority to redress adverse actions by other governmental actors, to score more highly on this index. Kim Holmes and coauthors develop an index of the security of property rights.[65] Christopher Clague and coauthors define "contract intensive money" (CIM) as the ratio of broad money (M2) minus currency to M2 and argue that CIM is a measure of the extent to which contracts are enforced.[66] They reason that CIM, unlike currency, represents a contract right, such as the right of the payee of a check to obtain money from the drawee bank. Second, although currency is well suited to simultaneous exchange, long-term contracting more frequently relies on CIM. The use of CIM in preference to currency, therefore, reflects confidence in the system of contract enforcement.

For the sake of completeness, I examine other measures of state intervention in the economy. Mauro uses BIC's "red tape" index that assesses the prevalence of bureaucratic obstacles to business activity.[67] Stephan Knack and Philip Keefer use the International Country Risk Guide's "rule of law" index that assesses adherence to legal procedures and "expropriation risk" index that assesses the risk of confiscation or nationalization of business assets.[68] In addition to the property rights measure, Holmes and coauthors provide a "business regulation" index that seeks to capture the extent of regulatory burdens on business activity.[69] Barro employs an index of civil liberties that assesses rights of speech and assembly and personal autonomy in matters such as religion, education, and physical movement.[70] James Gwartney and coauthors derive several measures of government involvement in the economy, including government consumption as a percentage of GDP, an index of the importance of state-owned enterprises in the national economy, government transfers and subsidies as a percentage of GDP, and top marginal tax rates.[71]

Each of these measures has some drawbacks. Many are survey based and accordingly subjective. Because the surveys are in all cases compiled by Anglophone firms or researchers, the compilers could be biased in favor of more familiar legal arrangements. The CIM ratio is a helpful addition because it is an objective measure, but it may reflect phenomena other than contract enforcement. The judicial quality, red-tape, rule-of-law, and expropriation-risk measures were compiled for use by foreign businesses and are therefore concerned principally with the government's treatment of foreign firms rather than of domestic firms and citizens. The measures of government size are noisy measures of intervention because governments can choose to engage in commercial activities directly or to heavily regulate the private sector. Either may have a retarding effect on growth, but the former would tend to produce larger measures of government spending and employment.

It is also obvious by inspection that rich countries score better than poor ones, on average, on each of these measures. I therefore begin by examining the partial correlations between each of these measures and the common-law dummy, controlling for starting real per capita GDP. These partial correlations are reported in table 3.4. As predicted, there are statistically significant partial correlations between the common law and the judicial quality, property rights, and contract rights (CIM) measures. The common law's partial correlation with the civil liberties measure is also large and significant. The common-law countries perform better (that is, the sign of the correlation coefficient is consistent with less intervention) for each measure except government consumption. Using multivariate analysis, La Porta and coauthors find a strong association between common-law origin and less interventionist government using several of these measures.[72]

On the basis of these results, I use legal origin as an instrumental variable for judicial quality, the security of property rights, and contract enforcement. I compute generalized method of moments (GMM) estimates for three regression equations using the BIC judicial quality index (JUDIC), the Holmes and coauthors property rights index (PROP), and

Table 3.4
Partial Correlations with Common Law

Variable	*Partial correlation coefficient*	*p-Value*
JUDIC	.296	.021
PROP	.218	.044
CIM	.303	.003
REDTAPE	.168	.196
RULELAW	.164	.124
EXPROP	.078	.604
CIVLIV	−.267	.007
BUSREG	.181	.096
MARG	−.124	.314
GOVCONS	.125	.264
SOE	−.104	.358
TRANSUB	−.107	.361

Note: All partial correlations control for starting real per capita GDP (PCG60 or PCG80, depending on the period for which the relevant variable is measured). The variable CIVLIB is defined so that a lower score implies more civil liberties. All other survey-based measures (JUDIC, PROP, REDTAPE, RULELAW, EXPROP, and BUSREG) are defined so that a higher score is better. For variable definitions, see appendix B.

the CIM ratio (CIM) of Clague and coauthors as endogenous variables. In order to have sufficient degrees of freedom to test for overidentifying restrictions, I use dummy variables for common law, French civil law, and German civil law as instruments (Scandinavian civil law is the omitted category).

I first estimate the GMM coefficients using a simple set of additional conditioning information consisting of initial per capita GDP, primary school enrollment, and ethnic fractionalization.[73] I then reestimate with an extended conditioning set that includes population growth and average investment. In each case, after computing the GMM estimates, I test for overidentifying restrictions by using a Lagrange multiplier test. As a check, I also estimate the same regressions using two-stage least squares and obtain consistent results.

Table 3.5 reports results for the instrumental variables regressions. Using the simple conditioning set, the judicial quality, property rights, and contract enforcement variables, each enters significantly at the 1 percent level. With the extended conditioning set, the estimated coefficient on the judicial quality index loses significance (when estimated using two-stage least squares, it is significant at the 10 percent level). The co-

TABLE 3.5
Common Law and Growth: Instrumental Variables

A. Simple conditioning set						
Variable	*Estimated coefficient*	*Standard error (White-corrected)*	*P-value*	*N*	*J-statistic*	*P-value, OIR*
JUDIC	.430	.128	.001	60	.032	.381
PROP	1.798	.372	.000	85	.004	.848
CIM	.116	.039	.004	91	.036	.193
B. Extended conditioning set						
Variable	*Estimated coefficient*	*Standard error (White-corrected)*	*P-value*	*N*	*J-statistic*	*P-value, OIR*
JUDIC	.270	.273	.328	60	.069	.127
PROP	1.756	.621	.006	85	.005	.807
CIM	.093	.031	.004	91	.019	.410

Note: OIR = overidentifying restrictions. The dependent variable for all regressions is GROW. The simple conditioning set includes PCG60, PRI60, and ETHNIC. The extended conditioning set includes, in addition, GPO and INV. The instruments are COM, FRCIV, and GERCIV. For variable definitions, see appendix B.

efficients on the other two variables are slightly reduced and remain significant at the 1 percent level. The weaker results in the extended regression may reflect the fact that judicial quality (in particular), property rights, and contract enforcement may affect growth in part directly and in part indirectly through investment. The investment variable is highly correlated with each of the three endogenous variables.

Looking at the Lagrange multiplier test for overidentifying restrictions, in no case can we reject the hypothesis that legal origin affects growth solely through its effect on the endogenous variables (in other words, that the legal origin variables are uncorrelated with the error term). Levine reaches a similar conclusion with respect to a set of endogenous variables that measure financial development.[74] The inability to reject the null hypothesis in any of these cases suggests that the overidentifying-restrictions test has low power with the sample sizes typical in cross-country growth studies. More important, the results support the hypothesis that legal origin affects growth through channels other than finance.

The data, then, are consistent with the notion that the common law produces improvements in property rights and contract enforcement, which in turn speed economic growth. The instrumental variables results also suggest that the strong association between secure property and contract rights and growth is causal, and not simply a consequence of simultaneity.

VI. Conclusion

Common and civil lawyers have long debated the relative merits of the two legal traditions. These discussions, like the law and finance literature, focus on differences in substantive rules. An alternative view, associated most notably with Hayek, focuses on legal tradition as a reflection of different philosophies of government. The common law and civil law, in this view, proceed from different views about the relative role of collective and individual action. These associations have to do with possibly chance connections between the judiciary and specific political problems of seventeenth-century England and eighteenth-century France, but once established, they have had continuing effects on institutional arrangements. Judges are invested with greater prestige and insulated more from political influence in common-law systems. Administrative bodies are insulated more from judicial influence in civil-law systems. These differences result in stricter protection for property and contract rights against government action in the common-law tradition.

This chapter's results suggest that the association between common law and growth is not an artifact of different rules of investor protection. Rather, it stems from a more fundamental divergence between the security of property and contract rights in the two systems.

Appendix A: Sample of Countries

Common-Law Countries

Australia, Bangladesh, Barbados, Botswana, Canada, Cyprus, Gambia, Ghana, Hong Kong, India, Ireland, Israel, Jamaica, Kenya, Lesotho, Liberia, Malawi, Malaysia, Malta, Mauritius, Nepal, New Zealand, Nigeria, Pakistan, Papua New Guinea, Sierra Leone, Singapore, South Africa, Sri Lanka, Swaziland, Tanzania, Thailand, Trinidad and Tobago, Uganda, United Kingdom, United States, Zambia, Zimbabwe

Civil-Law Countries

Algeria, Argentina, Austria, Belgium, Benin, Bolivia, Brazil, Burkina Faso, Burundi, Central African Republic, Chad, Chile, Colombia,

Congo, Costa Rica, Côte d'Ivoire, Denmark, Dominican Republic, Ecuador, Egypt, El Salvador, Finland, France, Gabon, Germany, Greece, Guatemala, Guinea-Bissau, Haiti, Honduras, Indonesia, Iran, Iraq, Italy, Japan, Jordan, Luxembourg, Madagascar, Mali, Mauritania, Mexico, Morocco, Netherlands, Nicaragua, Niger, Norway, Panama, Paraguay, Peru, Philippines, Portugal, Rwanda, Senegal, South Korea, Spain, Suriname, Sweden, Switzerland, Syria, Togo, Tunisia, Turkey, Uruguay, Venezuela

Appendix B

Variable Definition and Sources

AFRICA: Dummy for sub-Saharan African countries (Oxford Atlas of the World (2d ed. 1994))

BUDDHIST: Buddhists as percentage of population (Xavier X. Sala-i-Martin, I Just Ran Two Million Regressions, 87 Am. Econ. Rev. Papers & Proc. 178 (1997); data obtained from ⟨http://www.columbia.edu/~xs23/data.htm⟩)

BUSREG: Business regulation index (Kim Holmes, Bryan Johnson, & Melanie Kirkpatrick, 1997 Index of Economic Freedom (1997))

CATHOLIC: Roman Catholics as percentage of population (Xavier X. Sala-i-Martin, I Just Ran Two Million Regressions, 87 Am. Econ. Rev. Papers & Proc. 178 (1997); data obtained from ⟨http://www.columbia.edu/xs23/data.htm⟩)

CIM: Average ratio of broad money (M2) less currency to M2, 1969–90 (Christopher Clague *et al.*, Contract-Intensive Money: Contract Enforcement, Property Rights, and Economic Performance, 4 J. Econ. Growth 187 (1999))

CIVLIB: Index of civil liberties (Raymond D. Gastil, Freedom in the World (various years))

COMMONLAW: Dummy for common-law origin (Thomas H. Reynolds & Arturo A. Flores, Foreign Law: Current Sources of Codes and Basic Legislation in Jurisdictions of the World (1989))

CONFUCIAN: Adherents to Confucianism as percentage of population (Xavier X. Sala-i-Martin, I Just Ran Two Million Regressions, 87 Am. Econ. Rev. Papers & Proc. 178 (1997); data obtained from ⟨http://www.columbia.edu/~xs23/data.htm⟩)

ETHNIC: Ethnolinguistic fractionalization (William Easterly & Ross Levine, Africa's Growth Tragedy: Policies and Ethnic Divisions, 112 Q.J. Econ. 1203 (1997))

EXPORT: Average export share of GDP, 1960–89 (Ross Levine & David Renelt, A Sensitivity Analysis of Cross-Country Growth Regressions, 82 Am. Econ. Rev. 942 (1992); data obtained from Ross Levine)

EXPROP: Expropriation-risk index (International Country Risk Guides (various years))

FRCIV: Dummy for French civil-law origin (Thomas H. Reynolds & Arturo A. Flores, Foreign Law: Current Sources of Codes and Basic Legislation in Jurisdictions of the World (1989))

GERCIV: Dummy for German civil-law origin (Thomas H. Reynolds and Arturo A. Flores, Foreign Law: Current Sources of Codes and Basic Legislation in Jurisdictions of the World (1989))

GOVCONS: Government consumption as percentage of GDP (James Gwartney, Robert Lawson, & Walter Block, Economic Freedom of the World, 1975–1995 (1996))

GPO: Average annual population growth, 1960–89 (Ross Levine & David Renelt, A Sensitivity Analysis of Cross-Country Growth Regressions, 82 Am. Econ. Rev. 942 (1992); data obtained from Ross Levine)

GROW: Average annual growth in real per capita GDP, 1960–92 (Penn World Tables, Mark 5.6)

INFLATION: Average rate of change of GDP deflator, 1960–89 (Ross Levine & David Renelt, A Sensitivity Analysis of Cross-Country Growth Regressions, 82 Am. Econ. Rev. 942 (1992); data obtained from Ross Levine)

INV: Average investment share of GDP, 1960–92 (Penn World Tables, Mark 5.6)

JUDIC: Judicial quality index (Paolo Mauro, Corruption and Growth, 110 Q.J. Econ. 681 (1995))

LATINAM: Dummy for Latin American countries (Oxford Atlas of the World (2d ed. 1994))

MARG: Scaled measure of top marginal tax rates (James Gwartney, Robert Lawson, & Walter Block, Economic Freedom of the World, 1975–1995 (1996))

MUSLIM: Muslims as percentage of population (Xavier X. Sala-i-Martin, I Just Ran Two Million Regressions, 87 Am. Econ. Rev. Papers & Proc. 178 (1997); data obtained from ⟨http://www.columbia.edu/~xs23/data.htm⟩)

PCG60: Real per capita gross domestic product, 1960 (Penn World Tables, Mark 5.6)

PCG80: Real per capita gross domestic product, 1980 (Penn World Tables, Mark 5.6)

PROP: Property rights index (Kim Holmes, Bryan Johnson, & Melanie Kirkpatrick, 1997 Index of Economic Freedom (1997))

PROTESTANT: Protestants as percent of population (Xavier X. Sala-i-Martin, I Just Ran Two Million Regressions, 87 Am. Econ. Rev. Papers & Proc. 178 (1997); data obtained from ⟨http://www.columbia.edu/~xs23/data.htm⟩)

PRI60: Gross enrollment rate in primary education, 1960 (Ross Levine & David Renelt, A Sensitivity Analysis of Cross-Country Growth Regressions, 82 Am. Econ. Rev. 942 (1992); data obtained from Ross Levine)

REDTAPE: Bureaucratic delay index (Paolo Mauro, Corruption and Growth, 110 Q.J. Econ. 681 (1995))

RULELAW: Index of law and order (International Country Risk Guides (various years))

SEC60: Gross enrollment rate in secondary education, 1960 (Ross Levine & David Renelt, A Sensitivity Analysis of Cross-Country Growth Regressions, 82 Am. Econ. Rev. 942 (1992); data obtained from Ross Levine)

SOE: Index of importance of state-owned enterprises (James Gwartney, Robert Lawson, & Walter Block, Economic Freedom of the World, 1975–1995 (1996))

TRANSUB: Government transfers and subsidies as percentage of GDP (James Gwartney, Robert Lawson, & Walter Block, Economic Freedom of the World, 1975–1995 (1996))

Notes

Reprinted with permission from the Journal of Legal Studies, Paul G. Mahoney, and the University of Chicago as publisher.

I thank Kevin Davis; Ronald Gilson; Barry Ickes; Ross Levine; Julia Mahoney; Katharina Pistor; Andrei Shleifer; Todd Zywicki; Eric Posner; two anonymous referees; and seminar and conference participants at George Mason University, the University of Michigan, the University of Virginia, the American Law and Economics Association 2000 annual meeting, and the Latin American and Caribbean Law and Economics Association 2000 annual meeting. I am also grateful to Ross Levine for access to some of the data used in this chapter.

1. *See* Robert G. King & Ross Levine, *Finance and Growth: Schumpeter Might Be Right*, 108 Q.J. Econ. 717 (1993).

2. *See* Rafael La Porta et al., *Law and Finance*, 106 J. Pol. Econ. 1113 (1998); Rafael La Porta et al., *Legal Determinants of External Finance*, 52 J. Fin. 1131 (1997).

3. *See* Ross Levine, *Law, Finance, and Economic Growth*, 8 J. Fin. Intermediation 8 (1999); Ross Levine, Norman Loayza, & Thorsten Beck, *Financial Intermediation and Growth*: Causality and Causes, 46 J. Monetary Econ. 31 (2000).

4. *See* Friedrich A. Hayek, The Constitution of Liberty (1960); Friedrich A. Hayek, Law, Legislation, and Liberty: A New Statement of the Liberal Principles of Justice and Political Economy (1973).

5. *See* La Porta et al., *The Quality of Government*, 15 J.L. Econ. & Org. 222, 232 (1999).

6. *See* John Henry Merryman, The Civil Law Tradition: An Introduction to the Legal Systems of Western Europe and Latin America 18 (2d ed. 1985) (describing "[g]lorification of the state" as a central element in the civil-law tradition).

7. *See* La Porta et al., *supra* note 5.

8. *See* Douglass Cecil North, Structure and Change in Economic History (1981).

9. *See*, for example, Richard A. Posner, Economic Analysis of Law 399–427 (2d ed. 1977); George L. Priest & Benjamin Klein, *The Selection of Disputes for Litigation*, 13 J. Legal Stud. 1 (1984); George L. Priest, *The Common Law Process and the Selection of Efficient Rules*, 6 J. Legal Stud. 65 (1977); Paul H. Rubin, *Why Is the Common Law Efficient?* 6 J. Legal Stud. 51 (1977).

10. *See* Jürgen G. Backhaus, *Efficient Statute Law*, *in* 2 The New Palgrave Dictionary of Economics and the Law (Peter Newman ed., 1997).

11. *See* Gordon Tullock, The Case against the Common Law (1997).

12. *See* Henry G. Manne, *The Judiciary and Free Markets*, 21 Harv. J.L. & Pub. Pol. 11 (1997).

13. *See*, for example, Barry R. Weingast, *The Political Foundations of Democracy and the Rule of Law*, 91 Am. Pol. Sci. Rev. 245 (1997); Barry R. Weingast, *The Economic Role of Political Institutions: Market-Preserving Federalism and Economic Development*, 11 J.L. Econ. & Org. 1 (1995); Barry R. Weingast, *Constitutions as Governance Structures: The Political Foundations of Secure Markets*, 149 J. Inst. & Theoretical Econ. 286 (1993).

14. *See* Weingast, Constitutions as Governance Structures, *supra* note 13; Thorsten Persson, Gerard Roland, & Guido Tabellini, *Comparative Politics and Public Finance*, 108 J. Pol. Econ. 1121 (2000).

15. *See* Persson, Roland, & Tabellini, *supra* note 14.

16. *See* Sir Edward Coke, The First Part of the Institutes of the Laws of England (1979) (1628). *See* also Thomas Littleton, Tenures in English (1903) (1481).

17. *See* William Blackstone, 1 Commentaries on the Laws of England 22 (1765). David Hume sounds a similar note when he defines a judge as one "who in all disputed cases can fix by his opinion the possession or property of any thing." *See* David Hume, A Treatise of Human Nature 60 (1969).

18. *See* Douglass C. North & Barry R. Weingast, *Constitutions and Commitment: The Evolution of Institutions Governing Public Choice in Seventeenth-Century England*, 49 J. Econ. Hist. 803 (1989).

19. *See* Richard Pipes, Property and Freedom 30–38 (1999).

20. *See* James Harrington, The Commonwealth of Oceana (1992) (1656); Henry Neville, Plato Redivivus (1681); John Locke, Two Treatises of Government (1988) (1690).

21. *See* Darcy v. Allen (The Case of Monopolies), 11 Co. Rep. 84b, 77 Eng. Rep. 1260 (1603). Coke did not publish the case report until 1615, and he may have embellished it to make a stronger statement against royal power than he had in fact done in 1603. *See* Jacob Corre, *The Argument, Decision, and Reports of Darcy v. Allen*, 45 Emory L. Rev. 1261 (1996). This would not be surprising, as Coke's resistance to James I grew during the 1610s.

22. *See* Christopher Hill, The Century of Revolution, 1603–1714 (2d ed. 1980).

23. *See* Bailey Stone, The French Parlements and the Crisis of the Old Regime (1986).

24. *See* Robert B. Ekelund, Jr., & Robert D. Tollison, Politicized Economies: Monarchy, Monopoly, and Mercantilism (Texas A&M Econ. Ser. 14, 1997).

25. *See* Stone, *supra* note 23, at 56–58.

26. *See* Merryman, *supra* note 6, at 28–29.

27. *See* L. Neville Brown, John S. Bell, & Jean-Michel Galabert, French Administrative Law 46 (5th ed. 1998).

28. *See* Discours préliminaire prononcé par Portalis, le 24 thermidor an 8, lors de la présentation du projet arrêté par las commission du gouvernement, *in* P. A. Fenet, Recueil complet des travaux preparatoires du Code Civil 465 (1968) (1827): "[L]e désir exalté de sacrificier violemment tous les droits à un but politique, et de ne plus

admettre d'autre considération que celle d'un mystérieux et variable intérêt d'état." I thank John Portman for the translation in the text.

29. *See* Hayek, *supra* note 4, at 54–70 (The Constitution of Liberty (1960)).

30. Francis Lieber, *Anglican and Gallican Liberty*, *in* 2 Miscellaneous Writings 369, 382–83 (Daniel Coit Gilman ed., 1881) (emphasis in original). The essay was originally published in 1848.

31. *See* Pipes, *supra* note 19, at 39–44.

32. Note that George III's undermining of the independence of colonial judges was one of the grievances listed in the Declaration of Independence.

33. *See* René David & John E. C. Brierley, Major Legal Systems in the World Today: An Introduction to the Comparative Study of Law (3d ed. 1985).

34. Loi des 16–24.8.1790, Article 13, quoted in Brown, Bell, & Galabert, *supra* note 27, at 46.

35. *See* Charles Szladits, The Civil Law System, *in* 2 International Encyclopedia of Comparative Law 15, 41 (René David ed., 1974).

36. *See* Brown, Bell, & Galabert, *supra* note 27, at 176.

37. *See* Szladits, *supra* note 35, at 48–49.

38. *See* Davy v. Spelthorne Borough Council, [1983] 3 All Eng. Rep. 278, 285 (opinion of Lord Wilberforce).

39. *See* Peter de Cruz, Comparative Law in a Changing World (2d ed. 1999).

40. *See* A. V. Dicey, Lectures Introductory to the Study of the Law of the Constitution 178–79 (1886); Brown, Bell, & Galabert, *supra* note 27, at 4–5.

41. *See* Thorsten Beck, Asli Demirgüç-Kunt, & Ross Levine, Law, Politics, and Finance 13–14 (unpublished manuscript 2001) (available at ⟨http://www.csom.umn.edu/wwwpages/faculty/rlevine⟩); Szladits, *supra* note 35, at 35.

42. Grundgesetz, Article 97.

43. *See* Hayek (The Constitution of Liberty (1960)), *supra* note 4, at 193–204.

44. *See*, for example, La Porta et al., *Law and Finance*, *supra* note 2; La Porta et al., *Legal Determinants of External Finance*, *supra* note 2.

45. There have been some much less successful adopters, such as Russia and much of Eastern Europe, but these countries are socialist during my sample period and therefore excluded from the sample.

46. For a description of the Penn World Tables, *see* Robert Summers & Alan Heston, *The Penn World Tables (Mark 5): An Expanded Set of International Comparisons*, 1950–88, 106 Q.J. Econ. 327 (1991).

47. *See* Thomas H. Reynolds & Arturo A. Flores, Foreign Law: Current Sources of Codes and Basic Legislation in Jurisdictions of the World (1989).

48. *See* de Cruz, *supra* note 39, at 34–36.

49. This results in one difference between my assignments and that of some of the law and finance literature. I include Mauritius, a Commonwealth country that recognizes the jurisdiction of the Judicial Committee of the Privy Council, in the common-law category, whereas some studies assign it to the civil-law category.

50. *See* Ross Levine & David Renelt, *A Sensitivity Analysis of Cross-Country Growth Regressions*, 82 Am. Econ. Rev. 942 (1992), for a survey. Xavier Sala-i-Martin argues that a less restrictive test finds a larger set of robust variables. *See* Xavier X. Sala-i-Martin, *I Just Ran Two Million Regressions*, 87 Am. Econ. Rev. Papers & Proc. 178 (1997). I use some of these additional variables in robustness checks described below.

51. *See* William Easterly & Ross Levine, *Africa's Growth Tragedy: Policies and Ethnic Divisions*, 112 Q.J. Econ. 1203 (1997).

52. *See id.*

53. *See* Max Weber, The Protestant Ethic and the Spirit of Capitalism (1958).

54. *See* Robert J. Barro, Determinants of Economic Growth: A Cross-Country Empirical Study (1997). I obtained the data from Sala-i-Martin's Web page (⟨http://www.columbia.edu/~xs23/data.htm⟩).

55. These are the only religion variables that are robustly associated with growth. *See* Sala-i-Martin, *supra* note 50, at 181.

56. *See* Levine & Renelt, *supra* note 50.

57. *See id.*

58. *See* J. Bradford De Long & Lawrence H. Summers, *Equipment Investment and Economic Growth*, 106 Q.J. Econ. 445 (1991).

59. *See* Jeffrey Sachs & Andrew Warner, Economic Reform and the Process of Global Integration: Comments and Discussion (Brookings Papers Econ. Activity 1, 1995).

60. *See* Robert J. Barro & Jong-Wha Lee, *International Comparisons of Educational Attainment*, 32 J. Monetary Econ. 363 (1993).

61. *See* Robert J. Barro, *Economic Growth in a Cross-Section of Countries*, 106 Q.J. Econ. 407 (1991).

62. *See* Robert E. Hall & Charles I. Jones, *Why Do Some Countries Produce So Much More Output per Worker Than Others?* 114 Q.J. Econ. 83 (1999).

63. *See* Levine, *supra* note 3.

64. *See* Paolo Mauro, *Corruption and Growth*, 110 Q.J. Econ. 681 (1995).

65. *See* 1997 Index of Economic Freedom (Kim R. Holmes, Bryan T. Johnson, & Melanie Kirkpatrick eds., 1997).

66. *See* Christopher Clague *et al.*, *Contract-Intensive Money: Contract Enforcement, Property Rights, and Economic Performance*, 4 J. Econ. Growth 187 (1999).

67. *See* Mauro, *supra* note 64.

68. *See* Stephan Knack & Philip Keefer, *Institutions and Economic Performance: Cross-Country Tests Using Alternative Institutional Measures*, 7 Econ. & Pol. 207 (1995); *see* also Levine, *supra* note 3. The rule-of-law measure might seem to be at least as relevant as the property and contract enforcement measures. However, the rule-of-law assessment is problematic because, following the dominant intellectual trend in legal theory, the compilers focus only on whether the government acts with a high degree of procedural regularity. Thus the former Soviet Union and its client states, for example, score relatively high on this measure. Hayek frequently criticized legal positivists for their insistence that "legality" consists only in adherence to appropriate procedures, as opposed to respect for individual rights.

69. *See* 1997 Index of Economic Freedom, *supra* note 65.

70. *See* Barro, *supra* note 54, at 55–58. The data come from Raymond D. Gastil, Freedom in the World (various years).

71. *See* James D. Gwartney, Robert Lawson, & Walter Block, Economic Freedom of the World, 1975–1995 (1996).

72. *See* La Porta et al., *supra* note 5, at 246–50.

73. The procedure tracks Levine, *supra* note 3, at 26–31.

74. *See id.* at 29–31.

PART III

The Elements of Good Corporate Governance: Owners and Managers

CHAPTER FOUR

Russian Privatization and Corporate Governance: What Went Wrong?

Bernard Black, Reinier Kraakman, and Anna Tarassova

IN RUSSIA and elsewhere, proponents of rapid, mass privatization of state-owned enterprises (ourselves among them) hoped that the profit incentives unleashed by privatization would soon revive faltering, centrally planned economies. In Russia, the revival didn't happen. We offer here some partial explanations. First, mass privatization is likely to lead to massive self-dealing by managers and controlling shareholders unless (implausibly in the initial transition from central planning to markets) a country has a good infrastructure for controlling self-dealing. Russia accelerated the self-dealing process by selling control of its largest enterprises cheaply to crooks, who transferred their skimming talents to the enterprises they acquired and used their wealth to further corrupt the government and block reforms that might constrain their actions. Second, profit incentives to restructure privatized businesses and create new ones can be swamped by the burden on business imposed by a combination of (among other things) a punitive tax system, official corruption, organized crime, and an unfriendly bureaucracy. Third, while self-dealing will still occur (though perhaps to a lesser extent) if state enterprises aren't privatized, since self-dealing accompanies privatization, it politically discredits privatization as a reform strategy and can undercut longer-term reforms. A principal lesson: developing the institutions to control self-dealing is central to successful privatization of large firms.

I. INTRODUCTION

Rapid mass privatization of state-owned enterprises in formerly centrally planned economies hasn't turned out the way its creators hoped, in Russia or elsewhere. When Russian mass privatization began in the early 1990s, its proponents (including ourselves) hoped that the Russian economy would soon bottom out and then turn upward, as the efficiency incentives unleashed by privatization took hold.[1] That didn't happen.

Russia's mass privatization "voucher auctions" were moderately honest, but gave control to managers. This permitted insiders (managers and controlling shareholders) to engage in extensive self-dealing (transactions between insiders and the company, in which the insiders profit at the company's expense), which the government did nothing to control. Later privatization "auctions" were a giveaway of Russia's most important companies at bargain prices to a few well-connected "kleptocrats," who got the funds to buy these companies by skimming from the government and transferred their skimming talents to the enterprises they acquired.

At the macro level, the Russian economy stumbled along through mid-1998, then collapsed again, as it had in 1991–92 prior to privatization. Russia's medium-term prospects are only so-so. The Russian ruble has plunged; the Russian government has defaulted on both its dollar- and ruble-denominated debt, most banks are bankrupt, corruption is rampant, tax collection is abysmal, capital flight is pervasive, and new investment is scarce. The Russian economy rebounded somewhat in 1999 and 2000, but from a greatly shrunken base and mostly because oil prices soared. The fundamentals of nonextractive industries haven't changed that much. It remains to be seen whether Russia's new president, Vladimir Putin, will develop a coherent economic policy—none has emerged in his first year as prime minister and then president.

Russia's disappointment with mass privatization is mirrored in other former Soviet Union countries and, less severely, in the Czech Republic, which at one time seemed to be a model of the transition from central planning to a market economy. This suggests that the failure of privatization to jump-start the Russian economy may reflect structural flaws in mass privatization as a transition mechanism, not just Russia's specific circumstances.

This chapter joins an emerging literature that questions whether rapid mass privatization of large firms is an important element of the transition from central planning to a market economy.[2] We develop below a case study of what went wrong with large-firm privatization in Russia, using the Czech Republic as a comparison case study to assess the extent to which Russia's problems are generalizable. We bring to this task a reasonable mix of insiders' knowledge and outsiders' skepticism, gained through experience with privatization and capital markets reform in Russia and other countries.[3]

We leave to others the analysis of the macroeconomic steps that Russia might have taken and focus on microeconomic steps related to privatization and capital markets development. But the two are related. Russia's macro effort to balance the budget, control inflation, and attract investment was defeated, in large measure, by the micro failures we discuss below.

We see three main failures in the Russian privatization effort. First, mass privatization of large enterprises is likely to lead to massive insider self-dealing unless (implausibly in the initial transition from central planning to markets) a country has a good infrastructure for controlling self-dealing. The critical factor is lack of controls on self-dealing, and *not* the details of the privatization plan. If control is given to the current managers, as in Russian mass privatization, they often won't know how to run a company in a market economy. Some managers will loot their companies, perhaps killing an otherwise viable company. If outsiders can acquire control in the stock market, as in the Czech Republic, bad owners will often drive out good ones. A controlling stake is worth more to a dishonest owner who will extract all of a firm's value than to an honest owner who will share that value with minority shareholders.

To prevent this outcome, development of a decent legal and enforcement infrastructure must precede or at least accompany privatization of large firms. If privatization comes first, massive theft is likely to occur before the infrastructure to control it can develop. At the same time, important parts of this infrastructure require a base of existing private firms. For example, to learn to prosecute fraud and self-dealing, regulators need some fraud and self-dealing to practice on. Thus, privatization must to some extent be staged, lest the crooks simply outrun the regulators.

In a mythical thick market for corporate control, good owners could buy companies from bad owners if a company was worth more if run honestly than if run to maximize short-run skimming. But in fact, good owners don't exist in Russia in significant numbers or with the capital to buy large enterprises. If they existed, they wouldn't pay a bad owner anything close to fair value, because they couldn't verify what shape the business was in. Moreover, the business might be worth more to the bad owner, who has a comparative advantage in the important tasks of self-dealing, evading taxes, obtaining favors from the government, not paying workers, and using effective albeit unofficial means (read: the Mafia) to enforce contracts and scare off competitors. In contrast, an honest owner risks having the government expropriate his or her investment.

Second, the profit incentives to restructure privatized enterprises (instead of looting them), and to create new businesses that could draw workers from shrinking enterprises, can be swamped by a hostile business environment. In Russia, that environment includes a punitive tax system; official corruption; organized crime; an unfriendly bureaucracy; and a business culture in which skirting the law is seen as normal, even necessary behavior.

Third, corrupt privatization of large firms can compromise future reforms. In Russia, self-dealing was widespread before privatization began and would have continued if large enterprises had been privatized more slowly. But privatization can make self-dealing easier. In a vicious circle, dirty privatization also reinforces corruption and organized crime, as the new owners (some already with Mafia ties) turn their new wealth to the task of buying judges and government officials. Corrupt officials and company insiders join forces to resist future reforms, while the public comes to see privatization (and, by inference, other market reforms) as connected with self-dealing, corruption, and organized crime.

To be sure, Russia's economic problems weren't caused by privatization. Ukraine offers a sobering example. It hasn't privatized large firms, but is as corrupt as Russia and has done even worse economically. Comparing Russia with Ukraine suggests that if government is bad enough—badly enough corrupted, incapable of sustaining sensible policy—mass privatization won't affect economic performance very much, for better or worse. The assets of state-owned enterprises will be stolen whether they are privatized or not.

Our concerns here are with mass privatization of large enterprises, not with the other elements of the "shock therapy" prescription dispensed by Western advisors. There is much to be said, in the transition to a market economy, for the government's rapidly selling or giving away small shops and businesses to the people who work there, and apartments and land to the people who live there. These steps don't entail the separation of ownership and control that encourage self-dealing by controllers of large enterprises. But we believe that a concerted effort to control self-dealing is central to successful large firm privatization.[4]

An important piece of the overall puzzle: the largest Russian companies were sold in massively corrupt fashion to a handful of well-connected men, soon dubbed "kleptocrats" (клептоманы) by the Russian press, who made their first centimillions or billions through sweetheart deals with or outright theft from the government and then leveraged that wealth by buying major companies from the government for astonishingly low prices. The "reformers" who promoted privatization regretted the corruption, but claimed that any private owner was better than state ownership. Even if the new owners got their ownership in unfortunate ways, they would have incentives to increase company value. Many foreign advisors bought this story; viewed dirty privatization as better than no privatization; and supported Russia's privatization czar, Anatoli Chubais, as he pursued privatization by any available means.

Left unnoticed was that the new owners had two ways to make money—increase the company's value, or steal what value already existed. The first was difficult, perhaps beyond their ability, and uncertain in outcome. The second was easy; they were expert at it; and it was sure to produce a handsome profit that could be tucked away overseas, beyond the reach of a future Russian government. Most of the kleptocrats chose the second, easy approach.

An example: Bank Menatep (controlled by kleptocrat Mikhail Khodorkovski) acquired Yukos, a major Russian oil holding company, in 1995. For 1996, Yukos's financial statements show revenue of $8.60 per barrel of oil—about $4 per barrel less than it should have been.[5] Khodorkovski skimmed more than 30 cents per dollar of revenue while stiffing his workers on wages, defaulting on tax payments, destroying the value of minority shares in Yukos and its production subsidiaries, and *not* reinvesting in Yukos's oil fields.

It's doubtful that running Yukos honestly could have earned Khodorkovski a fraction of what he earned by skimming revenue, let alone offshore and tax free. He made a rational, privately value-maximizing choice. Even if running Yukos honestly was the best long-run strategy, Khodorkovski might have preferred present profit over future uncertainty. Besides, skimming was a business that he knew, while oil production was a tough business that he might fail in.

This example illustrates a general point: privatization is not enough. It matters who the owners are, what constraints on self-dealing they face, and the business climate they operate in. If it isn't politically feasible to import foreign owners, who are more likely to run privatized businesses honestly (though foreign owners must be watched too, as the Czechs learned) and to invest if profit opportunities exist, the government's second-best choice may be to first privatize selected firms with strong profits and reputedly honest managers, and watch these firms carefully once they are privatized, while building the legal and market institutions to control self-dealing.[6]

Even without immediate privatization, managers can be motivated to restructure by the promise of running a company that will be privatized if profitable. The government's ability to control theft will be higher if the enterprise is still state owned. And the enterprise's sale price will be far higher if it is sold in a stronger legal environment, in a fairer auction, and perhaps with more foreign participation than was politically acceptable in the near term. Ironically, Russia had such a "staged privatization" program in place in the early 1990s, through a program called enterprise leasing. The privatizers killed enterprise leasing because they thought it wasn't fast enough.

Proponents of fast privatization may respond that there is no assurance that the infrastructure to control self-dealing will develop anytime soon. This is indeed a risk. But the right response may be to stage privatization and work hard to develop this infrastructure, rather than privatize large firms anyway and hope that the outcome will somehow be acceptable.

Several countries on the fringes of the former Soviet Union created a reasonably friendly climate for new businesses and achieved corresponding economic success—among them Estonia, Hungary, Latvia, Poland, Slovenia, and the Czech Republic (which may have done reasonably well despite, rather than because of, mass privatization). Poland offers a nice contrast to Russia. It was slow to privatize its major businesses or its banks. It succeeded economically because it quickly privatized small businesses, created a climate in which new businesses could thrive, and built strong capital markets regulation that largely preceded large-firm privatization.[7]

This chapter proceeds as follows: in section II we survey Russian privatization and the sometimes astonishing corruption that accompanied the privatization effort. In section III we discuss the factors that affect how much self-dealing the controllers of privatized enterprises will engage in, the structural flaws in Russia's privatization efforts, and the often unhappy outcomes from privatization. In section IV we address the counterfactual question of what might have happened with staged privatization and greater effort to control self-dealing. In section V we evaluate Czech mass privatization, to assess the extent to which Russia's experience was rooted in large-firm privatization without controls on self-dealing, and to what extent that experience reflects Russia's unique problems. We offer in section VI some suggestions for future privatization efforts and future aid to Russia. Section VII concludes.

We seek to understand what went wrong with a plausible reform program, what reforms might have worked better, and what can be done now. We part company with critics of mass privatization who espouse implausible alternatives, such as Asian-style industrial policy (which Russia was incapable of carrying out), or seem mostly interested in assigning blame.[8]

II. A Cynic's Tour of Russian Privatization

This section surveys Russia's privatization history. Some of the stories that we report are well known; others are newly reported here. Taken together, they paint a grim picture of a government that privatized small, midsize, and many large companies in semihonest fashion through mass privatization, but tolerated virtual giveaways of majority stakes in the largest companies, where most of the value lay, as well as insiders' theft of the value of minority shares in most large companies.

A warning: The misdeeds that we report don't lend themselves to easy fact-checking. For all but one of the major stories we tell in section III, we have personal knowledge; this is indicated in notes. For the others, we rely on news stories or sometimes, even less satisfactorily, on "general knowledge"—for example, the general belief that Gazprom chief executive officer (CEO) Rem Vyakhirev owns a substantial percentage of Gazprom's shares. Thus, we may inadvertently tell a story that isn't true or, more likely, provides a partial picture. Still, we believe that our overall depiction of Russian business practices is accurate. The problem in recounting misdeeds by Russian insiders isn't finding true stories, but picking among the juicy stories that abound.

A. Mass Privatization: 1992–1994

Russia in 1992 was a huge country with a weak central government, which had neither will nor capacity to force privatization onto unwilling company managers. The prevailing Western advice called for "shock therapy"—rapid decontrol of prices, freeing of markets, and privatization of industry. Speed was thought critical, both to revive the economy and to reduce the state's role in the economy before popular tolerance for the dislocations that accompanied the shock was exhausted and reform lost its political momentum. As shock therapist Jeffrey Sachs wrote: "The need to accelerate privatization is the paramount economic policy issue facing Eastern Europe. If there is no breakthrough in the privatization of large enterprises in the near future, the entire process could be stalled for years to come. Privatization is urgent and politically vulnerable."[9]

Privatization of state-owned enterprises in developed countries has proceeded primarily through one-company-at-a-time auctions, generally with reasonable transparency.[10] But countries attempting the transition from centrally planned to market economies had thousands of state-owned enterprises to dispose of, many of modest size, only some of which were viable. One-at-a-time cash auctions couldn't meet the shock therapists' timetable and involved large transaction costs relative to enterprise value. Mass cash auctions were thought likely to exhaust the citizenry's funds and to risk political backlash if companies were sold to wealthy crooks, ex-government officials, or foreigners.[11]

Mass voucher privatization became the favored alternative. Citizens would be given vouchers, which they could use to buy shares of privatized companies. The Czech Republic showed the way. Czech voucher privatization began in 1991, was well under way in 1992 when Russia started down the same road, and was largely complete by 1994. Czech industry was mostly in private hands, and a new investment fund industry had sprung up to collect vouchers from citizens and invest in privatized firms. These "voucher investment funds" promised diversification, plus strong outside owners who could replace managers who couldn't make the transition to a market economy. And the wealth giveaway from voucher auctions made them initially popular.[12]

Russia followed in the Czech Republic's footsteps, with some important differences. In the Czech Republic, most of a company's shares were distributed in voucher auctions; only a limited number of shares were reserved for managers and employees. A small number of voucher investment funds accumulated most of the vouchers and bought large stakes in most major firms. This gave most Czech firms major outside owners.

The Russian government lacked the capacity to force privatization on unwilling managers. The political solution was to bribe them with cheap shares so they would pursue privatization voluntarily. Employees were also given large numbers of cheap shares, in a political bow to the communist ideology of worker ownership of the means of production. The result: most privatized firms were initially majority owned by workers and managers. A typical outcome was 60–65 percent manager and employee ownership, perhaps 20 percent ownership by individuals and voucher investment funds, and 15–20 percent still held by the state, which planned to sell its remaining shares for cash in the future. Given the passivity of Russian workers and their ignorance of free markets, this ownership structure led to manager control of most enterprises.

Russian managers' personal stake in their companies was often modest to begin with, but rose quickly. In Russia, vouchers were tradable. This let managers buy vouchers that they could trade for shares in their own companies. Managers often got the funds to buy vouchers by illegally "privatizing" company funds. They continued to accumulate shares after the voucher auctions were completed, by convincing or coercing employees to sell their shares cheaply.[13]

Some auctions were marked by other irregularities. Under the auction design, if fewer vouchers were bid for a company's shares, more shares would be distributed per voucher. This gave insiders an incentive to discourage others from bidding. There were various ways to achieve this result. The auction location could be hard to reach (Russia is a large country with limited transportation) or could be announced or changed at the last minute. In some cases, phone calls and air flights into the city where the auction took place were conveniently disrupted shortly before the auction, or armed guards excluded unwanted bidders from the auction. The more valuable the company, the more likely its managers (or well-connected outside investors) were to use tactics like these. And perhaps one thousand of the fifteen thousand mass-privatized firms cut special privatization deals with the government.

Finally, the largest enterprises were held out of voucher privatization, with the government distributing at most a minority stake. In several important industries, the government created pyramid structures, bundling controlling stakes in a number of operating companies into a few holding companies, and later sold controlling stakes in the holding companies. The government created seven oil holding companies: LUKOil, Sidanko, Sibneft, Rosneft, Tyumen Oil, Yukos, and VNK. Electric power (with United Energy Systems as the principal holding company) and telecoms (with Svyazinvest as the principal holding company) followed a similar pattern.

Pyramid structures everywhere are an invitation for controlling shareholders to siphon wealth from companies that they control, but have a limited economic stake in.[14] This risk is imperfectly controlled in other countries because the pyramid commonly begins as a wholly owned corporate group. The controlling family must develop a reputation for honesty, or no one will buy the noncontrolling shares that it wants to sell. The risk from pyramid structures was magnified in Russia by weak enforcement, plus controllers' ability to acquire control of a pyramid without first developing a reputation for honesty.

The privatizers knew that the auctions wouldn't be perfectly clean and that manager/worker control of privatized companies would limit shareholder oversight of managers. They saw this as an acceptable political price to pay for rapid privatization. Even bad private owners were better than state ownership. As Andrei Shleifer, a principal Western advisor to the Russian privatizers, and Dmitry Vasiliev, a top Russian privatizer, explained: "[Russian ownership] structures have been to a large extent determined by the political imperative of accommodating managerial preferences in the privatization program, since without manager support firms would have remained under political control. We believe that the ownership structures emerging from Russian privatization, while far superior to state ownership, still give managers too much control relative to what is needed to speed up efficient restructuring."[15] The privatizers ignored the special risks created by pyramid structures. We recall no discussion of this issue at the time, and it isn't mentioned in contemporaneous literature.

For our part, we don't doubt that privatization gave managers incentives to make profits. The harder question, to which we return in section III, was how many managers would seek to profit by improving their business, versus how many would steal the value that the business still had.

B. "Loans-for-Shares" and Other Rigged Auctions: 1995–Present

A story: The U.S. government owes $25 billion to Germany. To pay off the obligation, it gives $25 billion to Bank of America with instructions to wire the funds to the German government. The money never arrives. No one ever finds out where it went, or really tries to find out. No one at Bank of America goes to jail. The government never asks Bank of America to pay the money back, and the government continues to do business with Bank of America. Indeed, the president invites Bank of America's CEO to become a cabinet secretary, in charge of economic reform. For a time he agrees, before deciding that there is more profit to be made by dealing with the government than by helping to run it.

This story isn't remotely possible in the United States. But change the bank to Oneksimbank (owned by kleptocrat Vladimir Potanin), run the money not through Oneksimbank itself but through two affiliated banks, and reduce the amount to $502 million, which is a rough Russian equivalent of $25 billion as a proportion of GNP, and it becomes a true Russian story, less widely known than it ought to be.[16] It's no longer hard to understand how Oneksimbank accumulated enough money to become a principal proponent and beneficiary of the rigged "loans-for-shares" auctions of major companies, through which Russia sold its largest companies for a small fraction of fair value, beginning in 1995. The same deep corruption that let Potanin walk off with half a billion dollars can explain why the Russian government tolerated the obvious rigging of the loans-for-shares auctions, even though it was desperate for the revenue that honest auctions might have produced.[17]

Another popular way to instant wealth: arrange to hold and manage government funds, paying little or no interest to the government and reinvesting the funds at market rates, during a high-inflation period when interest rates were in triple or high-double digits. Vladimir Gusinski's MOST Bank got its start managing money in this manner for the Moscow city government; Potanin's Oneksimbank managed money for the Finance Ministry and the Foreign Trade Ministry; Mikhail Fridman's Alfa Bank managed funds for the Customs Service and distributed agricultural subsidies. Khodorkovski's Bank Menatep handled the funds that Russia spent on its 1996 military operations in Chechnya and later promised to spend on rebuilding Chechnya. A Russian government audit later estimated that some $4.4 billion of these funds never arrived at their intended destination.[18] As Pyotr Aven of Alfa Bank candidly explained: "To become a millionaire in our country it is not at all necessary to have a good head and specialized knowledge. Often it is enough to have active support in the government, the parliament, local power structures and law enforcement agencies. One fine day your insignificant bank is authorized, for instance, to conduct operations with budgetary funds. Or quotas are generously allotted . . . for the export of oil, timber, and gas. In other words, you are appointed a millionaire."[19]

Loans-for-shares was an audacious scheme to leverage wealth acquired in these dubious ways, by using it to acquire Russia's biggest companies for a small fraction of their value.[20] It began in 1995 with a proposal by Potanin, backed by most of the major new Russian banks. The Russian government wanted to raise revenue but found it politically hard to sell its stakes in these enterprises, which had been excluded from voucher privatization. The banks proposed to loan funds to the government for several years, with repayment secured by the government's controlling stakes in these enterprises. Everyone understood that the government would not repay the loans, and would instead forfeit its shares to the banks that made the loans.

Under loans-for-shares, the government auctioned its shares in a number of major oil, metals, and telephone companies, giving the shares to whoever would loan it the most money. But the auctions were peculiar indeed. The right to manage the auctions was parceled out among the major banks, who contrived to win the auctions that they managed at astonishingly low prices. The bid rigging that was implicit in divvying up the auction-managing role became explicit in the actual bidding. The auction manager participated in two separate consortia (to meet the formal requirement for at least two bids), each of whom bid the government's reservation price or trivially above that. No one else bid at all. Foreigners were either excluded formally or understood that it was pointless to try to bid.

In the few cases in which someone bid for a company intended to be won by someone else, pretexts were found to disqualify the high bidder. For example, Oneksimbank managed the Norilski Nickel auction, with a reservation price of $170 million. It arranged three bids from affiliates, all at $170 or $170.1 million. Unexpectedly, Rossiiski Kredit Bank offered $355 million, more than twice as much. Oneksimbank disqualified Rossiiski Kredit's bid on the grounds that the bid amount exceeded Rossiiski Kredit's statutory capital (the nominal value of its outstanding shares); Oneksimbank's affiliate won the bidding at $170.1 million. No matter that Oneksimbank's winning bid suffered from the same technical defect, or that Rossiiski Kredit's statutory capital didn't affect its ability to pay the bid amount, or that the auction rules required Oneksimbank to provide any objections in advance of the auction, to give bidders time to cure them. Not that either bid was more than a small fraction of the value of Norilski Nickel, which had annual profits of around $400 million.

The loans-for-shares auctions were auctions that the world was watching. Hopes that visibility, plus the government's desperate need for revenue, would instill some semblance of honesty were disappointed. Meanwhile, auctions that the world wasn't watching were often even worse. For example, Russia formed Zarubezhtsvetmet (which translates as "foreign nonferrous metals") to hold its 49 percent stake in a joint venture with the Mongolian government, which ran Mongolia's Erdenet copper mine. Zarubezhtsvetmet's market value was perhaps $250 million. It was sold for $150,000 to insiders with connections to the Russian Metallurgy Ministry. No matter that Mongolia had the right to approve any transfer of Russia's interest in Erdenet, and a right of first refusal to buy Russia's stake at the price at which it was offered to someone else. That right was ignored, despite Mongolia's official government complaint.[21]

Rather more of a nuisance was the Russian prosecutor who sued in 1997 to reverse the privatization of Zarubezhtsvetmet, on the grounds that Mongolia hadn't consented to Russia's transfer of its interest in Erdenet.[22] The prosecutor's error was soon corrected, and the suit has proceeded no further. A second official complaint by Mongolia in 1998 received a blunt response: "Что касаетса Вашево вопроса о российском участнике, то подтверждаем, что в соответствии с упомянутым межправительственным Соглашением им является открытое акционерное общество 'Внешнеэкономическое обьединение Зарубежцветмет'" (With regard to your question about the Russian participant [in Erdenet], this is to verify that in accordance with the [Russian-Mongolian agreement on creation of Erdenet], it is Zarubezhtsvetmet).[23] The fix was still in.

Another common tactic: Beginning in 1994, the government often required bidders in privatization auctions to promise specified future investments in the enterprise.[24] Once the winning bidder acquired the shares, the promised investments were often quietly shelved, or the shares were transferred to supposedly good-faith purchasers, who weren't bound by the investment promise. An honest purchaser couldn't use these dodges, so dishonest purchasers tended to win the auctions.

Another privatization rule gave a firm's managers the right to acquire 30 percent of its shares cheaply if they first secured an agreement with the employees that would prevent the enterprise from going bankrupt for one year. Since proof that the enterprise would go bankrupt without the agreement, or wouldn't go bankrupt for a year with it, was in the eye of the beholder, this was an all-but-open gift of a controlling stake to the managers, in return for a phony agreement with the employees.[25]

The rigged auctions continue. For example, in late 1999, an unknown offshore company, presumably controlled by LUKOil's managers, bought 9 percent of LUKOil's shares from the government for three dollars a share when the market price was eight dollars, marking the third time in five years that LUKOil management had bought a block of LUKOil shares from the government for less than the shares' market price.[26]

C. The Outcome: A Kleptocracy

Taken as a whole, Russian privatization led to several distinct outcomes. First, a kleptocracy emerged. A small number of individuals, who mostly achieved initial wealth through favorable deals with or outright theft from the government, ended up controlling most of Russia's major firms and, to a nontrivial extent, the government itself. Second, as we discuss in section IV, mass privatization hasn't measurably improved firm productivity.

Third, the Russian public came to associate privatization with corruption, increased crime, and fabulous wealth for a chosen few while workers and pensioners went unpaid. By 1992, Russia had a new slang term for privatization that combined the word for privatization (*приватизация* [*privatizatziya*]) with the verb *прихватить* (*prikhvatits*, "to grab, to take improperly") to form *прихватизация* (*prikhvatizatziya*), roughly translated as "grab-privatization." Top privatizer Anatoli Chubais was known as the *главный прихватизатор* (*glavní prikhvatizator*, the "chief grab-privatizer").[27] Popular disgust with privatization strengthened the Communists and those in other antireform political parties.

As the kleptocrats' power grew, many bought television stations, newspapers, and other media outlets to promote the election of friendly politicians and to blunt public criticism of their activities. They now control almost all major Russian newspapers and television stations. To follow a political debate in the Russian press, or a turf battle within the government, one must understand which kleptocrat owns which newspaper, and which kleptocrat is allied with which politician.[28]

Table 4.1 lists those most often named as among the kleptocrats and names their principal investments, government connections, and media outlets. Other recent or current major players include Roman Abramovich (Berezovski's apparent partner; chairman of Sibneft); Vladimir Bogdanov (Surgutneftegaz); the Chernoy brothers (aluminum companies); and Anatoli Chubais (former prime minister; head of the UES electric power company).[29]

III. Structural Flaws in Russian Privatization

Russian privatization was dirty. On the whole, the bigger the stakes, the dirtier the deal. Its advocates hoped that even if the manner of distributing the state's wealth was regrettable, the outcome would be salutary. New owners, motivated by profit, would improve the privatized companies' operations. The new owners would get rich, perhaps unde-

Table 4.1
Russia's Kleptocrats and Their Principal Holdings

Kleptocrats (known political connections)	*Principal companies*	*Media outlets*
Vagit Alekperov (ties to Moscow mayor Yuri Luzhkov)	LUKOil (largest Russian oil company); Bank Imperial (with Vyakhirev)	*Izvestia* newspaper (with Potanin); TV-6 (with Berezovski)
Boris Berezovski (ties to the family of former president Boris Yeltsin; former prime minister Viktor Chernomyrdin; Kremlin chief of staff Alexander Voloshin)	Sibneft (oil and gas holding company), Logo VAZ (auto distributor), Aeroflot and Transaero airlines; Avtovaz-bank, Obyedinenni Bank	ORT (with Fridman), TV6 (with Alekperov), and STS television stations; *Vremya* television program; NSN radio, *Nezavisimaya gazeta* *Novaya izvestia*, and *Kommersant* newspapers, *Ogonek* magazine
Viktor Chernomyrdin (former prime minister)	Gazprom (natural gas) (former chairman; reputed share owner ship) (Gazprom's ownership of other companies is listed below for Rem Vyakhirev)	
Mikhail Fridman (ties to Kremlin chief of staff Alexander Voloshin)	Alfa Group holding company, Alfa Bank, Tyumen Oil (oil holding company), Alfa Cement, various real estate, construction and oil export companies	Alfa TV, ORT television station (with Berezovski)
Vladimir Gusinski (ties to Moscow mayor Yuri Luzhkov)	Media Most holding company, Most Bank	Sevodnya, Novaya gazeta (with Smolenski), Obshchaya gazeta, 7 *dnei* and *Smena* newspapers; Ekho Moskvuy radio; NTV and NTV+ (with Vyakhirev) and TNT television stations, *Itogi* and *Lisa* magazines
Mikhail Khodorkovski (ties to former prime minister Yevgeni Primakov); former Fuel and Energy Ministry head Sergei Generalov)	Rosprom (holding company); Bank Menatep; Yukos and VNK oil and gas holding companies; various manu-facturing, copper, chemical, timber, and retail companies	*Moscow Times*, *St. Petersburg Times*, and *Literaturnaya gazeta* newspapers

(continued)

Table 4.1 (*continued*)

Kleptocrats (known political connections)	*Principal companies*	*Media outlets*
Yuri Luzhkov (Moscow mayor)	Through city of Moscow: Guta Bank, Bank Moskvuoy, Bank for Reconstruction and Development; also reputed to take a piece of every significant real estate deal in Moscow	*Moskovski komsomolets* news paper; TV Center televi sion station (owned by city of Moscow)
Vladimir Potanin (former deputy prime minister, ties to former deputy prime minister Anatoli Chubais)	Interros holding company; Oneksimbank; RosBank; MFK Renaissance investment bank; various insurance companies; Norilski Nickel (nickel and other nonferrous metals); Sidanko (oil and gas holding company); Novolipetsk (steel); 25% of Svyazinvest (telephone holding company); Perm Motors (aircraft); various metallurgical, shipping and industrial companies	*Izvestia* (with Alekperov), *Komsomolskaya Pravda* (with Vyakhirev) and *Russki telegraf* newspapers, *Ekspert* magazine
Aleksander Smolenski*	SBS-Agro Bank, Agromprom Bank, possible co-owner with Berezovski of Sibneft	*Novaya gazeta* (with Gusinski) and National News Service newspapers, *Dengi* magazine
Rem Vyakhirev (ties to former prime minister Viktor Chernomyrdin)	Gazprom (natural gas) (CEO, reputed share ownership), Bank Imperial (with Alekperov), Inkombank (minority stake), Gazprombank, National Reserve Bank, Promstroibank, Komitek oil company	Komsomolskaya pravda (with Potanin), NTV, and NTV+ television stations (with Gusinski); *Rabochaya tribuna*, *Trud*, and *Profil* magazines; various regional newspapers and television stations; minority stake in Media Most (see Gusinski)

*Smolenski is often listed as one of the kleptocrats, but there is evidence that he is partly a frontperson for Boris Berezovski, who rarely owns anything in his own name. Conversely, Berezovski's partner, Roman Abramovich, may be emerging as a first-tier kleptocrat in his own right. See Eduard Gismatullin, *Sibneft Director Steps into Kremlin Stage*, Moscow Times, June 1, 1999 (describing Abramovich's and Berezovski's joint control of Sibneft and related companies).

servedly, but the whole country would benefit from the productivity gains.

These hopes have not been fulfilled. In this section we investigate why. Sections A–D are the theoretical core of this chapter where we develop a framework for understanding why Russia's corporate owners and managers often chose self-dealing over company building and then apply that framework to the Russian environment. Sections E and F are the empirical core of the chapter. There we discuss the outcomes of voucher privatization and the kleptocrats' actions after they acquired control of Russia's biggest companies. In section IV we turn to the counterfactual: what might have happened with slower privatization and greater efforts to build market-supporting institutions.

A. The Controller's Dilemma: Build Value or Loot?

Consider a stylized account of the dilemma facing Russian managers or outside investors who acquire control of a privatized firm. The controllers wish to maximize their private return on investment. They are, we will assume, amoral, interested only in personal gain. In the short run, they have nearly absolute power over their firms' decisions and face no restrictions on self-dealing. In the case of enterprises that are not viable, our amoral controllers will steal what they can, leaving an empty shell behind. The more interesting case is when the firm is potentially profitable. How will a controller behave?

There are two basic ways for our hypothetical amoral controllers to earn private returns. The first (the "value-creating" strategy) is to increase the firm's value, and thus the value of the controller's fractional stake in the firm. The second (the "self-dealing" strategy) is to expropriate value from other claimants. For example, by self-dealing enough to extract all of the firm's free cash flow, the controller can appropriate the payments that would otherwise go to the government as income taxes and to minority shareholders as dividends. By self-dealing beyond this point, the controller can skim revenues that would otherwise go to pay the firm's suppliers, employees, or creditors.

If the value-creating and self-dealing strategies were independent, an amoral controller would maximize returns along each dimension independently. The controller would create as much value as possible *and* steal as much of that value as possible. The two strategies are not independent, however. A controller who skims revenues owed to suppliers and employees risks destroying the firm's going concern value. Suppliers and employees can't be defrauded indefinitely, even if they have no legal recourse. Sooner or later, they will stop doing business with the firm.

Even for self-dealing limited to a firm's free cash flow, there are tradeoffs between increasing value and self-dealing. For example, if the controller skims the firm's profits while continuing to pay its suppliers and employees, that person expropriates the government's income tax revenues and the value of minority shares without jeopardizing the firm's survival. But the firm will be unable to obtain external financing to pursue new business opportunities or support major investments. Nor can the controller use internal financing for these purposes without revealing the firm's profitability to the tax authorities and minority investors. Moreover, given the discretion exercised by the Russian tax authorities, it may be hard to skim tax payments without also stiffing suppliers and employees. A company that pays its suppliers and employees reveals that it can afford to pay some taxes (or bribes in lieu thereof), which the tax authorities will try to collect.

A controller also can't expropriate the value of minority shares and then sell the company at fair value to a new owner. The steps taken to expropriate the minority will conceal the firm's profitability. Potential buyers will heavily discount claims about true value by controllers who have proved themselves untrustworthy by expropriating minority shareholders. Finally, a controller may be skilled at self-dealing or creating value, but not both.

For all these reasons, self-dealing will decrease a profitable firm's value. Controllers can't independently maximize returns from creating value and self-dealing; they must maximize them jointly. With no enforcement, controllers are likely to pursue a mixed strategy. A controller who mostly maximizes value is likely to also extract some private returns. Conversely, a controller who mostly self-deals will likely keep a potentially viable firm alive. A firm that continues to operate can bring in new funds from suppliers, employees, creditors, and perhaps the government and shareholders, as long as it can find new contracting parties or pay the old ones just enough to keep their hopes of future payment alive. Moreover, keeping the firm alive lets the controller retain the option to sell the firm or build value in the future if business conditions improve.

The tension between creating value and looting increases as the risk of future sanctions grows. Consider the extreme case in which sanctions are certain, but won't be imposed for a while. Thieves who will be caught if they linger too long won't capture the firm's long-term value anyway. An amoral controller then has a sharp choice: create value (perhaps with self-dealing at a level unlikely to lead to sanctions), or steal as much as you can and then flee the jurisdiction before the police arrive.

In Russia, with enforcement uncertain, most controllers of viable enterprises will likely pursue a mixed strategy of enhancing firm value and grabbing the existing value. The critical question is, How much of each will they do?

In our view, three broad classes of factors shape controllers' choices. The first (section B) is the legal and institutional infrastructure that affects the level of self-dealing that is feasible and the risk that self-dealing will lead to sanctions. The second (section C) includes general regulatory and economic factors that affect all firms, especially the overall business climate. The third (section D) includes factors associated with particular firms or controllers.

B. Russia's Legal and Institutional Infrastructure

Consider first the legal and institutional constraints on self-dealing. The Soviet Union wasn't a very honest place to begin with. At the same time, the scale of dishonesty was limited. Managers and workers in stores could appropriate and resell some of the best goods, but there were others whose job was to control this petty theft. Managers of state-owned firms couldn't set up transfer pricing schemes with other companies that the managers owned because citizens couldn't own companies. Bureaucratic controls kept managers away from direct access to the payments that a company received for its goods, and provided oversight of those who had access to money.

Besides, the money from large-scale corruption couldn't buy very much—a new Russian car or a nice vacation (senior managers and government officials, however, already had cars and government-provided vacations), but not a fancy house, a fat savings account (which would be noticed), or a foreign vacation or bank account (generally not possible). And if you got caught being too greedy, you faced a lengthy term in a miserable Russian jail or gulag (work camp), which you certainly wouldn't enjoy and might not survive. Thus, we disagree with those who claim that Russia was so corrupt at the start of the 1990s that little could be done to control managers' theft of company assets.

At the same time, in the early 1990s, Russia wholly lacked the institutional infrastructure to control self-dealing by managers of private firms. Prosecutors, judges, and lawyers had no experience in untangling corporate transactions or understanding of the indirect ways in which company insiders can siphon off profits. Legal concepts of fiduciary duty and proscriptions against self-dealing didn't exist.[30] Russia had neither business lawyers who could advise managers on how to behave toward shareholders nor accountants who could ensure accurate financial disclosure. Its accounting rules were designed to meet the needs of central planners, not investors. The Finance Ministry is gradually updating Russian accounting rules, but often develops rules to determine how much tax a company owes rather than to help investors understand the company's cash flows.[31]

Basic commercial and capital markets laws didn't exist when voucher privatization was completed in 1994. The tax rules all but compelled managers to hide profits from tax inspectors and shareholders alike. A Securities Commission was created in 1994, but it has a tiny budget, can't pay its staff enough to keep qualified people, and lacks the political clout to investigate kleptocrat misdeeds.

Finally, the business culture is one of law avoidance. Under Communist rule, a good manager often had to obtain the parts and supplies needed to keep a factory running in unofficial ways.[32] In a market economy, those skills were easily transferred to the new tasks of asset stripping and self-dealing.

The weak legal and institutional framework was no secret to the privatizers. But writing good laws can take years and building good institutions takes decades. The privatizers weren't willing to wait. They chose to privatize immediately and hoped that the laws and institutions would follow later. The laws did indeed follow. The first two parts of a new Civil Code were adopted in 1995–96. A weak law on securities (since modestly strengthened) was adopted in 1995, a fairly strong law on joint stock companies in 1996, and decent laws on bankruptcy and limited liability companies in 1998. These laws have weaknesses, but no more so than do the laws in many other developing countries.

But the privatizers hoped for more than just decent laws. They hoped that broad private ownership would create a constituency for strengthening and enforcing those laws. That didn't happen. Instead, company managers and kleptocrats opposed efforts to strengthen or enforce the capital markets laws. They didn't want a strong Securities Commission or tighter rules on self-dealing transactions. And what they didn't want, they didn't get.

The tax rules are revised periodically but haven't improved much. Why isn't clear. Perhaps their vagueness lets most businesses escape with a modest payment to the tax inspectors (and little to the government). The Finance Ministry and the tax inspectors mostly oppose reform, perhaps because clear rules and reasonable rates would reduce bribes. Perhaps too, company managers aren't too unhappy with the current system. They must hide their income, but can then steal the hidden profits.[33]

International Monetary Fund (IMF) intervention didn't help. A core IMF condition for new loans was higher tax revenues *now*. Lower tax rates and less administrative discretion wouldn't achieve that. In contrast, reforming the tax system was a soft condition that the IMF never insisted on. But Russia's drive to collect more tax revenue was counterproductive. Tax revenue as a percentage of GDP declined while corruption intensified, as businesses responded to higher tax demands with larger bribes.

The kleptocrats were able to co-opt the Central Bank and the Finance Ministry into opposing a strong securities law or Securities Commission. The Central Bank's bureaucrats were none too honest themselves,[34] and didn't need much convincing that they, not the upstart Securities Commission, ought to control Russia's capital markets. As a result, the Securities Commission has limited powers and ended up in a protracted fight for political survival, which took most of what little resources it had.

The government's own behavior reinforced disrespect for rules. To survive, managers had to cheat on their taxes, bribe tax and customs inspectors, and avoid cash transactions. The government didn't pay its own bills to companies that provided it with goods and services, hardly an incentive for those companies to pay their tax bills. It became increasingly clear that corruption went right to the top—to the extended Yeltsin "family."[35]

Company managers soon learned that they could plunder their firms with negligible risk of prosecution. For example, in the two years after the 1998 ruble collapse exposed self-dealing at Russian banks and prompted a race to strip the assets that remained, not a single bank official had been charged with anything. Khodorkovski's Bank Menatep offers an example of how the bankers behaved. After Bank Menatep collapsed in mid-1998, Khodorkovski transferred its good assets to a new bank, Menatep–St. Petersburg, leaving depositors and creditors to pick at the old bank's carcass. To ensure that the transactions couldn't be traced, Khodorkovski arranged for a truck containing most of Bank Menatep's records for the last several years to be driven off a bridge into the Dybna River. Where presumably they will remain.[36]

Russia's core problem today is less lack of decent laws than lack of the infrastructure and political will to enforce them.[37] For example, the company law prohibits much of the rampant self-dealing by managers and large shareholders that occurs every day. But the courts respect only documentary evidence, which is rarely available, given limited discovery and the skill of managers in covering their tracks.

Moreover, a shareholder who sues a major company will usually lose at trial and first-level appeal, because of home-court bias, judicial corruption, or both. A shareholder with a strong case has a decent chance of getting an honest decision on further appeal, but that will take years. And judgments must be enforced (or, often, not enforced) by the same biased or corrupt lower court where the case began.[38]

A recent example: the bankruptcy proceedings for Sidanko, an oil holding company owned by kleptocrat Vladimir Potanin, and for Chernogoneft and Kondpetroleum, two key Sidanko subsidiaries. Chernogoneft and Kondpetroleum went bankrupt after selling oil to Sidanko, which failed to pay for the oil and was itself looted so severely that it went bankrupt. In the Chernogoneft bankruptcy proceedings, 98 percent of the creditors voted for one external manager, but the local judge appointed a different manager, with ties to Tyumen Oil, owned by kleptocrat Mikhail Fridman, which wanted to acquire Chernogoneft cheap. The court also rejected a Chernogoneft offer to pay all creditors in full! Tyumen was able to buy Chernogoneft for $176 million and Kondpetroleum for $52 million (a small fraction of the actual value), in what Potanin publicly called "an atmosphere of unprecedented pressure on the court system."[39] Which apparently means that Tyumen didn't merely bribe judges (Sidanko could have offered its own bribes), but threatened them as well. Indeed, a judge who issued an early ruling against Tyumen was beaten for his troubles.[40]

Sidanko's bankruptcy was marked by similar irregularities, some reflecting a battle between Potanin and Fridman for control of the proceedings.[41] Other prominent bankruptcy cases were also rigged by insiders, with the cooperation of the courts and (for bankrupt banks) the Central Bank.[42]

Prosecutors are no better than judges. The reported price to stall a criminal investigation into, say, a business-related Mafia hit: fifty thousand dollars in Moscow; less elsewhere.[43]

The privatizers, ourselves included, underestimated the extent to which functioning law requires honest courts and prosecutors that can redress gross violations. We called the Russian company law that we helped to draft a "self-enforcing" model because we thought that stating sensible rules would encourage corporate norms to coalesce around those rules (even with minimal enforcement) and that the courts could enforce simple procedural rules (for example, approval of self-dealing transactions by noninterested shareholders).[44] Instead, self-dealing transactions were hidden, courts were of little help even when self-dealing was obvious, and managerial culture coalesced around concealing self-dealing instead of disclosure and a noninterested shareholder vote.

We've thought since about ways to strengthen the constraints on self-dealing. For example, requiring a company's accountants to report to shareholders on any self-dealing transactions they find, and whether those transactions were completed in compliance with the company law, would make it harder to conceal self-dealing. But our central view is that if enforcement is weak enough, these and other possible changes to Russia's current not-so-bad rules won't matter much.

Having recounted Russia's many weak institutions, we should mention a problem that Russia didn't have in the early 1990s, at least in severe form. Theorists have speculated that social "trust"—the willingness of people to deal fairly with one another and expect others to do likewise—is an important market-supporting institution.[45] We have no sense that Russia was an especially low-trust country at the beginning of the 1990s. Russians didn't trust their government, but enterprise managers routinely dealt with one another on an oral basis (often to circumvent formal regulations). Indeed, these informal contacts helped to make extensive barter chains a feasible substitute for cash-based transactions. One of the tragedies of Russian misgovernment in the 1990s is that Russia is a far more corrupt and lower-trust place today than a decade ago, with all that implies for its future prospects.

C. Economy-Wide Factors

A second broad class of factors that influence a controller's choice between value creation and self-dealing are economy-wide factors that affect a firm's potential profitability, and thus the opportunity cost from self-dealing instead of creating value.

1. OVERALL BUSINESS CLIMATE

The worse the overall business climate, the smaller the expected gains from creating value, and thus the more likely controllers are to loot instead. Moreover, many state-owned enterprises will fail, and even viable enterprises will need to shed workers to improve productivity. New businesses must take up the employment slack. If they don't emerge, the market pressure on large firms to restructure will be weaker, and political pressure for firms to maintain employment and related social services will be stronger.[46]

Russia's business climate was lousy. We discuss the most important problems below, in rough order of estimated importance.

Tax. Perhaps the single most important regulatory obstacle to earning an honest profit is the Russian tax system. Russian tax law is both amazingly complex and quite simple. The complex part is the vague and constantly changing rules and administrative interpretations. The nominal tax rates aren't extreme, but apply to a measure of "income" that grossly overstates actual income. Actual taxes can easily exceed 100 percent of profits. In addition, tax inspectors have broad discretion to seize a company's bank accounts and other assets to pay whatever taxes the inspector claims are due. Companies can appeal, but they will be out of business long before the appeal is heard. Tax audits have become a potent political weapon, deployed by the government against businesses that don't support the incumbents.[47]

The simple part is how businesses behave: The confiscatory rates produce derisory revenues, because almost no one pays them. Instead, everyone hides income as best they can and bribes the tax inspectors to reduce whatever initial assessment the inspectors make. An important reason for Russia's development of an extensive barter economy is that cash in a bank account invites the tax inspectors to seize it.[48]

Falsified books preclude strong public capital markets. Companies that can't report income honestly to the tax inspectors also can't report honestly to investors. Investors therefore can't use a company's financial statements to check on management honesty and skill. They have to hope that the company is profitable and (usually in vain) that managers won't steal its hidden income. The frequent use of barter makes matters still worse. In a barter transaction that involves multiple intermediaries and is designed to hide true profits from the tax inspectors, the opportunities for insiders to skim profits are endless and the prospects of catching them are remote.

Hidden transactions also preclude using the courts to enforce contracts. If the true contract between two companies involves a large quantity of goods at a high price, while the nominal contract (prepared for the tax inspectors) specifies a small quantity at a much lower price, and one party defaults, the other can hardly go to court to enforce the true deal.

Corruption. The need to pay multiple bribes—to tax inspectors, to customs officials, to the police not to harass you, to the many bureaucrats from whom you need a permit to operate—has landed Russia near the bottom of most lists of official corruption.[49] Russia may be better than Nigeria, but not by much.

Moreover, while payoffs to organized crime provide protection against similar demands by competing Mafia groups, payoffs to government officials don't protect you against demands by other officials. The combined bribe demanded by multiple officials can be far larger than a "monopoly" official, seeking to maximize long-term income, would demand.[50] Corruption and an unfriendly bureaucracy are closely connected. Corrupt officials look for opportunities to enforce picky rules and add new rules.

Unfriendly Bureaucrats. Russian red tape, often dating from the Soviet era when businesspeople needed Planning Ministry permission to do almost anything, can be overwhelming. An average new business must obtain permission from "20–30 agencies and receive 50–90 approved registration forms."[51] On average, Russian shops take three months to register (versus three weeks in Poland), are inspected eighty-three times per year (versus half that in Poland), and are fined 19 percent of the time (versus 9 percent in Poland).[52] Disfavored (read: new) businesses are inspected far more often than these averages, and the price of not being fined is usually bribing the inspector.[53]

Organized Crime. If there is a street-level retail establishment in a major Russian city that doesn't pay a healthy share of revenue for "protection," we haven't heard of it. Arguing too strongly over how much to pay can reduce one's life expectancy, as can complaining to the police, who are likely to be in the pay of the Mafia. This leaves businesses to try to persuade their protectors to leave them enough profit to stay in business.

Many large businesses also engage private security forces. But private security is expensive, offers imperfect protection when goods are transported to market, and can be turned to pernicious use—enforcing price-fixing and market-division agreements with competitors or scaring off competitors. More generally, Russian managers can write off unpaid debts, try to enforce them through ineffective courts, or engage their *krysha* (*крьпна*, "roof," a slang term for Mafia protectors) to collect the bill. They can compete on price and quality or pay the *krysha* to put competitors out of business. They can pay the bribes demanded by local officials or hire the *krysha* to negotiate a lower payment.[54] Yet when managers rely on the Mafia for services like these, they strengthen the Mafia, strengthen government-Mafia ties, shorten managers' time horizons (you could be put out of business next), and contribute to a lawless environment.

If a company remains small, it has a better chance of staying out of sight of tax inspectors, other bureaucrats, and the Mafia. Russia is the only country we know where small businesses routinely avoid publicity and obtain customers only by word of mouth. Business cards commonly contain no telltale address and often not even a local phone number (the prefix will give away the business's approximate location). Retail businesses even often operate from behind unlabeled doors.

Subsidies to Unprofitable Firms. A rational capital market provides funds to profitable businesses and starves unprofitable ones. The Russian government usually did the opposite—funneling subsidies to money-losing businesses, often by accepting nonpayment of wages, taxes, and energy bills. Subsidies for losses let a controller loot the same asset multiple times.[55] The explicit and implicit government subsidies to money-losing firms are huge—around 15–20 percent of GDP.[56] Meanwhile, profitable Russian businesses are targets of opportunity for tax collectors, the Mafia, and bribe-seeking bureaucrats. And the products produced by subsidized competitors drive down market prices and lower the profitability of otherwise viable firms.

Urban Land. Starting a new business or growing an existing one requires land. In most Russian regions, urban land hasn't been privatized. Obtaining land requires bribing government officials, who can then collect taxes from you, tell their Mafia buddies about you, and revoke your land rights if you don't pay enough taxes or bribes. Moreover, insecure land rights mean that businesses won't invest much in immovable buildings or equipment, and thus won't grow very large or employ many people.

Lack of Capital. Russians have limited savings and don't trust banks. A recent good reason for both: In 1991–93, the government froze private savings held in the state savings bank and confiscated almost all of those savings by paying interest rates far below inflation. About $100 billion in savings that might have helped to found new businesses was wiped out, and Russians learned to keep savings away from domestic banks, often in hard currency, and hence unavailable to support new investment.

Those citizens who put savings into the new private banks, often run by kleptocrats, soon regretted that choice. During and after the 1998 ruble crash, a bank run ensued, and many banks refused to honor depositor demands for their funds. The Central Bank was in no hurry to straighten out the mess, and it allowed bank controllers to strip the banks of their remaining assets, leaving depositors and creditors with an empty shell.[57]

A Dysfunctional Banking System. It was not for nothing that Jeffrey Sachs once called Central Bank head Viktor Gerashchenko perhaps the worst central banker in history. He not only mishandled monetary policy, he also tolerated and perhaps personally benefited from a system in which, in the mid-1990s, the reported cost of (bribe for) transferring funds through the banking system from one part of Russia to another was around 15 percent of the amount transferred. That drove business activity underground and made it hard to conduct business across long distances at all.

Unfriendliness to Foreign Investment. Foreign investors face additional problems, including ever-changing currency regulations that make it hard to withdraw money once invested and ensure that the Central Bank takes a cut of every dollar that is withdrawn. The regulations don't stop capital flight, because the kleptocrats and other major players exploit loopholes or bribe their way out of compliance. Instead, they discourage honest capital from entering.

Labor Laws. Russia's labor laws, dating from its Communist days, formally prohibit most layoffs, and in practice make them expensive. Even top managers can't be easily fired. Standard practice is to pay employees to leave voluntarily. Many businesses don't pay their employees on time or in full, but honestly run or foreign-owned businesses can't escape so easily.[58]

2. MACROECONOMIC PERFORMANCE

A second key factor that affects firm controllers' expected gains from value creation, and thus the level of self-dealing they will engage in, is a country's macroeconomic performance. Macroeconomic performance interacts with the business climate and with asset stripping. The worse the business climate, the more asset stripping will take place and the worse macroeconomic performance will be. In a vicious circle, poor macroeconomic performance then further depresses firm profitability and encourages asset stripping.[59]

Our overall judgment is that Russia's macroeconomic policy decisions were sometimes poor but not terrible. Inflation was brought under reasonable control by around 1995, and the budget deficit was tolerable. However, high real interest rates chilled investment.[60] And from 1995 through 1998, Russia's Central Bank managed the ruble-dollar exchange rate, letting the ruble gradually slide against the dollar. The ruble's roughly 75 percent devaluation in 1998 suggests that the currency was overvalued before devaluation, which made Russian businesses less competitive.

Some evidence of the overall chill on business, from both microeconomic and macroeconomic factors: At a time when business opportunities should have been abundant and workers readily available, the number of small Russian businesses dropped from 877,000 in 1995 (many started in an early 1990s burst of enthusiasm) to 829,000 in 1997.[61] On a per capita basis, this is about a quarter of the number of small American businesses.[62] The Russian pattern of firms not paying workers for months on end is possible only because workers have no alternative. In successful post-Communist countries, even state-owned firms have shrunk payrolls and improved productivity. In Russia, it is common for a privatized firm to have cut production by 50 percent since 1991, but to have cut employment by only 10 percent.

Capital flight is another good measure of the investment climate. For those who follow Russia's woes, the $10 billion Bank of New York money laundering scandal that broke in 1999 was uninteresting. We merely learned how a small fraction of the money that left Russia (a ballpark estimate is $200 billion during the 1990s) happened to leave. The money is still leaving, just by another route.[63]

The lack of foreign investment is a further measure of the business climate. Russia's official statistics estimate cumulative foreign direct investment at a scant $13 billion from 1992 through 1999. Even the major oil companies, no strangers to tough political environments, have invested little and lost much of what they invested.[64]

3. OTHER FACTORS

Some additional important marketwide factors that affect the upside from a value creation strategy and thus the likelihood of looting:

An inefficient capital market. The harder it is to raise capital or sell one's stake at a fair price, the less there is an incentive to build firm value. In Russia, public offerings at fair value aren't possible because disclosing true profits to investors means disclosing them to tax inspectors also. A private buyer can be shown a company's true books. But the general prevalence of self-dealing makes it hard to persuade investors that a particular controller is (or will stay) honest. Russian firms also can't address investor suspicions by getting auditors to vouch for the company's books, since the real books are unofficial.

Uncertainty and controllers' effective time horizons (or implicit discount rates). A value-increasing strategy often requires investing capital in the near term, and generates additional cash only in the long run. Economic and political uncertainty makes long-term profits less certain and hence less valuable.

Product market competition. Strong competition provides incentives to restructure enterprises and reduces the rents that a controller can loot. In Russia, multiple factors weakened product market competition: privatized enterprises were often monopoly providers in their region, the poor business climate discouraged new entry, trade barriers limited import competition, and poor transportation and state-owned local distribution monopolies limited import and interregional competition.[65]

D. Firm-Specific and Controller-Specific Factors

In addition to these marketwide factors, a number of factors that are specific to particular firms or particular controllers affect the likelihood that a firm's controllers will choose self-dealing as their dominant strategy.

Firm Profitability. The more profitable a firm is (holding constant the marketwide factors discussed above), and the stronger its growth opportunities, the greater the opportunity cost from self-dealing. Privatizing nonviable firms was an open invitation to loot them.

Managerial Skill. Poor management reduces a firm's expected earnings and thus reduces the opportunity cost of self-dealing. Voucher privatization left Communist-era managers in control. Many could muster the skill to strip assets but were incapable of adapting to a competitive market, even if they wanted to.

Separation between Control and Cash Flow Rights. The smaller a controller's percentage holding of cash flow rights and the weaker the controller's hold on future control, the smaller the foregone gain from creating value, while the benefits of self-dealing remain the same. From this perspective, voucher privatization is inherently dangerous because it separates control from cash flow rights, not only for the largest firms, for which this separation is hard to avoid, but also for midsize firms that often have concentrated ownership in developed economies. Pyramid structures or dual-class voting structures that let controllers maintain control with a fraction of a firm's cash flow rights further encourage asset stripping. Yet pyramid structures were built into many of Russia's largest enterprises.

With no constraints on self-dealing, honest management and dispersed ownership are an unstable combination. A controlling stake is worth more to a self-dealer, who will extract 100 percent or more of the firm's value from 51 percent of the shares, than to an honest owner who will keep only his or her pro rata share of the firm's profits. Bad owners will thus tend to drive out good ones.[66]

Letting voucher investment funds aggregate the ownership stakes of individuals lets the funds provide a counterweight to managerial control of firms, but recreates the self-dealing problem at a different level—investment fund controllers can strip assets from both the funds and the companies that the funds control. As we argue in section V.C, investment fund managers are more likely than company managers to find asset stripping attractive.

Prosecution Risk and Effective Time Horizons. Economic and political uncertainty makes time horizons short (implicit discount rates high) for all managers. A controller who pursues a self-dealing strategy faces a still shorter horizon (a higher implicit discount rate), because of the risk that a future government will prosecute the controller for current self-dealing. The Russian kleptocrats, having got the money to buy major firms in questionable ways, already faced future prosecution risk, which enhanced the attractiveness of asset stripping.

The Controller's Morals. Our informal model of the asset-stripping decision assumes an amoral controller. In the real world, morals matter. Some controllers will seek to create value rather than steal it, as long as they have decent prospects for creating value. Others will see skimming as a quick way to generate a handsome return on investment and will not evaluate whether a value-creating strategy might be optimal in the long term. Give control of an enterprise to a crook and he or she is likely to loot it, whatever its long-term prospects.

In Russia, marketwide and firm-specific factors combined to make self-dealing the strategy of choice for many otherwise viable firms. Self-dealing was easy, running a business for profit was hard, growth prospects were dim, voucher privatization separated control from cash flow rights, controllers' time horizons were short, capital markets were rudimentary, managerial skill was scarce, unprofitable firms were subsidized while profitable ones were heavily taxed, and many businesses were sold to crooks who were predisposed to self-dealing.

E. Mass-Privatized Enterprises: Manager Theft and Incompetence

Voucher privatization left Communist-appointed managers in control of most privatized enterprises. The privatizers hoped that outside investors would invest in salvageable firms and profit by installing better management. That happened in a few cases. Sometimes outsiders reached an accord with the company's managers to buy a stake directly from the company; sometimes they bought controlling stakes in the market or by hiring agents to stand at the company's gates and make offers directly to employees. Occasionally, managers sought outside investors and accepted oversight in return.

But more often, enterprise managers acted in dubious ways to acquire more shares and thereby cement their control. Managers had the easiest access to employees' shares and often bought them at very low prices, sometimes by threatening retribution if the employees didn't sell. Sometimes shares were bought with company funds, but the managers ended up with the shares. Other times, managers siphoned funds from the company through self-dealing, funds that they used both to buy employee shares and to improve their own standard of living.[67]

Not infrequently, manager self-dealing compromised the viability of firms. Russia's coal industry offers an example. Many coal-mining firms were doomed to fail. But even potentially profitable firms were sometimes bankrupted by crooked managers. Common skimming techniques include selling the coal to an intermediary at below-market prices; buying mining equipment at inflated prices; and paying workers with vouchers redeemable at the company store, which sells goods to this captive market at above-market prices; with the managers in each case pocketing the difference. Coal workers and their unions, instead of asking where the cash went, periodically go on strike against the government for unpaid back wages, sometimes shutting down railways to dramatize their claims.

An irony: privatized land, while valuable for new businesses, would have been a mixed blessing if coupled with mass privatization. Land was the most valuable asset of many businesses. If salable, it often would have been sold cheaply to insiders, robbing shareholders of some of the value that their enterprises otherwise retain.

Not every privatized enterprise was run by crooks. But many were, and many managers who started out honest changed their minds, because they saw what their fellow managers were able to get away with; the tax system demanded that profits be hidden (which made them easy to steal); they saw the Mafia and dishonest managers becoming wealthy while they struggled to survive; and the authorities were too corrupt to do anything about obvious theft. Others, discouraged by the hostile business environment, sold out to crooks who could earn a swift return on investment in ways that honest managers couldn't. Honest and dishonest behavior alike can be contagious, and Russia fell into a dishonesty equilibrium.[68]

Hard data on the extent of looting of mass privatized enterprises isn't available. Our own qualitative sense: Transfer pricing schemes and other dodges to hide profits from tax collectors and minority shareholders are all but universal. A few controllers invest some of the hidden profits in new capital equipment, but many more pocket the profits, often offshore. Total business investment is very low. We discuss in section IV.B the mixed evidence on whether privatized firms show higher productivity than do nonprivatized firms.

F. Major Enterprises: Kleptocrat Looting

The enterprises that were privatized through voucher privatization were large in number, but often small in value. But there was enormous value in Russia's natural resources companies, related companies (steel and aluminum mills), and power and telephone companies. The government sold at most minority stakes in these companies during voucher privatization and sold controlling stakes later, through loans-for-shares and other "auctions." Estimates of the value of these companies, if permitted to sell their products at market value, run to maximize profit, and valued at developed country multiples, are often staggering. Table 4.2 gives some rough values (precise estimates aren't possible).

TABLE 4.2
Value Estimates for Major Russian Companies, September 1999

Company	*Industry*	*Value at Western multiples ($ Billions)*	*Market capitalization ($ Billions)*
Gazprom	Natural gas	1960	4
LukOil	Oil	195	5.5
Yukos	Oil	170	0.3
United Energy Systems	Electricity	110	3.1
Surgutneftegaz (producing co.)	Oil	91	4.4
Tatneft	Oil	75	0.4
Sberbank	Banking	60	0.4
Tyumen Oil	Oil	47	not traded
Mosenergo	Electricity	12	0.8
Irkutskenergo	Electricity	10	0.4
Norilski Nickel	Nickel	9	0.5
Rostelecom	Telephone	5	0.9
Bratsk Aluminum	Aluminum	2.3	0.03
Krasnoyarsk	Aluminum	2.2	0.08
Aeroflot	Airline	2	0.09
Magnitogorsk	Steel	1.8	0.04
Seversal	Steel	1.7	0.08
Total		2754	20.8

Source: James Fenkner, Troika Dialog investment bank.

Note: Rough value estimates for selected major Russian companies, if run to maximize profit, taxed on that profit at a 33 percent marginal rate, permitted to sell their products at world prices, and valued at developed market multiples. Value estimates for oil and gas companies are based on $13 per barrel of oil reserves (or gas equivalent); for electric companies on $795,000 per megawatt of generating capacity; for steel companies on $148 per ton of capacity; for aluminum companies on $2793 per ton of capacity; for Norilski Nickel on .085 × value of reserves at current commodity prices; for Rostelecom on 3.3 × book value of property, plant and equipment; for Sberbank on book value of 3.1 × assets; for Aeroflot on $16.5 million per plane.

How, then, can Russia have a total market capitalization in September 1999 of only around $20 billion? How can the government be unable to pay the $2 billion it owed to the IMF in 1999 and unable to pay in a timely manner its own pensioners and employees the modest amounts they are owed?

An inescapable answer is theft of these companies' value on a massive scale by the kleptocrats who acquired them. Theft at the time of sale, by buying controlling interests for a tiny fraction of fair value followed by extensive self-dealing, left many of Russia's most valuable companies unable (or unwilling) to pay taxes, pay their workers, or reinvest.

Russian share prices can be understood as out-of-the-money options: investors expect that the firm's entire value will likely go to the government or the firm's controllers. Minority shares still have some value because there is a small positive probability of realizing a return sometime in the future.

Privatization proponents argued that privatization would put control of Russia's major companies in the hands of competent businesspeople, who had incentives to restructure these enterprises, replace managers who couldn't make the transition to a market economy, and make the investments needed to improve productivity. The kleptocrats devoted themselves instead to skimming profits from their companies; starving them of funds (to the point where many were unable to pay their workers or their tax bills, let alone invest in new equipment); replacing managers who resisted the skimming (or threatening/bribing them into submission); and shooting managers and local government officials who resisted too strongly.

This story can be told only through anecdotes. We offer five below—hopefully enough to convince the reader that our strong words are justified. For the first four, we have firsthand knowledge of the shenanigans. The fifth, that of Gazprom, is simply too big to be left out.

Khodorkovski/Yukos. We recounted above the example of Yukos, whose reported 1996 oil revenues were $8.60 per barrel, about four dollars below what they should have been, with the rest presumably skimmed. But this was only part of Yukos's activity. The company owned several operating subsidiaries, each of which had large minority interests. Yukos purchased oil from these subsidiaries at even lower prices, averaging around $7.50 per barrel—low enough so that these subsidiaries, with combined pretax profits of around $1 billion before Yukos acquired control, were soon reporting minimal profits or outright losses and defaulting on their tax payments. Yukos had bled them of whatever cash they had had.[69] The subsidiaries' sale of oil to Yukos, without approval by the subsidiaries' minority shareholders, was a flagrant violation of the company law, but no matter. No one sued, and if they had, well, judges could be bought or their decisions ignored. The transactions were flagrant enough to prompt the Russian Securities Commission to investigate the dealings between Yukos and its subsidiaries. But the investigation went nowhere, perhaps because the commission didn't have the staff to pursue it, or because it was warned off by Khodorkovski's government allies.[70]

Khodorkovski's ambition exceeded his reach, however. In 1997 and 1998, he borrowed heavily from Western banks, using as collateral

Yukos shares and guarantees from Yukos's subsidiaries. When the Russian ruble collapsed in mid-1998, Khodorkovski's Bank Menatep, like most major banks, suffered heavy losses on ruble-denominated Russian government bonds. If one counts his offshore wealth, Khodorkovski surely could have weathered this storm, but he chose instead to let Menatep and Yukos sink. Yukos defaulted on its loan payments, which meant that 30 percent of its shares would soon be seized by Western lenders. But Khodorkovski still controlled Yukos for the moment, and he used that control to strip Yukos of its real value—ownership of its oil-producing subsidiaries.

At each major subsidiary—Tomskneft, Yuganskneftegaz, and Samaraneftegaz—each worth many billions of dollars based on their oil reserves—Yukos proposed for shareholder approval the following package of proposals, with minor variations:

(1) A massive new share issuance to obscure offshore companies, at prices that valued the companies at 1 percent or less of their true value, and perhaps 10 percent of their depressed trading prices. Even that modest amount would be paid not in cash but in promissory notes issued by other Yukos subsidiaries, of dubious legality and even more dubious value. Enough shares were to be issued (between 194 percent and 243 percent of the previously outstanding shares) to transfer control from Yukos to the offshore companies.

(2) A multiyear agreement obligating the subsidiary to sell its output to the offshore companies at the laughable price of 250 rubles per ton (around $1.30 per barrel at mid-1999 exchange rates, and headed lower as the ruble depreciates against the dollar).

(3) Shareholder approval of large asset transfers to still other obscure companies, including both past and unidentified future transactions.

Shareholders who opposed these proposals were given the opportunity to sell their shares back to the company at prices that valued the three companies, with proven oil and gas reserves of around 13 billion barrels of oil equivalent, at a total of $33 million—$.0025 per barrel of proven reserves. No, this is not a misprint.[71]

To be sure, Yukos needed shareholder approval for this raw theft. Yukos owned only 51 percent of the shares in the subsidiaries and needed 75 percent of the votes of the shareholders who participated in a shareholder meeting to authorize the share issuance (plus a majority of the votes of noninterested shareholders). Khodorkovski's solution was bold, if not exactly legal: The day before the subsidiaries' shareholder meetings, Yukos arranged for a compliant judge to declare that the minority shareholders were acting in concert, in violation of the Antimonopoly Law. The judge disqualified everyone but Yukos and its affiliated shareholders from voting. When minority shareholders arrived at the meetings, they were greeted by armed guards; most were barred from voting or attending on the basis of this court order. Yukos's shares were voted and were counted as noninterested; the proposals all passed. Having used Yukos's voting power to ram through these proposals, Khodorkovski then transferred Yukos's remaining shares in two of the three oil-producing subsidiaries to still other offshore companies.

Maybe, if oil prices stay strong, Khodorkovski will put Yukos back together. Maybe in a few years, an appellate court will rule that all this was illegal. But the initial lawsuits have been abandoned. And in the meantime, Khodorkovski will have stolen billions through below-market sales of the subsidiaries' oil.

Besides, opposing Yukos can be bad for one's health. The mayor of Nefteyugansk was murdered in 1998, shortly after he publicly demanded that Yukos subsidiary Yuganskneftegaz pay its local taxes and back wages.[72] In March 1999, Yevgeni Rubin, the head of a company that had won a lawsuit against Yukos, had his car blown up near his home, with armed attackers waiting to finish off anyone who survived the bomb. By chance, he wasn't inside, but his bodyguards were less fortunate.[73]

Khodorkovski's behavior didn't trouble senior Russian officials. In the middle of the scandal, Khodorkovski accompanied then prime minister Yevgeni Primakov on a trip to meet President Bill Clinton. It did trouble the Securities Commission, which launched an investigation. But the outcome of that investigation was hardly promising. The chairman of the Securities Commission resigned in disgust, after failing to get the cooperation he needed from other government agencies to bring a court action; the commission's remaining members approved the share issuances.[74]

Berezovski/Sibneft. Sibneis another major Russian oil holding company. So far as anyone can tell, it is controlled by Boris Berezovski and his partner Roman Abramovich (and perhaps also by Aleksandr Smolenski). But no one knows for sure, because Berezovski rarely owns shares in his own name, and he operates through obscure intermediary companies. Sibneft's main production subsidiary is Noyabrskneftegaz, which in 1997 was 61 percent owned by Sibneft. In round numbers, Noyabrskneftegaz earned $600 million in 1996, before Berezovski acquired control of Sibneft, and $0 in 1997. Most of the missing $600 million showed up as Sibneft profit, even though under the company law, transactions between parent and subsidiary require approval by the subsidiary's minority shareholders, which was never obtained.

Simply appropriating Noyabrsk's profits didn't satisfy Berezovski. At the 1998 Noyabrsk annual general meeting, shareholders were asked to approve a new charter and a proposal to increase the number of "announced" common shares that could be issued by decision of the board of directors. Management announced at the shareholder meeting that it proposed new announced shares equal to an astounding 1,963 times the current number of issued shares. Virtually no shareholder other than Sibneft voted to authorize these shares, but the authorization squeaked through with the necessary support from 75 percent of the shareholders who showed up and voted, perhaps because Sibneft hadn't previously disclosed how many shares it proposed to authorize and some minority shareholders didn't attend the meeting.

Noyabrsk's charter provided for preemptive rights, which let all shareholders buy newly issued shares in proportion to their current holdings. Thereafter, Noyabrsk's management ignored its charter and issued shares at roughly half of Noyabrsk's trading price (already severely depressed by Sibneft's expropriation of Noyabrsk's profits) to four purchasers with close relationships to Sibneft, ignoring along the way the company law requirements that shares be issued at "market value" and that any transaction with a 20 percent shareholder or its affiliated persons be approved by noninterested shareholders.

These actions enhanced Sibneft's trading price at the same time that they depressed Noyabrsk's trading price. Sibneft then announced an exchange offer to swap four Sibneft shares for each Noyabrskneftegaz share held by Noyabrsk's minority shareholders. This exchange rate had been around 4 percent of the relative value of Noyabrsk and Sibneft before this sorry saga started. Most minority shareholders accepted the offer—the alternative was no more attractive. One shareholder who sued found the local courts unreceptive. The local appellate court rejected the shareholder's appeal on the astonishing grounds that the lawyer's signature on the appeal papers differed from the signature on the original complaint (it didn't, and it would make no difference under Russian law if it had). The shareholder settled rather than fight a years-long battle in the upper appellate courts.[75]

Berezovski's behavior hasn't improved since. After consolidating Noyabrskneftegaz, Sibneft announced its intent to behave properly toward minority shareholders in the future, adopting a nonbinding "Corporate Governance Charter," and appointed a high-profile Corporate Governance Advisory Board.[76] But anyone who believed that one should have remembered the old lyric—"Fool me once, shame on you. Fool me twice, shame on me." In early 2000, a Sibneft affiliate stiffed the European Bank for Reconstruction and Development on a $58 million loan, by persuading a persuadable Russian court that it had paid the loan.[77]

Like Khodorkovski, Berezovski isn't a safe guy to sue, compete with, or write unflattering stories about. Those who try have a distressing tendency to end up beaten, jailed, or dead.[78]

Potanin/Sidanko. Sidanko is another major Russian oil holding company, which in 1998 was 96 percent controlled by Vladimir Potanin through Oneksimbank and its affiliates, especially MFK (Mezhdunarodnaya Finansovaya Kompaniya). Since MFK was trying to establish itself as the first major Russian-owned investment bank, one might think that Potanin wouldn't tarnish his reputation by diluting the already small minority interest in Sidanko. That expectation, like many Western expectations about how Russian businesspeople concerned about reputation ought to behave, turned out to be unjustified.[79]

In early 1998, Potanin decided to kill two birds with one stone—simplify the share ownership structure within the Oneksimbank financial-industrial group and dilute the 4 percent minority in Sidanko. The chosen means: Sidanko issued convertible bonds to Oneksimbank affiliates in exchange for their shares in other group companies. The conversion price was around 0.1 percent of Sidanko's current market price (this isn't a typo either). The effect was to more than triple Sidanko's outstanding shares, once the bonds were converted, and to dilute the 4 percent minority down to 1.3 percent.

This story had a temporarily not-too-unhappy ending for Sidanko's minority shareholders. The shareholders screamed, the Securities Commission launched an investigation into company law violations, and Sidanko agreed to issue enough shares to minority shareholders at the same low price to compensate for the dilution caused by the convertible-bond offering. But investor satisfaction didn't last long. After the ruble crash in mid-1998, Potanin found himself in financial trouble (not counting his offshore assets, anyway). He stripped Oneksimbank of most of its remaining assets and looted Sidanko and its subsidiaries as well. Sidanko's minority shareholders, including BP Amoco, which paid $571 million for 10 percent of Sidanko (after the shenanigans described above), found their shares nearly worthless.[80]

Zarubezhtsvetmet/Erdenet. We described above Russia's illegal sale of its $250 million stake in Erdenet for $150,000 by privatizing Zarubezhtsvetmet. Now that Zarubezhtsvetmet's (unknown) owners held 49 percent of Erdenet, how would they behave? Would they improve Erdenet's operations or invest in the new refining capacity that Erdenet wanted?

The answer was not long in coming. In early 1998, it was discovered that Erdenet was bankrupt, unable to pay either its taxes or its overdue bills for electric power. Some $30 million had disappeared, surely with the connivance of Erdenet's general director, Mr. Elbegdorj. The unpaid electric bills meant that the utilities couldn't pay Russia for fuel, leaving Mongolia's capital city, Ulaanbaatar, mostly without heat for several months of a bitterly cold Mongolian winter. The Mongolian government sought to fire Elbegdorj and trace the funds; the Russian members of Erdenet's board of directors refused to cooperate. Their resistance deadlocked the company (which has three Mongolian and three Russian board members) for the better part of a year. Mongolia finally used emergency legislation to wrest control of Erdenet away from Elbegdorj and his Russian accomplices.[81]

Gazprom. Gazprom's wealth is fabulous. Even a conservative $600 billion estimate of its market value implies that privatizing this one company, on the basis of one citizen, one share, could have delivered four thousand dollars in value to each citizen. That, plus honest management that delivered this value to shareholders, would have, without more, redeemed the promise of mass privatization—that the state was returning ownership of its property to the people. Continued state ownership would have let the government finance its payments to pensioners and employees, while permitting future privatization.

This was not to be. Who owns how much of Gazprom is a secret, but its managers received a huge cut. In early 2000, the government still owned 38 percent, while the managers' official stake was around 35 percent, most of it held by a small group of people who reportedly received stakes of 1 percent to 5 percent each—with each percentage point worth multibillions at Western valuations. That left another 25 percent in other hands. Some of that ownership can be traced, but much is hidden. Some of the hidden shares are likely also held by Gazprom insiders. Former Gazprom chairman and former Russian prime minister Viktor Chernomyrdin is rumored to be a major owner. Meanwhile, Gazprom pays little in taxes, despite its wealth and despite IMF complaints that Gazprom is seriously undertaxed.[82]

How (dis)honestly Gazprom has been run is impossible to know from the outside. Its reported revenues are around $30 billion a year. Its true revenues are hard to determine, because it faces political constraints on cutting off important nonpaying customers (including Ukraine and Belarus). Still, billions of dollars a year could easily be getting skimmed instead of appearing in Gazprom's financial accounts; Gazprom has also transferred reserves worth $30 billion or so to an unknown company that its managers presumably control.[83] Gazprom also spends money lavishly—including on building a glitzy new Moscow headquarters complex and buying top-of-the-line corporate jets.

Given the anecdotes we have recounted, and many others that we could have told instead (the better known ones include Berezovski's looting of AvtoVAZ and Aeroflot; Trans World Metals' tolling agreements with the Novolipetsk steel mill and all three of Russia's major aluminum refineries; Primorski Krai governor Yevgeni Nazdratenko's takeover of Far Eastern Shipping Company; and the reversal of the Lomonosov Porcelain Factory privatization after foreign investors bought control and sought to oust the factory's managers),[84] one might ask, Are there any honest major companies left in Russia?

Well, maybe. Some behave better than others. LUKOil and Surgutneftegaz are better respected than other Russian oil companies, and their shares trade at a higher price per barrel of reserves, though still at a small fraction of Western prices. Their managers still steal, just less egregiously. LUKOil's managers recently bought 9 percent of its shares from the government for a slender $200 million (with funds almost surely obtained by self-dealing); Surgutneftegaz recently proposed merging its holding company (which held 16 billion shares of its principal producing subsidiary) into the producing subsidiary, in exchange for 12 billion subsidiary shares—an instant 25 percent dilution of the holding company's minority shareholders.[85]

But gross misbehavior was the norm. The new investment that the privatizers hoped for rarely occurred. The kleptocrats often reneged on investment promises that they had made when acquiring shares, or that their companies had made before the kleptocrats acquired them.[86] The underlying question must be, If privatization of even the largest, clearly viable firms produced outcomes like these, can the alternative have been worse? We turn to that question next.[87]

IV. The Counterfactual: What Might Have Happened with Staged Privatization and More Institution Building?

Some early proponents of rapid privatization of large firms still defend this strategy; others have backed off.[88] The defenders have responded to the scandals with two principal assertions. First, they contend that massive theft would have occurred if firms hadn't been privatized. Second, they contend that privatization led to productivity gains at some firms. We consider these arguments to be only partial responses, for several reasons.

The first step in assessing what might have happened is to define a counterfactual. For us, the counterfactual is not *just* slower privatization of large firms. That might have reduced political backlash against market reforms, but wouldn't have helped the Russian economy or laid the groundwork for later privatization. Ukraine, for example, didn't privatize and is as corrupt as Russia and in even worse economic shape.

A more optimistic counterfactual, which we believe was attainable in the early reform period of 1991–93, would have included several interrelated steps:

- Staging privatization of large firms, while promising managers that their firm will be privatized if the firm performs well;
- Designing the privatization strategy (for example, enterprise leasing, cash auctions instead of voucher auctions, and sale of minority stakes to foreign firms) to produce concentrated ownership of all but the largest firms;
- Devoting the political energy that went into rapid privatization instead to building the institutions to control self-dealing, corruption, and organized crime; and
- Creating a friendlier business climate, especially a friendlier tax regime.

We discuss below why we believe these steps were at least partly attainable.

Some critics have argued to us that our counterfactual overstates the Russian government's capacity and honesty, even in the early 1990s. They believe that massive theft couldn't have been prevented, with or without privatization.[89] If they are right, that leaves us with our basic position: If the government is bad enough, large-firm privatization won't help or hurt the economy much, compared to available alternatives. But it will still poison the political climate against further reform; reinforce corruption; and, as we argue next, likely facilitate theft at the margin.

A. Did Large-Firm Privatization Make Self-Dealing Worse?

In Russia and other former Soviet Union countries, much theft from state-owned companies occurred prior to privatization. This theft was even given a polite name—"spontaneous privatization." The counterfactual question is whether theft would have been greater or less if large-firm privatization had proceeded more slowly and if higher priority had been given to controlling self-dealing.

We think the theft was likely worse in fact than in our counterfactual. To begin with, our counterfactual includes devoting political energy to a full-scale effort to control self-dealing, instead of to rapid privatization. That effort would include prosecuting raw theft and developing the enforcement institutions needed to attack spontaneous privatization less crude than simply walking off with the assets. There was ample public support for prosecuting managers who were lining their own pockets with state assets. Given the awful state of Russian prisons, it might not have taken many exemplar cases to turn many managers' risk-reward calculus toward more honest conduct.

Second, even without this redirection of political energy, there are cases in which theft increased as a result of privatization. The market price of Tomskneft, for example, plummeted in 1997 when Yukos acquired a controlling stake from the government, evidence that investors expected worse treatment from Khodorkovski than from the former managers. By mid-1999, the shares of Tomskneft, other Yukos subsidiaries, and Yukos itself had lost 98–99 percent of their former value. Similarly, the ratio of the market price of Noyabrskneftegaz to the price of Sibneft dropped from 100:1 in 1996 to 6:1 in mid-1998 after Sibneft acquired control, as minority investors incorporated ever-lower expectations about how much value Sibneft would leave for them. Sibneft then completed an exchange offer of four Sibneft shares for each Noyabrskneftegaz share. Sidanko also looted its subsidiaries, and then was looted itself, with both Sidanko and its principal subsidiaries ending up in bankruptcy.

Reported earnings tell the same story. Tomskneft, Noyabrskneftegaz, and other major enterprises reported large profits under government ownership, which turned to breakeven or outright losses after a kleptocrat acquired control.

Third, many privatized enterprises weren't viable in a competitive market. For these firms, liquidation was inevitable, but mass privatization still had pernicious consequences. Consider an unprofitable firm with assets worth one thousand dollars in piecemeal liquidation, and worth fifteen hundred dollars if sold to a competitor, who will close the firm but obtain some value from its customer relationships. The government could sell the firm for fifteen hundred dollars in a cash auction. If the firm isn't privatized, its managers will sell its movable assets cheaply to an intermediary, earning perhaps five hundred dollars. If the firm is mass privatized, the controllers, who may own only 10 percent of the firm's shares, will strip its assets as best they can. They will realize one thousand dollars from piecemeal liquidation, and perhaps another one thousand dollars in wealth transfers from employees who work but don't receive wages, suppliers who deliver goods but do not get paid, and customers who receive defective merchandise and have no recourse.

Fourth, if natural resource enterprises remained under government ownership, the current profits could be stolen, but the remaining resources could be recovered by a future government. With privatization at knock-down prices, not only the short-term flow, but also the full long-term stock, was stolen.

Fifth, control mechanisms under government ownership were weak, but still likely stronger than after privatization. Company managers still faced a chain of command to whom they reported. Gross theft might upset one's superiors. There was also possible embarrassment or even a jail term if theft became obvious and was publicly reported.

The theoretical case for privatization rests in part on removing enterprises from political oversight, so that managers' decisions are motivated by profit, not by whatever motivates politicians. As Shleifer and Vishny argue, "[P]rivatization widens the separation between the manager and the politician, and in this way stimulates restructuring."[90] But the same freedom from state control that facilitates restructuring also facilitates theft, if the manager wants to steal.

Indeed, it's hard to see how one could construct a theoretical model in which privatization promotes restructuring by freeing firms from state control, in which that diminished control does not also permit increased self-dealing. To prevent increased theft, the state would have to devote specialized resources (prosecutors, a strong Securities Commission) to controlling self-dealing. Russia didn't take these steps initially, and once managers and kleptocrats became strong, they opposed controls on self-dealing. The kleptocracy became self-reinforcing.

Moreover, the Russian government would be financially stronger today if it still owned Russia's major natural resources companies. Oil and gas revenues alone would easily cover its foreign debt service and pension and salary obligations. And there would be strong political pressure to use those revenues for these purposes.

B. Efficiency and Distributional Consequences of Large-Firm Privatization

Dirty privatization might be justified if it accelerated the restructuring of inefficient state-owned enterprises. Unfortunately, there is little evidence of this. Russian productivity fell sharply during the 1990s. The productivity of the average Russian worker fell from 30 percent of the U.S. level in 1992 to only 19 percent in 1999. Capital investment plunged as well, to only 13 percent of GDP (40 percent of the pre-1992 level).[91]

In many countries, case-by-case privatization of state-owned firms, often natural resources firms or monopolies such as railroads and telephone and electric utilities, increased productivity.[92] But evidence on postprivatization efficiency gains in Russia and other former Soviet Union countries that pursued mass privatization is mixed. As John Nellis concludes in a recent survey:

> Evidence—early and fragmentary, but impossible to ignore—from . . . Armenia, Georgia, Kazakhstan, the Kyrgyz Republic, Moldova, Mongolia, Russia, and Ukraine—shows less promising results:
>
> - Private ownership often does not lead to restructuring. . . .
> - Some partially state-owned firms perform better than privatized firms.
> - In some countries, there are few differences in performance between (wholly) state-owned and privately owned firms.

- In other countries, there are clear performance improvements only in those very few firms sold to foreign investors.[93]

The culprit appears to be, in part, the diffuse ownership created by voucher privatization. Diffuse ownership is associated with less restructuring than any other form of firm ownership, including continued state ownership.[94]

The evidence doesn't suggest that privatized companies perform worse than state-owned companies, on average. They merely don't perform much better, if at all. But that in itself is damning. Enormous political energy was devoted to large-firm privatization, which was seen as a key to economic revival. Ex post, the efficiency gains are so small that economists are debating whether they exist at all. This outcome suggests that political energy might have been better spent elsewhere.

Moreover, we often measure efficiency in terms of the size of the social pie, without regard to who owns which slice. That's too simple in Russia. One Russian tragedy is that wealth differences soared while the social pie was shrinking. Russia's per capita GDP declined by 40 percent in the 1990s, while a standard measure of inequality, the Gini coefficient, soared from 24 in 1988 to 47 in 1997 (compared to a U.S. level of about 43). The rising Gini coefficient tells us that the bottom half of the Russian population faced an income decline far greater than the 40 percent average decline. The percentage of Russians living in absolute poverty (by standard measures) grew from a small fraction of the population in 1989 to an estimated 55 million (37 percent of the population) in 1999.[95] The billions held offshore by a few kleptocrats have far less social value than the same amount distributed broadly among the Russian population.

Privatization doesn't have to be all or none. Our judgment is that Russia's privatization of small shops and businesses (basically given to their employees) was a positive step. Voucher privatization separates control from cash flow rights and encourages asset stripping. Even so, mass privatization of medium and larger enterprises was neither a clearly good nor a clearly bad step. It produced many viable companies and some decent owners, though with a tendency for bad owners to buy or squeeze out good ones. But loans-for-shares and other rigged sales of the largest enterprises were a failure both economically and politically. They produced bad owners who chose asset stripping over value creation, almost without exception.

C. Institution Building

Section B addressed whether rapid large-firm privatization is likely to produce productivity gains compared to continued state ownership, holding constant the (bad) institutional environment. However, our counterfactual does not hold constant the institutional environment. Instead, it assumes that the political energy devoted to privatization goes instead into building the institutions to support privatization.

There's no way to know by how much better laws and institutions could have reduced self-dealing, had they preceded or at least accompanied privatization. Good tax laws, a serious anticorruption program, and credible enforcement against insider theft of company assets might have made a major difference. Good (and sometimes enforced) capital markets laws might have helped to establish baseline expectations about behavior. Conversely, their early absence contributed to a lawless climate, in which managers could justify self-dealing by claiming (sometimes correctly) that they had done nothing illegal.

Perhaps enforcement of capital markets rules would have been equally minimal if the rules and regulators had come first. Or perhaps Russia would have found a different path-dependent equilibrium, with better and more vigorously enforced capital markets laws, had good laws and a strong securities commission preceded privatization. We cannot say. What we can say is that bad owners reinforce corruption and create pressure for weak enforcement, and this pressure contributed to the nonenforcement of capital markets laws that is the norm today.[96]

At the margin, stronger controls on skimming would have reduced the expected return to skimming, while improving the firm's expected long-term value (because the same government that was building stronger institutions was less likely to expropriate that value). That would have changed at least some managers' decisions to skim instead of build value.

D. Staged Privatization: Enterprise Leasing and Alternatives

Our counterfactual also assumes a program of *staged privatization*, in which companies whose managers have proved both the company's viability and their own honesty are privatized first, and privatization is designed to produce concentrated rather than dispersed ownership. These steps would have reduced the likelihood that enterprise controllers would strip them rather than build value; would have given the enforcers a less overwhelming task; and would have facilitated the virtuous cycle that the privatizers hoped for, in which managers of privatized enterprises become political supporters of good (and enforced) commercial and capital markets laws, and these managers' mostly good behavior establishes norms for manager conduct.

Staged privatization can produce value-creation incentives similar to immediate privatization. If the government credibly promises managers that their firm will be privatized if the firm's results justify this, that promise of future wealth, if believed, can provide incentives similar to those created by immediate privatization, without the loss of state control over self-dealing that privatization entails.[97] Such a promise won't be fully credible, but semicredible promises could have been made, *and were being made*, prior to mass privatization. For example, the government could reserve a percentage of a company's shares for its managers. The expectation of receiving shares in the future can create incentives similar to restricted stock or stock options that vest over time, which are commonly used as incentive compensation in developed countries.

For us, staged privatization has four key features:

- The promise of future privatization, contingent on performance, can create profit incentives comparable to those created by immediate privatization.
- Bureaucratic controls are loosened first on operating decisions, and only later on self-dealing, as the infrastructure to control self-dealing within fully private enterprises is created.
- Privatization is designed to produce concentrated ownership of all but the largest firms, to reduce controllers' incentives to expropriate minority shareholders.
- If only successful, honestly run enterprises are privatized, a virtuous spiral that encourages good managerial behavior can emerge, instead of the downward spiral that resulted from mass privatization without controls on self-dealing.

Staged privatization would not have been perfectly clean. Some companies would have been privatized as a result of bribery rather than performance. But the tilt would still have been toward privatizing successful firms first.

1. ENTERPRISE LEASING

A promise of future privatization of profitable firms could take many forms. But we need not speculate on its exact form because such promises were being made during the perestroika era, through a program called "enterprise leasing" that began in 1989. The privatizers killed enterprise leasing in 1992, so we don't know how it would have turned out. But we know how it started, and the start was promising.[98]

Enterprise leasing involved a contract between the state, as enterprise owner, and the enterprise or a legal entity created by the enterprise's labor collective. The lease contract promised the enterprise greater freedom to make investment and operating decisions, to pay higher wages, and to retain profits and held out the potential to eventually buy ownership of the enterprise from the state—all conditioned on the enterprise producing profits that could be reinvested, used to pay higher wages, or saved toward an eventual buyout.

This scheme created complex but, on the whole, promising incentives and information-revelation mechanisms. The incentives were similar to those created by leveraged buyouts (an analogy that the privatizers missed). Saved profits were the *only* funds that could be used for an eventual buyout, so there was a powerful incentive to run the firm efficiently and not to squander profits through higher wages. Conversely, managers who didn't generate (and then save) enough profits to buy their own firm faced the risk that the state would replace them or sell the firm to outside owners.

The firm's accounts were open to its workers, who could therefore watch the managers. The workers had incentives to monitor the managers, lest the managers pay high salaries to themselves or skim profits. The workers could police self-dealing by complaining through the existing administrative chain of command. Managers, in turn, knew that they could be fired or jailed, or privatization could be withheld, if they ran the enterprise crookedly.

Privatization, then, would be available to those managers who proved their skill by earning profits and proved their honesty by not self-dealing. A managerial culture of honesty would be reinforced. The state, meanwhile, could collect a fraction of the reported profits as taxes. Managers who hid profits would deprive themselves of the chance for a future buyout. And the state would have a strong incentive to honor the privatization promise when the time came. Privatization would raise revenue today while still promising tax revenue down the road. With a respectable tax base in place and privatization revenue also flowing in, the government would have been less inclined to turn to draconian tax rules in a desperate attempt to raise revenue. Slower privatization of large enterprises would also have given Russia time to develop a better infrastructure to police self-dealing when full privatization occurred.

The early returns from enterprise leasing were positive. It began in 1990, based on an April 1989 decree and a November 1989 law,[99] and soon proved highly popular with managers and workers. Enterprises that entered the leasing program—self-selected to be sure—often did well. By early 1992, about ninety-five hundred leased enterprises accounted for 8 percent of total Russian employment and 13 percent of industrial production. The privatizers then shut down the leasing programs, lest too many profitable firms choose leasing and be unavailable to be privatized.

Some nuances of the choice between staged and immediate privatization: First, some firms could become profitable only under new management. Enterprise leasing wouldn't directly lead to replacement of the old managers. But mass privatization as actually carried out, with control given to workers and managers, also produced only limited managerial turnover. The turnover that occurred wasn't always for the better; sometimes bad owners bought shares in privatization auctions or the market and ousted or co-opted honest holdover managers. Moreover, with leasing, the state retained the power to install new managers or to sell unsuccessful enterprises to new owners.

Second, enterprise leasing won't work for nonviable enterprises. For these enterprises, the managers' best option will be to skim what they can while they can. But for these enterprises, privatization only accelerated the plunder by loosening the bureaucratic controls on theft from state-owned enterprises. The government could more usefully have retained ownership of nonviable enterprises, not subsidized them further, and ideally supervised their liquidation.

Third, for Russia's huge natural resources and utility companies, leasing would have openly conveyed too much wealth to a few lucky managers to be politically feasible. Honest privatization auctions might have been preferable. But even for these enterprises, leasing would likely have been better than the dirty privatization that actually took place.

It's ironic that the Russian Communists of a decade ago, knowing that central planning was a dead end but not fully trusting markets either, likely built through enterprise leasing a better means to manage privatization than the privatize-now approach that Western advisors later promoted and Russian reformers enthusiastically followed. The Russians who blame Western advice for destroying their economy are not entirely wrong.

2. OTHER APPROACHES TO STAGED PRIVATIZATION

Enterprise leasing is only one example of a staged privatization strategy. We discuss below several other approaches to privatization that are consistent with this overall approach.

Cash Auctions. Enterprise leasing is one way to sell enterprises for cash—where the current managers are the only permitted bidders and can pay only with the firm's own accumulated profits. Another way is cash auctions, designed to produce concentrated ownership. A realistic reservation price, measured perhaps as a multiple of the book value of the company's assets, can segregate viable from nonviable firms and ensure that insiders don't steal viable firms for a small fraction of true value. Firms for which no one bids the reservation price can be left in state hands, where controls on theft are likely to be stronger. The government can still give their managers incentives to build value by promising to sell the enterprise if its prospects improve, as well as incentives to pursue an orderly liquidation if that is the best alternative.

Russians had enough wealth to make cash auctions viable. At the start of the 1990s, they held about $100 billion in savings accounts. The government froze these savings accounts and then inflated the currency, wiping out almost all their value before they were unfrozen. Once the savings were gone, only crooks and the nomenklatura had the money to buy large enterprises. But cash auctions were feasible ex ante.

Privatizing Leveraged Companies. Russia privatized companies free of debts to the government. Having firms issue debt to the government as part of privatization could have ensured a realistic minimum price when the companies were sold in cash auctions, because the government's net receipt would be the payment for the equity plus the present value of the debt. By reducing the firm's equity value, it would reduce the amount that the managers could expropriate from minority shareholders. And if the government were willing to promptly seize and resell firms that defaulted on their debt payments, this would give managers incentives to generate enough cash to make those payments.[100]

Two caveats: First, selling leveraged companies is a form of seller-financing that enables the buyers to leverage their limited cash. That's valuable as an antidote to limited citizen funds, but also dangerous because leverage creates asset-stripping incentives not too dissimilar from partial equity ownership. So leverage makes sense only for clearly viable firms, and the debt should be limited to a moderate percentage of firm value. Second, either control must automatically revert to the state if the debt isn't paid,[101] or the government must have both the means and the will to quickly seize companies that don't pay their debts (the Russian government lacked the will for tax debts), or the strategy will collapse.

Selling Minority Stakes to Foreign Firms. For Russia's very large natural resources companies, domestic sales for cash weren't feasible. There wasn't enough cash around to pay more than a fraction of their value, and the largest cash hoards were often obtained in dubious ways. Selling controlling stakes to foreigners was a political nonstarter. But it might have been politically possible to sell to a foreign firm a significant minority stake in, say, a government-owned oil company, with the expectation that the foreign firm would manage the company in the near term and would coinvest in new projects and the government would sell its remaining stake through a public offering a few years hence, once the Russian securities market had developed enough to make that a viable option.[102]

At the same time, foreign ownership is no panacea. The wrong foreigners can strip assets too. A corrupt government that can't conduct honest auctions or control self-dealing isn't likely to do a good job of screening investors, domestic or foreign.

Staged privatization would not have been perfectly clean. Some companies would have been privatized as a result of bribery rather than performance. But the tilt would still have been toward privatizing the more successful firms first. Whether that tilt, coupled with institution building, would have fostered a different managerial culture, we'll never know. This is, after all, a counterfactual.

E. The Political Consequences of Dirty Privatization

Russians themselves do not distinguish sharply between voucher privatization (in which most received worthless shares) and the corrupt sales of the largest enterprises. Both have left a residue of popular distrust of privatization and a market economy, which has already slowed other reforms and will affect future market reforms for decades to come. That is a heavy price to pay for the uncertain economic benefits of fast privatization.

Even if insiders would loot privatized and state-owned firms equally, the political consequences are very different if it occurs within government ownership, rather than after privatization. In the former case, the public associates managers' theft of assets with continued state ownership. The political case for eventual privatization becomes stronger and is coupled with political pressure to control self-dealing. In the latter case, the political case for market reforms is undermined, as the public associates privatization with theft of company assets and company insiders become potent opponents of efforts to control them.

An important political goal of voucher privatization was to build popular support for privatization by distributing share ownership broadly. What irony that the exact opposite happened! Conversely, staged privatization, starting with successful firms, could have given privatization a good name, encouraging future reform efforts.[103]

In addition, one hoped-for consequence of privatization was faster restructuring of major enterprises. Restructuring through new management or new investment was the exception. But restructuring through layoffs, wage arrears, and shedding of social obligations to maintain housing, kindergartens, medical clinics and the like was common.

The shedding of excess costs was inevitable. It might have been politically acceptable if the government had provided the social services that enterprises were shedding, plus some unemployment, retraining, and relocation benefits, especially in company towns where new jobs were scarce. The social consequences would have been milder if the business climate had been friendlier, so that more laid-off workers could land jobs at newly created firms. Without these ameliorating factors, shedding of social obligations led to a huge increase in seriously poor people, a sharp increase in death rates, and political unhappiness with market reforms.

The privatizers sometimes offer a political defense for the corrupt sales of Russia's major firms: the kleptocrats used their wealth and media outlets to buy Yeltsin's reelection as president in 1996; otherwise, the Communists would have returned to power. We aren't persuaded by this "better crooks than Communists" argument. First, the poisonous mix of corruption, dirty privatization, rampant self-dealing, and Mafia-government ties was a major reason why Yeltsin was desperately unpopular and hence a Communist victory was a serious risk. Better policies might have let Yeltsin (or another reform or center candidate) win easily. Second, by 1999, as it became apparent that the kleptocrats virtually owned the Kremlin, it was no longer so clear that Zyuganov would have been a worse leader than a sick, ineffectual, corruption-tolerating Yeltsin.

F. Toward a Friendlier Business Climate

The final and perhaps most challenging part of our counterfactual involves creating a friendlier overall business climate. Creating a friendly business climate is a complex task. We list here only a few steps that we think were politically viable and could have improved the business climate if given high priority.

Political attention is a scarce resource. The reformers focused on rapid large-firm privatization and thus foreclosed the opportunity to accomplish much along other lines.

One step would have been to waive enterprise-level income taxes on businesses below a certain size, such as one thousand employees. The actual confiscatory taxes that Russia levied are hugely counterproductive. They raise negligible revenue, promote corruption, drive small businesses underground and sometimes out of business, and force businesses to hide their profits (which promotes skimming).

Even rich countries have little success in collecting income taxes from small businesses. The United States recently gave up and now allows nonpublic firms to pass through all profits and losses to their owners, without firm-level income tax. If the United States can't collect these taxes, Russia would have done better not to try. Eliminating income taxes on small businesses has an obvious constituency and would have been politically feasible if tried.

A second critical step would have been to attack corruption and organized crime. If an aggressive attack on corruption had been a top priority for internal reformers and a key condition for outside financial aid, the attack might have been launched and if launched would likely have been partly successful. Such an effort is harder today, because corruption is more deeply entrenched and many privatized businesses support the corrupt status quo. The political viability of an attack on corruption and the Mafia is not in doubt, only the political will to carry it out.

An attack on bureaucratic interference and on the sheer size of the bureaucracy would have helped. Central-government employment expanded rapidly during the 1990s, when it logically should have contracted to reflect the government's reduced role in managing the economy.

V. Insider Self-Dealing in the Czech Republic

The Czech Republic offers an interesting comparison to Russia that can help isolate which aspects of the Russian experience with rapid mass privatization were unique to Russia, and which may reflect deeper problems that arise when privatization precedes development of legal and institutional controls on self-dealing.

The Czech Republic was the first formerly communist country to plunge into voucher privatization, through auctions that took place in two stages, in 1991–92 and 1993–94. By 1994, more than two thousand state-owned firms had been privatized through the voucher program; around five hundred voucher investment funds had emerged to collect vouchers and invest in the privatized firms; most of Czech industry was in private hands; competing stock markets had emerged; and the Czech economy was growing briskly, with rapid formation of new businesses and low unemployment. As late as 1996, the Czech Republic seemed to be "the success story of Eastern European mass privatization."[104]

Today, no one is so sanguine. The early Czech stock market success was replaced by a scramble for control of privatized enterprises, stock prices that collapse once control is attained, and insider looting of many privatized companies and voucher investment funds. The Czechs invented their own term—*tunneling*—for various ways of stripping companies and funds of their assets. Widespread tunneling drove the Czech Republic into recession in 1997 and 1998, while neighboring Poland and Hungary, which were slower to privatize large firms but built better controls on self-dealing, continued to expand briskly.

A. The Czech Experience with Tunneling

Czech mass privatization sparked the emergence of voucher investment funds, which collected vouchers from citizens and invested in the companies that were being privatized. The voucher investment funds often took sizeable stakes in a limited number of firms, enough to give them influence and sometimes control. This seemed at first to encourage restructuring. When holdover management couldn't make the transition to a market economy, the funds could install new managers. There was, however, concern that the not-yet-privatized Czech banks, which owned some of the largest investment funds, would use their equity stakes to cement lending relationships, rather than to promote restructuring.[105]

The bank-run investment funds indeed didn't generate much restructuring. But that was the *good* news. A retrospective analysis by the Czech Ministry of Finance found a *negative* correlation between post-privatization firm performance and the percentage of shares held by nonbank voucher investment funds. The principal reason was that the voucher investment funds used their influence not to restructure firms, but to tunnel away the firms' profits.[106]

As scandals proliferated, foreign investors withdrew—net foreign direct and portfolio investment dropped from $103 million in 1995 to $57 million in 1996 and turned negative in 1997. The Czech stock market imploded. Total listed companies dropped from a peak of around 1,700 in 1994 to 283 at year-end 1998. The number of companies on the "main exchange," the only one with significant liquidity, dropped from sixty-two in 1995 to ten in 1998. And there has not yet been a single Czech initial public offering (IPO).

The minimal regulation of investment funds, companies, and securities markets was by design. The Czech government was dominated by fervent free-marketeers who believed that market participants would largely regulate themselves.[107] They were simply wrong. The scams that quickly developed offer a tutorial in the ways that fraudsters can extract value from both companies and investment funds. A Czech Ministry of Finance report identified fifteen common techniques:

- *the interconnection of several companies*—especially investment companies, investment funds and securities dealers, pension funds, banks and other companies. These interconnections are informal, hard to identify, and utilize puppets.
- *large conventional fines*—conventional fines are agreed on in agreements on securities transfer, the amount often being a multiple of the value of the agreed deal. . . . Simultaneously, failure to comply with conditions is ensured by the above interconnection of persons in the contracting parties.
- *purchases of worthless shares*—persons controlling investment companies or investment funds found a normal joint-stock company, whose shares are based on worthless property (e.g., receivables, know-how) and then these shares are purchased [by the] investment fund or unit trust.
- *concluding unfavorable options and futures contracts*—such agreements do not cover the [market price] risks associated with [the] securities held by the in-

vestment fund or unit trust [that are subject to the option or futures contract]. . . .

- *transfer of advances for the purchase of securities*—the investment company or investment fund transfers [funds to] a securities dealer; this cash is not subject to payment of interest by the dealer. . . . [T]he dealer makes use of this money for dealing in his own name and . . . [may have] negligible assets. . . .
- *long settlement periods for securities sold*—an investment company sells securities . . . and sets a [very] long settlement period. . . . In the meantime the company owing the money declares bankruptcy and is liquidated.
- *loans of securities*— . . . securities are loaned from the assets of an investment fund or a unit trust without any guarantees and even without any payment for the loan.
- *poorly drawn-up agreements on the transfer of securities*—the agreements do not cover basic obligations, such as the date of supply of the security [or the] date of settlement of advances for the purchase of the securities. . . .
- *irrational movements of securities*—there are entire chains of trades in a single type of security; over a few days or weeks or even months, the respective security is owned by a whole series of companies and then returns to the fund at an entirely different price than that when it left. . . .
- *trading in securities at ridiculous prices*—such operations can be carried out especially because there is no objectively determinable price for most securities as the price-creating function of the public market fails to operate. . . . [Czech law] prohibits funds from loaning money from their assets to other (i.e., third) parties. Funds evade this restriction by concluding an agreement on the sale of securities from their assets to some other legal entity, usually an associated one, at a very low price. A verbal agreement is then made that this associated person will sell the securities back to the fund after a certain period of time. . . .
- *disadvantageous purchases and sales of securities*—[funds may purchase new issues of a company's shares] for large sums while these shares can be purchased on the market at much lower prices. . . .
- *trading by management on its own account*—these practices . . . [are] associated with the misuse of confidential information, obtained on boards of directors of joint-stock companies, whose shares are part of the assets of the fund; this information is supplied to the [fund's] management, employees, or relatives, or the [company's] shares are sold to such persons at low prices.
- *concentration of considerable amounts of cash in the accounts* of investment funds or unit trusts in banks. This method formed the basis for subsequent "tunneling" into unit trusts managed by the CS Fund [which] gradually sold securities from the assets of the unit trust and when the entire assets were transferred in the form of deposits to a bank, the deposits were withdrawn and transferred to an account abroad. . . .
- *failure to comply with limits for restricting and spreading risks*—[Czech law] sets forth limits for holding securities [of a single issuer] in relation to the total

volume of assets owned by an investment fund or unit trust. . . . Cases have been registered in which investment funds . . . exceeded the limits. . . . Simultaneously, the [companies] whose shares were owned by the funds encountered difficulties, . . . their shares fell to zero value and the investment funds often suffered considerable losses. . . .

- *"tunneling" into companies is a frequent phenomenon*—Current "corporate raiders" have discovered a risk-free method of removing money from companies. This method consists of holding a general meeting of shareholders, in which the "raiders" have a voting majority; this meeting passes a decision on a transaction involving company property . . . and the board of directors of the company then carries out this operation, with consequent damage to the company. No (minority) shareholder can blame the board of directors of the company for this operation as it is bound by the decision of the general meeting. . . .

These ways of "handling" the assets of investment funds and unit trusts are combined in practice and are very difficult to demonstrate and penalize.[108]

The ardent free-marketeers who resisted calls to regulate Czech capital markets may have been sincere in the beginning. But by the late 1990s, many had been bought, as company managers turned to bribery to ward off regulation or prosecution. The Klaus government fiercely resisted calls for an anticorruption probe; Klaus himself simply denied (against all evidence) that the Czech Republic had a problem with corruption or tunneling.[109]

The Czech Republic, unlike Russia, responded to the scandals. A corruption scandal brought down the Klaus government in 1997; a Securities Commission, which Klaus had long opposed, was installed the same year; the new government launched an anticorruption drive, which has been at least a partial success; and legal controls on investment funds and majority shareholders were tightened. Much remains to be done, but these efforts give hope of improved long-term performance. Still, for now, the government is shutting the barn door after many valuable horses have been removed and much harm has been done to the economy.

B. Comparing Russia and the Czech Republic

The Czech Republic privatized without controls on self-dealing, but otherwise provided a reasonably good business environment. In 1995, when the self-dealing frenzy really took off, Czech macroeconomic performance and macroeconomic policies were both strong. The country had been communist for only about forty years, not seventy-five as had Russia; its economy was never as thoroughly centrally planned; some memories of how to run a private business survived; it was close to major export markets in Western Europe; and Czech firms faced strong import competition.

That environment, far better than Russia's in many ways, was sufficient to nourish self-dealing. One central reason: The shares of a privatized company were worth more to crooks, who would use 50 percent control to extract 100 percent of value, than to honest owners who would run the company for the benefit of all shareholders. At the same time, the Czech Republic's friendlier business climate meant that for insiders, building long-term value, or selling to someone else who would do so, was sometimes more attractive than looting. In Russia, theft of company assets became the norm; in the Czech Republic, it merely became distressingly common.

Still, the many Czech cases in which insiders skimmed from viable enterprises, instead of restructuring them, demonstrate—as the Russia example alone cannot—that strong controls on insider self-dealing are a necessary precondition for successful large-firm privatization. In neither country did many entrepreneurs both run the business to maximize long-term profit and skim profits in the near term. In the Czech Republic, that may reflect looters' assigning a low weight to the firm's long-term value, given the risk that a future government will investigate their near-term theft.

The Klaus government turned, between 1992 and 1997, from a collection of apparently honest free-market ideologues into corrupt opponents of restrictions on tunneling. Proposed regulations and proposed indictments of the tunnelers were routinely quashed. A (secondhand, thus unverifiable) story from a Finance Ministry official: The ministry staff's record in getting Klaus and other senior officials to approve proposed criminal cases against tunnelers was 0/26. In the Czech Republic, as in Russia, privatization without controls on self-dealing fostered corruption, as the self-dealers bought government officials, both to permit continued self-dealing and to ward off prosecution.

Growth in labor productivity offers a good measure of a country's overall success in privatization and transition policy. Table 4.3 shows the striking contrasts between Hungary and Poland, which stumbled into something resembling our staged privatization/institution building proposal; the Czech Republic, which had the capacity to do likewise but pursued mass privatization instead; and Russia, which started from a worse place and pursued mass privatization.

C. The Special Case of Voucher Investment Funds

In both Russia and the Czech Republic, the privatizers hoped that voucher investment funds would become strong outside owners, who

TABLE 4.3
Labor Productivity in Selected Transition Countries, 1989–98

Country	*Change in labor productivity (%)*
Hungary	36
Poland	29
Czech Republic	6
Russia	−33

Source: Economic Commission for Europe, Economic Survey of Europe 1999 No. 3 (1999)

could replace bad managers and force restructuring of enterprises. That sometimes happened, but more often, the voucher investment funds were part of the problem, not the solution. Many looted the companies in which they invested and were looted themselves. Roughly a quarter of Czech investment funds were looted so thoroughly that they went bankrupt; another quarter were converted into unregulated holding companies, with likely adverse consequences for their minority investors. In Russia, too, many investment funds simply disappeared, and their assets were never traced.

Our theoretical analysis in section III of an amoral controller's choice between value creation and self-dealing can help to explain why. First, fund controllers hold only a modest fraction of the cash flow rights (through their management fee). Second, a value-creating strategy is most likely to maximize the controller's private value for a company with strong growth prospects. For voucher investment funds, growth prospects are limited. They receive a one-shot infusion of capital at the time of voucher privatization, which won't be replicated through private investment for a long time, if ever.[110] This virtually ensures that if self-dealing isn't policed, an amoral controller will be better off stealing the fund's value than keeping a partial claim on that value through management fees. All the more so if the fund can first tunnel into operating companies that it controls.[111]

The incentive to loot created by the separation of ownership and control is exacerbated at the level of the companies in which the fund invests. Investment fund control of operating companies is a pyramid structure under another name. Suppose that the fund manager collects an annual fee equal to 2 percent of assets. That might represent, in present value, a claim on 15 percent of the fund's assets. If the fund owns 20 percent of an operating company, the fund manager's claim on the operating company's profits is a scant 15 percent × 20 percent = 3 percent.[112]

Just as crooks can outbid honest owners for control of operating companies, making dispersed ownership unstable if self-dealing is easy, so too for investment funds. An example: The Austrian bank Creditanstalt sponsored a major Czech investment fund. But Czech citizens who thought they were safe entrusting funds to Creditanstalt soon discovered otherwise. Motoinvest bought 11 percent of the fund's shares in the market, called a special shareholder meeting, replaced Creditanstalt as manager, and proceeded to loot the fund.[113]

It also was never realistic to expect even honest fund managers to devote much attention to restructuring portfolio firms. The same pyramid structure that creates incentives to loot creates *disincentives* to pursue restructuring: the fund manager will realize only a small fraction of the resulting gains in company value. Nor were voucher funds a source of the new capital that many firms needed.[114]

D. A Czech Counterfactual: Mass Privatization with Institution Building

The Czech Republic chose to privatize in a hurry and not to build institutions to control self-dealing. That hands-off policy gave the tunnelers a six-year head start; the regulators have not yet caught up. A difficult counterfactual: What if the Czech Republic had vigorously pursued both mass privatization and institution building?

Our own judgment: The tunnelers would still have largely outrun the regulators. In the early 1990s, Czech regulators and prosecutors were completely inexperienced in how to regulate capital markets or control self-dealing. Czech courts were and remain overloaded and unsophisticated. Neither could deal with the misdeeds of the controllers of thousands of enterprises and voucher funds. Mass privatization, even if coupled with an immediate effort to build these and other needed institutions, would have given the crooks a critical head start. The crooks would then have used the funds generated by that head start to compromise the regulators, ensuring that the government wouldn't run too fast to catch up.[115]

VI. Implications for Future Privatization Efforts

Mass privatization was motivated, in important respects, by faith. As Andrei Shleifer and Robert Vishny, key Western advisers on Russian privatization, wrote as recently as 1998, "We believe that managerial discretion problems are usually minor relative to political discretion problems. Privatization works because it controls political discretion."[116]

For Russia, we once shared that belief.[117] So did the Western advisors who pushed the Czech Republic, Russia, and many other countries to plunge ahead with mass privatization. But they and we were wrong. The faith that any private owner was better than state ownership rested on an unexamined premise—that a country has the will and infrastructure to control managerial discretion manifested through overt self-dealing. If the state cannot control this form of white-collar crime, then the balance between the problems of managerial discretion and political discretion is uncertain.

We have learned that Western-style capitalism is more fragile than we thought. It will not emerge—certainly not quickly, perhaps not at all—if seeds are simply scattered widely through mass privatization, to grow in the thin soil of an institutionally impoverished country. Instead, the institutions that control theft in its myriad forms, especially self-dealing by managers and controlling shareholders, are an essential fertilizer.

The task of creating fertile soil in which privatized companies can take root is not a simple one. We don't yet know how strong the infrastructure must be before large-firm privatization is likely to significantly promote economic growth. Moreover, many of the necessary institutions can develop only as the market develops. The securities commission and criminal prosecutors need fraud to practice on, if they are to become skilled at combating fraud. Accountants, investment bankers, and other reputational intermediaries also learn from their mistakes—from the frauds they didn't catch.

What we do know is discouraging. The necessary tasks can't be completed quickly. Controlling corruption is essential, but not enough. Ironically, the countries that have made the worst hash of managing their state-owned enterprises are least likely to possess the institutions that would let them gain from rapidly privatizing large firms.[118]

A. Steps Toward Successful Large-Firm Privatization

What then should a country with weak institutions do, with its not-yet-privatized firms or its already privatized firms? For not-yet-privatized firms, the counterfactual that we offered in section IV, including attacking corruption, building institutions to control self-dealing, staged privatization, and a privatization plan that produces concentrated rather than dispersed ownership where feasible, offers a guide on how one might proceed.

For both already privatized and not-yet-privatized firms, Russia needs a serious, top-down effort to control corruption, organized crime, and self-dealing; adopt a rational tax system; reduce the broad administrative discretion that invites corruption; shrink the bloated bureaucracy; enforce existing rules that limit self-dealing; remove the principal loopholes in those rules; and improve financial reporting by major firms (which isn't feasible until the tax system permits firms to report results honestly). The relevant "top" could be a central government or a regional government. No one of these steps is sufficient by itself, but each will help, and progress on any one can reinforce progress on others.

No sensible person could be against these changes, and many Russians understand their importance. But none is yet at the top of the Russian government's agenda. They all need to be. Otherwise, Russia risks going the way of Nigeria—another oil-rich country whose government is thoroughly corrupt and its population impoverished, while a favored few skim billions into offshore accounts. There's hope that Russia's new president, Vladimir Putin, will mount a serious attack on corruption, but as yet no solid evidence that he will do so. His public anticorruption, antikleptocrat rhetoric hasn't thus far been matched by his behind-the-scenes actions.[119]

B. The Case for Selective Renationalization and Reprivatization

For already privatized firms with bad owners, there are no easy solutions, but here is one unconventional proposal. Western advisors are reluctant to propose renationalization as a remedy, no matter how corrupt the initial privatization. In contrast, we see possible merit in selective renationalization, followed promptly by reprivatization. When—and only when—the government develops the will and ability to reprivatize promptly and honestly, it could make sense to both prosecute corporate thieves and to renationalize companies that were, for all practical purposes, stolen.

The case for renationalization and reprivatization will depend on company-specific misdeeds that justify this remedy. Here are two examples. Suppose that Mikhail Khodorkovski transfered all value from Yukos and its subsidiaries to shadowy offshore companies. Renationalization and reprivatization would harm no one but Khodorkovski and his accomplices; could produce better owners who would pay workers, pay taxes, and invest in Yukos's oil fields; and raise serious revenue for the government. A reprivatization auction that raised 20 percent of the value of a comparably sized Western firm could raise $35 billion, an amount that exceeds the government's current annual tax revenue. Similarly, renationalization of Zarubezhtsvetmet would harm only its current crooked owners, benefit the Erdenet copper mine and the entire country of Mongolia, and permit Russia to earn the revenue from privatization that it should have earned the first time.

The appropriate analogy is to thieves who steal government property. The government should put the thieves in jail (unless they flee the country first) *and* seize and resell their ill-gotten property. As long as the government seizes property only from thieves, we shouldn't worry too much that honest owners would be scared off from investing, lest the government treat them the same way.

Indeed, the antirenationalization advice now proffered by the multilateral institutions is internally inconsistent. The IMF and the World Bank are encouraging governments around the world to seize insolvent financial institutions (often made so by bad loans to insiders). They have missed the analogy between seizing a financial institution that has been stripped by insiders and seizing a nonfinancial institution that has been stripped by insiders.

We propose renationalization *plus* prompt reprivatization, *when and only when* the government can do a better job both in reprivatizing and in controlling insider self-dealing.[120] We have no opinion on whether renationalization without privatization could make sense. That depends on whether a Russian government that can't conduct honest auctions of major companies can nonetheless run these companies better than their current owners. That is a tough choice between two bad owners. Moreover, reprivatization auctions make sense only if they will be more honest than the initial privatization. In Russia today, there is not yet a basis for those beliefs.

Renationalization has costs. It can cause bad owners to accelerate the plundering of the enterprises that they control. If it extends beyond clear cases of theft, it can lead managers who might otherwise manage firms with at least one eye toward long-term value to plunder instead. But if limited to clear cases of theft (of which Russia has no shortage), and accompanied by criminal prosecution of the crooks, renationalization can also convey an important message to managers about the limits of acceptable behavior and the long-term risk from plundering. In the end, the response to theft cannot be to turn a blind eye to all crooks, for fear that prosecuting some will cause others to steal faster before their turn comes.

C. Strengthening Product Market Discipline

Competition and trade policy are essential accompaniments to privatization. The more competitive the market, the greater the pressure to improve operational efficiency, the fewer the rents to be skimmed, and the shorter the time period for which skimming can be sustained.[121] Discussion of Russia's competition and trade policies is beyond the scope of this chapter, but Russia has a long way to go. The European

Bank for Reconstruction and Development rates Russia as 2+ on a 1–5 scale for competition policy.[122] And Russia's trade policy has been moving in the wrong direction—toward higher customs duties and tighter restrictions on oil exports. The state monopoly over distribution that still exists in much of Russia is especially pernicious, because it blocks competition across a whole range of industries.

Just as it helps to install controls on self-dealing together with privatization, lest the managers of privatized firms defeat subsequent efforts to install these controls, so too with competition and trade policy, lest the private owners defeat efforts to reduce their monopoly rents.

D. How Can the Outside World Help Russia?

What the world outside Russia can do now to help isn't clear. Decades of foreign aid to corrupt governments show that shoveling money at them doesn't help economic development and indeed might hurt by financing the society's corrupt elements and imposing a repayment burden (since most aid is in the form of loans).[123] IMF aid was supposed to buy time for Russia to reform its tax system so it could collect the revenues it needed to balance its budget; instead, aid permitted the existing system to survive a bit longer by substituting for revenues that the government didn't collect, while its tax reform promises went unkept. Most of the proceeds were apparently siphoned off by kleptocrats and government officials, leaving Russia to choose between the burden of repayment and official default (Russia has thus far mostly chosen the latter).

It might help to promise aid that is conditioned on promises being kept, not merely made. A government that first adopted simple, enforceable tax rules, put a respectable number of corrupt officials and kleptopcrats in jail, and solved a few of the many murders of politicians and businesspeople might be worth trusting to use aid funds to support development or to assist the losers from the switch to a market economy. In the interim, useful steps are scarce and the payoff will be measured in decades. Here are a few modest ideas.

Efforts to support legal reform are worthwhile. Good laws on the books are a background condition that will become important when and if an honest government emerges. Aid that helps Russia to develop enforcement capacity could be useful. For example, judges and prosecutors need training to handle complex corporate cases, and the Securities Commission needs all the enforcement resources it can get. Training won't help when prosecutors are bought off by company managers or called off by politicians, but not every corporate crook has as much political clout as the kleptocrats.

It could help to fund smart young Russians to study law, business, and accounting in Western countries. Many would stay (benefiting their new home country but not Russia), but some would return, and more would return in a decade or two, by then highly skilled, if opportunities improve. The return of foreign-trained professionals has aided development of other countries, including China, Taiwan, India, and Ireland. It could help Russia too.

A small example: Funding five hundred top Russian law students to get Western legal training (in the United States and Europe) would cost perhaps $20 million a year initially, and less over time if students who took law firm jobs (as most will) had to repay their tuition loans. Many of these lawyers would return to Russia, either immediately or if business conditions improved. In twenty years, Russia would have a pool of ten thousand well-trained lawyers, who understood how market-supporting laws worked. Some would become bar leaders, law teachers, government officials, and political leaders who could help to bring such a system about.

An equally long-run project would be to develop new private Russian law and business schools. Russia's current law schools are far too small to meet its need for business lawyers and are often dominated by communist-era holdovers. Business schools scarcely exist—the Soviet Union didn't need them.

Foreign pressure aimed at opening Russia's markets to competition could be useful, because strong product market competition can police much self-dealing. But the advice to open markets to imports and foreign investment must be coupled with the advisors' willingness to open their own markets to Russian exports—willingness that has sometimes been absent.

VII. Conclusion

A central economic lesson of the twentieth century is the huge difference between well-run, mostly market-centered economies and badly run, often government-centered economies. That experience demonstrates the boost that good government can give to economic performance, and the difficulty of escaping from a legacy of bad government.

A central lesson from the past decade is that mass privatization offers no escape from that general lesson. A weak government can't build the institutions that are needed to control self-dealing and support a complex market economy. Yet without that infrastructure, rapid large-firm privatization won't help the economy much, if at all. Initial conditions, especially the quality of institutions, matter more, and privatization matters less, than we thought in the early 1990s.

In the artificial world of the Coase Theorem, neither these institutions nor the manner of privatization would matter much. Bad owners would quickly sell enterprises to good owners, who would build long-term value. In the real world, bad initial owners loot enterprises instead and corrupt the government while they are at it. Call it the triumph of Hayek over Coase—of Hayekian respect for endogenously developed traditions over the abstract promise of the Coase-influenced mass privatization schemes.[124]

More generally, mass privatization was part of the shock therapists' effort to destroy the existing structure of state control, quickly and irrevocably. In the political sphere, as Edmund Burke taught us two centuries ago, destructive revolutions often come to bad ends.[125] That lesson has been relearned many times since (not least in Russia under the Communists). Economic revolutions that destroy existing institutions before new ones can be built are similarly likely to founder, as those without scruples take advantage of the resulting institutional vacuum.

Notes

Reprinted from Stanford Law Review, vol. 52, B. Black et al, *Russian Privatization and Corporate Governance: What Went Wrong?* p. 1731, copyright 2000, with permission from Stanford Law Review.

We thank Harry Broadman, Jason Bush, Kevin Covert, Richard Craswell, George Crawford, Simeon Djankov, Alexander Dyck, John Earle, David Ellerman, Itzhak Goldberg, Dale Gray, Barry Ickes, Gregory Jedrzejczak, Tarun Khanna, Miriam Klipper, Michael Klausner, Branco Milanovic, David Moss, Peter Murrell, John Nellis, Hugh Patton, Katharina Pistor, Russell Pittman, Gerhard Pohl, Harold Rogers, Andrew Schwartz, Andrei Shleifer, Christopher Stone, Lee Wolosky, Alexander Yushkevich, and Lena Zezulin. We also thank participants in workshops at the American Law and Economics Association; George Mason Law School, Harvard Business School; an OECD Conference on Corporate Governance in Russia; the International Monetary Fund; Stanford Center for Russian and East European Studies; Stanford Law School; University of California, Berkeley (Haas School of Business); University of Michigan (William Davidson Institute); and the World Bank for helpful discussions and comments. Special thanks go to James Fenkner of Troika Dialog for the data on Russian market capitalization and comparable Western values for Russian companies reported in sec. III of this chapter, and to Brian Fonville for research assistance. The research for this chapter was substantially completed in September 1999; we updated partially through June 2000, primarily to correct statements that were inaccurate by then.

1. The best statement of the optimists' view is Maxim Boycko, Andrei Shleifer, & Robert Vishny, Privatizing Russia (1995). Boycko was one of the Russian architects of mass privatization. Shleifer and Vishny are American economists who helped to design the Russian privatization program. They and their collaborators

recruited us (Tarassova beginning in 1992, Black and Kraakman beginning in 1993) to work on the legal infrastructure for Russia's capital markets. One outgrowth of that effort was the Russian law on joint stock companies. *See* Bernard Black & Reinier Kraakman, *A Self-Enforcing Model of Corporate Law*, 109 Harv. L. Rev. 1911 (1996); Bernard S. Black, Reinier Kraakman, & Anna S. Tarassova, Guide to the Russian Law on Joint Stock Companies (1998).

2. Early doubters about rapid privatization include Janos Kornai, The Road to a Free Economy: Shifting from a Socialist System; the Example of Hungary (1990); Stephen S. Cohen & Andrew Schwartz, *Privatization in the Former Soviet Empire: The Tunnel at the End of the Light*, Amer. Prospect, Spr. 1993, at 99; Peter Murrell, *What Is Shock Therapy? What Did It Do in Poland and Russia?* 9 Post-Soviet Aff. 111 (1993); Peter Murrell & Yijiang Wang, *When Privatization Should Be Delayed: The Effect of Communist Legacies on Organizational and Institutional Reforms*, 17 J. Comp. Econ. 385 (1993). Recent work includes Gerard Roland, Transition and Economics: Politics, Markets, and Firms (2000); David Ellerman, *Voucher Privatization with Investment Funds: An Institutional Analysis* (World Bank Pol'y Research Paper No. 1924, 1998); Janos Kornai, *Ten Years after "The Road to a Free Economy": The Author's Self-Evaluation*, working paper presented at the Annual Bank Conference on Development Economics (World Bank 2000); Joseph E. Stiglitz, *Whither Reform? Ten Years of the Transition*, working paper presented at the Annual Bank Conference on Development Economics (World Bank 1999); John Nellis, *Time to Rethink Privatization in Transition Economies?* Fin. & Dev., June 1, 1999, at 16.

3. Anna Tarassova was a senior legal advisor to the Russian Privatization Ministry during mass privatization and later a senior legal advisor to the Russian Securities Commission. She participated in drafting many of the basic laws and presidential decrees that support Russia's capital markets. Bernard Black and Anna Tarassova worked together on several Russian capital markets laws and decrees, including joint stock company law, securities law, limited liability company law, and a decree on investment funds; Reinier Kraakman assisted in developing the theoretical structure for the Russian joint stock company law. Black has also been an advisor on privatization, corporate governance, and capital markets legislation in Armenia, the Czech Republic, Indonesia, Mongolia, South Korea, Ukraine, and Vietnam; Kraakman has advised on company law in Vietnam; Tarassova has advised on capital markets and commercial legislation in Armenia, Belarus, Kazakhstan, Macedonia, and Ukraine.

4. We do not assess in this chapter where the line should be drawn between small enterprises, for which rapid privatization seems desirable, and large enterprises, for which it is problematic.

5. This assumes that Yukos exported roughly 25 percent of its production, at world prices of around $18/barrel, and sold the balance at domestic prices of around $10.50/barrel. Yukos's revenue is based on translated Yukos financial statements provided to us by Graham Houston of National Economic Research Associates. Houston's numbers are also reported in Jeanne Whalen, *Shareholders Rights: Round 2*, Moscow Times, Feb. 17, 1998, ⟨http://www.moscowtimes.ru/archive/issues/1998/Feb/17/story44.html⟩.

6. It is beyond the scope of this chapter to discuss which institutions are most important to control self-dealing. That topic is addressed in Bernard S. Black, *The Legal and Institutional Preconditions for Strong Securities Markets*, 48 UCLA L. Rev.

781 (2001), *available in* Social Science Research Network at ⟨http://papers.ssrn.com/paper.taf?abstract_id=182169⟩.

7. For a case study that attributes Poland's economic success partly to strong capital markets regulation, see Simon Johnson & Andrei Shleifer, *Coase v. the Coasians* (working paper 1999), *available in* Social Science Research Network at ⟨http://papers.ssrn.com/paper.taf?abstract_id=193776⟩.

8. For an industrial policy proposal, see Alice H. Amsden, Jacek Kochanowicz, & Lance Taylor, The Market Meets Its Match: Restructuring the Economies of Eastern Europe (1994). For a blaming effort, see Janine R. Wedel, Collision and Collusion: The Strange Case of Western Aid to Eastern Europe, 1989–1998 (1998).

9. Jeffrey Sachs, *Accelerating Privatization in Eastern Europe: The Case of Poland*, 1 New Eur. L. Rev. 71, 71 (1992); *see also* Jeffrey Sachs, Poland's Jump to the Market Economy (1993). For other statements of the prevailing Western wisdom, see Anders Aslund, How Russia Became a Market Economy (1995); Joseph R. Blasi, Maya Kroumova, & Douglas Kruse, Kremlin Capitalism: Privatizing the Russian Economy (1997); Boycko, Shleifer, & Vishny (1995), *supra* note 1. For an argument that Poland's economic success came from building on existing institutions, not the shock of discarding them, see Grzegorz W. Kolodko, From Shock to Therapy: The Political Economy of Postsocialist Transformation (2000).

10. *See, e.g.*, Steven L. Jones, William L. Megginson, Robert C. Nash, & Jeffry M. Netter, *Share Issue Privatizations as Financial Means to Political and Economic Ends*, 53 J. Fin. Econ. 217 (1999).

11. *See* Boycko, Shleifer, & Vishny (1995), *supra* note 1, at 71–72; Maxim Boycko, Andrei Shleifer, & Robert W. Vishny, *Voucher Privatization*, 35 J. Fin. Econ. 249 (1994). In hindsight, some of the arguments against mass cash auctions seem thin. Foreign participation in cash auctions could have been limited, as it was for voucher auctions. Ill-gotten wealth could be used to buy vouchers (Russian vouchers were tradable) as easily as to buy companies in cash auctions. And Russians were not that poor. They had more than $100 billion in the state savings bank, at least before the government froze savings accounts and then destroyed their value through inflation.

12. We discuss the Czech Republic's experience with mass privatization in sec. V *infra*. Our discussion of Russian privatization relies primarily on Blasi, Kroumova, & Kruse (1997), *supra* note 9; Boycko, Shleifer, & Vishny (1995), *supra* note 1; and the personal knowledge of Black and Tarassova.

13. *See* Blasi, Kroumova, & Kruse (1997), *supra* note 9, at 193 (management ownership rose, on average, from 7 percent in 1994 to 10 percent in 1996, with the general director's stake rising from 2 percent to 4.5 percent).

14. See Lucian Bebchuk, Reinier Kraakman, & George Triantis, *Stock Pyramids, Cross-Ownership, and Dual Class Equity: The Creation and Agency Costs of Separating Control from Cash Flow Rights*, *in* Concentrated Corporate Ownership (Randall Morck ed., 2000), *available in* Social Science Research Network at ⟨http://papers.ssrn.com/paper.taf?abstract_id=147590⟩.

15. Andrei Shleifer & Dmitry Vasiliev, *Management Ownership and Russian Privatization*, *in* 2 Corporate Governance in Central Europe and Russia: Insiders and the State 62, 76–77 (Roman Frydman, Cheryl W. Gray, & Andrzej Rapaczynski eds., 1996); *see also* Nellis, *supra* note 2, at 18 (For the IMF and the World Bank, "[t]he immediate need was to create a basic constituency of property owners: to build capitalism, one needed capitalists—lots of them, and fast").

16. *See* Matt Bivens and Jonas Bernstein, *The Russia You Never Met* (informally circulated English version; Russian version was published in Demokratizatziya (1999)) (on file with authors) (available without footnotes at ⟨http://www.wayan.net/journal/russia/feb_22.htm⟩); Matt Bivens & Jonas Bernstein, *Russian Finance: Byzantium Inc.*, Economist, July 19, 1997, at 62.

17. For a more recent example, see *Funds Sent to Kemerovo Missing?* Radio Free Europe/Radio Liberty Newsline, May 21, 1999, ⟨http://www.rferl.org/newsline/1999/05/1-rus/rus-210599.html⟩ ($100 million foreign loan, intended for the coal industry in Kemerovo Oblast, never arrived at its destination). On general Kremlin corruption, see Celestine Bohlen, *Russian Says He Has Proof Bribes Were Paid to Kremlin*, N.Y. Times, Aug. 31, 1999, at A8; Celestine Bohlen & Michael R. Gordon, *Lawmakers Turn Back Another Attempt by Yeltsin to Dismiss His Chief Prosecutor*, N.Y. Times, Oct. 14, 1999, at A6; Geoffrey York, *Kremlin Kills Corruption Probe of Highly Placed Officials*, Globe & Mail (Toronto), June 26, 1999, at A16.

18. On Gusinski and Potanin, see Bivens & Bernstein (1999), *supra* note 16. On Fridman, see Craig Mellow, *The Oligarch Who Knew Better*, Inst. Investor, June 1999, at 95. On Khodorkovski, see *The Abuses of "Authorized Banking,"* Radio Free Europe/Radio Liberty (Jan. 1998) ⟨http://www.rferl.org/nca/special/rufinance/authorize.html⟩.

19. Igor Baranovsky, *Terror Is a Fact of Russian Competition*, Moscow News, July 22, 1994, at 22 (quoting Mr. Aven).

20. Our discussion of the loans-for-shares auctions relies primarily on Ira W. Lieberman & Rogi Veimetra, *The Rush for State Shares in the "Klondyke" of Wild East Capitalism: Loans-for-Shares Transactions in Russia*, 29 Geo. Wash. J. Int'l L. & Econ. 737 (1996), and the personal knowledge of Black and Tarassova.

21. Our discussion of Erdenet and Zarubezhtsvetmet is based on conversations of 1996–98 between Bernard Black and Z. Enkhbold, head of the State Property Committee of Mongolia, and on the Erdenet joint venture agreement, Соглашение между правительством монгольской народной республики и правительством союза своетских социалистических республик о деятельности монголо-советского совместного горно-обогатутельного предприятия "ЭРДЭНЭТ" [Agreement between the Government of the Mongolian Peoples' Republic and the Government of the Union of Soviet Socialist Republics on the Activity of the Mongol-Soviet Joint Mining-Concentrating Enterprise ERDENET] (June 5, 1991) (on file with authors).

22. Исковое заявление о признании недействительным плана приватизации ВО Зарубежцветмет [Court complaint on deeming invalid the privatization plan for Zarubezhtsvetmet], filed by the general prosecutor in the Moscow Arbitration Court (May 6, 1997) (on file with authors).

23. Letter from Yuri Maslyukov, first deputy prime minister of the Russian Federation, to Prime Minister Elbegdorj of Mongolia (Oct. 29, 1998) (on file with authors).

24. *See* Basic Provisions of the State Programme of Privatization of State-Owned and Municipal Enterprises in the Russian Federation after July 1, 1994 §3.4.2, *approved by* Decree of the President of the Russian Federation No. 1535 of July 22, 1994 (Lexis, Intlaw Library, RFlaw file).

25. *See* Regulations for the Procedure of Concluding an Agreement for Acquiring Shares with the Group of an Enterprise's Workers Who Have Undertaken to

Implement the Privatization Plan and to Prevent the Bankruptcy of the Enterprise to be Privatized, *approved* by Order of the State Committee for State Property Management of the Russian Federation No. 862-R of Nov. 23, 1992 (Lexis, Intlaw Library, RFlaw file).

26. *See* Matt Bivens, *Cyprus Company Buys LUKOil Share*, Moscow Times, Oct. 30, 1999.

27. Stiglitz, *supra* note 2, also notes the chilling effect that dirty privatization had on other market reforms. On the possibility that a rule, although efficient in the near term, may be inefficient in the long run because it produces political backlash, see Mark J. Roe, *Backlash*, 98 Colum. L. Rev. 217 (1998).

28. *See, e.g.*, Laura Belin, *A Year of Discord, in* Annual Survey of Eastern Europe and the Former Soviet Union: 1997—the Challenge of Integration, at 276 (Peter Rutland ed., 1998); Laura Belin, *Changes in Editorial Policy and Ownership at Izvestiya, in id.* at 291; Floriana Fossato & Anna Kachkaeva, *Russian Media Empires III*, Radio Free Europe/Radio Liberty (May 26, 1998) ⟨http://www.rferl.org/nca/special/rumedia3/index.html⟩.

29. Sources for table 4.1 include many of the articles cited above, personal knowledge, a chart made public by the U.S. State Department section on Intelligence and Review titled *Russia's Business Magnates: Their Empires and Interrelationships* (July 1998); Juliet Johnson, *Russia's Emerging Financial-Industrial Groups*, 13 Post-Soviet Aff. 333 (1997); Donald N. Jensen, *Russia's Financial Empires*, Radio Free Europe/Radio Liberty (Jan. 1998) ⟨http://www.rferl.org/nca/special/rufinance/index.html⟩; and Kirsten Vance, *FIGs Rx Figures*, Russia Rev., July 31, 1998, at 24. We used our best judgment in resolving conflicts between sources about who owns what. On the LUKOil-Luzhkov connection, see "*Party of Exporters" to Be Victor in Upcoming Parliamentary Elections*, Russia J., May 24–30, 1999. ⟨http://www.russiajournal.com/start/opinion/article_17_450.htm⟩. On Gazprom, Chernomyrdin, and Vyakhirev, see, e.g., Aleksandras Budrys, *Ex-Russia PM Chernomyrdin Returns to Gazprom*, Reuters, June 30, 1999; *Gazprom and Regions Cozy Up*, Russia J., May 24–30, 1999 ⟨http://www.russiajournal.com/start/business/article_17_466.htm⟩; John Lloyd, *The Russian Devolution*, N.Y. Times, Aug. 15, 1999, §6 (magazine), at 34, 51 (discussing Chernomyrdin's reputed ownership of Gazprom shares). On Berezovski's media interests, see *Get Gusinsky*, Economist, Nov. 20, 1999, at 58; Andrew Higgins, *Russian Newspaper Finds Itself in a Tug of War over Ownership*, Wall St. J., Aug. 9, 1999, at A15. On Luzhkov, see Paul Klebnikov, *Who Will Be the Next Ruler of Russia? The Slick City Boss or the Rough-Edged Populist General*, Forbes, Nov. 16, 1998, at 152; Mark Whitehouse, *Moscow Mayor Steals Political Spotlight*, Wall St. J., May 20, 1999, at A14.

30. In drafting the Russian Law on Joint Stock Companies, we had to adapt an existing word that didn't quite fit (заинтересованный; zainteresovannuy) to refer to a person who has a conflict of interest for a transaction by a company. We were unable to employ the concept of fiduciary duty to behave in the company's interests rather than one's own interests, because we couldn't find an acceptable way to state this concept in Russian legal language.

31. *See* Interview with Sergey Shatalov, First Deputy Minister of Finance, *in No More Delays, in the Move to IAS*, Acct. Rep. (Int'l Center for Acct. Reform, Moscow), Jan./Feb. 2000, at 1 (discussing Finance Ministry delays in moving to accounting rules based on International Accounting Standards; Shatalov explains that the IAS

rules "do not specify in detail individual transactions . . . and the way to account for them for tax purposes").

32. *See, e.g.*, Rozalina V. Ryvkina, *What Kind of Capitalism Is Being Created in Russia?*, Russian Pol. & L., May–June 1998, at 5, 21.

33. On the political economy of Russian tax reform, see Andrei Shleifer & Daniel Treisman, Without a Map: Political Tactics and Economic Reform in Russia (2000).

34. An example: the Central Bank's use of an obscure offshore firm to manage some of the bank's foreign currency reserves, including keeping two sets of books to hide what it was doing. *See* Celestine Bohlen, *Secrecy by Kremlin Financial Czars Raises Eyebrows*, N.Y. Times, July 30, 1999, at A8.

35. *See, e.g.*, Michael Wines, *Yeltsin Son-in-Law at Center of Rich Network of Influence*, N.Y. Times, Oct. 7, 1999, at A1; *supra* note 17.

36. *See* Глеб Пьяных Концы в Воду: Документы МЕНАТЕПа Покоятся на дне Дубны, Коммерсантъ [Gleb Pyannuyx, *Endings in the Water: Menatep Documents Come to Rest at the Bottom of the Dybna*, Kommersant], May 29, 1999, at 1.

37. *See* Katharina Pistor, Martin Raiser, & Stanislaw Gelfer, *Law and Finance in Transition Economies* (European Bank for Reconstruction and Development Working Paper No. 48, 2000), *available in* Social Science Research Network at ⟨http://papers.ssrn.com/paper.taf?abstract_id=214648⟩ (reporting Russia's weakness on a variety of "rule of law" measures; finding a correlation between these measures and the strength of a country's capital markets).

38. For appraisals of Russian judicial corruption, see Jeffrey M. Hertzfeld, *Russian Corporate Governance: The Foreign Direct Investor's Perspective*, at 6–7, *in* Organization for Economic Co-operation and Development, Corporate Governance in Russia (Conference Proceedings 1999) ⟨http://www.oecd.org/daf/corporate-affairs/governance/roundtables/in-Russia/1999/index.htm⟩ ("In many cases, the most likely explanation [for court decisions] is that improper influence has been exerted either through inducements or coercion. . . . [Among other problems], Russian courts have been regularly refusing to recognize and enforce international arbitration awards rendered against Russian parties"); Lee S. Wolosky, *Putin's Plutocrat Problem*, Foreign Aff., Mar./Apr. 2000, at 18, 27 ("In cases involving the oligarchs, trial and appellate judges are routinely bribed. Failing that, judges who evince a dangerous predisposition to impartiality are reassigned without explanation by superiors who are presumably on the take").

39. Jeanne Whalen & Bhushan Bahree, *How Siberian Oil Field Turned into a Minefield*, Wall St. J., Feb. 9, 2000, at A21 (quoting Potanin). Bernard Black was an advisor to a minority shareholder in Kondpetroleum in litigation against Sidanko and BP Amoco (a large Sidanko shareholder) for looting Kondpetroleum. For other pieces of the Chernogoneft bankruptcy story, see Igor Semenenko, *Siberian Oil Company Fights Hostile Takeover*, Moscow Times, May 29, 1999; Alan S. Cullison, *Russia's Tyumen Oil Seeks to Expand with Some Assets of Troubled Sidanko*, Wall St. J., July 8, 1999, at A12; Neela Banerjee, *From Russia, with Bankruptcy*, N.Y. Times, Aug. 13, 1999, at C1.

40. *See Rules of War*, Economist, Dec. 4, 1999, at 65 (Tyumen rival alleges that Tyumen intimidated local judges and complains, "If they just stuck to bribing judges, we could play that game too."); Wolosky, *supra* note 38, at 30 (reporting the beating).

41. *See, e.g.*, Gary Peach, *Sidanko Squabbles Give Investment a Bad Name*, Moscow Times, June 1, 1999 (court rejects external manager proposed by 80 percent of Sidanko's creditors).

42. During the election of the principal creditor committee in Tokobank's bankruptcy, Tokobank disallowed foreign creditors' ballots on flimsy grounds, while accepting massive fraudulent claims by obscure offshore companies. This let the offshore companies control the creditor committee even though their claims were later disallowed. All without objection from the Central Bank, which was overseeing the bankruptcy proceeding. *See* Andrew Higgins, *The Lion's Share: As One Bank Shows, Bankruptcy in Russia Is a Real Cat Fight*, Wall St. J. Apr. 5, 1999, at A1.

43. *See* Wolosky, *supra* note 38, at 27.

44. *See* Black, Kraakman, & Tarassova, *supra* note 1; Jonathan R. Hay & Andrei Shleifer, *Private Enforcement of Public Laws: A Theory of Legal Reform*, 88 Am. Econ. Rev. (Papers & Proceedings), May 1998, at 398.

45. On trust and the related concept of social capital, see, e.g., Francis Fukuyama, Trust: The Social Virtues and the Creation of Prosperity (1995); Jonathan Temple & Paul A. Johnson, *Social Capability and Economic Growth*, 113 Q.J. Econ. 965 (1998); Paul S. Adler and Seok-Woo Kwon, *Social Capital: The Good, the Bad, and the Ugly* (working paper 1999), *available in* Social Science Research Network at ⟨http://papers.ssrn.com/paper.taf?abstract_id=186928⟩; Luigi Guiso, Paola Sapienza, & Luigi Zingales, *The Role of Social Capital in Financial Development* (Ctr. for Research in Sec. Prices Working Paper No. 511, 2000), *available in* Social Science Research Network at ⟨http://papers.ssrn.com/paper.taf?abstract_id=209610⟩. Russia doesn't appear on published multicountry rankings of trust or social capital, because of lack of data, so we can't use these rankings to verify or refute our intuition that Russia was a moderate-trust society in 1990.

46. *See* Olivier Blanchard, The Economics of Post-Communist Transition (1997).

47. *See, e.g.*, Paul Goble, *Repression by Selective Prosecution*, Radio Free Europe/Radio Liberty (May 2000) ⟨http://www.rferl.org/newsline/2000/05/120500.html⟩ (discussing tax police inspection of Media-MOST offices, presumably ordered by Russian President Vladimir Putin).

48. On barter generally, see David Woodruff, Money Unmade: Barter and the Fate of Russian Capitalism (1999). On barter as a tax-avoidance strategy, see Kathryn Hendley, Barry Ickes, & Randi Ryterman, *Remonetizing the Russian Economy, in* Russian Enterprise Reform: Policies to Further the Transition 101 (Harry G. Broadman ed., 1999) (World Bank Discussion Paper No. 400); Alan Reynolds, *Russia and Japan in the Shadow of Tax Policy*, Jobs and Capital (Milken Inst.), Summer/Fall 1998, at 50. For a nontax explanation for barter, see Clifford G. Gaddy & Barry W. Ickes, *Russia's Virtual Economy*, Foreign Aff., Sept./Oct. 1998, at 53.

49. *See, e.g.*, Transparency International, *The 1999 Transparency International Corruption Perceptions Index (CPI)* ⟨http://www.transparency.de/documents/cpi/index.html⟩ (ranking Russia eighty-second of ninety-nine ranked countries, with a corruption rating of 2.4 on a 1–10 scale, with lower ratings indicating higher corruption).

50. *See* Andrei Shleifer & Robert W. Vishny, *Corruption*, 108 Q.J. Econ. 599 (1993).

51. Harry G. Broadman, *Reducing Structural Dominance and Entry Barriers in Russian Industry*, 17 Rev. Ind'l Org. 155 (2000).

52. *See* McKinsey Global Institute, Unlocking Economic Growth in Russia (1999), exhibit 33.

53. *See* Guy Chazan, *Russian Entrepreneurs Fret over Putin*, Wall St. J., Mar. 21, 2000, at A23 ("Many small-scale entrepreneurs say their biggest headache is a plethora of overlapping and often competing bureaucracies. In many cases, [regulations are used as] a tool against firms that have fallen out of favor with local authorities").

54. *See* Neela Banerjee, *Tough Times in Crime Too*, Bus. Rev., Apr. 1999, at 16, 17 ("A krysha offers its clients everything from "office renovations to killing off a business rival, though that costs extra,' says Pavel, a women's clothing importer"); Simon Johnson, John McMillan, & Christopher Woodruff, *Contract Enforcement in Transition* (working paper 1999) (in survey on contract enforcement, 48 percent of Russian firms report using "an informal agency specializing in such disputes" to help resolve the dispute).

55. *See* McKinsey Global Institute, *supra* note 52, at 24 ("The continuous flow of implicit government subsidies . . . makes the endless milking of [nonviable] assets (with the complicity of local authorities) a more attractive proposition to managers than selling cheap to industry consolidators").

56. *See* Brian Pinto, Vladimir Drebentsov, & Alexander Morozov, *Give Growth and Macroeconomic Stability in Russia a Chance: Harden Budgets by Eliminating Nonpayments* (working paper 2000).

57. On the Central Bank's ineffective response to bank failures, see Mark Whitehouse, *Frustration Soars for Russian Bank Depositors: Moscow Does Little to Resolve Crisis*, Wall St. J., Apr. 8, 1999, at A14. For an asset stripping example, see text accompanying note 36 *supra*.

58. As one Western law firm recently warned its clients, when "Russian employees sue foreign companies in Russian courts for wrongful termination, they usually win." Mary Holland and Olga Kozyr, *Downsizing Russian-Style*, CIS LawNotes (Patterson Belknap Webb and Tyler), Mar. 1999, at 6, 7.

59. *See* Simon Johnson, Peter Boone, Alasdair Breach, & Eric Friedman, *Corporate Governance in the Asian Financial Crisis* (working paper 1999) (arguing that such a vicious circle can help to explain the 1997–98 financial collapses in a number of countries).

60. The exchange-rate problem was suggested to us by Gerhard Pohl. He sees the too-high ruble as central to Russian firms' troubles. In contrast, we see it as only one factor that affected profit opportunities. Also, the decline in the sustainable ruble-dollar exchange rate partly reflects the declining productivity of Russian industry. Thus, the ruble's overvaluation may be as much a result of other factors as an independent cause of low profitability.

61. *See* Robert Orttung, *Newly Elected Regional Governors Grapple with Moscow*, *in* Annual Survey of Eastern Europe and the Former Soviet Union: 1997—the Challenges of Integration 285 (Peter Rutland ed., 1998).

62. Employment data tell a similar story. *See* Broadman, *supra* note 51 (small and medium Russian enterprises employ only 13 percent of workers, compared to 53 percent in the United States and 37–58 percent in selected other transition economies).

63. On the Bank of New York scandal, see, e.g., Andrew Higgins, Alan S. Cullison, Michael Allen, & Paul Beckett, *Brash Russian Banker and His Deals Are Key to Laundering Probe*, Wall St. J., Aug. 26, 1999, at A1; Andrew Higgins, Paul Beckett, & Ann Davis, *A Scheme for Ducking Taxes May Be a Key in Russia Money Probe*, Wall St. J., Sept. 15, 1999, at A1. For capital flight estimates, see Timothy L. O'Brien, *Follow the Money, If You Can*, N.Y. Times, Sept. 5, 1999, §3, at 1. On continued capital flight, see Mark Whitehouse, *In Russia, Capital Flight Continues Unabated*, Wall St. J., Apr. 19, 1999, at A19.

64. On overall foreign direct investment, see Troika Dialog Research, Foreign Direct Investment (2000) (reporting data from the State Statistics Committee). On oil sector investment, see Jeanne Whalen & Bhushan Bahree, *How Siberian Oil Field Turned into a Minefield*, Wall St. J., Feb. 9, 2000, at A21 (estimating foreign investment in the oil sector at $3.9 billion since 1990).

65. On barriers to competition, see Broadman, *supra* note 51. On the correlation between competition and productivity, see J. David Brown & John Earle, *Competition and Firm Performance: Lessons from Russia* (Stockholm Inst. of Transition Econ. Working Paper No. 154, 2000), *available in* Social Science Research Network at ⟨http://papers.ssrn.com/paper.taf?abstract_id=222229⟩.

66. *See* Lucian Arye Bebchuk, *A Rent-Protection Theory of Corporate Ownership and Control* (Nat'l Bureau of Econ. Research Working Paper No. W7203, 1999), *available in* Social Science Research Network at ⟨http://papers.ssrn.com/paper.taf?abstract_id=203110⟩.

67. For a list of twenty-seven techniques used by Russian managers to cement their control, "apart from the purely criminal ones," see Alexander Radygin, *Ownership and Control of the Russian Industry*, *in* Organization for Economic Co-operation and Development, Corporate Governance in Russia (Conference Proceedings 1999) ⟨http://www.oecd.org/daf/corporate-affairs/governance/roundtables/in-Russia/1999/index.htm⟩.

68. *See* Paul J. Zak & Stephen Knack, *Trust and Growth* (working paper 1998), *available in* Social Science Research Network at ⟨http://papers.ssrn.com/paper.taf?abstract_id=136961⟩ (modeling a separating equilibrium, in which countries can be characterized as either high or low trust).

69. *See* Joseph Kahn & Timothy L. O'Brien, *For Russia and Its U.S. Bankers, Match Wasn't Made in Heaven*, N.Y. Times, Oct. 18, 1998, at A1 (reporting on Yukos's dealings with subsidiaries).

70. *See* Geoff Winestock, *The Quixotic Technocrat*, Moscow Times, Mar. 31, 1998 (Securities Commission head Dmitri Vasiliev says that he was dissatisfied with Yukos's response to the commission's investigation, but the commission had no power to do any more).

71. For pieces of this story, see *Selected Documents in Regard to Minority Shareholders Rights Abuses in YUKOS's Production Subsidiaries* (May 31, 1999) (materials presented by Michael Hunter, President of Dart Management Inc., a major investor in the Yukos subsidiaries, at the OECD Conference on Corporate Governance in Russia (Moscow, 1999)); Alan S. Cullison, *Russian Firm Bars Minor Holders, Passes Contentious Share Increase*, Wall St. J., Mar. 24, 1999, at A21; David Hoffman, *Out of Step with Russia? Outsider's Battle over Stake in Oil Giant Offers a Glimpse of Nation's Uncertain Capitalist Ways*, Wash. Post, Apr. 18, 1999, at H1; Alan S. Cullison, *Yukos*

Transfers Two Oil Units to Offshore Firms, Wall St. J., June 4, 1999, at A12; Alan S. Cullison, *Vanishing Act: How Oil Giant Yukos Came to Resemble an Empty Cupboard*, Wall St. J. Eur., July 15, 1999, at 1; Alan S. Cullison, *Russian Share Shuffle Maddens Investors*, Wall St. J., July 23, 1999, at A12. Yukos eventually settled with Kenneth Dart, reportedly buying his shares for more than $100 million—far above market value, but still far below their true value. See Jeanne Whalen, *Russia's Yukos to Buy Dart Stock, Ending Long Feud*, Wall St. J., Dec. 21, 1999, at A16. Bernard Black was an advisor to the Dart Group in connection with the Yukos transactions described in the text.

72. *See* Сергей Топов & Юрий Коначоков, *Конфликт из-за нефтеюганского рынка закончился убийством мэра*, Коммерсанть June 27, 1998 [Sergei Topov & Yuri Konachokov, *Conflict over Nefteyugansk Market Ends in Mayor's Assassination*, Kommersant] (reporting the murder and the mayor's conflicts with Yukos); Владимир Ладний, *Кров и Нефть*, Комсомольская правда, July 8, 1998 [Vladimir Ladni, *Blood and Oil*, Komsomolskaya Pravda], at 2 (speculating that Khodorkovski and Yukos were likely to be behind the attack).

73. *See* Grigori Mkrtchyan & Oleg Luriye, *Holiday Contract*, Совершенно Секретно [Top Secret], Mar. 1999 (interview with the intended victim, Yevgeni Rubin, about the attack, a prior attack on his life three months earlier, and his conflicts with Yukos).

74. *See* Alan S. Cullison, *Russian Watchdog Sues Oil Giant, Seeks Probe of Share Shufflings*, Wall St. J., July 22, 1999, at A22 (Securities Commission to investigate Yukos); Neela Banerjee, *Frustrated, Russian Securities Regulator Resigns*, N.Y. Times, Oct. 16, 1999, at B1 (Vasiliev explains his resignation, saying, "It's perfectly clear that we haven't gotten the support of other Government agencies we need in connection with some recent shareholder disputes."); David Hoffman, *Russia's Rookie Capitalists Can't Count on Law*, Wash. Post, Nov. 4, 1999, at A1 (Securities Commission, without Vasiliev, approves share issuance by Yukos subsidiary).

75. Bernard Black was an advisor to a minority shareholder in Noyabrskneftegaz in the matters described in the text. A fuller account of the litigation can be found in Bernard Black, *Shareholder Robbery, Russian Style*, Issue Alert (Institutional Shareholder Serv.), Oct. 1998, at 3. On the exchange rate offered by Sibneft, see Christina Ling, *Russia Sibneft Swap Riles Minority Investors*, Reuters, July 2, 1998.

76. *See* Sebastian Alison, *Russian Oil Co Sibneft Sets Out Policy*, Reuters, July 16, 1998.

77. *See* Andrew Higgins, *EBRD Says Dispute Tests Russian Legal System*, Wall St. J., Feb. 11, 2000, at A12.

78. *See* Wolosky, *supra* note 38, at 30 (head of the Omsk refinery, who opposed Sibneft's takeover of Omsk, was killed; Noyabrskneftegaz's head of oil exports was jailed for months without charges); James Michaels, *Keeping the Old KGB Busy*, Forbes, Dec. 30, 1996 ("After you've read the [accompanying Forbes expose of Berezovski, *Godfather of the Kremlin*, Forbes, Dec. 30, 1996], you will understand why we have omitted [the reporters'] names. . . . Berezovsky stands tall as one of the most powerful men in Russia. Behind him lies a trail of corpses, uncollectible debts, and competitors terrified for their lives"); Mark Taibbi & Mark Ames, *All Fired Up: Interview with Leonid Krutakov of Moskovsky Komsomolets*, Exile, Oct. 23, 1999 ("Q: You were beaten twice? Krutakov: Yes, once very severely, after my article on Bere-

zovsky came out. A bunch of guys caught me outside my doorway and beat me there, breaking bottles over my head. . . . And of course they didn't take my wallet, didn't ask for anything. Clearly they were just sending a message").

79. Bernard Black and Reinier Kraakman advised a minority Sidanko shareholder in connection with the dilution effort described in the text. For pieces of the Sidanko story, see Jeanne Whalen, *Sidanko Bond Issue Tests Legal Water*, Moscow Times, Feb. 10, 1998; Jeanne Whalen, *Sidanko Talks Tackle Bond Dispute*, Moscow Times, Feb. 12, 1998; Jeanne Whalen, *Shareholders Rights: Round 2*, Moscow Times, Feb. 17, 1998; Jeanne Whalen, *Sidanko President, Top Managers Quit*, Moscow Times, Mar. 17, 1998.

80. On the Sidanko bankruptcy, see sec. III.B *supra*. On Oneksimbank, see Guy Chazan, *Russia's Uneximbank Is Close to a Deal on Debt*, Wall St. J., Nov. 12, 1999, at A15.

81. Bernard Black was an advisor to the Mongolian State Property Committee in connection with its efforts to regain control of Erdenet and prepared a legal opinion on the legality of Mongolia's actions in replacing Mr. Elbegdorj.

82. On potential tax revenues from Gazprom, see Dale F. Gray, *International Monetary Fund, Evaluation of Taxes and Revenues from the Energy Sector in the Baltics, Russia, and Other Former Soviet Union Countries* (Int'l Monetary Fund Working Paper 98/34, 1998) ⟨http://www.imf.org/external/pubs/cat/longres.cfm?sk&sk=2527.0⟩.

83. On Gazprom's cash flow, see Adell Karian, *Russia's Dirtiest Secret: Where the Money Goes*, Russia J., Aug. 23, 1999 ⟨http://www.russiajournal.com/start/business/article_26_70.htm⟩ ("Where [Gazprom's] cash flow winds up is anybody's guess, and whether the company's numbers even remotely reflect reality is a question that securities analysts would far prefer to avoid"); *Aksenenko Complains Gas Exports Too Cheap*, Radio Free Europe/Radio Liberty Newsline, Aug. 30, 1999 (First Deputy Prime Minister Nikolai Aksenenko complains that Gazprom is selling gas cheaply to middlemen, who are making "enormous profits"). On transfer of Gazprom's reserves, see Craig Mellow, *Putin's Problem*, Inst. Investor, Apr. 2000, at 44, 50.

84. On AvtoVAZ and Berezovski, see [authors omitted by Forbes because of concern for their safety], *Godfather of the Kremlin?* Forbes, Dec. 30, 1996, at 90. On Aeroflot, see Paul Klebnikov, *The Day They Raided Aeroflot*, Forbes, Mar. 22, 1999, at 106; John Tagliabue, *Swiss Ask Whether Russian Used Aeroflot to Siphon Millions*, N.Y. Times, Sept. 15, 1999, at A8; Elif Kaban, *Russia Suspects $600 Mln Aeroflot Cash Laundered*, Reuters, Oct. 20, 1999. On Trans World Metals, see Erin Arvedlund, *Investors, Factory Face Off Over Board*, Moscow Times, Feb. 11, 1997; Tom Warner, *The Supply Wars of Ukrainian Aluminum*, N.Y. Times, Aug. 23, 1999, at C2; Neela Banerjee, *Swiss Expand Inquiry on Russian Money Flow*, N.Y. Times, Oct. 14, 1999, at A6. On Nazdratenko and Far Eastern Shipping Co., see Russell Working, *Cloak, Dagger and Strong-Arming in the Russian Far East*, N.Y. Times, June 24, 1999, at C4; Bruce Ramsey, *Red Faces Here over Visit by a Russian Official*, Seattle Post-Intelligencer, July 24, 1999. On Lomonosov, see Jeanne Whalen, *Russia Ousts Foreign Owners of Prized Factory*, Wall St. J., Oct. 12, 1999, at A19; David Lynch, *Investor Caught in Russian Tug of War*, USA Today, Dec. 17, 1999, at 1. For a recounting of many more scandals, see Radygin (1999), *supra* note 67.

85. For the market capitalization of LUKOil and Surgutneftegaz, see table 4.2.

On the sale of LUKOil shares, *see supra* note 26 and accompanying text. On Surgutneftegaz's dilution of holding company shareholders, see Neela Banerjee, *Shareholder Value in a Russian Oil Stock?* N.Y. Times, Jan. 27, 2000, at C4.

86. Yukos again provides an example. Shortly after acquiring control of Yukos, Khodorkovski renounced Yukos's contract with Amoco to jointly develop the Priobskoye oil field in West Siberia. *See* Jeanne Whalen, *Pena: Russia Should Respect its Oil Deals*, Moscow Times, Sept. 24, 1997; Jeanne Whalen, *Amoco Eyes Sale of Stake in Far North Oil Project*, Moscow Times, Nov. 14, 1998.

87. Sec. III ends our storytelling. This may be an appropriate place to answer a question that readers knowledgeable about Russia have frequently asked us: Having written this article, are we scared to return to Russia? A glib yet serious answer—it's a nice place to visit (quietly), but we wouldn't want to live there anytime soon. And we've chosen for now not to publish in Russia a Russian-language version of this chapter.

88. The defenders include Andrei Shleifer and Anders Aslund. *See* Andrei Shleifer & Daniel Treisman, *supra* note 33; Anders Aslund, *Russia's Collapse*, Foreign Aff., Sept./Oct. 1999, at 64. The backtrackers include Jeffrey Sachs, who now concedes being "overly optimistic about . . . mass privatization" and explains: "When privatization was rushed through via mass voucher schemes, as in Czechoslovakia in 1991 and Russia in 1993, the result all too often was corrupt asset grabs, managerial plunder of enterprises, and paralysis of firms. The voucher holders often ended up with nothing." Jeffrey D. Sachs, *Life after Communism*, Wall St. J., Nov. 17, 1999, at A22.

89. This is the principal defense of mass privatization offered by Dmitri Vasiliev, deputy minister in the Russian Privatization Ministry during mass privatization and later head of the Russian Securities Commission, in commenting at a 1999 conference on the paper that became this chapter. Vasiliev defends only Russia's 1993–94 mass privatization, however. He opposed loans-for-shares and similar "auctions" of Russia's largest companies. Andrei Shleifer has also argued to us that our counterfactual is unrealistic, there was "tremendous looting from state enterprises by their managers," and privatization didn't make the looting worse. Letter from Andrei Shleifer to Bernard Black (Sept. 29, 1999) (on file with authors).

90. Andrei Shleifer & Robert W. Vishny, The Grabbing Hand: Government Pathologies and Their Cures 147 (1998).

91. *See* McKinsey Global Institute, *supra* note 52.

92. For a current survey, see William L. Megginson & Jeffry M. Netter, *From State to Market: A Survey of Empirical Studies on Privatization* (N.Y. Stock Exchange Working Paper No. 98–05, 2000), *available in* Social Science Research Network at ⟨http://papers.ssrn.com/paper.taf?abstract_id=158313⟩.

93. Nellis, *supra* note 2, at 16; *see also* Simeon Djankov & Peter Murrell, *Enterprise Restructuring in Transition: A Quantitative Survey* (working paper 2000) (finding no statistically significant effect of privatization on firm restructuring for former Soviet Union countries); Megginson and Netter, *supra* note 92 (abstract) ("[T]hose countries which have chosen the mass (voucher) privatization route . . . face ongoing efficiency problems as a result").

94. *See* Djankov & Murrell, *supra* note 93, fig. 1.

95. On inequality and Gini values, see Branko Milanovic, Income, Inequality, and

Poverty During the Transition from Planned to Market Economy (1998) ⟨http://www.worldbank.org/research/transition/inequal.htm⟩; Stiglitz, *supra* note 2, fig. 2; Elizabeth Brainerd, *Winners and Losers in Russia's Economic Transition*, 88 Am. Econ. Rev. 1094 (1998). On poverty rates, see Milanovic, *supra*; Michael R. Gordon, *Hardened by Their History of Hardship, Russians Simply Stretch the Rubles Further*, N.Y. Times, Aug. 22, 1999, at A1.

96. For a generalization of this argument, see Gerard Roland, *Corporate Governance Systems and Restructuring: The Lessons from the Transition Experience*, working paper presented at the Annual Bank Conference on Development Economics (World Bank 2000).

97. *See* Michael Ian Cragg & I. J. Alexander Dyck, *Management Control and Privatization in the United Kingdom*, 30 Rand J. Econ. 475, 477 (1999) (reporting that productivity gains by privatized British firms were achieved primarily in the five years *prior to* privatization).

98. We thank David Ellerman for calling to our attention the potential promise of enterprise leasing as a strategy for staged privatization. Our discussion of enterprise leasing relies primarily on Anna Tarassova's personal knowledge of enterprise leasing in the Moscow region during 1991–92. For discussions that convey the reformers' antipathy to a program that they saw as half a loaf, see, e.g., Roman Frydman, Andrzej Rapaczynski, & John S. Earle, The Privatization Process in Russia, Ukraine, and the Baltic States 20–22, 63–64 (1993); Aslund, *supra* note 9, at 225. Ellerman discusses leasing as one form of privatization in David P. Ellerman, *Management and Employee Buy-Outs as a Technique of Privatization: Overview*, *in* Management and Employee Buy-Outs as a Technique of Privatization 31, 42–49 (David P. Ellerman ed., 1993).

99. *See* Decree of the Presidium of the Supreme Soviet of the USSR on Lease and Lease Relations in the USSR (Apr. 1989) (on file with authors); Fundamentals of Legislation of the USSR and the Union Republics on Lease (Nov. 1989) (on file with authors).

100. This alternative was suggested to us by Dale Gray.

101. For example, upon payment default, the debt could automatically gain voting rights or convert into voting common stock.

102. This alternative was suggested to us by Janos Kornai.

103. *Cf.* Vincent Benziger, *The Chinese Wisely Realized That They Did Not Know What They Were Doing*, Transition, July–Aug. 1996, at 6, 7 (in China, "small reforms, aimed at relatively easy problems, led to economic expansion, which, in turn, led to increased political support for further reform").

104. John C. Coffee, Jr., *Institutional Investors in Transitional Economies: Lessons from the Czech Experience*, *in* 1 Corporate Governance in Central Europe and Russia: Banks, Funds, and Foreign Investors 111, 111 (Roman Frydman, Cheryl W. Gray, & Andrzej Rapaczynski eds., 1996).

105. Our discussion of the Czech experience relies on the personal knowledge of Bernard Black and our research assistant, Brian Fonville, and on Coffee, *supra* note 104; John C. Coffee, Jr., Inventing a Corporate Monitor for Transitional Economies: The Uncertain Lessons from the Czech and Polish Experiences, *in* Comparative Corporate Governance: The State of the Art and Emerging Research 68 (Klaus Hopt, Hideki Kanda, Mark Roe, Eddy Wymeersch, & Stefan Prigge eds.,

1998); John C. Coffee, Jr., *Privatization and Corporate Governance: The Lessons from Securities Market Failure*, chapter 7, *infra*; Czech Ministry of Finance, *Current Aspects of the Czech Capital Market* (informally circulated report, 1997) (on file with authors); Raj M. Desai, *Reformed Banks and Corporate Governance in the Czech Republic, 1991–1996*, 37 Post-Soviet Geography & Econ. 463 (1996); Andrew Weiss and Georgiy Nikitin, *Performance of Czech Companies by Ownership Structure* (working paper 1998); Organization for Economic Cooperation and Development, OECD Economic Surveys 1997–1998: Czech Republic (1998) and OECD Economic Surveys, 1999–2000: Czech Republic (2000); Johnson & Shleifer, *supra* note 7.

106. *Cf.* Weiss & Nikitin *supra* note 105 (finding no correlation between performance and ownership by either bank-run or nonbank investment funds).

107. *See* Václav Klaus, Renaissance: The Rebirth of Liberty in the Heart of Europe (1997) (Klaus was Czech prime minister during mass privatization).

108. Czech Ministry of Finance, *supra* note 105, at 4–9.

109. *See* Peggy Simpson, *Some Confess Mistakes in Velvet Revolt, but Not Czech's Klaus*, Warsaw Bus. J., Oct. 25, 1999. On the Klaus government's growing corruption, see Andrew Harrison Schwartz, The Best-Laid Plan: Privatization and Neoliberalism in the Czech Republic (1999) (Ph.D. dissertation, University of California (Berkeley)) (on file with authors).

110. In Russia, the inability of voucher investment funds to attract new investment was guaranteed by fund-level taxation that proved politically impossible to remove.

111. Thus, we disagree with arguments that stronger oversight by voucher investment funds could have ameliorated Russia's problems with manager control of privatized firms. *See* Raj M. Desai & Itzhak Goldberg, *The Vicious Circles of Control: Regional Governments and Insiders in Privatized Russian Enterprises* (working paper 1999), *available in* Social Science Research Network at ⟨http://papers.ssrn.com/paper.taf?abstract_id=190570⟩.

112. *See* David Ellerman, *Lessons from Voucher Privatization* (working paper 2000).

113. *See* Bruce Kogut & Andrew Spicer, *Institutional Technology and the Chains of Trust: Capital Markets and Privatization in Russia and the Czech Republic* (working paper 1999) ⟨http://eres.bus.umich.edu/docs/workpap-dav/wp291.doc⟩.

114. *See* Bernard S. Black, *Shareholder Passivity Reexamined*, 89 Mich. L. Rev. 520, 575–84 (1990) (modeling money managers' incentives to monitor); Ellerman, *supra* note 2 (discussing reasons why voucher funds weren't a promising source of restructuring effort).

115. *Accord*, Schwartz, *supra* note 109, at 209; *see also* Kogut & Spicer, *supra* note 113. Thus, we mostly disagree with Merritt Fox and Michael Heller, who argue that the details of Russian mass privatization were central to subsequent mismanagement and asset stripping. *See* Merritt Fox and Michael Heller, *Corporate Governance Lessons from Russian Enterprise Fiascos*, 75 N.Y.U. L. Rev. 1720 (2000) and Merritt Fox and Michael Heller, Conclusion: The Unexplored Role of Initial Conditions, chapter 9, *infra*.

116. Shleifer & Vishny, *supra* note 90, at 150.

117. Black and Kraakman did, anyway. Tarassova disclaims ever having done so.

118. Black, *supra* note 6, discusses the institutions that underlie strong securities markets.

119. *See* David Hoffman, *Putin's Actions Seem to Belie Promises on Tycoons*, Wash.

Post, May 7, 2000, at A21; Nick Wadhams, *Putin Reappoints Chief-of-Staff*, Assoc. Press, May 27, 2000.

120. For a proposal that the Russian government swap tax obligations for additional company shares, which it will then promptly sell to investors, see Desai & Goldberg, *supra* note 111. In our judgment, Desai & Goldberg don't sufficiently question whether the Russian government's auctions of shares that it received in exchange for tax obligations would be more honest or produce better owners than recent past auctions.

121. On the empirical correlation between competition policy and outcomes from privatization, see John Nellis, *Competition and Privatization: Ownership Should Not Matter—but It Does*, 4 Revista do Instituto Brasileiro de Estudos Das Relacoes de Concorrencia e de Consumo 211 (1997); Pankaj Tandon, *The Efficiency of Privatized Firms: Evidence and Implications* (Boston Univ., working paper 1994) (on file with authors).

122. European Bank for Reconstruction and Development, Transition Report 1999 (2000), at 24; *see also* Broadman, *supra* note 51.

123. *See, e.g.*, World Bank, Assessing Aid: What Works, What Doesn't, and Why (1998); Jonathan Isham & Daniel Kaufman, *The Forgotten Rationale for Policy Reform: The Productivity of Investment Projects*, 114 Q.J. Econ. 149 (1999).

124. *See* Kornai (2000), *supra* note 2, at 127 (contrasting the roots of his own work in Hayek and Schumpeter to the "vulgar Coase-ism" of the shock therapists). For Hayek's views, see Friedrich A. Hayek, 1 Law, Legislation, and Liberty: Rules and Order (1973). For Coase's views about what he meant by the Coase Theorem, see Ronald H. Coase, The Firm, the Market, and the Law chs. 5–6 (1988).

125. *See* Edmund Burke, Reflections on the Revolution in France (Thomas H. D. Mahoney ed., 1955) (1790).

References

Paul S. Adler & Seok-Woo Kwon, *Social Capital: The Good, the Bad, and the Ugly* (working paper 1999), *available in* Social Science Research Network at ⟨http://papers.ssrn.com/paper.taf?abstract_id=186928⟩.

Alice H. Amsden, Jacek Kochanowicz, & Lance Taylor, The Market Meets Its Match: Restructuring the Economies of Eastern Europe (1994).

Anders Aslund, How Russia Became a Market Economy (1995).

Anders Aslund, *Russia's Collapse*, Foreign Aff., Sept./Oct. 1999, at 64.

Lucian Arye Bebchuk, A *Rent-Protection Theory of Corporate Ownership and Control* (Nat'l Bureau of Econ. Research Working Paper No. W7203, 1999), *available in* Social Science Research Network at ⟨http://papers.ssrn.com/paper.taf?abstract_id=203110⟩.

Lucian Bebchuk, Reinier Kraakman, & George Triantis, *Stock Pyramids, Cross-Ownership, and Dual Class Equity: The Creation and Agency Costs of Separating Control from Cash Flow Rights*, *in* Concentrated Corporate Ownership (Randall Morck ed., 2000), *available in* Social Science Research Network at ⟨http://papers.ssrn.com/paper.taf?abstract_id=147590⟩.

Laura Belin, *Changes in Editorial Policy and Ownership at Izvestiya*, *in* Annual Survey of Eastern Europe and the Former Soviet Union: 1997—the Challenge of Integration, at 291 (Peter Rutland ed., 1998).

Laura Belin, *A Year of Discord*, *in* Annual Survey of Eastern Europe and the Former Soviet Union: 1997—the Challenge of Integration, at 276 (Peter Rutland ed., 1998).

Vincent Benziger, *The Chinese Wisely Realized That They Did Not Know What They Were Doing*, Transition, July–Aug. 1996, at 6.

Matt Bivens & Jonas Bernstein, *The Russia You Never Met* (informally circulated English version; Russian version was published in Demokratizatziya (1999)) (available without footnotes at ⟨http://www.wayan.net/journal/russia/feb_22.htm⟩).

Bernard S. Black, *The Legal and Institutional Preconditions for Strong Securities Markets*, 48 UCLA L. Rev. 781 (2000), *available in* Social Science Research Network at ⟨http://papers.ssrn.com/paper.taf?abstract_id=182169⟩.

Bernard Black, *Shareholder Passivity Reexamined*, 89 Mich. L. Rev. 520 (1990).

Bernard Black, *Shareholder Robbery, Russian Style*, Issue Alert (Institutional Shareholder Serv.), Oct. 1998, at 3.

Bernard Black & Reinier Kraakman, *A Self-Enforcing Model of Corporate Law*, 109 Harv. L. Rev. 1911 (1996).

Bernard S. Black, Reinier Kraakman, & Anna S. Tarassova, Guide to the Russian Law on Joint Stock Companies (1998).

Olivier Blanchard, The Economics of Post-Communist Transition (1997).

Joseph R. Blasi, Maya Kroumova, & Douglas Kruse, Kremlin Capitalism: Privatizing the Russian Economy (1997).

Maxim Boycko, Andrei Shleifer, & Robert Vishny, Privatizing Russia (1995).

Maxim Boycko, Andrei Shleifer, & Robert W. Vishny, *Voucher Privatization*, 35 J. Fin. Econ. 249 (1994).

Elizabeth Brainerd, *Winners and Losers in Russia's Economic Transition*, 88 Am. Econ. Rev. 1094 (1998).

Harry G. Broadman, *Reducing Structural Dominance and Entry Barriers in Russian Industry*, 17 Rev. Ind'l Org. 155 (2000).

J. David Brown & John Earle, *Competition and Firm Performance: Lessons from Russia* (Stockholm Inst. of Transition Econ. Working Paper No. 154, 2000), *available in* Social Science Research Network at ⟨http://papers.ssrn.com/paper.taf?abstract_id=222229⟩

Edmund Burke, Reflections on the Revolution in France (Thomas H. D. Mahoney ed., 1955) (1790).

Ronald H. Coase, The Firm, the Market, and the Law chs. 5–6 (1988).

John C. Coffee, Jr., *Institutional Investors in Transitional Economies: Lessons from the Czech Experience*, *in* 1 Corporate Governance in Central Europe and Russia: Banks, Funds, and Foreign Investors 111 (Roman Frydman, Cheryl W. Gray, & Andrzej Rapaczynski eds., 1996).

John C. Coffee, Jr., *Inventing a Corporate Monitor for Transitional Economies: The Uncertain Lessons from the Czech and Polish Experiences*, *in* Comparative Corporate Governance: The State of the Art and Emerging Research 68 (Klaus Hopt, Hideki Kanda, Mark Roe, Eddy Wymeersch, & Stefan Prigge eds., 1998).

John C. Coffee, Jr., *Privatization and Corporate Governance: The Lessons from Securities Market Failure*, 25 J. Corp. L. 1 (1999).
Stephen S. Cohen & Andrew Schwartz, *Privatization in the Former Soviet Empire: The Tunnel at the End of the Light*, Amer. Prospect, Spr. 1993, at 99.
Michael Ian Cragg & I. J. Alexander Dyck, *Management Control and Privatization in the United Kingdom*, 30 Rand J. Econ. 475 (1999).
Czech Ministry of Finance, *Current Aspects of the Czech Capital Market* (informally circulated report, 1997) (on file with authors).
Raj M. Desai, *Reformed Banks and Corporate Governance in the Czech Republic, 1991–1996*, 37 Post-Soviet Geography & Econ. 463 (1996).
Raj M. Desai & Itzhak Goldberg, *The Vicious Circles of Control: Regional Governments and Insiders in Privatized Russian Enterprises* (working paper 1999), *available in* Social Sciences Research Network at ⟨http://papers.ssrn.com/paper.taf?abstract_id=190570⟩.
Simeon Djankov & Peter Murrell, *Enterprise Restructuring in Transition: A Quantitative Survey* (working paper 2000).
David Ellerman, *Lessons from Voucher Privatization* (working paper 2000).
David Ellerman, *Voucher Privatization with Investment Funds: An Institutional Analysis* (World Bank Pol'y Research Paper No. 1924, 1998).
David P. Ellerman, *Management and Employee Buy-Outs as a Technique of Privatization: Overview*, *in* Management and Employee Buy-Outs as a Technique of Privatization 31 (David P. Ellerman ed., 1993).
European Bank for Reconstr. and Dev., Transition Report 1999 (2000).
Merritt Fox & Michael Heller, *Corporate Governance Lessons from Russian Enterprise Fiascoes*, 75 N.Y.U. L. Rev. 1720 (2000).
Roman Frydman, Andrzej Rapaczynski, & John S. Earle, The Privatization Process in Russia, Ukraine, and the Baltic States 20 (1993).
Francis Fukuyama, Trust: The Social Virtues and the Creation of Prosperity (1995).
Clifford G. Gaddy & Barry W. Ickes, *Russia's Virtual Economy*, Foreign Aff., Sept./Oct. 1998, at 53.
Dale F. Gray, *International Monetary Fund, Evaluation of Taxes and Revenues from the Energy Sector in the Baltics, Russia, and Other Former Soviet Union Countries* (Int'l Monetary Fund Working Paper 98/34, 1998) ⟨http://www.imf.org/external/pubs/cat/longres.cfm?sk&sk=2527.0⟩.
Luigi Guiso, Paola Sapienza, & Luigi Zingales, *The Role of Social Capital in Financial Development* (Ctr. for Research in Sec. Prices Working Paper No. 511, 2000), *available in* Social Science Research Network at ⟨http://papers.ssrn.com/paper.taf?abstract_id=209610⟩.
Jonathan R. Hay & Andrei Shleifer, *Private Enforcement of Public Laws: A Theory of Legal Reform*, Am. Econ. Rev. (Papers & Proceedings), May 1998, at 398.
Friedrich A. Hayek, 1 Law, Legislation, and Liberty: Rules and Order (1973).
Kathryn Hendley, Barry Ickes, & Randi Ryterman, *Remonetizing the Russian Economy*, *in* Russian Enterprise Reform: Policies to Further the Transition 101 (Harry G. Broadman ed., 1999) (World Bank Discussion Paper No. 400).
Jeffrey M. Hertzfeld, *Russian Corporate Governance: The Foreign Direct Investor's Perspective*, *in* Organization for Economic Co-operation and Development, Corporate Governance in Russia (Conference Proceedings 1999) ⟨http://www.oecd

.org/daf/corporate-affairs/governance/roundtables/in-Russia/1999/index.htm⟩.

Mary Holland & Olga Kozyr, *Downsizing Russian-Style*, CIS LawNotes (Patterson Belknap Webb & Tyler), Mar. 1999, at 6.

Jonathan Isham & Daniel Kaufman, *The Forgotten Rationale for Policy Reform: The Productivity of Investment Projects*, 114 Q.J. Econ. 149 (1999).

Juliet Johnson, *Russia's Emerging Financial-Industrial Groups*, 13 Post-Soviet Aff. 333 (1997).

Simon Johnson and Andrei Shleifer, *Coase v. the Coasians* (working paper 1999), *available in* Social Science Research Network at ⟨http://papers.ssrn.com/paper.taf?abstract_id=193776⟩.

Simon Johnson, Peter Boone, Alasdair Breach, & Eric Friedman, *Corporate Governance in the Asian Financial Crisis* (working paper 1999).

Simon Johnson, John McMillan, & Christopher Woodruff, *Contract Enforcement in Transition* (working paper 1999).

Steven L. Jones, William L. Megginson, Robert C. Nash, & Jeffry M. Netter, *Share Issue Privatizations as Financial Means to Political and Economic Ends*, 53 J. Fin. Econ. 217 (1999).

Václav Klaus, Renaissance: The Rebirth of Liberty in the Heart of Europe (1997).

Bruce Kogut & Andrew Spicer, *Institutional Technology and the Chains of Trust: Capital Markets and Privatization in Russia and the Czech Republic* (working paper 1999) ⟨http://eres.bus.umich.edu/docs/workpap-dav/wp291.doc⟩.

Grzegorz W. Kolodko, From Shock to Therapy: The Political Economy of Postsocialist Transformation (2000).

Janos Kornai, The Road to a Free Economy: Shifting from a Socialist System; the Example of Hungary (1990).

Janos Kornai, *Ten Years after "The Road to a Free Economy": The Author's Self-Evaluation*, working paper presented at the Annual Bank Conference on Development Economics (World Bank 2000).

Ira W. Lieberman & Rogi Veimetra, *The Rush for State Shares in the "Klondyke" of Wild East Capitalism: Loans-for-Shares Transactions in Russia*, 29 Geo. Wash. J. Int'l L. & Econ. 737 (1996).

McKinsey Global Institute, Unlocking Economic Growth in Russia (1999), exhibit 33.

Branko Milanovic, Income, Inequality, and Poverty During the Transition from Planned to Market Economy (1998) ⟨http://www.worldbank.org/research/transition/inequal.htm⟩.

William L. Megginson & Jeffry M. Netter, *From State to Market: A Survey of Empirical Studies on Privatization* (N.Y. Stock Exchange Working Paper No. 98–05, 2000), *available in* Social Science Research Network at ⟨http://papers.ssrn.com/paper.taf?abstract_id=158313⟩.

Peter Murrell, *What Is Shock Therapy? What Did It Do in Poland and Russia?* 9 Post-Soviet Aff. 111 (1993).

Peter Murrell & Yijiang Wang, *When Privatization Should Be Delayed: The Effect of Communist Legacies on Organizational and Institutional Reforms*, 17 J. Comp. Econ. 385 (1993).

John Nellis, *Competition and Privatization: Ownership Should Not Matter—but It Does*,

4 Revista do Instituto Brasileiro de Estudos Das Relacoes de Concorrencia e de Consumo 211 (1997).

John Nellis, *Time to Rethink Privatization in Transition Economies?* Fin. & Dev., June 1, 1999, at 16.

Organization for Economic Cooperation and Development, OECD Economic Surveys 1997–1998: Czech Republic (1998).

Organization for Economic Cooperation and Development, OECD Economic Surveys 1999–2000: Czech Republic (2000).

Robert Orttung, *Newly Elected Regional Governors Grapple with Moscow*, *in* Annual Survey of Eastern Europe and the Former Soviet Union: 1997—the Challenges of Integration 285 (Peter Rutland ed., 1998).

Brian Pinto, Vladimir Drebentsov, & Alexander Morozov, *Give Growth and Macroeconomic Stability in Russia a Chance: Harden Budgets by Eliminating Nonpayments* (working paper 2000).

Katharina Pistor, Martin Raiser, & Stanislaw Gelfer, *Law and Finance in Transition Economies* (Eur. Bank for Reconstr. and Dev. Working Paper No. 48, 2000), *available in* Social Science Research Network at ⟨http://papers.ssrn.com/paper.taf?abstract_id=214648⟩.

Alexander Radygin, *Ownership and Control of the Russian Industry*, *in* Organization for Economic Co-operation and Development, Corporate Governance in Russia (Conference Proceedings 1999) ⟨http://www.oecd.org/daf/corporate-affairs/governance/roundtables/in-Russia/1999/index.htm⟩.

Alan Reynolds, *Russia and Japan in the Shadow of Tax Policy*, Jobs and Capital (Milken Inst.), Summer/Fall 1998, at 50.

Mark J. Roe, *Backlash*, 98 Colum. L. Rev. 217 (1998).

Gerard Roland, *Corporate Governance Systems and Restructuring: The Lessons from the Transition Experience*, working paper presented at the Annual Bank Conference on Development Economics (World Bank 2000).

Gerard Roland, Transition and Economics: Politics, Markets and Firms (2000).

Rozalina V. Ryvkina, *What Kind of Capitalism Is Being Created in Russia?* Russian Pol. & L., May–June 1998, at 5.

Jeffrey Sachs, *Accelerating Privatization in Eastern Europe: The Case of Poland*, 1 New Eur. L. Rev. 71 (1992).

Jeffrey Sachs, Poland's Jump to the Market Economy (1993).

Andrew Harrison Schwartz, The Best Laid Plan: Privatization and Neo-liberalism in the Czech Republic (1999) (Ph.D. dissertation, University of California (Berkeley)).

Andrei Shleifer & Daniel Treisman, Without a Map: Political Tactics and Economic Reform in Russia (2000).

Andrei Shleifer & Robert W. Vishny, *Corruption*, 108 Q.J. Econ. 599 (1993).

Andrei Shleifer & Robert W. Vishny, The Grabbing Hand: Government Pathologies and Their Cures 147 (1998).

Andrei Shleifer & Dmitry Vasiliev, *Management Ownership and Russian Privatization*, *in* 2 Corporate Governance in Central Europe and Russia: Insiders and the State 62 (Roman Frydman, Cheryl W. Gray, & Andrzej Rapaczynski eds., 1996).

Joseph E. Stiglitz, *Whither Reform? Ten Years of the Transition*, working paper pre-

sented at the Annual Bank Conference on Development Economics (World Bank 1999).
Pankaj Tandon, *The Efficiency of Privatized Firms: Evidence and Implications* (Boston Univ. working paper 1994) (on file with authors).
Jonathan Temple & Paul A. Johnson, *Social Capability and Economic Growth*, 113 Q.J. Econ. 965 (1998).
Transparency International, *The 1999 Transparency International Corruption Perceptions Index* (CPI) ⟨http://www.transparency.de/documents/cpi/index.html⟩.
Troika Dialog Research, Foreign Project Investment (2000).
Janine R. Wedel, Collision and Collusion: The Strange Case of Western Aid to Eastern Europe, 1989–1998 (1998).
Andrew Weiss & Georgiy Nikitin, *Performance of Czech Companies by Ownership Structure* (working paper 1998).
Lee S. Wolosky, *Putin's Plutocrat Problem*, Foreign Aff., Mar./Apr. 2000, at 18.
David Woodruff, Money Unmade: Barter and the Fate of Russian Capitalism (1999).
World Bank, Assessing Aid: What Works, What Doesn't, and Why (1998).
Paul J. Zak & Stephen Knack, *Trust and Growth* (working paper 1998), *available in* Social Science Research Network at ⟨http://papers.ssrn.com/paper.taf?abstract_id=136961⟩.

CHAPTER FIVE

Why Ownership Matters: Entrepreneurship and the Restructuring of Enterprises in Central Europe

Roman Frydman, Marek Hessel, and Andrzej Rapaczynski

In this chapter, based on a study of midsize firms in the Czech Republic, Hungary, and Poland, we seek to explain the reasons behind the marked impact of ownership on firm performance that has been observed in a number of studies in Eastern Europe and other parts of the world. Focusing in particular on the differential impact of ownership on revenue and cost performance, we argue that privatized firms controlled by outside investors are more entrepreneurial than those controlled by corporate insiders or the state. We provide evidence that all state and privatized firms in transition economies engage in similar types of restructuring, but that product restructuring by firms owned by outsider investors is significantly more effective (in terms of revenue generation) than that by firms with other types of ownership. We also examine the impact of managerial turnover on revenue performance, as well as differences between managers of firms with different types of ownership, and conclude that the more entrepreneurial behavior of outsider-owned firms is caused primarily by incentive effects, rather than human capital effects, of privatization. More specifically, we argue that the success of outsider-owned firms is caused by their greater readiness to accept risks (as evidenced by the higher variance of the revenues generated by restructuring) and a lesser need to defend, and account for, their managerial decisions.

I. Introduction

There exists, by now, growing empirical evidence that ownership affects company performance. Much of it comes from studies of privatization. Megginson and coauthors document improvements in postprivatization performance of sixty-one large firms in eighteen countries.[1] La Porta and López-de-Silanes provide evidence from Mexico,[2] while Frydman and coauthors[3] and Pohl and coauthors[4] examine medium-size and large firms, respectively, in central and Eastern Europe. Earlier findings provide evidence of the effectiveness of privatization of retail shops and other small businesses in central Europe and Russia, respectively.[5]

The difference between state and private ownership is not the only one that affects firm performance; different types of private owners also generate different returns. Evidence has been presented that managerial ownership below certain levels improves performance (as measured by Tobin's Q), but is associated with lower performance at higher levels.[6] Numerous studies have dealt with the impact of worker ownership on firm productivity, investment, capital raising ability, and so on.[7] Frydman and coauthors provide evidence that firms privatized to different types of owners differ significantly in postprivatization performance, with especially pronounced differences between firms controlled by corporate insiders and outside investors.[8]

Not only do firms owned by different owners perform differently, but also some aspects of firm performance are more affected than others by differences in ownership. Thus, firms controlled by outsider owners outperform those owned by corporate insiders or the state in terms of their revenue performance, but that ownership does not appear to make a significant difference in terms of (labor and material) cost performance.[9]

That ownership makes a difference is very important. But can we explain *why*? There are several types of explanations advanced in the literature. Some commentators focus on the difference between state-owned and privately owned firms and attribute the inferior performance of state firms (in terms of the standard criterion of value maximization) to the fact that state officials are prone to impose on the management of state companies a variety of goals, such as minimization of layoffs, political patronage, or protecting other state firms' markets.[10] A similar change in the objective function of a firm may also be associated with some forms of private ownership: employees, for example, may be interested in minimizing layoffs and be prepared to compromise, to achieve this end, the value-maximization objective.

Other explanations focus on different levels of entrepreneurship that may be associated with different types of ownership, and thus on the readiness of firms with certain types of owners to accept higher levels of risk, their willingness to innovate, and the skills that allow them to accomplish better the objectives they pursue. In particular, some have argued that the success of firms with certain types of owners is the result of a better incentive structure of persons charged with making business decisions. Others have attributed the same performance differences to the fact that firms with certain types of owners are controlled by people whose superior human capital allows them to achieve better results.[11]

In this chapter, we present the results of empirical analyses of medium-size firms in three transition countries in central Europe and seek to clarify the way ownership affects a firm's revenue and cost performance by focusing on behavioral differences between firms owned by the state, outside investors, and corporate insiders (managers and employees). In particular, we examine the restructuring activities undertaken by different types of firms from the point of view of the differences they may reveal with respect to the degree of entrepreneurship that may characterize firms with different types of owners.

Grosfeld and Roland[12] hypothesized that firms with different types of owners may, when faced with new challenges, engage in different types of adaptive behavior, and they distinguished between "strategic" (revenue-oriented) and "defensive" (cost-oriented) restructuring. Interestingly, we found no significant differences in the frequency or general type of product restructuring engaged in by firms with different types of owners, indicating that the difference in the success rate of different owners is not to be accounted for in terms of *what* their firms do: in fact, all of them attempt to revamp their product offerings by undertaking broadly the same types of measures, such as introducing new products, changing design or packaging, or improving quality by new production processes.

The relationship between restructuring and performance is, apparently, more complicated. Although engaging in specific forms of product restructuring is not a sufficient condition of success in improving performance, neither can success be achieved without extensive revamping of the firm's operations: we find that firms that do not restructure their products, whether owned by outsiders, insiders, or the state, do not experience significant improvements in revenue performance. But among the firms that do restructure, some—those owned by outsiders—tend to generate significantly higher revenues, while others do not. What determines, therefore, the success of some firms, and not others, in their restructuring efforts seems to lie more in who does it, and *how*, rather than in *what* they are doing.

This should not be surprising, if—as we shall argue—it is the degree of entrepreneurship that makes some firms more successful than others. The very nature of entrepreneurship is likely to lie in factors—such as a talent for spotting opportunities not seen by others, a willingness and ability to act on often idiosyncratic "hunches" and intuitions that cannot be easily communicated to others (but that ultimately turn out to be correct), and the ability to take risks in order to succeed—that do not lend themselves to being captured by the "what" of an activity. Indeed, were we able to specify some general, objectively reproducible criteria of what an entrepreneur does (such as the frequency of restructuring or types of product changes), the advantages of entrepreneurship would disappear, to be replaced by a system of rules that could be followed by anyone. Only if such rules do not exist can ownership be truly indispensable.

We proceed, therefore, to analyze the relationship between ownership and entrepreneurship by testing the hypothesis[13] that firms controlled by certain owners are more successful in restructuring their products (and consequently outperforming other firms in terms of their sales) because the *quality of the human capital* of their decision makers is simply higher than in other firms. Although there are reasons to believe that in a developed society, firms with certain types of owners might, over time, attract better managers than others, there is no evidence of this in our sample (perhaps because the managerial labor market has not yet had enough time to operate). Moreover, we find evidence in our data that the performance differences we observe between firms with different types of owners are not primarily caused by differences in the quality of the human capital of their decision makers, and that firms in which the principal decision makers remain unchanged experience significant changes in their performance upon a change of owners.

We therefore argue in favor of linking the better performance of firms with certain types of owners to the *incentive effects of ownership*. Although entrepreneurship is clearly in part a matter of human ability—perhaps even largely innate ability—certain ownership arrangements appear to allow it better to thrive and manifest itself in performance. We associate this aspect of ownership with different attitudes toward risk and different degrees of accountability that various control structures impose on the decision makers responsible for major restructuring. We then test this hypothesis by examining the variance of the performance of firms with different types of ownership (which should reflect their ability and willingness to accept risk) and find significant differences among them. In particular—as expected—the performance of outsider-owned firms is characterized by significantly higher variance than that of the firms owned by either insiders or the state.

II. The Data

The present study is based on a survey of 506 manufacturing firms in the Czech Republic, Hungary, and Poland conducted in the fall of 1994. To avoid the special problems of the industrial "dinosaurs" of the communist era, the sample was drawn from midsize firms employing between one hundred and fifteen hundred persons; the median 1993 sales were just above US$6 million. The firms were drawn randomly from the list provided by the central statistical office in each country, but when a maximum of firms with a certain type of owners was reached, further firms with the same ownership type were excluded from the drawing.[14] In this sense, the ownership composition of the sample may not reflect the composition of the parent populations.

Since we are interested in behavioral differences between firms that are similar in all respects but their ownership, we focus here on firms that were all state owned at the beginning of the sample period. We therefore eliminated from the original sample 88 private firms that were never state owned. The ownership structure of 87 other firms was in doubt, and we excluded them from the subsample as well.[15] Of the remaining 331 state and privatized firms,[16] 87 firms did not provide complete enough data to allow for an analysis of any aspect of their performance,[17] and 29 firms provided unusable or dubious data. Thus, the largest available sample, used to evaluate revenue performance, consists of 215 firms, 90 of them state and 125 privatized.

In terms of country distribution, 36 percent of the firms were in the Czech Republic, 42 percent in Hungary, and the remaining 22 percent in Poland. The firms operated in both consumer (food and beverages, clothing, and furniture) and industrial (nonferrous minerals, chemicals, textiles, and leather) goods sectors, with 58 percent of privatized firms and 48 percent of state firms in consumer goods sectors. Practically all state (90 percent) and privatized (93 percent) firms faced domestic or foreign competition for their products.

In the overwhelming majority of cases, the privatized firms in our sample had a very concentrated structure of ownership,[18] allowing us to identify the firm's ownership type with that of its largest shareholder.[19] Insiders (managerial or nonmanagerial employees) and foreign investors were the most frequent owners (each the largest shareholders in about 25 percent of privatized firms), followed by privatization funds (20 percent of privatized firms). Although division of ownership and management was the norm, the owners seem to be relatively active in monitoring their firms: almost all (94 percent) of the managers of privatized companies in the sample consult "regularly" (74 percent) or "occasionally" (20 percent) with their main shareholders. (Full distributions of sample firms by ownership type, country, size, and industrial sector are in appendix A.)

Table 5.1 presents the summary statistics of the annual rates of growth of revenues and (labor and material) costs per unit of revenues for the firms in our sample over the 1990–1993 period. The statistics clearly show the extent to which the early stages of the postcommunist transition were characterized by a downward pressure on revenues for

Table 5.1
Average Annual Rate of Growth of Firms, 1990–93

	State firms	Insider-owned firms		Outsider-owned firms	
		Preprivatization	Postprivatization	Preprivatization	Postprivatization
Revenue					
Mean	−19.47	−13.29	−11.75	−19.48	−4.00
Standard deviation	20.37	23.26	19.66	20.16	25.87
Minimum	−67.16	−52.56	−62.80	−57.35	−71.88
25th percentile	−32.67	−25.50	−25.05	−34.93	−21.48
Median	−21.82	−15.42	−11.75	−18.50	−6.33
75th percentile	−7.70	−7.38	−1.69	−5.68	11.15
Maximum	89.15	58.03	52.10	45.49	80.41
Number of observations	224	34	41	62	151
Cost per unit of revenue					
Mean	3.73	3.90	6.61	0.95	−2.90
Standard deviation	14.93	13.84	23.13	18.32	18.68
Minimum	−26.69	−16.21	−57.77	−35.98	−55.90
25th percentile	−4.81	−5.64	−7.80	−12.71	−11.01
Median	2.60	0.26	2.77	0.00	−2.39
75th percentile	11.02	11.31	21.10	15.27	5.04
Maximum	59.89	41.72	59.42	41.69	58.22
Number of observations	138	26	35	40 107	

all types of firms. The collapse of the COMECON market for the products of many postcommunist enterprises and the loss of other previously captive markets shrank the revenue base of most firms: in each year between 1990 and 1993, more than 80 percent of state and more than 64 percent of privatized firms lost revenues, with most of them losing more than 25 of their sales in 1990–1991 period alone. With the employment reductions and cost cutting often insufficient to catch up with the collapse of the sales, the pressure of the transition drove up the costs per unit of revenue.[20]

III. Ownership and Performance

The effects of ownership on firm performance, which may be glimpsed from the statistics in Table 5.1, were analyzed in detail by Frydman and coauthors.[21] A breakdown of the results showed that the impact of different types of private owners on firm performance was too diverse to allow for meaningful generalizations at the level of a "privatized firm"; instead, the appropriate level of generality seemed to call for less inclusive groupings of "insider-owned" firms (i.e., those owned by employees, managers, or both) and privatized firms owned by outside investors. Using fixed-effects panel regressions to estimate the impact of ownership type on firm performance, studies found that outsider-owned privatized firms had significantly (nearly 10 percentage point) higher annual revenue growth than either state- or insider-owned firms,[22] but that no significant differences could be detected in terms of (labor or material) cost performance between any two groups of firms (see table 5.2). The performance of state- and insider-owned firms was statistically indistinguishable, both in terms of revenue and cost performance.

These results were controlled for differences in the macroeconomic environment of the three countries; they persisted across all industrial sectors in which the sample firms operated and could not be attributed to possible performance "dips" in the years immediately preceding privatization. They were not driven by either a handful of well-performing firms or a few poorly performing firms (remaining virtually unchanged when the data set was trimmed at the 5th and 95th percentiles); and they were controlled for possible selection bias, both at the firm and the ownership-type level.[23] They thus provide robust evidence of a differential impact of ownership on firm performance, both in terms of a significantly better revenue performance of outsider-owned firms and the contrast between the effect of ownership on revenue and cost performance.

TABLE 5.2
The Effects of Privatization on Outsider- and Insider-Owned Firms

	Annual rate of growth of revenue	*Annual rate of growth of cost per unit of revenue*
Privatization effects		
Outsiders[a]	**9.70*** (3.64)	−4.36 (3.33)
Insiders[a]	0.68 (5.28)	1.12 (4.45)
Test statistics for the model	$n = 513, F = 7.05$* adj $R^2 = 0.13$	$n = 347, F = 5.27$* adj $R^2 = 0.14$
Test statistics for the equality of group effects	$F = 1.24$ $p = 0.29$	$F = 0.42$ $p = 0.66$

Source: Full statistics are reported in Frydman et al. (1999). See note 3, present chapter.

Note: Standard errors in parentheses, significant coefficients in bold face. Group-effects estimates. Group effects and coefficients on initial values of performance measure and country-year variables not reported here.

[a]A dummy variable set to 1 for the postprivatization performance of privatized firms where the given type of owner is the largest shareholder, 0 otherwise. State-owned enterprises are the reference group.

*$p \leq 0.01$; **$p \leq 0.05$; ***$p \leq 0.10$.

IV. Ownership, Restructuring, and Entrepreneurship

There are two basic ways in which firms can improve their overall performance: they may cut costs or increase their revenues. It has been suggested that, in the environment of the postcommunist transition, there may be significant differences in the restructuring activities required to succeed in these two objectives.[24] Grosfeld and Roland therefore distinguish between a "defensive" (cost-focused) and "strategic" (revenue-focused) restructuring, and they hypothesize that a firm's ownership may affect the type of restructuring the firm selects.[25]

To cut costs, the notorious waste of the communist production system must be reduced, as must be the equally notorious overstaffing. Hoarding, made necessary by the constant shortages of the old regime, must give way to modern inventory management; assets unrelated to the main line of business must be shed; unprofitable production lines must be closed; materials must be used more rationally; and often the use of floor space must be redesigned. Whatever else is involved in this type of defensive restructuring, it usually revolves around a relatively straightforward application of the established principles of management, and faced with a hardening of the budget constraints, all firms, regardless of ownership, must engage in it or perish. The finding that ownership does not affect cost performance of firms in our sample in fact means that firms with different ownership types do not differ between themselves in terms of the success of their defensive restructuring.

There are reasons to believe, however, that the restructuring necessary to improve the revenue side of a firm's operation is of a different nature. Indeed, the skills required to improve sales of most companies in the transition environment—when the old markets have collapsed, imports have introduced overnight competition from the most advanced world producers, and buyers have become more careful and demanding—are not that different from those needed to start a new business: with some additional constraints (such as the existing labor force or the already available machinery), the postcommunist firms must reinvent their products and find markets in which they can be sold. Discovering an area of a firm's comparative advantage calls for much more innovation and involves much greater uncertainty than eliminating the relatively obvious waste and laying off excess labor.

The difference between strategic and defensive restructuring is particularly stark in the circumstances of the postcommunist transition because the inefficiencies of the old enterprises are quite obvious, while their products are mostly worthless, and thus the company's future depends primarily on finding a new niche in the completely new environment of competitive markets. Nevertheless, the difference between cost and revenue restructuring probably has wider application and reflects principles of more universal significance. Although uncertainty is quite ubiquitous in corporate practice, the results of cost-related changes tend to be generally known to company insiders with a relatively higher degree of certainty than those related to revenue generation. The reason for this is that cost-cutting measures, while not always routine, are more a matter of managerial skill, based on techniques involving relatively predictable risks. Revenue generation, by contrast, is inherently oriented toward anticipating future decisions of other agents (customers and competitors) and, for this reason, is not only risky, but also subject to risks that are hard or impossible to compute on the basis of past history.[26]

At the root of the difference between cost and revenue restructuring may thus lie a difference between handling largely predictable (i.e., objectively recognizable) risks and dealing with unpredictable or radical uncertainty—something that might involve two different skills of great importance in every economy, and not just in the special circumstances of the postcommunist transition. While the first skill is one of managerial "science" (i.e., a discipline based on generally applicable principles) the second involves the rather ill-defined combination of abilities often referred to as "entrepreneurship."[27]

The nature of entrepreneurship is sometimes explained in terms of different attitudes toward risk[28] and in terms of the agents' ability to spot and pursue business opportunities.[29] But the concept remains somewhat vague and the relationship between entrepreneurship and ownership remains largely unexplored. In what follows we explore, therefore, the nature of entrepreneurship as manifested in the revenue restructuring of firms in the process of transition.

V. Product Restructuring and Its Effectiveness

We asked the chief production officers (CPOs) of our sample firms to list four product groups that contributed most to the firm's gross annual revenues in each sample year.[30] We also asked them to identify changes in each of these groups introduced in the subsequent years and to list all new product groups (regardless of their contribution to revenue) introduced during each year.

On the basis of these questions, we constructed a category of *major product-restructuring measures* by grouping together the following: (1) introduction of new product groups; (2) introduction of major new products within an existing product group; (3) major changes in design or packaging of existing products; and (4) introduction of major new production processes. The rationale behind this grouping was to isolate those changes in the firm's product portfolio that are aimed at gaining new markets or retaining the vanishing old ones, rather than straightforward cost-cutting operations.[31] An introduction of new or improved products may or may not increase sales, but it is likely to require outlays that may contribute to a deterioration of a firm's cash flows, balance sheet position, or both.[32] Undertaking such innovations is more likely to involve a substantially higher degree of uncertainty and higher business risk than implementing most cost-reduction measures.

Table 5.3 presents summary measures of revenue-restructuring activities among firms with different types of owners. Over the entire sample period, the proportion of firms that introduced at least one major product restructuring measure is very similar among all ownership groupings (with no statistically significant differences between any two types of firms).[33] To be sure, this statistic counts only changes implemented by privatized firms *after* they had been privatized (while for state firms, changes throughout the sample period are recognized) and thus could hide a greater frequency of major product changes among privatized firms. But the average number of major product restructuring measures per firm per year—probably the most accurate measure of the frequency of major changes—also shows no significant differences among firms with different types of owners.[34]

TABLE 5.3
Major Product-Restructuring Measures Undertaken by Firms with Different Types of Owners (1990–93)

	State firms	*Outsider-owned firms*[a]	*Insider-owned firms*[a]
Number (percentage) of firms with major product-restructuring measures[b]	69 (77%)	73 (75%)	18 (60%)
Average number of major changes[c]	3.51	1.87	2.30
Average number of years with major changes[c]	1.86	1.28	1.40
Average number of major changes per year[c]	1.17	1.00	1.27

[a]Values for postprivatization periods only.
[b]Over the entire sample period (1990–94).
[c]For firms that introduced at least one major product change.

We also looked into patterns, as opposed to mere frequency, of product-restructuring measures among firms with different types of owners, and, again, we were unable to discover any significant differences that could explain differences in performance. The incidence of particular types of product-restructuring measures (the introduction of new products or product groups or of changes in design, packaging, or production processes) was very similar in all ownership groupings, as was the occurrence of a large number of combinations of measures we tested.

The fact that differences in neither frequency nor pattern of major product restructuring explain differential revenue performance of firms with different types of owners raises the question of whether the measures of product restructuring we have chosen are indeed components of the "strategic restructuring" that is supposed to help improve the sales performance of firms in the postcommunist transition. We have therefore tested the impact of the activities we identified as "major product-restructuring measures" on the revenue performance of firms in our sample by estimating a fixed-effects regression in which the firms were split according to their ownership type and variables were included to control for initial firm size and country-year effects.[35] Since our revenue data are for calendar years, and privatization occurred, of course, at different times of the year, the effect of postprivatization restructuring in the year of privatization may be expected to be less (since it is given a shorter period of time to be felt) than when the firm operates as a private company for an entire year. As this could affect the averages (especially when the postprivatization period is generally short), we separated the year of privatization effects from the subsequent years' effects.

The results, reported in table 5.4, indicate that the product-restructuring measures we identified as potentially responsible for the superior revenue performance of outsider-owned privatized firms, as compared with their state- or insider-owned counterparts, are indeed an important factor in explaining their success, since outsider-controlled firms that did *not* restructure their products (in the sense we have identified) performed similarly to state- and insider-owned firms, while those that did significantly outperformed their state- ($p < .01$) and insider-owned ($p < .05$) counterparts.[36] The outsider-owned firms that restructured their products also performed in subsequent years significantly better than those that did not ($p < .05$).

But if major product-restructuring measures are a necessary condition of significant improvements in revenue performance, they are not sufficient, since essentially the same restructuring measures that allow outsider-owned firms to better their performance lead to no improvement in either state- or insider-owned firms—indeed, major product restructuring seems to make no difference in their case.[37] In other words, it is an *interaction of ownership and restructuring*, rather than restructuring alone, strategic or not, that seems to be the key to a firm's ability to gain new markets and ensure long-term survival.

From a theoretical point of view this may at first seem a disappointing result, since the concept of strategic restructuring does not appear, after all, to explain the advantages of ownership; quite the other way around, ownership seems to be, in the end, needed to explain why some firms succeed where others fail in their restructuring efforts. But on reflection, the fact that the difference made by ownership cannot be reduced to an objectively ascertainable combination of restructuring measures or their frequency should not be surprising: if the advantages of ownership could be explained in this way, they would be ipso facto explained *away*, for it is difficult to see why the management of any firm, regardless of ownership, could not be charged with undertaking the same types of measures and deliver the same sort of performance.

The familiar theory of the firm as a nexus of contracts suggests that ownership is a solution to the problem of the inherent incompleteness of contracts and thus probably *substitutes* for an unavailable system of objectively ascertainable rules of behavior (which could be used to bind contractually the agents responsible for company performance). This

Table 5.4
The Impact of Major Product-Restructuring on Revenue Growth (panel regressions, group fixed-effects specification)

	Annual rate of revenue growth
State firms	
With no major product restructuring	—
With major product restructuring	−1.09
	(3.06)
Outsider-owned privatized firms[a]	
With no major product restructuring	
Year of privatization	4.57
	(5.69)
Subsequent years	4.84
	(4.83)
With major product restructuring	
Year of restructuring	**10.13****
	(5.25)
Subsequent years	**15.62***
	(4.43)
Insider-owned privatized firms[a]	
With no major product restructuring	
Year of privatization	−4.53
	(7.71)
Subsequent years	4.01
	(7.1)
With major product restructuring	
Year of restructuring	−0.99
	(9.04)
Subsequent years	−2.21
	(8.09)
Country-year effects	
Czech Republic	
Year 2	**15.94***
	(4.77)
Year 3	**16.14***
	(4.65)
Hungary	
Year 1	3.52
	(4.52)
Year 2	**13.89***
	(4.47)
Year 3	**9.52***
	(4.54)

(*continued*)

Table 5.4 (*continued*)

	Annual rate of revenue growth
Poland	
Year 1	2.90
	(5.66)
Year 2	**10.06***
	(5.44)
Year 3	**9.42****
	(5.17)
Initial level of revenues	**−0.17***
	(0.05)
Test statistics for the model	$n = 501$ $F = 4.88^*$, adj. $R^2 = 0.13$
Test statistics for the equality of group effects	$F = 0.62,\ p = 0.54$

Note: Standard errors in parentheses, significant coefficients in bold face. Revenues measured in constant local prices; initial levels of revenue are in US$ millions.

[a]A dummy variable set to 1 for the postprivatization performance of firms where the given type of owner is the largest shareholder, 0 otherwise.

$^*p \leq 0.05$; $^{**}p \leq 0.10$.

suggests, in turn, that an explanation of the role of ownership in corporate experience is not likely to lie in the *what* of corporate practice, like an explanation of what needs to be done, say, to put together the components of a machine (although here too a whole variety of complex skills is assumed). Rather, an account of ownership can be expected to resemble an account of what it means to be an artist or a sportsperson. Even if a number of things, such as training, perseverance, and devotion, without which artistry or sporting behavior is not possible, can be specified (and followed by all aspiring artists or sportspeople), there will always remain an element of "how" (i.e., a *tacit*, perhaps even *ineffable*, skill or knowledge that may be brought out and clarified to some extent, but that resists a reduction to an objectively available system of rules).

It is this element of at least partially tacit skill or knowledge, which gives the firms controlled by certain types of owners an advantage in improving revenue performance, that we identify with *entrepreneurship*. We have mentioned already that entrepreneurship has been associated with certain attitudes toward risk and an ability to spot and pursue business opportunities. We will attempt to clarify this concept further, but whatever the precise nature of the skill involved, we would like to examine first a recently advanced hypothesis concerning the contribution of ownership to the entrepreneurial behavior of firms and their managers.

VI. Why Ownership Matters: The Human Capital Hypothesis

Like every skill, entrepreneurship is likely to be, to some extent, a personal characteristic: some people may be naturally more prepared than others to accept risks or be able to spot business (or other) opportunities. Since these two characteristics are commonly seen as essential components of entrepreneurship, some people thus may be naturally more entrepreneurial than others. Indeed, it would not be surprising if this characteristic were, to a large extent, innate. But as with other skills or talents, people who are capable of entrepreneurship may not be able to develop or exercise it unless the conditions are right. Thus, the incentive systems under which businesspeople operate may also play an important role. Are the advantages of firms with certain types of owners related to the fact that people in control of them are simply more skillful at what they do than those in other firms, or are they related to a better incentive structure that some types of ownership provide? In recent literature, Barberis and coauthors have advocated the view that performance differences between firms with different types of ownership in the postcommunist environment are primarily attributable to fact that certain types of privatization "select owners and managers who are better at running firms efficiently" (i.e., to the superior human capital of the persons in control of the better-performing firms).[38]

It is important to clarify what it would mean to deny that human-capital improvements are the engine of success of the firms privatized to outsiders. First, it should be clear whose human capital is at issue. Most obviously, successful firms may have more skillful managers (whether or not they own equity) who run firms on a day-to-day basis. But privatization may also lead to a transfer of ownership to new persons whose superior skills *as owners* may perhaps be decisive for the firm's success. These skills may vary from the ability to choose managers (thus leading to higher average managerial human capital) to all kinds of other qualities an owner may exhibit in making basic corporate decisions.

In what follows, we will be mostly concerned with the relative importance of managerial human-capital differences, as compared to different incentive structures of these corporate decision makers. To the extent that owners themselves are managers (as was predominantly the case in the sample of shops and other small businesses examined by Barberis and coauthors),[39] or as far as differences in the owners' human capital manifest themselves in their choice of managers, our evidence concerning the importance of managerial human capital will also bear on the importance of the human capital of the owners. We will have no opportunity, however, to assess the importance of the quality of nonmanagerial owners' human capital insofar as these owners may be involved in a host of other corporate decisions where their skill may contribute to the firms' success. Although ownership is very concentrated in our sample of firms and there are reasons to believe that the nonmanagerial owners are consulted about major corporate decisions, we assume that the basic skills involved in running the firms in which management and ownership are separated lies with the managers, not the owners. To the extent that the owners are not passive, we assume that their role, beyond that of choosing management, is limited to monitoring and that the assumption of risk for major decisions is proposed and executed by the management.

Second, it would be foolish to deny that entrepreneurship is largely a matter of personal skill: some people are surely better than others at making the risky, often idiosyncratic restructuring decisions allowing their firms to conquer new markets and increase their revenues. In the absence of such skills, no amount of incentives will make a firm really successful, much as no amount of promised rewards will make most people run a four-minute mile or become world-class tennis players. Certainly, successful entrepreneurship is a matter of human capital in *this* sense.

But while human capital is a necessary condition of success, it would also be improbable if incentives did not matter: even the most skilled manager would not be likely to succeed, if success were punished, for example, rather than rewarded. Moreover, if different types of firms offered different incentives to people possessing certain types of skills (say, some rewarded entrepreneurship, while others put a premium on the ability to cut costs or run large organizations), one would expect managers with different types of skills to allocate themselves, over time, among different types of firms. As a result, to the extent that firms with different types of owners rewarded, say, different managerial skills, one would expect differences in the type of managerial human capital to track differences in ownership types, thus making it very difficult to separate the impact of incentives from the impact of managerial human-capital improvements.

The question of incentives versus human capital must, therefore, be one of their relative contribution. In particular, it would be interesting to find out, on the one hand, whether some owners, independently of the incentive structure they provide for their management, are indeed better than others at picking better managers and, on the other hand, whether different incentive structures associated with different types of ownership yield differences in performance even in the absence of human capital differences.

We explore these issues in two ways. First, although in a mature economy one may expect differences in human capital and incentive structures to go together, in a transition economy, especially in the early period, the market for managerial talent may not have had time to operate, and we may therefore be able to observe that ownership-related performance differences are not paralleled by differences in the characteristics of persons in control (which would indicate that other factors, in particular, incentives provided by the firms for their management,[40] are driving the differences in performance). Second, we examine the performance of firms in which the type of ownership has changed (as a result of privatization), but that continue to be managed by the *same* persons.

Our survey provides extensive information about the managers of both state and privatized firms, including their age, education, length of tenure, previous occupation, political beliefs, attitudes toward market economy and political changes since 1989, opinions about the role of the state and about the importance of various business objectives. All in all, despite substantial efforts, we have been unable to identify any systematic differences between enterprises with different types of owners. Since it has often been assumed that the old communist managers, who had been picked more for their ideological loyalty and their ability to maneuver within the Byzantine communist hierarchy, were less competent than the new people appointed after the change of the regime, the data concerning managerial turnover, presented in table 5.5, may be of special interest.[41] What they show is that, unlike in Russia (where the small businesses studied by Barberis and coauthors were located),[42] the managerial turnover in central Europe has been high (though predictably somewhat lower in insider-controlled firms) and that the rate of replacement of the old managers was not significantly higher in the better-performing outsider-controlled privatized firms than in, say, the lagging state firms. It is also noteworthy that the proportion of promotions from within (which may have been more likely to pick up members of the old nomenklatura) among the firms privatized to outside investors is not significantly different from that in state firms. Nor are the managers of firms privatized to outsiders likely to be any younger than their counterparts in state- and insider-controlled firms.

But perhaps the data on the rate of managerial turnover or the "profiles" of managers do not really capture the effectiveness of managerial changes in firms with different types of owners. Therefore, in order to examine more precisely the relative impact of ownership change and managerial turnover, we contrasted the performance of state-, insider-, and outsider-owned firms that did not change their management during the sample period with the pre- and postchange performance of firms in which the management did change.[43] We also controlled for the countries in which the firms were located, macroeconomic changes, and initial firm size. The results are presented in table 5.6. (In the left-hand column under "Annual Rate of Revenue Growth," for the firms that did change their management during the sample period, only the

Table 5.5
CEOs of State and Privatized Firms

	State firms	*Outsider-owned firms*	*Insider-owned firms*
Number of firms	72	85	29
Firms in which new CEO appointed during 1990–94 (%)	75	72	55
Of these firms, CEO promoted from within (%)	61	54	31
Privatized firms in which present CEO appointed at or after privatization (%)	—	49	45
Average age of present CEO	46	47	49
Firms in which present CEO is			
less than 40 years old (%)	21	14	11
between 40 and 50 years old (%)	51	46	41
more than 50 years old (%)	28	40	48

first managerial change is recognized; in the right-hand column, only the *last* managerial change is recognized.)

Even on the assumption that old managers were, by and large, incompetent and that managerial turnover, at least in the case of firms controlled by some types of owners, is among the most basic forms of postcommunist restructuring,[44] performance comparisons of firms with new and old management are not likely to yield interesting results. If a given type of owner is expected to be able to identify bad managers and replace them with good ones, then, when the wave of pruning is completed (as, given the size of the turnover in the first three years, seems to be the case in our sample), the retained old managers are likely to be the ones who are not incompetent and the firms they control should not perform worse than those in which the management did change. If, however, the owner is presumed to be unable to separate the wheat from the chaff, then the new managers should not be expected to be better than the old. The estimates reported in table 5.6 support this conjecture. When the postchange performance of firms that changed management (i.e., those in which the owners presumably considered the performance of the incumbents unsatisfactory) is compared to that of firms that did *not* change management at all (i.e,. to those in which the owners were presumably satisfied), no statistically significant difference is found, regardless of whether the first or the last managerial change is recognized (although the size of the coefficients indicates that the firms under new management may be somewhat more successful).

Table 5.6
The Impact of Managerial Change on Revenue Growth
(panel regression, group fixed-effects specification)

	Annual rate of revenue growth	
	First managerial change recognized	*Last managerial change recognized*
State firms		
With no managerial change	—	—
Prior to managerial change	−4.47	−5.57
	(4.28)	(3.95)
Following managerial change	−0.21	3.08
	(3.98)	(4.25)
Outsider-owned Firms[a]		
With no managerial change	**10.99***	**11.30***
	(4.50)	(4.46)
Prior to managerial change[b]	9.57	8.61
	(6.26)	(5.94)
Following managerial change[b]	**15.67***	**18.51***
	(5.88)	(6.03)
Insider-owned firms with no managerial change[a]	−6.76	−6.38
	(6.17)	(6.13)
Czech Republic		
Year 2	**17.33***	**17.13***
	(4.88)	(4.83)
Year 3	**14.10***	**13.54***
	(4.74)	(4.70)
Hungary		
Year 1	4.19	4.52
	(4.58)	(4.55)
Year 2	**13.80***	**13.93***
	(4.57)	(4.53)
Year 3	**10.62***	**10.13***
	(4.61)	(4.57)
Poland		
Year 1	1.39	3.19
	(6.35)	(6.37)
Year 2	7.94	9.35
	(5.85)	(5.81)
Year 3	**8.99****	**9.11****
	(5.33)	(5.26)
Initial level of revenues	**−0.17***	**−0.17***
	(0.05)	(0.05)

(*continued*)

Table 5.5 (*continued*)

	Annual rate of revenue growth	
	First managerial change recognized	Last managerial change recognized
Test statistics for the model	$n = 413, F = 5.25$* adj. $R^2 = 0.16$	$n = 413, F = 5.69$* adj. $R^2 = 0.17$
Test statistics for the equality of group effects	$F = 1.09, p = 0.35$	$F = 1.09, p = 0.35$

Note: Standard errors in parenthesis; significant coefficients on nonconstant terms in bold face. Revenues measured in constant local prices, initial revenues in US$ millions.

[a]A dummy variable set to 1 for the postprivatization performance of privatized firms where the given type of owner is the largest shareholder, 0 otherwise.

[b]Postprivatization periods only.

*$p \leq 0.05$; **$p \leq 0.10$.

This does not mean, however, that managerial changes are not beneficial; just that their effect is not likely to be gauged by comparison with firms that did not change managers. The proper yardstick is the difference between the pre- and postchange performance of firms that did change their management. According to this criterion, managerial change is probably beneficial in both state- and outsider-controlled firms: although the postchange improvement is not significant when performance before and after the *first* managerial change is compared, it becomes significant for both types of firms when performance before and after the *last* change is compared (which allows the owners to change managers more than once if the first change does not bring the desired effects).[45] But since the improvements from managerial turnover are significant and of similar magnitude in both state- and outsider-controlled firms, they do not seem to be ownership related.[46] Whatever the impact of ownership, it must be felt elsewhere.

Comparisons of firms with different types of owners in which *no* managerial change took place since the fall of the communist regime are much more relevant—and telling—with respect to the question of the impact of ownership. Outsider-owned privatized firms that did *not* change their management still outperform their state- and insider-owned counterparts by significant margins—indeed, with respect to state-owned firms, the margin is roughly the same as that separating *all* outsider-owned privatized firms from all state firms.[47] Moreover, the superior performance of outsider-owned firms cannot be explained by any selection bias attributable to the fact that new private owners of these firms might have kept only good managers in place and fired the bad ones (while perhaps the state was not equally skillful in its staffing decisions). Although such selection is likely to have occurred, it does not account for the superior performance of this group of privatized firms. Not only do panel regressions correct for such bias, but the group effects for the outsider-owned firms with no managerial change are virtually identical to those for state-owned firms.[48] Since those effects gauge preprivatization performance of privatized firms, the identity implies that prior to their privatization, the outsider-owned firms' performance was, on average, the same as that of their state-owned counterparts, and thus the managers in charge of them did not seem to stand out in any way prior to privatization. In the wake of privatization, however, even though the *same* managers remained in charge, the performance of their firms shot upward in comparison to their state-owned counterparts, indicating that something other than differences in the quality of managerial human capital is primarily responsible for the differences in the performance.

In summary, then, differences in the quality of managerial human capital (or in the owners' skill in picking managers) are not likely to be responsible for the bulk of the performance differences between outsider-controlled privatized firms and their state- or insider-owned counterparts. Both state and privatized firms seem to appoint new managers in firms that lag in performance behind their peers, and in both types of firms such changes seem to lead to performance improvements. But the performance differentials of firms controlled by different types of owners are essentially independent of their (basically similar) managerial appointment policies: the outsider-owned firms, whether or not they change management, outperform state firms by similar margins *in every category* (including prechange performance of firms that changed management).

VII. Ownership and Entrepreneurship

We argued that cost restructuring is primarily a matter of political will and managerial skills, while revenue generation requires entrepreneurship. Given the disappearance of previously captive markets for the inferior products of most firms, and the need of the postcommunist firms to "reinvent" themselves in product markets, strategic, revenue-oriented restructuring is inherently risky.[49] This, in turn, makes two factors—which we see as the defining characteristics of entrepreneurship—of special importance: (1) the risk attitudes of the decision makers and (2) the constraints on the types of risks they can justify.

Both these factors are related to incentives, and not just skills, and the incentives may depend on the ownership structure. Different payoffs faced by decision makers as an outcome of their decisions may be different in firms with different types of owners. Furthermore, regardless of the payoffs attached to different outcomes of particular decisions, the control structure of firms with different types of owners may impose different degrees of accountability, and this, in turn, may narrow the range of opportunities that managers of certain types of firms may be expected to pursue.

To begin with risk attitudes, the incentive structure induced by state ownership may be the most serious problem. Managers of state companies have their human capital heavily invested in their jobs and are thus exposed to the downside of risky projects, the failure of which may threaten their positions. However, they have only a limited expectation of participating in the potential upside of their decisions. As a result, they are likely to be generally risk averse, except when their firms are close to collapse (or when their jobs are already threatened because of the firm's inferior performance). In the latter case, managers of state firms may become risk prone because the downside of risky decisions becomes low to them (though not to the firm), while an even small chance of success promises to save their jobs.[50]

The incentives of the persons in control of insider-owned firms are somewhat more conducive to risk taking, as the upside of risky decisions may bring significant payoffs to the decision makers. But the problem of undiversified, firm-specific investment of both the human and financial capital of insider-owners is even more severe than in the case of state-owned firms and may be a serious impediment to their willingness to bear the degree of risk required for success in the uncertain environment of the transition, except when the survival of the firm is already seriously endangered.

A different pattern of behavior may be expected in a firm owned by an outside investor. As we already noted, most of such firms in our sample have very concentrated ownership, and their owners are likely to be actively involved in ratifying major managerial decisions.[51] At the same time, the most successful outsider-owned firms are controlled by institutions, such as privatization funds and foreign investors, who are also able to diversify their risks. They are thus both likely to be less risk averse and to impose their risk preferences on the managers in control of daily operations. Benefiting fully from the upside and paying for the downside of all decisions, these owners may be expected to maximize the value of the firm and will be prepared to ratify risky decisions, if the payoffs justify the risks. Unless the firm is heavily leveraged (as few privatized firms in our sample are; see note 47), these owners are also less likely to play Russian roulette with the firm when it is in financial difficulties, since the firm will have some residual value to them even if the business is not going well.

This pattern of risk attitudes is quite consistent with the different effectiveness of product-restructuring measures we observe in our sample. If outsider-owned privatized firms engage in more risky types of restructuring, introducing radical changes and seizing the opportunities that present themselves, they can expect consistently higher returns than the firms controlled by more risk averse owners. Similarly, if the latter undertake the more risky forms of major product restructuring, not in response to opportunities that arise when their firms do relatively better and can focus on changing their offerings, but when they are in distress and have to fight for survival, the results may be expected to be inferior.

The second, much less commonly observed factor that we believe to be constitutive of entrepreneurship is related to the absence of constraints that a control structure may impose on the ability to make idiosyncratic decisions. Entrepreneurship is not a science: it does not proceed in accordance with well-understood rules or a knowledge that can be objectively demonstrated.[52] Instead, entrepreneurial decisions involve a large measure of ineffable skills and an often quite idiosyncratic evaluation of the situation that may be very difficult or impossible to explain to an outside observer. If the control structure of a firm requires, therefore, that decision makers be able to *justify* what they do, this may severely restrict the opportunity set out of which a feasible project must be chosen. The very feature of an approach taken by entrepreneurs that allows them to succeed by breaking the mold of routine, rule-governed behavior makes it very difficult for them to convey their "hunches" or "intuitions" to others whose views are within the prevailing consensus.

Again, the manager of a state firm or a bureaucrat charged with its supervision is at the greatest disadvantage here. It is the modus operandi of the state, for which there is ample justification in the political sphere, that officials must be *accountable* for what they do in terms of intersubjectively accessible principles. But in the context of business decisions, the rule of bureaucratic accountability is likely to restrict the possibility of entrepreneurship. An assignment of probabilities, for example, is required to assess the expected payoff from a creative project, such as a bet on a new product or a far-reaching design change. Under conditions of change and uncertainty, an objective (statistical) assignment of probabilities is likely to be extremely difficult or impossible. In such situations, an idiosyncratic, subjective assignment of probabilities to future events that turns out to be accurate after the fact is a paradigmatic example of entrepreneurship that allows some to increase their chances of success where others are most likely to fail.

But precisely because the assignment is subjective, it is difficult for decision makers in firms in which the principle of bureaucratic accountability is the rule to pursue such entrepreneurial projects. Even if a decision is right, the decision makers might be unable to clear it in advance with their monitors or, if they take full responsibility for it, explain it adequately if things go wrong.[53] Moreover, this difficulty is not the result of any "deficiency" of the monitors to whom the decision maker is accountable. Precisely because entrepreneurship involves idiosyncratic, subjective insights, the monitors who are unpersuaded by them are not only perfectly within their rights to reject them, but would be derelict in their duty if they accepted them against their own best judgment. Decisions that are worth making, therefore, including many product innovations that owners, who need not account to anyone for what they do, will be likely to ratify, may for this very reason not be taken by decision makers in state enterprises.

The constraint of accountability is not an obstacle in a managerially owned firm, but there are few of those in our sample of firms for which we have sufficiently complete product-restructuring data.[54] Most of the insider-dominated firms in our sample are worker owned, and the problem of accountability is potentially serious here. The principals of worker-owned firms suffer from collective action problems, aggravated by conflicts of interest whenever the workforce is also not homogeneous.[55] As a result, decisions are likely to require discussion and consensus, where entrepreneurship calls for a hierarchically imposed resolution with no accountability beyond the rewards and punishments delivered by the market.

By contrast, an outsider-owned firm with highly concentrated ownership apparently entails a control structure conducive to entrepreneurial decisions. Although the management of these firms is in control of day-to-day decisions, major risky projects need to be ratified by the owner. Owners, however, need not base their approval on objectively verifiable principles—it is enough that they trust their managers or have an independent sense of the appropriateness of the decision to be able to ratify it without further explanation and to assume all the risks it involves.

If the explanations proposed here to account for the superior effectiveness of product restructuring by outsider-owned firms is correct, the difference that ownership makes with respect to corporate performance should—according with our expectations—be observable not in the broad categories of restructuring undertaken by firms with different types of ownership, but rather in the different degrees of risk attached to various projects. This, in turn, suggests an empirical test capable of capturing the risk differentials of decisions made by firms with different types of owners: if the opportunity set that accountable decision makers are likely to face is narrower than that of the decision makers who need not explain their actions, and if outside owners are generally more likely to take justifiable risks than the insiders and state officials, the performance of firms with outside owners should be characterized not only by higher averages, but also by a significantly greater *variance* of outcomes than that of the other types of firms.

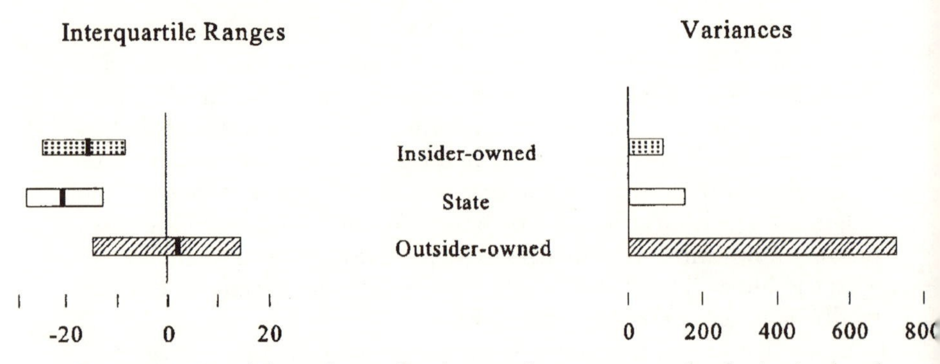

Figure 5.1 Variability of annualized rates of revenue growth of privatized and state firm with major product changes.

Figure 5.1 summarizes the differences in the variability of the annualized rates of revenue growth between the firms with different types of ownership that had introduced major product-restructuring measures. The left part of figure 5.1 shows the interquartile ranges of the annualized rates of revenue growth of firms with different ownership types, with the thick marks indicating the mean values. The rightward shift of the mean value of performance for outsider-owned firms is accompanied by a pronounced lengthening of the interquartile range, which (at 27.82) is nearly twice as large as that of state- (16.22) or insider-owned (15.50) firms.

The differences in the variability of annual rates of revenue growth are captured by the variances of the corresponding distributions, shown in the right part of figure 5.1: the differences in both moments between outsider-owned and the other types of firms are significant at p-values less than to 0.01, regardless of the time period over which the performance of state firms is evaluated. By contrast, in the absence of major product changes the variance of annualized rates of revenue growth for outsider-owned firms is statistically indistinguishable from that for state- ($p = 0.27$) or insider-owned ($p = 0.52$) firms.

These results are consistent with our hypothesis that the superior results of product restructuring by firms privatized to outside owners are a function of their greater willingness to accept risks and their freedom to make decisions without having to justify them to employee owners or a hierarchy of state officials. Entrepreneurship certainly involves skills and abilities—risk taking and nonaccountability pay off only when the decision maker uses them to good purpose. But entrepreneurial skills may also be inherently tied to certain types of ownership because only the incentives provided by such ownership may create the proper conditions for their exercise.

Appendix A: Sample Description

Table 5.A1
Distributions of Sample Firms by Year of Privatization and Firm Size

		Number of firms[a] privatized					*Average revenues (US$ mil, constant prices)*		*Average employment (full-time employees)*	
	All	*1990*	*1991*	*1992*	*1993*	*1994*	*1990*	*1993*	*1990*	*1993*
All countries										
State firms	90						17.6	11.0	876	573
Outsider-owned firms	95	12	16	37	26	4	22.5	16.2	882	647
Insider-owned firms	30	1	4	12	10	3	6.0	5.1	404	325
Czech Republic										
State firms	23						22.2	13.0	1343	797
Outsider-owned firms[b]	50	—	5	29	15	1	25.4	17.1	1203	790
Insider-owned firms[b]	6	—	—	4	2	—	9.8	5.6	725	339
Hungary										
State firms	26						29.5	13.1	605	416
Outsider-owned firms	39	10	7	8	11	3	20.7	14.6	671	461
Insider-owned	24	1	4	8	8	3	5.6	5.0	376	323
Poland										
State firms	41						8.0	8.6	734	544
Outsider-owned firms[c]	6	2	4	—	—	—	—	19.5	—	914

[a]The sample descriptions given in this and other tables in this appendix pertain to the sample of firms in the growth of revenue regressions.

[b]In the Czech Republic, the year of privatization refers to the year in which the new owners assumed control rather than the year during which the shares were formally distributed.

[c]For Polish privatized firms, the 1990 revenue and employment levels were not provided.

TABLE 5.A2
Sectoral Distribution of Sample Firms

Industrial Sector (two-digit sic code)	*State firms*	*Outsider-owned firms*	*Insider-owned firms*
Food and beverages	18 (20%)	36 (38%)	7 (23%)
Clothing	12 (13%)	9 (10%)	10 (33%)
Furniture	13 (15%)	6 (6%)	3 (10%)
Textile	8 (9%)	13 (14%)	4 (13%)
Leather	7 (8%)	3 (3%)	3 (10%)
Chemicals	13 (14%)	8 (8%)	1 (3%)
Non-ferrous minerals	15 (16%)	19 (20%)	2 (7%)
Other	4 (4%)	1 (1%)	—
All	90 (100%)	95 (100%)	30 (100%)

TABLE 5. A3
Ownership Structure of Privatized Firms

Shareholder	*Firms in which the shareholder is the largest owner*	*Mean holdings when the shareholder is the largest owner (%)*
Foreign company	28	75
Czech Republic	9	66
Hungary	17	86
Poland	2	40
Private financial company	25	22
Czech Republic	24	20
Hungary	1	71
Domestic nonfinancial company	12	71
Czech Republic	5	76
Hungary	5	71
Poland	2	60
Domestic individual	12	63
Czech Republic	2	73
Hungary	9	58
Poland	1	80
State (in privatized firms)	18	41
Czech Republic	10	33
Hungary	7	49
Poland	1	60
Managerial employees	19	77
Czech Republic	6	92
Hungary	13	71
Nonmanagerial employees	11	69
Hungary	11	69

Appendix B: Methodological Note on Panel Regressions

The main results of this chapter are based on regression analyses of revenue and cost performance panel data provided by the sample firms. Although the panel regressions reported in different sections of the chapter vary in terms of variables used, the main features of most specifications are common, and we describe them here to avoid unnecessary repetitions.

We use a standard panel data treatment evaluation procedure[56] with the characteristic of interest (e.g., restructuring, managerial change) viewed as the "treatment" variable.[57] In all regressions, the outcome variable is the annual rate of growth of performance (revenues or costs) of a firm, and the effects of the treatment are controlled for differences in the initial levels of a firm performance as well as the macroeconomic conditions in the three countries.

All panel regressions are fixed-effects specifications. Let i index individual firms, j index their ownership grouping (e.g., state or privatized), k index the treatment (e.g., product restructuring, managerial change), and t index time (year). If y_{ijt}, the outcome variable, is the rate of growth of performance measure for firm i between $(t - 1)$ and t, the following is the group fixed-effects specification of performance equations involving comparisons of state and privatized firms:

$$y_{ijt} = \alpha_j + (P_{ijt} \times T_{ikt})\beta_{jk} + X_{ijt-1}\,\gamma + D_{ct}\delta_{ct} + \varepsilon_{ikt}. \qquad (1)$$

P_{ijt} is the ownership indicator variable equal to 1 if firm i operates as ownership type j firm in period t and 0 otherwise, and T_{ikt} is the treatment variable equal to 1 for posttreatment performance of firm i and 0 otherwise. X_{ijt-1} is the level of performance at the beginning of the period for which the rate of growth is computed (e.g., if the rate of growth of revenue is computed for the 1991–92 period, X_{ijt-1} is the level of revenues for 1991), included to control for differences in the initial conditions (such as firm size or extent of inefficiency), and D_{ct} is a set of country-year dummies controlling for possible differences in the macroeconomic environment of the three countries.

For evaluating the effects of a particular treatment (e.g., product restructuring) within a single ownership group of firms (e.g., state firms only), we restrict the sample to that group of firms and estimate equation (1) with the treatment variable T_{ijt} included and the ownership variable P_{ijt} excluded; similarly, for comparisons of the effects of ownership changes among firms with the same treatment, we restrict the sample to firms that either receive or do not receive the treatment and use equation (1) with the ownership variable P_{ijt} included and the treatment variable T_{ijt} omitted. (This is the equivalent of treating privatization as the only treatment variable.)

Equation (1) specifies fixed effects at the ownership group level. It thus assumes that firms grouped by ownership types have similar distributions of unobservable characteristics that influence performance outcomes , and therefore controls for possible selection bias stemming from nonrandom selection of firms for privatization to particular types of owners. In the firm fixed-effects specifications, group fixed effects α_j are replaced by firm fixed effects α_i. The firm fixed effects specification controls for possible selection bias stemming from the fact that firms grouped within a given ownership category may differ between themselves with respect to some unobserved characteristics correlated with performance outcomes.

Except for the predictable consequences of the loss of degrees of freedom associated with the firm fixed-effects specification, the two sets estimates were virtually identical in our sample. Inasmuch as in some cases comparisons of pretreatment performance of state and privatized firms are of interest, we discuss group fixed-effects estimates throughout the chapter. We do report, however, differences between the two sets of estimates whenever they arise.

Notes

One of the authors, Marek Hessel, died after this chapter was written, but before it was published. In grateful acknowledgment of his contributions, as well as his priceless friendship, Roman Frydman and Andrzej Rapaczynski dedicate this study to the memory of their coauthor.

This chapter is part of a larger study undertaken jointly by the Privatization Project and the World Bank. Cheryl Gray has participated in the design of the study and contributed ideas at all stages of the research project. The authors would like to thank Joel Turkewitz for his contributions to the design and implementation of the survey instrument, and Mihaela Popescu for her extraordinary assistance in the analysis of the data. Andrei Shleifer provided insightful comments on an earlier draft of this chapter, and his suggestions led us to substantial revisions. Helpful conversations with Joel Hellman, Sam Peltzman, Edmund Phelps, and Christoph Ruehl are also gratefully acknowledged.

The authors are grateful to the CEU Foundation, the Open Society Institute, and the World Bank for supporting research on this chapter. CV Starr Center for Applied Economics at New York University has provided additional support for Roman Frydman's research. None of these institutions are responsible for the opinions expressed in this chapter.

1. *See* William L. Megginson, Robert C. Nash, and M. van Randenborgh, *The Financial and Operating Performance of Newly Privatized Firms: An Empirical Analysis*, 49 J. Fin. 403–52 (1994).

2. *See* R. La Porta & F. López-de-Silanes, The Benefits of Privatization: Evidence from Mexico (Nat'l Bureau of Econ. Research Working Paper No. 6215, 1997).

3. *See* Roman Frydman, Cheryl W. Gray, Marek Hessel, and Andrzej Rapaczynski, *When Does Privatization Work? The Impact of Private Ownership on Corporate Performance in the Transition Economies*, Q.J. Econ. 1153–92 (1999).

4. *See* Gerhard Pohl, R. E. Anderson, S. Claessens, and Simeon Djankov, Privatization and Restructuring in Central and Eastern Europe (The World Bank Technical Paper No. 368, 1997).

5. *See* John Earle, Roman Frydman, Andrzej Rapaczynski, and Joel Turkewitz, Small Privatization: The Transformation of Retail Trade and Consumer Services in the Czech Republic, Hungary, and Poland (1994). See also N. Barberis, Maxim Boycko, Andrei Shleifer, and N. Tsukanova, *How Does Privatization Work? Evidence from the Russian Shops*, 104 J. Pol. Econ. 764–90 (1996).

6. *See* Randall Morck, Andrei Shleifer, and Robert Vishny, *Management Ownership and Market Valuation: An Empirical Analysis*, 20 J. Fin. Econ. 293–315 (1988).

7. *See* H. Hansmann, The Ownership of Enterprise (1996) for a review.

8. *See supra* note 3.

9. *See id.*

10. *See* Andrei Schleifer & Robert Vishny, *Politicians and Firms*, 109 Q.J. Econ. 995–1025 (1994).

11. *See* Barberis et al., *supra* note 5.

12. *See* I. Grosfeld & Gerard Roland, *Defensive and Strategic Restructuring in Central European Enterprises*, 3 J. Transforming Econ. & Societies 21–46 (1997).

13. *See* Barberis et al., *supra* note 5.

14. We imposed this restriction to ensure the presence of firms with different types of owners. No deviations from random drawing turned out to be necessary in Hungary.

15. Sixty firms in Hungary listed ownership types that we could not classify as either state or private (primarily because of the presence of corporate entities with unknown ownership), and one firm did not provide the identity of the largest owner. We also excluded all (twenty-six) firms privatized through leasing. The nature of leasing in Poland and employee stock ownership plans in Hungary made it difficult for us to categorize unambiguously the leased firms according to their ownership, especially when they were not employee owned. We verified, however, that the inclusion of these firms produced no significant changes in the results reported in this chapter.

16. By a privatized firm we mean an enterprise (partially or totally) privatized through a privatization of a predecessor state-owned company (or its part) in which the combined holdings of private parties give them a blocking power. We consider private parties to have blocking power if they control the percentage of votes formally sufficient to block major decisions at the general shareholder meeting. Note that this means that in some (15 percent) of the firms classified as privatized in this paper, the state remains a majority shareholder. But otherwise the high concentration of holdings in our sample makes the difference between blocking and majority power of little significance.

17. We have no reason to believe that the incompleteness of data for certain firms introduces any systematic bias "in favor" or "against" any group of firms. The most

common reason for incompleteness was lack of availability or an obvious misunderstanding of the meaning of certain questions.

18. Except for privatization funds, the average holdings of private parties in the position of the largest owner were majority holdings. All privatization funds were in the Czech Republic, where legal regulations at the time of the survey capped their individual holdings in any one firm at 20 percent. Even then, the combined holdings of different funds in a single firm typically added up to a majority.

19. This opens the possibility that some of the differences between state and privatized firms we observe may be the result of the particular type of concentrated ownership in our sample, and firms with smaller (and less active) owners may not behave in the same way. The owners= behavior may also be affected by the degree of the diversification of their investments. There are indications that most outsider owners of the firms in our sample are diversified.

20. The decline in output and employment of state firms in the region has been discussed by, among others, Olivier Blanchard, S. Commander, & F. Coricelli, *Unemployment, Restructuring, and the Labor Market in Eastern Europe*, *in* Unemployment, Restructuring, and the Labor Market in Eastern Europe and Russia (S. Commander & F. Coricelli eds., 1994); Brian Pinto & S. van Wijnbergen, "Ownership and Corporate Control in Poland: Why State Firms Defied the Odds (World Bank Policy Research Working Paper No. 1308, 1994); and L. Balcerowicz, Cheryl W. Gray, and I. Hashi, Exit Processes in Transition Economies: Downsizing, Workouts, and Liquidation (1997). Olivier Blanchard, The Economics of Post-Communist Transition (1997) reviews the evidence and provides further references.

21. *See supra* note 3.

22. *See id.*

23. *See id.*

24. *See supra* note 12.

25. *See id.*

26. This does not mean, of course, that there are no risks involved in cost-cutting measures, such as when, for example, decreased maintenance may raise the risk of breakdowns, or that such risks are insignificant. What is being claimed here is that these risks, not involving predictions concerning the behavior of other parties such as customers or competitors, tend to be better known and to involve less *radical* uncertainty.

27. For a recent discussion of the importance of incorporating entrepreneurship into the neoclassical theory of the firm, its measurement, and significance for understanding the demise of the planned economies, *see* S. Rosen, *Austrian and Neo-Classical Economics: Any Gains from Trade*? 11 J. Econ. Perspectives 139–52 (1997).

28. *See* F. Knight, Risk, Uncertainty, and Profit (1921).

29. *See* Friedrich Hayek, Individualism and Economic Order (1948); *see also* I. Kirzner, Perception, Opportunity, and Profit (1921).

30. We defined a *product group* as products that are produced using essentially the same type of equipment and production process, and do not differ substantially in the basic design. Examples of product groups include leather shoes, soaps, canned fruits, baked goods, beverages, and so on.

31. In the context of the transition economies, we treat the introduction of major new production process as primarily proxies for product quality improvements akin

to the introduction of new products. The changes we attempted to capture with the concept of major product restructuring corresponds to what Grosfeld and Roland label "strategic restructuring." *See supra* note 12.

32. Seventy-eight percent of the firms (83 percent of state and 74 percent of privatized) in our sample financed investments between 1990 and 1994 primarily from retained earnings. The level of long-term debt among the firms that introduced major product restructuring measures is also very low: the median is 3 percent of 1993 revenues. Major product restructuring thus is very likely to have a direct impact on a firm's cash position.

33. That nearly eight out of every ten state firms introduced major product restructuring changes may be surprising, but it is consistent with previous reports of extensive restructuring among all types of firms, including state enterprises, in the transition environment. *See* Brian Pinto, M. Belka, & S. Krajewski, *Transforming State Enterprises in Poland: Evidence on Adjustment by Manufacturing Firms*, 1 Brookings Papers on Economic Activity 213–69 (1993).

34. If anything, the number of major changes by the best-performing (outsider-owned) firms is slightly lower, indicating perhaps that frequency of change may be to some extent a function of a failure, rather than success, of restructuring measures, and that firms that introduce successful changes may focus on consolidating their results, while those that make unsuccessful changes may try again. But overall, the frequency of the introduction of major product restructuring measures has no explanatory value with respect to revenue performance.

35. We also tested, but do not report here, for a number of sectoral effects, and found none.

36. In the firm fixed effects specification, the effect of major product restructuring changes in postprivatization years for outsider-owned firms retains its magnitude (15.33 v. 15.62 in group fixed effects specification) but with more than twice the standard error (9.72 v. 4.43). The loss of precision results from the fact that the firm fixed effect model uses up a lot of degrees of freedom, and, *ceteris paribus*, inflates the standard errors of all estimates. When a constant term is used instead of firm-level fixed effects, the OLS estimate of the restructuring effect has virtually the same magnitude as in the fixed effect model (15.80) but with much lower standard error (3.60).

37. The evidence concerning the ineffectiveness of product restructuring by insider-dominated privatized firms should be treated with some caution. Since nine of the twelve insider-owned firms that restructured their products were owned by workers, as the estimate in table 5.4 is based almost entirely on the performance of worker-owned firms, since of the twelve insider-owned firms that restructured their products over the sample period, nine were worker owned. With only three manager-owned firms in the sample restructuring their products, we could not obtain meaningful separate estimates of the effectiveness of restructuring in these firms. (Note: The data in that the first row of table 5.3 contains instances of restructuring occurring in 1994, for which no postrestructuring performance results are available, and which therefore could not be included in the regressions reported in table 5.4.) The disadvantages of employee-ownership have been discussed extensively elsewhere, and our data suggest that, at least in the environment of the early postcommunist transition, those costs may completely neutralize the benefits of private own-

ership. *See supra* note 7. The most relevant contrast in the postrestructuring performance of firms with different types of ownership is thus between state-owned firms and those privatized to outside owners.

38. *See* Barberis et al., *supra* note 5.

39. *See id.*

40. Barberis and coauthors take equity ownership as the only measure of incentives. We take a broader view and treat all performance differences between firms with various types of ownership as caused by different incentive structures, unless they can be accounted for in terms of better human capital. What these incentives actually are will be considered further in the following section. *See id.*

41. *See id.*

42. *See id.*

43. For privatized firms, we have recognized managerial changes since privatization only (including any change occurring at the time the firm was privatized). This was done to focus on managerial choices made by the private owners and to exclude the possibly incompetent changes introduced by the state. Because the number of insider-owned firms that changed their managers was too small to allow for meaningful estimates, we included only those that did not change managers.

44. *See* Roman Frydman, Katharina Pistor, and Andrzej Rapaczynski, *Investing in Insider-Dominated Firms: A Study of Russian Voucher Privatization Funds, in* Corporate Governance in Central Europe and Russia (Roman Frydman, Cheryl W. Gray, and Andrzej Rapaczynski eds., 1996); *see also* Barberis et al., *supra* note 5.

45. Again, data limitations do not allow us to gauge directly the postchange performance of the insider-controlled firms.

46. This suggests, incidentally, that state firms= appointments under the new regime seem to be made primarily for business, rather than political, reasons.

47. *See supra*, table 5.2; *see also supra* note 3.

48. The group effects (not reported in table 5.6) for state- and outsider-owned firms with no managerial changes are, respectively, −23.08 (with a standard error of 5.17) and −24.74 (4.80) for the specification involving the first managerial change, and −23.39 (5.13) and −24.66 (4.76) for the specification involving the last managerial change.

49. To a large extent, this is also true of market economies, particularly in periods of rapid demand changes when a firm's sales, far from being predictable of the basis of an exogenously given demand curve, depend on its ability to accommodate the largely unpredictable decisions of potential customers and consumers.

50. The monitors of the managers of state firms have similar payoffs to the managers themselves. Like the managers, they derive limited benefits from the upside potential of risky decisions. On the downside, however, they are more likely to encounter political problems if the firms under their supervision go bankrupt (or require big bailouts) than if their "scrap" value is wasted (so that they are willing to undertake very risky projects to keep the firms afloat).

51. We note that almost all (94 percent) of the managers of privatized companies in the sample consult "regularly" (74 percent) or "occasionally" (20 percent) with their main shareholders.

52. *See* Kirzner, *supra* note 29.

53. *See* Hayek, *supra* note 29.

54. Our sample of managerially controlled firms for which revenue data is complete is sufficient, however, to show that these firms underperform their outsider-owned competitors. Thus, although the problem of accountability is not decisive here, the incentive structure of these firms, resulting in risk averseness and entrenchment, appears to be enough to depress their performance. *See supra* note 6.

55. *See supra* note 7.

56. *See* O. Ashenfelter & D. Card, *Using the Longitudinal Structure of Earnings to Estimate the Effects of Training Programs*, 67 Rev. Econ. & Stat. 648–60 (1985); *see also* J. J. Heckman & V. J. Hotz, *Choosing among Alternative Nonexperimental Methods for Estimating the Impact of Social Programs: The Case of Manpower Training*, 84 J. Am. Stat. Ass'n. 862–80 (1989).

57. Recent applications of this procedure include the evaluation of the effects of strengthening workers' incentives on productivity in Chinese state-owned enterprises, *see* T. Groves, Y. Hong, J. McMillian, & B. Naughton, *Autonomy and Incentives in Chinese State Enterprises*, 109 Q.J. Econ 183–209 (1994), and the effects of arrests on employment and earnings of young men, *see* J. Grogger, *The Effects of Arrests on the Employment and Earnings of Young Men*, 110 Q.J. Econ. 51–71 (1995).

PART IV

The Elements of Good Corporate Governance: Stock Markets

CHAPTER SIX

Corporate Governance in Transitional Economies: Lessons from the Prewar Japanese Cotton Textile Industry

Yoshiro Miwa and J. Mark Ramseyer

Observers of the formerly communist economies urge firms there to obtain funds from a relatively few sources. They note the problems the firms face: dysfunctional courts, markets, and statutes. Because these firms cannot rely on the courts to discipline managers, they predict that firms will do best if they raise their capital only from a few sources. Firms in Japan at the close of the nineteenth century similarly faced dysfunctional courts, markets, and statutes. Yet the firms that succeeded in Japan were not the ones that took the tack proposed by modern observers. They were the ones that used little debt and raised their equity from a large number of investors. In this chapter, we outline how concentrated finance can introduce problems potentially as severe as the ones it mitigates, and discuss why dispersed equity did not reduce firm efficiency in late nineteenth-century Japan.

Dysfunctional courts, nascent markets, nonexistent statutes, and firms controlled by communist hacks—for many observers, that combination characterizes modern "transitional economies." For firms in that environment, these observers prescribe concentrated finance: they suggest that rather than relying on broadly dispersed shareholdings (with their well-known collective action problems), entrepreneurs will need to raise capital from a few sources and to rely heavily on bank debt. Because managers often lack the skills they need and the courts provide little protection, firms with broadly dispersed investors will find themselves adrift with incompetent and unconstrained managers. If only to discipline themselves, they will need to restrict themselves to more concentrated sources of funds.

In this chapter, we use data from turn-of-the-century (that is, turn of the last century) Japan to test this hypothesis. We do not purport to have data on all firms or industries, nor do we try to estimate comprehensively how well the capital markets worked. Yet dysfunctional courts, nascent markets, nonexistent statutes, and firms controlled by people without a clue—all this, overstated to be sure, arguably describes late nineteenth-century Japan about as well as it does present-day Eastern Europe. Within this "transitional" Japan, we pick the largest industrial sector, cotton spinning, and ask what capital and governance structures the more successful firms in the industry adopted.

Consistently, we find that the most successful spinning firms relied on equity and raised it from many shareholders. Although they often did have investors with 5–15 percent interests in the firm, they did not focus on highly concentrated sources of equity capital or bank debt. Instead, they used bank debt only for their short-term needs, raised equity from hundreds of shareholders, and deliberately structured their governance to cripple the ability of unwanted shareholders to intervene in firm management. To induce their managers to maximize firm value, they then tied managerial pay to profits; turned to reputational sanctions in the managerial labor market; committed themselves to high-dividend policies; restricted managerial discretion by charter and statute; and recruited well-known industrialists to the board and induced them to place their reputations, connections, and expertise behind the firm.

Corrupt and badly informed dominant shareholders can present risks potentially as large as corrupt, inept, or lazy managers—and Japanese entrepreneurs recognized the risk. Some major investors could indeed provide value: for example, those with broad reputations among investors, those who could monitor firm performance well, or those who could provide (or recruit) the necessary technological talent. These investors the Japanese firms actively recruited. Other large-block shareholders, the firms did their best to stymie.

We begin by summarizing the current literature on corporate governance in transitional economies in section I. In section II we then describe the institutional environment of late nineteenth-century Japan, the cotton-spinning firms that dominated this economy, and the capital structure of the most successful of these firms. In section III we conclude by investigating how these firms mitigated the conflict of interest between shareholders and managers, and why they adopted the governance structures that they did.

I. Finance in Transitional Economies

A. The Trade-Offs

In studying the modern transitional economies, several observers argue that firms there will need to structure themselves in ways radically different from the ways firms structure themselves in the United States. Rather than to raise funds on the stock or bond markets, they will need to obtain the bulk of any investment from a relatively few places: through intermediated (generally, bank) debt, or from large-block shareholders. As Erik Bergloef wrote in a recent World Bank study:

- Most of the external funding will have to come from control-oriented finance. . . .
- Stock and bond markets are not going to play a major role in the provision of funds during early phases of economic transition. . . .
- Holdings of debt and equity will be concentrated, with little turnover in control blocks. . . .
- Both mutual funds and commercial banks will be needed, but banks are likely to be more important in corporate governance.[1]

The logic is straightforward. For expositional simplicity, assume that at each firm there is an "entrepreneur" who chooses its investment structure. These entrepreneurs choose how much debt to issue, and how much stock. They choose how much stock to hold themselves and how much to issue to others. They choose how much of the earnings to reinvest and how much to distribute in dividends. Whether debt or equity, however, they also choose whether to try to raise the funds from a large number of sources or to raise them from only a few investors. They could, for example, try to borrow $10 million broadly from a wide variety of bondholders or to borrow it from a small number of banks. They could try to sell $10 million in stock to hundreds of diversified investors or sell it to a few plutocrats.

In choosing between dispersed and concentrated sources of capital, the entrepreneurs trade off liquidity against monitoring. If they obtain their money from a wide group of investors, they can offer a more liquid claim: an investment they can more easily sell and more readily fit within a diversified portfolio. All else equal, investors will prefer more liquid and diversified investments to less. If the entrepreneurs obtain their money from a small group of investors, the investors can more effectively constrain managers: because the investors each hold a large interest in the firm, they face fewer collective action problems in monitoring or intervening; because they can more readily monitor and intervene, they can better prevent managers from doing silly or crooked things. All else equal, investors will prefer honest and effective managers to the foolish and dishonest.

Given this calculus, all entrepreneurs everywhere will not prefer the same capital strategy. As Harold Demsetz and Kenneth Lehn explained many years ago, entrepreneurs will choose the strategy that maximizes firm value—but which strategy does so will vary by firm.[2] All else being equal, for example, an entrepreneur who needs more money than even the rich can easily spare will tend to raise capital broadly. An entrepreneur who finds it hard to be committed to not cheating investors will tend to turn to fewer investors.

B. Transitional Economies

Within transitional economies, observers point to two factors that they believe will favor entrepreneurs who raise money from a relatively few sources. First, stock and bond markets work best if investors have access to sophisticated courts.[3] Not only can investors use courts to enforce their property rights to these stocks and bonds; given the risk of managerial misconduct, they can also use them to enforce the claims they derivatively hold against incumbent managers. Such claims, however, raise sensitive legal questions that are not usually amenable to bright-line rules—questions that go to the market value of illiquid assets sold by investors to the firm, or to whether managers exercised "reasonable" care in making business decisions that eventually went bad.[4] Unfortunately, most transitional economies have few lawyers and judges, and those they have come with precious little experience.

Second, many firms in these transitional economies are run by people who obtained their jobs at best by luck and sometimes through ties to the old communist bureaucracy or the new mob.[5] Often, they lack much business sense or technical education, let alone reputations for integrity. As a result, they present massive monitoring problems. Only investors with concentrated interests, explain observers, will be able to make investments in these firms profitable. As Masahiko Aoki and Hyung-Ki Kim wrote: "In the transitional economies . . . both competitive capital and labor markets are lacking. Managers have established strong control within their enterprises; there is no external agent with the decisive power to dismiss them for poor management performance or moral hazard behavior. . . . Outsiders would then anticipate substantial agency costs to investing in insider-controlled enterprises. Therefore, the funds necessary for restructuring formerly state-owned enterprises would be difficult to come by from the capital market."[6]

The conclusion follows straightforwardly—or so it would initially seem. "Taking into account present-day conditions in the East European region," conclude Roman Frydman, Edmund S. Phelps, Andrzej Rapaczynski, and Andrei Shleifer, "one class of mechanisms, namely, outsider control by banks and other financial intermediaries, is well-designed to promote enterprise performance." By contrast, "some of the other mechanisms, such as a stock market or foreign investment, will not be strong enough in the near future, if ever, to be a major source of outside governance."[7] On corporate governance, it seems, the transitional economies yield a corner solution: not a Demsetz-Lehn mix of concentrated and dispersed ownership patterns, but an overwhelming focus on bank debt and large-block shareholders.

C. The Japanese Analogy

If firms in transitional economies will tend to focus on concentrated capital sources, one need not read far to intuit the next step: learn from Japan. After all, most scholars place large-block shareholders and large bank loans at the center of postwar Japanese finance. For example, a World Bank study cites a prominent economist for the proposition that "the Japanese financial model [may be] a better fit for a capitalist economy at an earlier stage of development when information problems, including the lack of business reputations and sophisticated market analysis, make stock or bond-based finance exceedingly difficult."[8]

Similarly, in their plea that these countries not ditch their socialist heritage completely, Pranab Bardhan and John E. Roemer urge them to ape their vision of Japan if they must ape capitalism at all:

> [W]e are skeptical that the option of the "real thing," Western-style capitalism, is available to some of the East European countries, China, or Vietnam, however much some people in these countries may crave it. The institutions of Western capitalism, including its legal, political, and economic infrastructure, evolved over a long period. Some of them are not easily replicable. In fact, the bank-centric organization . . . is a way of mitigating an historical handicap in capital market institutions. . . . Even in the case of Japan, . . . the main bank system originated in the highly imperfect financial markets and economic uncertainties of the immediate postwar period.[9]

In this chapter, we test these predictions against the Japanese experience, but not the postwar experience.[10] Instead, we believe that the current transitional economies face predicaments far closer to those Japan faced between the Meiji Restoration and World War II. Many of the problems said to characterize these economies parallel the problems said to have characterized Japan during various parts of this period: insufficient and inadequately trained lawyers, accountants, bankers, and other professionals; novice judges; an absence of economically knowledgeable regulators; (during the early years) a dysfunctional statutory framework; an absence of large and smoothly functioning stock and bond markets; even an absence of a working managerial labor market.

Crucially, by looking at prewar Japan, we can look at a "transitional economy" and ask which firms succeeded in the long run. Because we are only a few years into the current European transition, we cannot yet tell which types of firms do best. But in deciding what governance structures to recommend, we do not want to know what structures current Russian firms adopt. We want to know which structures facilitate long-term Russian economic success. Toward that end, we need to know which firms have the highest odds of ultimately succeeding. For that, we need to be able to view the entire period retrospectively. Prewar Japan gives us that retrospective view. And to focus our inquiry, we examine the industry that most radically revolutionized the prewar economy: cotton textiles.

II. The Cotton Textile Industry in Prewar Japan

A. Legal Structure

Although it hardly harbored a brood of recovering Leninists, Japan at the end of the nineteenth century underwent a transition every bit as radical as anything that occurred among the formerly communist states at the end of the twentieth. When Commodore Perry crossed Uraga Bay in 1853, he sailed into a country that had deliberately rejected the West for two centuries. It had not been a splendid isolation.

The national government was badly in disarray and had been for decades. Even in the best of times, it had not maintained a very effective legal system. Although the domain governments had maintained their own courts too, these courts used rules that varied widely, and jurisdiction was haphazard at best. In this vacuum, merchants did create a sophisticated customary commercial law system. Crucially, they never developed firms with transferable equity stakes.

In the name of the young Meiji emperor, a coalition of regional military leaders overthrew this government in 1868. For several years they faced continuing threats to their control, but they quelled the last major rebellion in 1877. Despite their only haphazard control over the country, they organized the first national courts in 1872.[11] Ostensibly on behalf of the emperor, they passed a constitution in 1889. Through the new parliament, they then enacted a Civil Procedure Code in 1890[12] and a Civil Code (essentially contract, tort, property, agency, and family law) in 1896 and 1898.[13] They passed one version of the Commercial Code (consider it the Uniform Commercial Code, the Uniform Partnership Act, an insurance act, and a corporations code rolled into one) in 1890 with the corporate law provisions taking effect in 1893. They then abandoned it and passed an almost entirely new one in 1899.[14]

B. The Cotton-Spinning Industry

Cotton spinning had not been a significant industry in Japan, but come the new regime, matters changed. The government of Satsuma province opened the first "modern" cotton-spinning mill in 1867 with several British spinning machines. The national Ministry of Home Affairs imported more machines in 1878, and still more in 1879. None of these government-run operations succeeded, nor did the government offer firms in the industry any other targeted help. Instead, because the "unequal treaties" forced it to keep trade barriers minimal, the government did little more than subject its textile firms to international competition.[15]

From these inauspicious beginnings, the industry grew rapidly. After some early false starts, Japanese firms soon became major international competitors. When World War I closed the Suez Canal, Japanese textile firms made enormous profit in the Asian market. By the 1920s, they consumed more raw cotton than did British firms. Despite a deep recession in the industry after the war, Japanese textile firms in the 1930s still produced a quarter of all domestic manufactured goods and employed 40 percent of all factory workers.[16] By 1934, the three largest cotton-spinning firms in the world were all Japanese: Toyo boseki (1,372,000 spindles; *boseki* means "spinning"); Dai-Nippon boseki (1,023,000 spindles); and Kanegafuchi boseki (generally called Kanebo; 823,000 spindles). The fourth largest was the American firm Amoskeag Manufacturing with 687,000 spindles. The largest British firm was Riverside and Dan River Mills, at 467,000 spindles.[17]

Other than the Mitsui family's initial interest in Kanebo (more on this in Section III.C.2) the major *zaibatsu*—those prewar conglomerate predecessors to the modern *keiretsu*—invested almost nothing in this industry. As of about 1930, the Mitsui owned only 6.7 percent of Kanebo, 40–50 percent in four much smaller spinning firms, and under 6 percent in a couple of other small firms. The Mitsubishi held equity interests in only two firms—both under three percent. The Sumitomo and Yasuda had interests in only one each, both under one percent.

C. Capital Structure

Entrepreneurs began forming private cotton-spinning firms in earnest soon after the government mills failed. These firms required massive amounts of capital: Kurashiki boseki, for example, began with paid-in capital of 150,000 yen—this at a time when the incorporators anticipated paying the chief executive officer (CEO) a salary between 15 and 30 yen. About the capital structure of the firms that failed, little information survives. About those that succeeded, several points stand out.

1. EARLY FORMATION

Entrepreneurs formed these firms quickly. Indeed, they had already formed most of the firms that would eventually dominate the industry (or their principal predecessors) by 1890. They had formed them, in other words, before any corporate law had taken effect.[18]

The Amagasaki boseki and Settsu boseki firms, for instance, began in 1889. Eventually, they would constitute the core of the giant Dai-Nippon boseki, in 1925 the largest Japanese spinning firm (at 672,000 spindles; the merger was in 1918). Mie boseki and Osaka boseki began in 1886 and 1882, respectively. Together, they would become Toyo boseki, in 1925 the second-largest firm (660,000 spindles; the merger was in 1914). The third-largest (498,000 spindles) Japanese spinning firm in 1925 was Kanebo, incorporated in 1887. Fuji boseki and Tokyo gasu boseki (to become Fuji gasu boseki in 1906; at 416,000 spindles the fourth largest in the industry in 1925) both began in 1896. Kurashiki boseki (216,000 spindles by 1925; seventh-largest firm) started in 1887. And Fukushima boseki (184,000 spindles by 1925; eighth-largest firm) was incorporated in 1892.

Spinning firms were not unusual in incorporating early. As of 1890, government statistics recorded more than five thousand firms. The four-thousand-plus nonbank firms had 224,000 investors and paid-in capital of 90 million yen. Slightly more than half the firms were corporations, and the rest were partnerships.[19]

2. BROAD OWNERSHIP

Entrepreneurs sold the stock in these spinning firms to a broad array of investors. In most cases no single shareholder or group of shareholders held a very large interest, though the lion's share of the investors in any one firm often came from a few towns and cities—a point that obviously facilitated trust. Take Kazuo Yamaguchi's study of the sixty-odd spinning firms in 1898.[20] On average, the firms had 331 shareholders. The largest investor held about 8 percent of the stock, the five largest together held 24 percent, and the ten largest held 33 percent. Only 11 percent of the firms (seven firms) had fewer than one hundred shareholders, while 52 percent (32 firms) had three hundred shareholders or more. In no firm did the largest shareholder hold 50 percent or more of the stock, and in only three firms did a shareholder hold 20 percent of the stock or more. In 76 percent of the firms (forty-seven firms), the largest shareholder held less than 10 percent of the stock. In no firm did the ten largest shareholders hold 70 percent or more of the stock, and in only six firms did they hold 50 percent or more. By contrast, in 66 percent of the firms (thirty-nine firms), the ten largest shareholders together held less than 35 percent of the stock.

Table 6.1
Shareholding Patterns

A. Mean number of shareholders per corporation, by industry

	Manufacturing			Transportation			
Year	*All*	*Cotton Spinning*	*Agriculture*	*All*	*Railroads*	*Commercial*	*Total*
1886	35.1	NA	188.2	110.5	1,598	113.2	65.4
1887	33.8	115.5	190.2	98.5	1,550	95.7	61.3
1888	40.5	94.8	148.8	75.7	863	65.1	57.3
1889	27.0	148.9	167.7	92.9	904	61.1	55.2
1890	29.0	120.7	663.2	96.1	939	57.7	56.9
1891	22.0	139.5	200.3	96.1	832	57.2	53.2
1892	22.1	171.5	188.8	103.6	769	56.3	49.4
1893	16.8	136.4	184.0	181.1	714	59.2	40.2
1894	59.0	222.1	144.9	188.9	669	53.1	74.0
1895	63.3	255.4	90.2	163.4	719	45.1	65.8

B. Stock-exchange-listed cotton-spinning firms

Firm	*Incorporated*	*Listed*
Settsu	1889	1891 (OSE)
Amagasaki	1889	1892 (OSE)
Mie	1886	1888 (OSE) 1889 (TSE)
Osaka	1882	1887 (OSE)
Kanebo	1887	1889 (TSE)
Tokyo gas	1896	1897 (TSE)
Fukushima	1892	1895 (OSE)

Sources: Panel A, Toshimitsu Imuta, Meiji ki kabushiki kaisha bunseki josetsu (Introduction to the Analysis of the Meiji-era Corporations) 57–59 (1976); panel B, Daikabu 50 nen shi (A 50-Year History of the Osaka Stock Exchange) (Osaka kabushiki torihiki sho ed. 1928); and Tokyo kabushiki torihiki sho 50 nen shi (A 50-Year History of the Tokyo Stock Exchange) (Tokyo kabushiki torihiki sho ed. 1928).

Note: NA = Not available; OSE = Osaka Stock Exchange; TSE = Tokyo Stock Exchange.

The average number of shareholders varied by industry during this period. While spinning firms had more shareholders than most, some firms—most particularly the railroads—had even more. Panel A of table 6.1 gives the mean number of shareholders per corporation in different sectors.

Within a few years, most of the spinning firms that would become the eventual industry leaders had listed their stock on a national exchange.

Indeed, as panel B of table 6.1 shows, they typically listed their stock with the Tokyo or Osaka Stock Exchanges (both founded in 1878) by the early 1890s, still before Japan had settled on its eventual corporate law. More generally, on the eve of Japan's first corporate law (1893), the Tokyo Stock Exchange already listed the stock of sixty-two firms and the Osaka Stock Exchange thirty-five firms.[21]

3. HEAVY EQUITY

The spinning firms rarely relied on debt, much less bank debt. This lack of bank debt should not surprise, for Japanese banks in the late nineteenth century seldom lent to firms of any sort. Instead, they lent to individuals and took security interests directly. In 1896, for instance, nationally chartered private banks in Osaka[22] made 72 percent of their loans to merchants, generally wholesalers. In Tokyo, they made 80 percent of their loans to borrowers whom the records catalog as "miscellaneous," much of it apparently to individual aristocrats. In both cities, the banks secured more than 70 percent of the loans with stocks or bonds.[23] This does not mean that borrowers did not invest in firms—they probably often did. It means that banks did not lend directly to firms and therefore seldom had the means to monitor corporate governance.

This near absence of bank debt appears directly in the balance sheets of the firms themselves. The classic study of Japanese long-term economic statistics divides the principal spinning firms of the period into four groups, roughly on the basis of descending size (or the size of their successor firms). Table 6.2 gives their debt-to-total-assets ratio for three selected years. Although the firms did borrow some funds, in all size categories they relied primarily on equity finance.

D. Success

Firms such as Toyo boseki and Kanebo did not come to dominate the industry just by steady growth, though they did steadily grow.[24] They also came to dominate it by relentlessly acquiring their more inefficiently managed competitors—so much for the notion that Japanese business executives have a cultural aversion to mergers and acquisitions. Even as they built and expanded their own factories, aggressive spinning-firm managers strategically bought their rivals.

Toyo boseki, for example, was formed in 1914 from the merger of Mie boseki and Osaka boseki.[25] Osaka had been formed in 1882. In 1906 it acquired Kanakin, which had acquired Heian in 1905, which had acquired Fushimi in 1900. In 1907, Osaka also acquired Hakuseki, which had acquired Uwa in 1902. Mie began in 1886. It then bought Owari

TABLE 6.2
Debt-to-Asset Ratios, Cotton-Spinning Firms

Year	*Group I* (%)	*Group II* (%)	*Group III* (%)	*Group IV* (%)
1905	10.9 (50,071)	3.3 (1,988)	NA	NA
1910	17.1 (102,060)	17.5 (4,430)	NA	NA
1915	15.1 (138,721)	8.6 (8,106)	4.8 (3,107)	22.1 (488)

Source: Choki keizai tokei: Sen'i kogyo (Long-Term Economic Statistics: The Textile Industry) 74–81 (Shozaburo Fujino, Shiro Fujino, & Akira Ono eds. 1979).

Note: Debt is both bank debt and bonds; total assets (given in parentheses at × 1,000 yen) are the sum of paid-in capital, accumulated reserves, debt, current reserves, and carryforwards. NA = Not applicable.

(1905), Nishinari (1906), Tsushima (1906), Kuwana (1907), Chita (1907), and Shimotsuke (1911). Toyo also acquired Tokai penii in 1919, Hamamatsu in 1920, Ise boshoku in 1923, Nogoya kenbo in 1926, and Osaka godo in 1931—which in turn had acquired Tenma in 1900, Chugoku and Meiji in 1902, and Imabari in 1923.

Formed in 1887, Kanebo pursued a similarly aggressive strategy. In 1899, it acquired Kashu, Shibajima, and Jokai. The following year, it acquired Awaji. In 1902, it acquired Hakata kenmen, Nakatsu and Kyushu—which in turn had acquired Kurume, Miike, and Kumamoto in 1899. In 1907, Kanebo acquired Nippon kenmen, and in 1911 acquired Nankai and Kenshi. Kenshi had acquired Okayama and Bizen in 1907. Okayama had acquired Saidaiji in 1898. In 1913, Kanebo acquired Asahi boshoku; in 1921, Kokka seishi; in 1922, Nippon kenshi; in 1923, Nansei—and so it went, year after year, even through the war.

Generally, these firms could profitably acquire their competitors because they were better—because the managers of the acquiring firms could more efficiently use the target's capital stock than the target's own managers. To illustrate this point, in table 6.3 we compare the profitability of the targets and the acquiring firms. More specifically, we take all acquisitions in the industry between 1903 and 1911 involving firms for which profitability data remain, and calculate the mean semiannual profits per spindle for acquiring firms and targets during the three years before the acquisition.[26] Of the fourteen acquisitions, according to public records, in only one case did the target have a higher premerger profitability than the acquiring firm. Using a simple probit model to predict the likelihood that a firm will be acquired (Target = 1) as a function of total spindles (per 1,000) and profits per spindle, we obtain:

TABLE 6.3
Acquisitions in the Cotton-Spinning Industry, Profits per Spindle, 1903–11

Acquirer	*Profits per spindle*	*Target*	*Profits per spindle*	*Date*	*Acquirer-target*
Osaka boseki	4.812	Kanakin	2.532	September 1906	2.280
Kanakin	2.361	Heian	−4.778	1905	7.139
Mie	2.185	Shimotsuke	2.144	November 1911	.041
Mie	2.765	Owari	1.239	October 1905	1.526
Mie	4.877	Kuwana	4.506	August 1907	.371
Mie	3.828	Tsushima	1.592	1906	2.236
Mie	4.877	Chita	2.724	August 1907	2.153
Nihon boseki	3.383	Ichinomiya	2.775	July 1907	.608
Settsu	4.834	Koriyama	4.745	June 1907	.089
Kanebo	2.525	Kenshi	−.161	March 1911	2.686
Sakai	4.174	Awa	3.906	February 1907	.268
Fukushima	2.957	Kasaoka	1.548	November 1909	1.409
Fukushima	1.811	Harima	2.175	May 1912	−.364
Wakayama orimono	4.484	Wakayama boseki	.437	November 1911	4.047

Sources: Calculated from data found in Menshi boseki jijo sanko sho (Reference Materials on Cotton Spinning) (Dai-Nippon boseki rengo kai ed., appropriate years); Choki keizai tokei: Sen'i kogyo (Long-Term Economic Statistics: The Textile Industry) (Shozaburo Fujino, Shiro Fujino, & Akira Ono eds. 1979).

Note: In each case, we give the semiannual stated profits (yen) per spindle (mule spindles are converted to ring equivalents at 1.3 mules per ring). Profits are for the six semiannual accounting periods ending immediately prior to the acquisition. For Heian, we have data only for calendar year 1903. For the Owari-Mie merger, we have data only on the five preceding accounting periods; for the Fukushima-Kasaoka and Fukushima-Harima mergers, we lack the data on the last two accounting periods.

$$\underset{}{\text{Target}} = \underset{(0.49)}{-0.0480} - \underset{(2.32)}{0.0175} \times \text{Total Spind} - \underset{(6.10)}{0.0192} \times \text{Prof/Spin} + e,$$

where the absolute value of the z-values are in parentheses, the pseudo $R^2 = .13$, and $N = 531$. The targets were disproportionately the smaller and less efficient firms.

III. Corporate Governance in Cotton Spinning

A. Introduction

Return, now, to the question at the heart of this essay: Why did these successful firms find it advantageous to disperse their shareholdings broadly? Given the primitive courts and almost nonexistent statutory framework, the logic of the modern corporate governance literature suggests that they should have been closely held. They were not. Instead, they were both publicly held and economically successful. How were they able to mitigate the conflicts of interest between shareholders and managers? Why did apparently unmonitored managers create such smoothly running and eminently profitable firms? How could the entrepreneurs sell shares broadly without a corporate law?

To explore these questions, we first briefly identify the source of the efficiency gains (Section III.B). We then turn to the ways the firms mitigated the incentive misalignments between managers and shareholders (Section III.C).

B. Managerial Efficiency in the Spinning Firms

1. MONOPOLY GAINS?

Consider, initially, why the large firms were so successful. Their gains were not monopoly gains. In 1900, there were more than seventy firms in the industry trade association; even in 1925 there were still more than fifty.[27] At that size, any attempt to fix profits was almost bound to fail. More to the point, the firms did not try. Although price-fixing agreements would not have been illegal, the firms never made them.

To be sure, the spinning firms did sometimes agree to idle spindles or to cut back hours. Yet, for several reasons, the agreements would not have earned monopoly rents. First, the firms never banned investments in new equipment. So long as they could increase production by increasing their investment, they were unlikely to earn monopoly rents—even if they had been only a handful of firms.[28]

Second, the agreements involved fewer than all members of the industry. As of 1927, eleven spinning companies controlling 6 percent of the cotton spindles remained outside these agreements.[29] Third, new entry remained feasible to the end. Although most of the ultimately successful firms were early entrants, not all were. Formed in 1907, by 1910 Nisshin boseki was in the second quintile of firms. By 1930, it was the sixth-largest firm in the country. Other firms continued to form and compete throughout the period.[30]

Last, the cotton market was an international market, and—big as they were—Japanese firms faced fierce competitors overseas. Some thread they sold directly in the overseas market. Other thread they sold domestically or wove in vertically integrated loom operations. Eventually, however, much of that woven product went overseas. So long as downstream buyers (here, the Japanese weaving firms) sell their products on competitive markets, any cartel among less than all upstream sellers (a cartel only of Japanese spinners) will not likely raise prices.

2. SCALE ECONOMIES?

Neither were their gains scale economies of factory size. In cotton spinning, the scale economies to factory size disappeared at scales far smaller than those of the largest Japanese firms. With several hundred thousand (and in some cases more than a million) spindles, the Japanese firms were much bigger than necessary to capture the scale economies to factory size. According to one 1957 British study, the "technical limit" to spinning mills rose "as we go to finer counts from 9000 to 10,000 m.e. [mule equivalent] spindles for a mill balanced at 10's counts to 25,000–30,000 spindles for a mill balanced at 30's counts, and so on." Even in the 1940s, few British mills had more than 150,000 spindles. Concluded the same author, "[T]he main economies arising from increasing size are reached at about 30,000 spindles and . . . above 60,000 spindles, if they exist, they are more than offset presumably by increasing managerial difficulties."[31]

The onetime president of Toyo similarly calculated the minimum efficient scale at 20,000 spindles for 20's count thread, 40,000 spindles for 40's count, and 60,000 spindles for 60's count.[32] Panel A of table 6.4 gives his estimates. For 20's count yarn (and in the 1920s, Japanese yarn averaged 20–21 count),[33] as factory size rose from 10,000 spindles to 30,000, production costs fell 21 percent; as it rose from 30,000 spindles to 60,000, it fell only another 6 percent.

As this discussion should make clear, the successful Japanese firms were already far larger than factory scale economies warranted. And true to these considerations, they did not use new machines to expand their factories. Instead, they kept any firms they acquired as separate factories. Throughout this period, the mean number of ring spindles per factory at the largest firms remained above the minimum efficient scale, but well within range of the smaller firms as well (see panel B of table 6.4). In short, the acquisitions did not change factory size. They changed factory management.

3. MANAGERIAL EFFICIENCIES?

a) Technical Expertise. The reason behind the acquisitions and behind the success of the largest firms apparently lay in their managerial talent: the way the largest firms (1) mastered both spinning technology and management practices, (2) learned how to govern a multi-unit firm, and (3) now leveraged technological and organizational sophistication over a bigger capital base. Begin with the technological expertise. So crucial was this expertise that top engineers could sometimes command higher pay than even the company president. When Kurashiki began operations, for example, it paid its CEO fifteen yen a month, but its two top engineers eighteen and thirty yen.[34]

TABLE 6.4
Scale Economies in Cotton Spinning

A. Indexed cost of production by factory size

Spindles	*Materials*	*Wages (labor)*	*Amenities (labor)*	*Operating costs*	*Total*
5,000	21.77	104.14	16.92	22.37	165.20
10,000	21.77	73.59	11.95	19.34	126.65
20,000	21.77	57.66	9.35	18.84	107.64
30,000	21.77	51.53	8.37	18.33	100.00
40,000	21.77	49.25	8.00	18.09	97.11
50,000	21.77	47.97	7.79	17.93	95.46
60,000	21.77	47.14	7.66	17.83	94.40

B. Mean ring spindles per factory, selected firms

	1919	*1927*	*1937*
Toyo boseki	34,595	41,948	52,366
Kanebo	30,740	37,269	66,795
Dai-Nippon	43,910	54,259	82,185

Sources: Panel A, Keizo Seki, Nihon mengyo ron (A Theory of the Japanese Cotton Industry) 103, 204, table 10 (1954); panel B, Takeshi Abe, Mengyo—senkanki ni okeru boseki kigyo no doko wo chushin ni (The Cotton Industry: Principally Concerning the Changes in the Spinning Firms during the Interwar Years), in Nihon sangyo hatten no dainamizumu (The Dynamism of Japanese Industrial Development) (Haruhito Takeda ed. 1995).

Note: The calculations in panel A are for 20's count yarn.

Cotton textile production involved almost completely foreign technology.[35] Rightly or wrongly, the British firms had believed that they could rely on on-the-job training. Even in 1950, the fifty-one textile firms in Manchester employed a total of only seventy-four university graduates.[36] Japanese firms had no such luxury. They needed expertise they did not have. Toward that end, the most successful firms were the firms that aggressively hired university graduates.

Like much in the industry, the practice may have begun at Kanebo.[37] For Kanebo, its first years were bad years. As the firm's largest shareholder (this being virtually the only time a *zaibatsu* had invested heavily in a spinning firm), the Mitsui family stepped in. From the Mitsui Bank, it brought in Keio University graduate Sanji Muto in 1893. Muto quickly began hiring other university graduates and placing them in managerial slots. Initially, he hired them away from his competitors. Soon, he went directly to the schools. By 1914, he was hiring a dozen

TABLE 6.5
Cotton-Spinning Firms with Largest Number of University Graduates, 1914

Firm	*A. University graduates*	*B. Factory workers*	*A/B*
Kanebo	269	24,323	.0111
Toyo	136	32,441	.0042
Fuji gas	87	10,172	.0042
Osaka godo	61	9,400	.0065
Amagasaki	48	9,525	.0050
Kurashiki	45	3,135	.0143
Settsu	33	10,176	.0032
Naigai	32	2,220	.0144

Source: Shin'ichi Yonekawa, University Graduates in Japanese Enterprises before the Second World War, 26 Bus. Hist. 193, 195–99 (1984).

graduates a year and had filled virtually all branch-manager posts with university graduates.[38]

At the firms, these graduates noticeably raised profitability.[39] Table 6.5 gives the textile firms with at least twenty university graduates as of 1914. Recall the firm-profitability data used to calculate table 6.3. If we regress firm profits on total spindles (per one thousand) and the number of university graduates, we obtain[40]

$$\underset{}{\text{Profits}} = \underset{(1.64)}{19{,}373} + \underset{(6.93)}{1{,}781} \times \text{Total Spind} + \underset{(6.23)}{1{,}732} \times \text{Grads} + e,$$

where the absolute value of the t-statistics are in parentheses, the adjusted $R^2 = .48$, and $N = 531$. Holding firm size constant, the firms with the most university graduates were more profitable than their competitors.

b) Firm Size. For recent graduates, the bigger firms offered the jobs of choice. New graduates faced a nontrivial risk that the firm to which they went would fail. By joining a bigger and more profitable firm, they could minimize that risk. Overwhelmingly, they chose the bigger firms.[41]

Technological expertise eventually cascaded into the smaller firms, but only as the graduates moved on the interfirm managerial market. Toyo adopted modern management practices, for example, only after it hired away a team of managers from Kanebo. When it laid off its own managers, they moved to smaller firms and took those practices with them.[42]

All told, about half the 1900–1915 graduates who joined Kanebo soon after school left the firm within twenty years. Generally, they left for higher-ranking positions at lesser firms. After improving management there, they often moved to yet other firms, some ex-Kanebo managers working at two, three, or even four other firms during their careers.[43] In effect, the larger firms adopted much the same strategy that high-prestige law firms use today: hire a large corps of graduates, train them, pick the most promising, and induce the rest to leave.

Kanebo was not the only firm with sophisticated managerial talent. Mie had Kozo Saito, a university engineering graduate who worked at the Osaka mint before moving to textiles and becoming the equivalent of a director by age thirty-three. Amagasaki had Kyozo Kikuchi, likewise a university engineering graduate with experience at the Osaka mint. He became a director by age thirty-five. Indeed, he was in such demand that he served simultaneously as chief engineer at Amagasaki, Settsu, and Hirano. Toyoharu Wada graduated from Keio University, and through the course of his career worked at NYK (the Mitsubishi shipping firm), Kanebo, Fuji (as director), and its successor Fuji gasu—where he became president. Throughout, the firms that came to dominate the industry were generally ones where the early entrepreneurs were lucky or shrewd enough to recruit technologically and organizationally sophisticated people to prominent positions.[44]

c) Managerial Expertise. The big-firm advantage was not just in engineering—it was also in management. Not only did Kanebo (most prominently of the large firms) hire university graduates for technological positions, it hired them for management too. As of 1914, most firms used universities only as a source for engineers: of the seven firms other than Kanebo with at least twenty university graduates, 72 percent of the graduates had science backgrounds. At Kanebo only 48 percent did.[45]

Under Muto, Kanebo self-consciously imported modern management theory. Frederick W. Taylor published his *Principles of Scientific Management* in 1911. By 1912, Muto had announced his own "Principles of Scientific Operations," and the Taylorite motion studies soon followed.[46] But Muto went further. Developing his own "psychological" theories of management, he reasoned that workers worked best if they liked their jobs and had few personal distractions.[47] Just as Henry Ford cut absenteeism by doubling wages and hiring social workers, Muto hiked wages and built dormitories, schools, and health clinics.[48] Compare, for example, wages—the mean Kanebo daily wages (in current sen) with the average wage among spinning firms in the trade association (the Dai-Nippon boseki rengo-kai, generally called the Boren; see table 6.6). Historians sometimes belittle Muto's efforts, just as they

TABLE 6.6
Mean Kanebo and Boren Wages

Year	*Boren (Mean)*	*Kanebo (Mean)*	*Kanebo (premium; %)*
1898	14.99	19.60	30.8
1908	24.89	29.00	16.5
1919	80.51	84.10	4.5

Source: J. Mark Ramseyer, Odd Markets in Japanese History: Law and Economic Growth 150, table 7.6 (1996).

Note: Wages are in current sen; 1918 data are not available.

sneer at Ford. But in belittling either, they miss the essence of efficiency wages: workers work hardest and most carefully if they earn more than the market-clearing wage, and sometimes that additional productivity more than offsets the wage premium.

Indeed, Kanebo's wage premium relative to other spinning firms eventually faded (as table 6.6 shows) but only because other firms raised their wages too. In 1898, female workers in the spinning firms (most spinning workers were young women recruited from peasant families) earned annual wages that were 1.17 times the annual wages female workers earned in the agricultural sector. By 1908 that ratio had risen to 1.90. In 1918 the spinning/agricultural annual wage ratio fell to 1.57 from the 2.21 it had been in 1914, but by 1920 it was back up to 2.74.[49]

To preserve the incentive effects of these efficiency wages, the firms worked hard to commit themselves to a policy of not hiring away blue-collar workers from rival firms. During the earliest years of the industry, the firms used the trade association Boren for just that purpose. Indeed, for precisely that reason Kurashiki waited to join the Boren until after it had hired away the workers it wanted from its rival firms. And lest nonmember firms hire away their employees, they worked hard to induce the newer and smaller spinning firms to join the Boren too.[50]

d) Multiunit Leverage. To exploit the efficiency gains to modern engineering and management, the larger firms learned to master the multidivisional firm. Even in the West, managers did not tackle multiunit firms until the railroads arrived with their distinctive challenges.[51] Yet it was primarily by learning to leverage their technological sophistication over multiple factories that the larger Japanese spinning firms could exploit their technological and managerial lead.

This leverage took many forms. At Kanebo, the trained, educated managers centralized such tasks as buying raw materials, allocating cotton among factories, making managerial personnel decisions, and selling finished tread. At Toyo, central managers used the data they collected on intrafirm performance to induce factories to compete among themselves. The larger firms also circulated their managers among the factories. Having aggressively acquired less efficiently run factories, they now had to integrate them into the firm and improve both their efficiency and their quality. Toward that end, they regularly moved managers from factory to factory. Even central-office managers could spend time supervising work on the shop floor, and firms often rotated factory heads every two to three years.[52]

C. Misaligned Incentives

1. CONSTRAINING MANAGERS

a) Introduction. In arguing that firms in transitional economies should rely on concentrated sources of capital, corporate governance theorists focus on the potential for managerial and shareholder incentives to diverge. Managers can steal or shirk, they note, and only if investors hold large interests in the firm will they have the power or incentives to constrain them. Accordingly, they continue, closely held firms will more tightly monitor their managers; closely held firms will suffer fewer losses from managerial fraud and indolence; and necessarily in competitive markets, closely held firms will out-compete their more widely held competitors.

In turn-of-the-century Japan the most successful firms had hundreds of shareholders. To succeed, these publicly held firms used a variety of devices to help align managerial and investor incentives: (1) they tied managerial pay to profits; (2) given a fluid managerial labor market among a limited number of firms, they relied on reputational sanctions; (3) they restricted managerial discretion by charter and statute; (4) they subjected their major investment decisions to the discipline of the capital market by committing to high-dividend payout policies; and (5) they recruited well-known industrialists and technologically sophisticated professionals onto the board, effectively inducing them to place their own reputations, connections, and expertise behind the firm. We now turn to each.

b) Profit Sharing. Cotton-spinning firms often tied managerial compensation to firm profits. They did this in a variety of ways, but perhaps the most direct was that used by Mie boseki. Mie explicitly provided in its corporate charter that 13 percent of its net profits would go to its officers as compensation, and another 7 percent to its blue-collar workers. Other companies included similar provisions in their charter—

Kanebo, for example, and Kurashiki, Amagasaki, and Osaka. Indeed, the Boren (the trade association) even included such a provision in its model charter.[53]

c) Managerial Labor Market. Managers worked within a fluid labor market. We noted earlier the way they regularly moved among the larger firms, and moved from larger firms to smaller. They did this, moreover, within an industry with a limited number of firms. Given the constrained number of cotton-spinning firms (generally fifty to seventy), they necessarily worked within a world where reputations traveled quickly. Should they shirk or steal, they, necessarily, jeopardized their prospects on the lateral market.

d) Restrictive Charters. By corporate charter, the early entrepreneurs sometimes limited managerial discretion severely. The Kurashiki charter (1888), for example, specified even the number of spindles the company would use and required that shareholders approve any changes in that investment level.[54] The 1899 Commercial Code then limited managerial discretion in several other ways as well: it mandated a special shareholders' meeting if the company lost half its stated capital (Section 174), required managers to close a firm if its debts exceeded its assets (Section 174), forced shareholder votes on bond issues (Section 199), and forbade firms from issuing bonds in an amount greater than their capital (Section 200).

e) Dividends. The firms with widely dispersed investors paid high dividends. By informally (or formally) committing to high-dividend policies, they forced themselves to return to the capital market to fund large new projects. In the process, they subjected their major investment decisions to the discipline of the market. For some firms, the commitment was a tradition they worked hard to keep. Late in life, Muto recalled the accounting games Kanebo had played to maintain dividends even when times had been bad.[55] For some firms, the commitment was explicit: Amagasaki, for instance, formally agreed to a dividend payout rate of 70 percent of profits in its charter. Kurashiki likewise included a mandatory payout (provided it had accounting profits) in its charter, and so did the Boren in its model charter. Osaka maintained high dividend payout rates almost from the year of its founding: Formed in 1892, in the second half of 1883 it paid dividends of 7,950 yen on profits of 11,191 yen (8.4 percent of paid-in capital); by the second half of 1886 it was paying 48,000 yen on 88,641 yen profits (29.5 percent); and by the second half of 1889 it was paying 120,000 yen on 177,030 yen (29.5 percent).[56]

Several years ago, Frank H. Easterbrook explained how dividends subject managers to the discipline of the capital market, but his logic applies most strongly to firms with dispersed shareholdings.[57] If a firm is closely held, a team with a majority of stock can intervene directly in management anyway. Such controlling shareholders need not bleed the firm of its extra cash. Because smaller firms are more likely to be closely held, we posit that dividends will be a smaller fraction of income among smaller firms; because listed firms are more likely to have dispersed shareholdings, we posit that dividends will be a larger percentage of profit where the firm is listed on a national stock exchange.

To test these hypotheses, return to the data set we used to create table 6.3: measures of profit for the spinning firms, 1903–11. To this, we add data on dividends paid, and regress firm dividends on firm profits, on a dummy equal to one if the firm is listed on either the Tokyo or the Osaka Stock Exchange, and on total spindles. The results confirm both hypotheses (see table 6.7): (1) profits held constant, larger firms paid higher dividends than smaller firms, and (2) profits held constant, firms listed on the Tokyo Stock Exchange and Osaka Stock Exchange paid higher dividends than did unlisted firms.

f) Prominent Industrialists. Entrepreneurs actively recruited well-known industrialists or technologically sophisticated professionals as shareholders and board members. Eiichi Shibusawa, for example, not only founded Osaka boseki in 1882, but also helped raise capital for Mie boseki.[58] A national figure, he had earlier founded the Dai-ichi Bank (predecessor to the Dai-ichi Kangyo Bank), and built around himself a financial empire that historians sometimes call the Shibusawa *zaibatsu*.

Other textile investors were less in the public eye, but no less prominent within the industry. They were experienced businessmen, and if anyone could monitor spinning-firm managers, they were the ones. Prominent Amagasaki director Kyozo Kikuchi served on the boards of two other firms, Katsuzo Ukita served as statutory auditor (a senior position mandated by the 1899 Commercial Code, Section 133) on three firms, Kyohei Magoshi served as auditor for two firms and a director of a third, and so forth. In his study of spinning-firm shareholders, Toshimitsu Imuta identifies twenty-eight industrialists with significant investments in multiple firms, who often held officer or director posts as well.[59]

These prominent shareholders and board members performed several roles. Most obvious, some provided the imprimatur necessary to attract other investors and corporate officers. When in 1886 entrepreneurs tried to organize Mie boseki, for example, potential investors still remembered the debacle that befell the early government-run mills.

TABLE 6.7
Dividend Payouts in the Cotton-Spinning Industry, 1903–11

A. Summary statistics

	Minimum	*Mean*	*Maximum*
Dividends	0	99,471.26	876,580
Profits	−2,486,857	142,564.80	1,559,085
Listed	0	.43	1
Total spindles	0	48,333.80	377,920

B. Regression results

	Left-hand-side variable		
	Dividends	*Dividends*	*Dividends*
Profits	.520 (37.43)	.390 (24.20)	.390 (24.23)
Listed	46,790.41 (6.754)		13,563.21 (2.06)
Total spindles	.937 (14.00)	.875 (11.96)	
Constant	−7,333.98 (1.68)	−11,475.18 (3.21)	−14,391.9 (3.73)
SE	69,660	60,558	60,437
Censoring ($x < 0$, uncensored)	(87,444)	(87,444)	(87,444)
Pseudo R^2	.067	.077	.077

Sources: Calculated from data found in Menshi boseki sanko jijo (Reference Materials on Cotton Spinning) (Dai-Nippon boseki rengo kai ed., various years); Tokyo kabushiki torihiki sho 50 nen shi (A 50-Year History of the Tokyo Stock Exchange) (Tokyo kabushiki torihiki sho ed. 1928); Daikabu 50 nen shi (A 50-Year History of the Osaka Stock Exchange) (Osaka kabushiki torihiki sho ed. 1928).

Note: Because dividends are censored below at zero, the regressions use tobit. Profits and total spindles are for each firm for each half year from the second half of 1903 to the first half of 1911. Mule spindles are converted into ring equivalents at 1.3 mules per ring. Listed takes the value of one if the firm was listed on either the Tokyo or Osaka Stock Exchange at the time, zero otherwise. For panel B, N = 531.

Faced with potential investors who would not invest, Shibusawa placed his family's money (it bought two hundred of the twenty-two hundred shares) and national reputation (as head of the Dai-ichi Bank) behind the project—and the other money then followed.[60]

The logic loosely resembles that which J. Bradford de Long used to explain the role the House of Morgan played in the United States.[61] By inducing Morgan to place one of its partners on its board, a firm could significantly raise its value. In effect, in placing a partner on the board, the House agreed to monitor managerial performance and posted its own reputation behind it—and earned a return for the service by handling the firm's investment banking needs. We suspect that prominent industrialists played a similar (subject to important qualifications) role in Japan.

Particularly during the troublesome early years at the firms, prominent shareholders and board members also provided crucial expertise or access to expertise. Involving as it did radically new production technology, cotton spinning often proved far harder than the firms' first entrepreneurs anticipated. At this point, people like Shibusawa could use their ties to industrialists elsewhere to recruit the talent a firm desperately needed.[62] In Kurashiki, for example, it was a prominent shareholder who located the engineers the company needed when it found, soon after starting operations, that its initial engineers were not up to the job. Similarly, when early in the history of Fuji boseki that firm found itself adrift, it was prominent shareholder Ichizaemon Morimura (of Noritake China) who convinced Tokyo gasu boseki founder Heizaemon Hibiya to restructure the firm.[63]

Other prominent investors were simply corporate officers who had done well for the firm. Spinning firms paid successful officers and engineers well, and those men often then invested in their firm. Muto, again, bought large amounts of Kanebo stock. Kikuchi, who simultaneously worked as a head engineer at Settsu, Hirano, and Amagasaki, used his salary to buy large shareholdings in each. That these men chose to do so, of course, itself provided a quality imprimatur—for that an insider chooses to invest heavily (and not as part of a balanced portfolio) in his own company is exactly the type of news outside investors like to hear.

The incentive for these industrialists to monitor their firms came in several forms. First, depending on the firm, they could earn a compensation package tied directly to firm performance. Some prominent investors were also directors or officers and earned profit-based pay through those roles. Other firms, like Kurashiki, by its 1893 amended charter, could explicitly commit themselves to paying a stated percentage of their profits to their incorporators.[64] Second, even if not on a profit-sharing plan, prominent directors often held nontrivial (though not controlling) equity interests in the firm.

Last, because these industrialists often worked in a variety of roles at a variety of firms, how well they performed at one firm directly affected their overall earnings. How tightly they monitored one firm, for example, could affect whether they obtained high-paying board spots elsewhere. Whether they saved one troubled firm could affect the aggregate business they obtained as investment bankers, and so forth. The exact ramifications depended on the industry with which they were most closely involved, but the basic logic remained constant.

2. CONSTRAINING SHAREHOLDERS

a) Introduction. When modern observers focus on managerial fraud and indolence in the transitional economies, they miss half the corporate governance problem: how to constrain dominant shareholders. It was not a half lost on turn-of-the-century Japanese entrepreneurs. Investors can lose money when managers misbehave, but they can also lose money when controlling shareholders misbehave. If managers can steal from the corporate till, so can controlling shareholders. In urging closely held capital structures on Eastern European firms, observers today merely substitute one problem for another, often roughly comparable, problem.

Although Japanese entrepreneurs recognized the value that the right kind of investor could bring (monitoring, strategic intervention, access to talent), they also saw the threat that the wrong large-block investors posed—and structured their governance accordingly. To the right large-block investors, they offered paid corporate positions. When unwanted large-block investors sought board positions or tried to intervene in governance, they fought them off.

b) Kanebo. Again, the best-known example was Kanebo. In the early 1920s, at Muto's urging, the firm amended its charter to require that the company president and representative director have at least five years' experience at Kanebo. By charter, in others words, it expressly banned outside directors from the top two posts.

Behind Muto's move lay the attempt by a team of outside shareholders to intervene.[65] Early in its history, the Mitsui family had controlled Kanebo. In 1905, it decided to sell its Kanebo stock. Soon, a thirty-year-old named Kyugoro Suzuki bought much of what the Mitsui had sold. Once he acquired a quarter and his allies another quarter or so, he turned to corporate policy.

Suzuki wanted to merge several spinning firms into one large firm and export aggressively to China. When Muto opposed the stock issue necessary to pay for the expansion (he was not particularly opposed either to acquiring other firms or to exporting), Suzuki called a special shareholders' meeting and pushed through his policy. Anticipating this, Muto and all directors and officers peremptorily threatened to resign. As Suzuki could not run Kanebo without experienced personnel, he pleaded with them not to leave. In the end, only Muto left. For unrelated reasons Suzuki soon lost his fortune, however, and his Kanebo stock passed to the Yasuda Bank. By 1908 Muto was back as representative director. In 1921 he became president, and he promptly initiated the charter amendment to ban outside presidents and representative directors.

Lest readers think the Kanebo charter illustrates how persistently Japanese firms favor employees over shareholders, note that Kanebo returned regularly—and successfully—to the capital market for new funds.[66] Apparently, to Kanebo investors, the risk of intervention by unsophisticated or devious shareholders exceeded the risk of unmonitored officers.

c) Deviations from One-Share-One-Vote. If Kanebo's ban on outside corporate leaders was unusual (recall that many firms sought out prominent industrialists for top positions), other firms also adopted strategies designed to limit the power of large-stake investors. Most commonly, they installed charter voting rules that slashed the power of lead shareholders. Although the Commercial Code (both the 1893 code, Section 204, and the 1899 code, Section 162) provided a one-share-one-vote default rule, firms could legally reduce the voting power of the largest shareholders. Many—particularly during the earliest years—did just that.

Take the 1887 Hirano boseki charter, typical for its time: for any shareholder, the first ten shares had one vote each, the next forty shares had one-fifth of a vote, and any additional shares had one-tenth of a vote. Consequently, a shareholder with ten shares had 10 votes, one with fifty shares had 18 votes, one with one hundred shares had 23 votes, and one with one thousand shares had 113 votes. The 1883 Enshu boseki charter gave all shareholders with more than five shares one-fifth of a vote for the additional shares; the 1888 Kurashiki charter specified a graduated scale falling to one-tenth of a vote for all shares beyond one hundred.[67]

One might have thought prominent shareholders would try to avoid these rules by placing shares in trust with others. Apparently, they seldom did, for only a very few accounts of such tactics survive. The Jugo Bank distributed its shares in the Nippon Railroad to forty-five of its directors and officers prior to the railroad's 1898 special shareholders' meeting, and major shareholders in the Kyushu Railroad are said to have done the same in 1899. Exactly why other major shareholders avoided this tactic is unclear. Certainly, it could generate bad publicity (as the Jugo Bank's tactics did), and it was not unambiguously legal. Whatever the reason, major shareholders seem rarely to have used the tactic.[68]

Curiously enough (given the discussion of corporate governance in transitional economies), Japanese firms were most likely to limit the power of concentrated investors prior to the first Commercial Code (1893)—precisely when the legal regime was weakest. Imuta surveyed 271 corporate charters from the late nineteenth century. Of the 134 pre-1893 charters, only 22 (16.4 percent) used one-share-one-vote rules; of the 137 charters from 1893 to 1900, a full 89 (65.0 percent) did.[69] For late nineteenth-century entrepreneurs, it seems the problem presented by a weak legal system less involved misbehavior by managers; it more involved misbehavior by controlling shareholders.

D. The Effect of Governance Structures

1. INTRODUCTION

Finally, consider the effect various governance structures had on the profitability of a firm. To study the issue, we regress firm profits on several indexes of governance. We focus on two questions. First, were the firms that raised equity capital more broadly less efficient? After all, that seems the hypothesis implied by modern observers of transitional economies. To test this first hypothesis, we examine the effect that the number of shareholders had on firm profitability.

Second, were firms able to attract the prominent shareholders that they wanted? Recall that the firms typically adopted two cross-cutting strategies: At the same time that they tried to attract prominent industrialists and professionals to the firm (section III.C.1.f), they adopted charter rules that limited the power that large-block shareholders could wield (Section III.C.2). The point, of course, is that they wanted—and wanted to empower—only the "right" kind of large-block shareholder.

More specifically, firms wanted shareholders who would monitor the firm, help in a crisis, and work hard at building it. Those shareholders they would name to the board. At the same time, they emphatically did not want investors with little value-added (and who might try to use the firm for private gain) to intervene in firm management. To test whether the firms with large-block shareholders had the right kind of investor, we regress firm profits on measures of shareholder concentration.

2. THE VARIABLES

We define the following variables:

Profits = semiannual accounting profits in one thousand yen. We start our data in the second half of 1903, when the data became public;

Total Spin = the total number of spindles. We convert mule spindles into ring-spindle equivalents by dividing by 1.3. Because spindles become a misleading measure of firm size once firms invest heavily in vertically integrated weaving operations, we close our data at the end of the Meiji era (the first half of 1911);

Total S/h = the total number of shareholders, as of about 1898;

Largest S/h = the percentage of the firm's shares held by the shareholder with the largest interest, as of about 1898;

Larg5 S/h = the percentage of shares held by the five largest shareholders, as of about 1898;
Larg10 S/h = the percentage of shares held by the ten largest shareholders, as of about 1898.

3. THE RESULTS

We report the coefficients and the absolute value of the *t*-statistics from the regressions in the columns of table 6.8. First, the coefficient on Total S/h is consistently positive and is significant in two of the three specifications: firm size (Total Spin) held constant, the firms with more shareholders were more profitable than those with fewer. Second, the coefficients on Large S/h, Larg5 S/h, and Larg10 S/h are positive and significant in all specifications: firm size held constant, the firms with large-block shareholders were more profitable than those without.

Hence, the conclusion: firms with more shareholders were more successful, but firms in which the largest shareholders owned more stock were also more successful. Recall, however, that the firms with prominent lead shareholders did not concentrate large percentage interests with these shareholders. As of about 1898, the average spinning firm had 330 shareholders, and the largest shareholder held 8 percent of the stock. Some firms dispersed their stock among perhaps five hundred to eight hundred shareholders; some firms had a lead shareholder with perhaps 10–20 percent of the stock. In only three firms did the lead shareholder have more than 20 percent of the stock, and in only one did that person have more than 30 percent.

Within this world, the firms with more shareholders and with the heavily invested lead shareholder did better than the rest. As obviously ambiguous as the implications are, when viewed together with the other strategies the firms adopted, we suspect they point to the importance of attracting the "right" investors. After all, these firms (1) self-consciously tried to attract investors who would provide monitoring, technical expertise, or access to help, but simultaneously (2) fought to keep unsolicited large-block shareholders at bay. The combination of these two factors (1 and 2) suggests that they believed that some, but only some, large-block investors added value. Table 6.8, in turn, suggests (obviously does not prove) that the firms with the large-block shareholders had largely found the investors they wanted.

IV. Conclusions

Observers of modern transitional economies argue that the firms there should raise their capital from a few concentrated sources and rely heav-

Table 6.8
Shareholdings and Profitability in the Cotton-Spinning Industry, 1903–11

A. Summary statistics

	Minimum	*Mean*	*Maximum*
Profits	−126,05	4154,083	1,559,085
Total Spin	1,539	51,546	377,920
Total S/h	29	407	907
Largest S/h	.020	.087	.486
Larg5 S/h	.077	.223	.560
Larg10 S/h	.113	.316	.608

B. Regression results

	Left-hand-side variable		
	Profits	*Profits*	*Profits*
Total spin	2,609 (16.2)	2,883 (20.0)	2,973 (21.7)
Total S/h	85.4 (2.01)	75.5 (1.71)	63.2 (1.43)
Largest S/h	482,728 (4.67)		
Larg5 S/h		239,984 (2.98)	
Larg10 S/h			165,283 (2.32)
Constant	−57,143 (2.83)	−78,700 (2.82)	−77,118 (2.40)
Adjusted R^2	.63	.62	.61

Sources: Menshi boseki jijo sanko sho (Reference Materials on Cotton Spinning) (Dai-Nippon boseki rengo kai ed., appropriate years); Kazuo Yamaguchi, Meiji 31 nen zengo boseki gaisha no kabunushi ni tsuite (Regarding Spinning-Firm Shareholders at around 1898) 15 [Meiji daigaku] keiei ronshu 1 (1968).

Note: The regression uses ordinary least squares. N = 380. For variables, see text.

ily on intermediated debt finance. And yet, faced with a similar institutional environment (dysfunctional courts, nascent markets, nonexistent statutes), the successful cotton-spinning firms in late nineteenth-century Japan were the firms that in some important ways did the opposite. The successful firms did have prominent investors, but they also relied heavily on equity raised from hundreds of shareholders.

These modern observers reason that in weak legal environments only large-block shareholders and banks will effectively constrain managers. Faced with such an environment, however, the successful cotton-spinning firms used banks only for short-term funds and manipulated corporate charters to keep large-block shareholders at bay. They did this for a simple reason: they had other ways to control managers, and they needed to protect their firms against intervention by shareholders who either had foolish ideas or, more likely, would manipulate the firms for private gain. They did not keep all major investors powerless. After all, some investors they actively recruited to the firm, but the investors they wanted, they could, and did, empower by naming to the board. Other major investors they kept at arm's length.

Maybe we should not be surprised by all this. Although diversified shareholders need ways to induce managers to keep their bargains, so do creditors and majority shareholders. Creditors, too, need to be able to demand repayment, to force auctions, to enforce security interests, to acquire title to collateral, to sell their collateral on the open market. And so, too, do controlling shareholders. An investor may own two-thirds of a firm's stock, but if incumbent officers and directors will not call a shareholders' meeting, the investor cannot vote. If the officers and directors rig the vote, the investor's shares will not matter. If officers and directors will not leave, a successful vote is so much hot air. And if the officers and directors rob the till on the way out, their eviction is simply hollow. Absent promissory credibility, investors become even controlling shareholders at their peril.

The point, rephrased, is that entrepreneurs need some way of enabling managers credibly to commit themselves to their promises—but they can choose from a broad portfolio of means. A sophisticated legal system is one such mechanism, but in worlds with only nascent courts entrepreneurs have access to other mechanisms besides. To align managerial incentives—to make managerial commitments credible—Japanese entrepreneurs used profit-sharing compensation schemes, relied on the incentives created by the lateral job market, restricted managerial discretion by charter and statute, committed themselves to high dividend rates that forced managers to subject their plans to the discipline of the capital market, and recruited well-known industrialists to the board.

Entrepreneurs can do all this to align managerial and shareholder incentives, but simultaneously they must do what recent observers ignore: protect the firm from incompetent or corrupt controlling shareholders. In a world with sophisticated courts staffed by judges accustomed to making judgment calls in corporate cases, perhaps entrepreneurs can rely on courts to police the duties of care and loyalty. In late nineteenth-century Japan, the successful cotton-spinning firms chose to structure their firms in ways that stymied unwanted shareholder intervention instead.

Notes

 Published originally as Yoshiro Miwa & J. Mark Ramseyer, *Corporate Governance in Transitional Economies: Lessons from the Pre-War Japanese Cotton Textile Industry*, 29 J. Legal Stud. 171 (2000).

We gratefully acknowledge the generous financial assistance of the Sloan Foundation and the John M. Olin Center for Law, Economics, and Business at the Harvard Law School and the helpful comments and suggestions of Serguey Braguinsky, Eisuke Daito, John Haley, William Klein, Curtis Milhaupt, Eric Posner, Tom Roehl, Gary Saxonhouse, Masayuki Tanimoto, Kip Viscusi, Kazuo Wada, Mark West, Noriyuki Yanagawa, participants in a workshop at the University of Tokyo, and an anonymous referee.

1. Erik Bergloef, *Corporate Governance in Transition Economies: The Theory and Its Policy Implications, in* Corporate Governance in Transitional Economies: Insider Control and the Role of Banks 59, 81–82 (Masahiko Aoki & Hyung-Ki Kim eds., 1995).

2. Harold Demsetz & Kenneth Lehn, *The Structure of Corporate Ownership*, 93 J. Pol. Econ. 1155 (1985).

3. Thus, Rafael La Porta, Florencio Lopez-Silanes, Andrei Shleifer, and Robert W. Vishny argue that firms in legal systems that offer less shareholder protection will tend—all else equal—to have more concentrated ownership structures. Rafael La Porta *et al., Law and Finance*, 106 J. Pol. Econ. 1113 (1998).

4. Bernard Black & Reinier Kraakman, *A Self-Enforcing Model of Corporate Law*, 109 Harv. L. Rev. 1911 (1996).

5. Black and Kraakman, *id.* at 1915, find this independence of managers in transitional economies one of the pivotal problems facing firms there: "[A]n acute problem in Russia is protecting minority investors against exploitation by managers or controlling shareholders. Protection of minority investors has also emerged as a central political issue in the most successful post-Communist economy, the Czech Republic, and is at the core of recent reforms in Israeli corporate law." The comparison to Japan is not that Japanese firms consistently recruited better managers; rather, it is that only Japanese firms that did recruit able managers survived. We discuss below the many difficulties Japanese firms faced in assembling the talent pool they needed.

6. *Overview, in* Corporate Governance in Transitional Economies: Insider Control and the Role of Banks, xi, xiii (Masahiko Aoki & Hyung-Ki Kim eds., 1995). For the argument that concentrated debt financing would not be appropriate for the transitional economies, *see* Peter Dittus & Stephen Prowse, *Corporate Control in Central Europe and Russia: Should Banks Own Shares? in* 1 Corporate Governance in Central Europe and Russia: Banks, Funds, and Foreign Investors 20 (Roman Frydman, Cheryl W. Gray, & Andrzej Rapaczynski eds., 1996); for a discussion of the problems posed by institutional investors in the Czech Republic, *see* John C. Coffee, Jr., *Institutional Investors in Transitional Economies: Lessons from the Czech Experience, in* Frydman, Gray, & Rapaczynski eds., *supra*, at 111.

7. Roman Frydman *et al., Needed Mechanisms of Corporate Governance and Finance in Eastern Europe*, 1 Econ. Transition 171, 200 (1993).

8. John M. Litwack, Corporate *Governance, Banks, and Fiscal Reform in Russia, in* Corporate Governance in Transitional Economies: Insider Control and the Role of Banks 99, 100 (Masahiko Aoki & Hyung-Ki Kim eds., 1995) (citing David Scharfstein). Roman Frydman, & Andrzej Rapaczynski, Privatization in Eastern Europe: Is the State Withering Away? 37–38 (1994), argue that "the East European economies need precisely [the German and Japanese] kind of institutions to supervise the restructuring effort," provided agency problems are solved.

9. Pranab Bardhan & John E. Roemer, *Market Socialism: A Case for Rejuvenation*,

6 J. Econ. Persp. 101, 103 (1992). For an analysis of the putative "main bank system," see Yoshiro Miwa & J. Mark Ramseyer, The Fable of the Keiretsu: Urban Legends of Modern Japan (Chicago: University of Chicago Press, forthcoming 2005); Yoshiro Miwa & J. Mark Ramseyer, *Does the Relationship Banking Matter? The Myth of the Japanese Main Bank*, 2 J. Empirical Legal Stud. 261 (2005).

10. Although we are also skeptical whether the postwar Japanese experience provides any evidence in favor of the recommendations offered by transitional economy observers. *See generally* Yoshiro Miwa, *"Market" and "Marketization": From the Japanese Experience*, Finansharu rebiyu (Ministry of Finance financial review), March 1999, at 18; Yoshiro Miwa, Firms and Industrial Organization in Japan, chs. 5–7 (1996).

11. Shiho shokumu teisei (Rules Regarding Judicial Functions), *Dajokan* unnumbered *tatsu*, August 3, 1872. These institutions did not begin to look recognizably modern until the late 1880s. Saiban sho kansei (Court Organization), Chokurei No. 40 of 1886; and Saibansho kosei ho (Judicial Organization Act), Law No. 6 of 1890.

12. Minji sosho ho (Code of Civil Procedure), Law No. 29 of 1890.

13. Minpo (Civil Code), Law No. 89 of 1896 and Law No. 9 of 1898.

14. Shoho (Commercial Code), Law No. 32 of 1890; Shoho (Commercial Code), Law No. 48 of 1899.

15. Eventually the national government sold off all of its machines to private operators. *See generally*, J. Mark Ramseyer & Frances M. Rosenbluth, The Politics of Oligarchy: Institutional Choice in Imperial Japan 137 (1995); Naosuke Takamura, Nihon boseki gyo shi josetsu: Jo (1 Introduction to the History of the Japanese Spinning Industry) (1971); Tetsuro Nakaoka, *Gijutsushi no shiten kara mita Nihon no keiken (The Japanese Experience, Seen from the Perspective of Technological History), in* Kindai Nihon no gijutsu to gijutsu seisaku (The Technology and Technological Policy of Early Modern Japan) 49 (Tetsuro Nakaoka, Tadashi Ishii, & Hoshimi Uchida eds., 1986).

16. Ramseyer & Rosenbluth, *supra* note 15, at 136–37; on employment in the industry, *see* Gary R. Saxonhouse, *Country Girls and Communication among Competitors in the Japanese Cotton-Spinning Industry*, *in* Japanese Industrialization and Its Social Consequences 97 (Hugh Patrick & Larry Meisner eds., 1976).

17. Toyo boseki, K. K., Toyo boseki kabushiki kaisha yoran (A Survey of Toyo boseki, K. K.) 5 (Supp. 1934). This survey excludes the "trusts" in England that were, as combined operations, larger than the Japanese firms.

18. The information on firm foundings in this paragraph and the following is taken from Choki keizai tokei: Sen'i kogyo (Long-Term Economic Statistics: The Textile Industry) 39–42 (Shozaburo Fujino, Shiro Fujino, & Akira Ono, eds., 1979). The 1925 size information is taken from the Dai-Nippon boseki rengo kai geppo (Great Japan Spinning Federation Monthly Newsletter) (Dai-Nippon boseki rengo kai, ed., July 1925), hereafter cited as Geppo. Total spindles are calculated by discounting mule spindles by 1.3. Entrepreneurs who met specified conditions could obtain limited liability by application to the local prefectural governor, albeit with some uncertainty. Junzo Yoshida, Nihon no kaisha seido hattatsu shi no kenkyu (A Study of the Developmental History of the Japanese Company System) 11 et seq. (1998).

19. Toshimitus Imuta, *Meiji chuki ni okeru "kaisha kigyo" no kosei (The Structure of "Company Firms" during Mid-Meiji)*, 25 Osaka shiritsu daigaku, Kenkyu to shiryo 20, 26–31 (1967).

20. Kazuo Yamaguchi, *Meiji 31 nen zengo boseki gaisha no kabunushi ni tsuite (Regarding Spinning-Firm Shareholders at around 1898)*, 15 (2) Meiji daigaku Keiei ronshu 1 (1968).

21. Toshimitsu Imuta, Meiji ki kabushiki kaisha bunseki josetsu (Introduction to the Analysis of Meiji-Era Corporations) 17–18 (1976).

22. That is, the *kokuritsu ginko*, the first category of private banks.

23. Toshimitsu Imuta, *Sangyo shihon kakuritsu katei ni okeru kokuritsu ginko kashitsuke kin no kosei (The Structure of Nationally Chartered Bank Loans during the Establishment of Industrial Capital)*, 27 Kenkyu to shiryo 31, 39, 66–67 (1967). Note that the need to pay interest on these loans may have contributed to shareholder pressure on the firms to pay high dividends, as discussed below. For an analysis of financial intermediation through trade credit in turn-of-the-century Japan, see Yoshiro Miwa & J. Mark Ramseyer, *Japanese Industrial Finance at the Close of the 19th Century: Trade Credit and Financial Intermediation*, 43 Explorations Econ. Hist. 94 (2006).

24. Merger information is from Fujino, Fujino, & Ono, *supra* note 18, at 39; Kanebo, K. K., Kanebo hyakunenshi (A 100-Year History of Kanebo) (1988); Toyo boseki, *supra* note 17.

25. Under the 1899 Commercial Code, mergers took effect, inter alia, only upon a favorable vote among a majority of shareholders and among those shareholders holding a majority of the shares. Commercial Code, §§ 222, 209, or after amendment by Law No. 72 of 1938, §§ 408, 343.

26. We do not carry the data further forward because shortly after 1911 (the end of the Meiji period), Japanese firms expanded aggressively into weaving operations. This, of course, makes it hard to construct a simple metric of operating efficiency like profits/spindle.

27. Geppo, *supra* note 18 (relevant years).

28. For details of the mandated restraints, *see* J. Mark Ramseyer, Odd Markets in Japanese History: Law and Economic Growth 139, table 7.2 (1996).

29. Nippon kangyo ginko chosaka, Menshi boseki gyo ni kansuru chosa (An Investigation into the Cotton-Thread-Spinning Industry) 55–58 (1928).

30. Nisshin boseki K. K., Nisshin boseki hyakunen shi (A 100-Year History of Nisshin Spinning) (1969); Geppo, *supra* note 18 (various years).

31. R. Robson, The Cotton Industry in Britain 134, 135, 137 n.1 (1957). The same source calculates a ring spindle as equivalent to 1.5 mule spindles at 20s count yarn (*id.* at 49 n.*). Lars G. Sandberg, however, describes the 1 ring = $1\frac{1}{3}$ mule conversion ratio as "the accepted practice" of the period in Lancashire in Decline: A Study in Entrepreneurship, Technology, and International Trade 122, 27 (1974). Ring spindles were the newer technology and required less expertise but were less suited for the finer (higher-count) yarn.

32. Purged by the U.S.-run occupation, Keizo Seki was invited to lecture at the University of Tokyo Economics Department, where he wrote what became one of the classic histories of the Japanese textile industry.

33. Menshi boseki jijo sanko sho (Reference Materials on Cotton Spinning) 21–22 (Dai-Nippon boseki rengo kai, ed., 1925).

34. Kurashiki boseki, K. K., Kaiko 65 nen (Sixty-five-Year Recollections) 36–37 (1953); similarly (for Settsu), *see* Nichibo, K. K., Nichibo 75 nenshi (The 75-Year History of Nichibo) 128, 130 (1966).

35. For an insightful discussion of the various factors that facilitated the adoption of this technology, *see* Gary R. Saxonhouse, *A Tale of Japanese Technological Diffusion in the Meiji Period*, 34 J. Econ. Hist. 149 (1974).

36. Shin'ichi Yonekawa, *University Graduates in Japanese Enterprises before the Second World War*, 26 Bus. Hist. 193, 215 (1984); Shin'ichi Yonekawa, Bosekigyo no hikaku keiei shi kenkyu (A Comparative Management History of the Spinning Industry) 180–83 (1994).

37. Other spinning firms had not entirely ignored educated technicians, of course. *See* Hidemasa Morikawa, Keieisha kigyo no jidai (The Age of Managerial Firms) 43 (1981). On technology transfer in the industry, *see* Gary R. Saxonhouse, *Mechanisms for Technology Transfer in Japanese Economic History*, 12 Managerial & Decision Econ. 83 (1991). For an analysis of the pre-war zaibatsu and the post-war keiretsu, see Yoshiro Miwa & J. Mark Ramseyer, *Banks and Economic Growth: Implications from Japanese History*, 45 J. Law & Econ. 127 (2002); Yoshiro Miwa & J. Mark Ramseyer, *The Fable of the Keiretsu*, 11 J. Econ. & Mgmt. Strategy 169 (2002).

38. Yonekawa, *University Graduates*, *supra* note 36, at 211–12.

39. Note, however, that in a careful early econometric study Saxonhouse did not find that an increase in the number of university-trained graduates in cotton-spinning firms led to higher profits. Gary R. Saxonhouse, *Productivity Change and Labor Absorption in Japanese Cotton Spinning* 1891–1935, 91 Q.J. Econ. 195 (1977).

40. Much the same results obtain by using the percentage of university graduates on the payroll. For these estimations we set the number of university graduates at firms not on Yonekawa's list at zero, where in fact they may have ranged from zero to 20. If we simply exclude all firms not on Yonekawa's list, we obtain (N = 124)

$$\text{Profits} = \underset{(1.64)}{75{,}839} + \underset{(2.06)}{1{,}120} \times \text{Total Spind} + \underset{(3.81)}{2{,}088} \times \text{Grads} + e.$$

Because Toyo resulted from the merger of Mie (a highly successful firm) and Osaka boseki (a failing firm) in 1914, we attribute the Toyo graduates to Mie. For a discussion of the lack of educated personnel at Osaka and the contrast at Mie, see Yonekawa, Bosekigyo no hikaku keiei shi kenkyu, *supra* note 36, at 180–83.

41. Yonekawa, *University Graduates*, *supra* note 36, at 212.

42. Shin'ichi Yonekawa, *Senkanki sandai boseki kigyo no gakusotsu shokuin so (The University Graduate Class at the Three Largest Spinning Firms in the Interwar Years)*, 108 Hitotsubashi Ronso 673, 617, 683 (1992).

43. Yonekawa, *University Graduates*, *supra* note 36, at 212; Yonekawa, *supra* note 42, at 692–93.

44. Morikawa, *supra* note 37, at 41, 43, 141.

45. Yonekawa, *University Graduates*, *supra* note 36.

46. Kanebo, *supra* note 24, at 130–33; Yonekawa, *supra* note 42, at 677.

47. Kanebo, *supra* note 24, at 134–36.

48. Gary J. Miller, Managerial Dilemmas: The Political Economy of Hierarchy 67–74 (1992).

49. Ramseyer, *supra* note 28, at 152 table 7.8.

50. Toyo boseki, K. K., Toyo boseki 70 Nenshi (A 70-Year History of Toyo boseki, K. K.) 234–35 (1953); Kurashiki boseki, *supra* note 34, at 58.

51. Oliver Williamson, The Economic Institutions of Capitalism, ch. 11 (1985).

52. Yonekawa, *supra* note 42, at 677, 684.

53. Yonekawa, Bosekigyo no hikaku keiei shi kenkyu, *supra* note 36, at 198; Kanebo, *supra* note 24, at 985; Yukio Okamoto, Meiji-ki boseki kankei shiryo (Materials Relating to Meijiera Spinning) 323, 357, 365 (1996); Kurashiki boseki, *supra* note 34, app. 11.

54. Kurashiki boseki, *supra* note 34, app. 3 (§ 4).

55. Sanji Muto, Watashi no minoue banashi (Stories of My Life) 153 (1934).

56. Okamoto, *supra* note 53, at 357, 365; Kurashiki boseki, *supra* note 34, app. 11; Takamura, *supra* note 15, at 107–9.

57. Frank H. Easterbrook, *Two Agency-Cost Explanations of Dividends*, 74 Am. Econ. Rev. 650 (1984). The application to our chapter here depends, of course, on the existence of other constraints against self-dealing by controlling shareholders.

58. Takamura, *supra* note 15, ch. 1. On the use of prominent directors at these firms, see Yoshiro Miwa & J. Mark Ramseyer, *The Value of Prominent Directors: Corporate Governance and Bank Access in Transitional Japan*, 31 J. Legal Stud. 273 (2002).

59. Imuta, *supra* note 21, at 12–13. Note that the firms facilitated monitoring by such industrialists by collectively (through the Boren) publishing information on firm performance that made evaluating managerial performance much easier. *See generally*, Geppo, *supra* note 18, and the material used to construct table 6.3.

60. Hatsu Murakami, *Mie boseki kaisha (The Mie boseki Firm)*, *in* Nihon sangyo kin'yu shi kenkyu (Studies in Japanese Industrial Financial History) 393, 393–97 (Kazuo Yamaguchi et al. eds., 1970).

61. J. Bradford de Long, *Did J. P. Morgan's Men Add Value: An Economist's Perspective on Financial Capitalism*, *in* Inside the Business Enterprise: Historical Perspectives on the Use of Information 205 (Peter Temin ed., 1991). We discuss these issues in more detail and note the differences to DeLong's account of Morgan in Miwa & Ramseyer, *supra* note 58.

62. Nor was this peculiar to Japan, of course. Others have documented the importance of connections and kin ties in a wide variety of economies. *See*, for example, Naomi R. Lamoreaux, Insider Lending (1994); Jack Carr & Janet Landa, *The Economics of Symbols, Clan Names, and Religion*, 12 J. Legal Stud. 135 (1983).

63. Fuji boseki 50-nen shi (A 50-Year History of Fuji Boseki) 37–88 (Fuji boseki, K. K., ed., 1947).

64. Kurashiki boseki, *supra* note 34, app. 4 (§ 37).

65. Accounts of this battle appear in, for example, Hidemasa Morikawa, Nihon keiei shi (Japanese Management History) 100–101 (1981); Kanebo, *supra* note 24, at 103–5.

66. Note that company records show increases in stated capital (generally, but not necessarily, a sign of additional stock issues) for 1922, 1923, 1924, 1934, and 1937 (twice). See Kanebo, *supra* note 24, at 995.

67. Imuta, *supra* note 21, at 193–203.

68. *Id.* at 242–43.

69. *Id.* at 206. This possibly reflects the fact that the Commercial Code itself reduced the power of majority shareholders by requiring that many corporate changes follow not just a vote of the majority of shares, but of a majority of shareholders as well. *See supra* note 25.

CHAPTER SEVEN

Privatization and Corporate Governance: The Lessons from Securities Market Failure

John C. Coffee, Jr.

A PARADIGM SHIFT is now under way in the manner in which financial economics views corporate governance, with the new scholarship emphasizing both the centrality of legal protections for minority shareholders and the possibility that regulation can outperform private contracting. However, substantive differences in corporate law may be less important than the differences in the level of regulation that different nations impose on their securities markets. Under this latter hypothesis, the focus shifts from the minority shareholder to the investor generally. The critical question becomes, does local law establish adequate disclosure and market transparency standards, restrict insider trading, and regulate takeovers and corporate control contests adequately? If it does, then arguably the exposure of shareholders to unfair self-dealing transactions at the corporate level may have only a second-level significance. This chapter reveals that considerable evidence in the Polish and Czech experiences is consistent with the hypothesis that inadequate securities regulation plays the primary role in explaining privatization failures.

I. Introduction: Corporate Governance Rediscovered

A specter is haunting the neoclassical theory of the corporation.[1] It is the specter that law matters—that a positive theory of the firm is incomplete unless it incorporates and explains the role of legal variables. Recent research on corporate governance has found systematic differences between nations in ownership concentration, capital market development, the value of voting rights, and the use of external finance.[2] More important, these differences seem to correlate closely with the strength of the legal protections given minority to investors.[3] In turn, this level of legal protection seems to depend upon, and vary systematically with, the nature and origins of each nation's legal system. In particular, common-law legal systems seem to vastly outperform civil-law legal systems (and particularly French civil-law systems) in providing investor protections and, in turn, encouraging capital market growth and ownership dispersion. Most important, this new scholarship has found that the size, depth, and liquidity of securities markets correlates directly with the quality of the legal protections given to shareholders.[4] In consequence, because the nature and quality of legal protection differs widely across nations, the corporate world subdivides today into rival systems of dispersed ownership and concentrated ownership, with different structures of corporate governance characterizing each.[5]

A paradigm shift is now under way in the manner in which financial economics views corporate governance, with the new scholarship emphasizing both the centrality of legal protections for minority shareholders and the possibility that regulation can outperform private contracting.[6] Although in this chapter I recognize the importance of this transition, I am far more skeptical about whether this new scholarship has identified the critical elements that have given the "common law" nations a comparative advantage over the "civil law" world. Here, a mystery remains. One possibility is that substantive differences in corporate law may matter far less than differences in enforcement practice. In turn, enforcement may depend more upon the strength of the incentives to assert legal remedies than upon the availability of legal remedies themselves. Even this hypothesis, however, oversimplifies, because once one closely examines the differences between various systems of corporate governance, the assumed homogeneity of even common-law legal systems begins to break down. Another possibility is that differences in substantive corporate law are less important than the differences in the level of regulation that different nations impose on their securities markets.[7] Under this latter hypothesis, the focus shifts from the minority shareholder to the investor generally. The critical question becomes, does local law establish adequate disclosure and market transparency standards, restrict insider trading, and adequately regulate takeovers and corporate control contests? If it does, then arguably the exposure of shareholders to unfair self-dealing transactions at the corporate level may have only a second-level significance. This chapter finds considerable evidence in the Polish and Czech experiences that is consistent with this hypothesis. Inadequate securities regulation plays the primary role in explaining privatization failures, but some evidence also exists to suggest that deficiencies in Czech corporate law contributed to the systematic looting of Czech companies by their controlling shareholders.

Even if the critical protections upon which minority shareholders depend have not yet been clearly identified, the available data still strongly support the interpretation that law matters; that in some not yet well-understood manner, certain legal systems have encouraged dispersed ownership, while other systems have rendered it an unstable and transient phenomenon. This new emphasis on legal variables has potentially subversive implications for at least some aspects of neoclassical corporate finance theory. Much of the modern law-and-economics literature on corporate governance has assumed that financial-market regulation was unnecessary and that the role of corporate law was simply to offer a model form contract to investors to enable them to economize on contracting costs. This conclusion that regulation was superfluous, or worse, rested on twin premises: (1) sophisticated parties could write financial contracts that were far more detailed, sophisticated, and fine-tuned to their specific circumstances than any body of standardized regulations could hope to be;[8] and (2) entrepreneurs had adequate incentives to minimize agency costs (in part by bonding themselves and otherwise limiting their discretion) in order to maximize the value for their stock when they brought their fledgling firm to the capital markets.[9] In short, because, under the standard Jensen and Meckling model of the firm,[10] entrepreneurs bore the weight of agency costs, they had good reason to surrender any discretion to expropriate wealth from their investors and to bond themselves to serve their shareholders faithfully; hence, regulation seemed unnecessary. From this perspective, the survival of regulation could be explained best by reference to public choice theories about interest groups and rent-seeking.[11]

This claim that financial contracting largely renders regulation irrelevant cannot explain, however, the close correlation between a given country's level of capital market development and the nature of its legal system. The more logical conclusion is that law does matter, and regulation can somehow better promote economic efficiency than can reliance on financial contracting alone. By themselves, private contracting and the voluntary incentives for disclosure seem incapable of producing the level of continuing disclosure necessary to sustain active securities markets.

More important, standard economic models of financial contracting within firms do not fit the privatization context. Chiefly, this is because privatized firms do not evolve over time from smaller firms, beginning with the usual incubation period at the venture capital stage and progressing through the initial public offering (IPO), but instead are created Minerva-like by governmental fiat. Typically, voucher privatization (which has been the preferred technique) simply distributes shares (or coupons to purchase shares) to all or most of the adult citizens in the country. Dispersed ownership is more transient and vulnerable in this context, because it arrives overnight at the outset of the firm's existence. Hence, managers neither contract with shareholders nor pledge a reputational capital that they have carefully built up over years of service; rather, managers and shareholders are thrown together as legal strangers.[12]

This point has important implications for a policy debate that has begun among scholars who have studied the transitional process: Should privatization be "fast" or "slow"?[13] Should policymakers adopt a "Damn the torpedoes, full speed ahead" approach that accepts the inevitability of some overreaching by controlling shareholders, but justifies this cost as necessary to realize and expedite the efficiency gains incident to privatization? Or should privatization proceed more cautiously because of the risks of market failure and political corruption that may result when control seekers are tempted to bribe and seduce the judicial and regulatory systems to achieve the private benefit of control? These tempting private benefits arise, of course, precisely to the extent that privatization preceded the creation of an adequate legal foundation. The cases examined in this chapter illustrate this tension and lead toward favoring a prudential course of phased privatization, which does not make a hasty and potentially corrupting scramble to control the likely consequence of creating a dispersed-ownership structure.

This chapter will proceed through four stages. In section II I examine some of the difficulties in attempting to distinguish common-law from civil-law systems in terms of any critical factors that lead one to outperform the other. I then focus, in section III on the Czech and Polish experiences, along with earlier, more tentative efforts at privatization, in order to understand what has chiefly gone wrong. In section IV I discuss the techniques recently used for expropriating value from privatized firms and suggest that these techniques reveal some deficiencies in the corporate governance norms of civil-law systems. Finally, in section V I suggest functional reforms and priorities, but these proposals will not give primary emphasis to specific doctrinal rules. Indeed, the premise will be that wholesale adoption of U.S. or U.K. legal rules is not feasible and might not be effective in any event.

II. Are Common-Law Systems Homogenous?

The new comparative research on corporate governance has found that some legal systems give minority shareholders greater protection from fraud and expropriation than others and has assumed that the critical differences largely inhere in the statutory law of these rival systems.[14] This assumes, however, what is to be proved. For example, differences in substantive law could be far less important than differences in enforcement practice. But once we focus on enforcement practice, a blunt, but overlooked, truth quickly confronts us: common-law legal systems may not be that much alike. Thus, while it has been an implicit premise of this new learning that the United States and the United Kingdom, as the two leading common-law systems and the two leading economies characterized by dispersed share ownership, are highly similar, this premise is very debatable. To be sure, both systems share a common legal history. But to stop at this point is to ignore volumes of more recent and highly relevant history over which their two paths have diverged. For much of the late nineteenth-century robber baron era in the United States, controlling shareholders regularly overreached and plundered minority shareholders and creditors. Colorful rogues—such as Jay Gould, Jim Fisk, and Daniel Drew—regularly manipulated the market and perfected the legal technology for "watering" the stock of minority shareholders.[15] Meanwhile, these predators battled for control of railroad empires against even more imperious barons, such as Commodore Vanderbilt, with each side buying and corrupting local judges.[16] Throughout that period, much of which seems to have been recently replayed in Russia and central Europe, the common law proved a frail reed upon which minority shareholders could not safely rely. Over time, investment bankers (most notably, the House of Morgan) and the New York Stock Exchange brought some semblance of law and order to this Wild West environment, and legal standards (particularly those applicable to stock issues and fiduciary standards) were consciously tightened by courts and state legislatures. Still, as of 1900, little suggested that shareholders in the United States received greater protection than shareholders in, say, France.

Another aspect of this puzzle emerges if we look at the legal system in contemporary Russia. Although the Russian legal environment seems even closer to the Hobbesian state of nature, with the looting of corporations and financial institutions being a fairly common event, Russian corporate law has largely borrowed (in a simplified fashion) the principal features and protections of U.S. and U.K. corporate law.[17] Apparently, expropriation can occur even when the "law on the books" is nearly optimal. Perhaps this should not surprise us, as the legal realists have taught us for most of the twentieth century that the "law on the books" is often different from, and less important than, the "law in practice."

One likely answer to this puzzle of when law matters (and why) may lie in the hypothesis that what really counts is not the content of the substantive law, but the adequacy of the enforcement mechanisms that underlie it.[18] The concept of enforcement mechanism needs, however, to be understood in a broader sense than simply as the availability of specific legal remedies. For example, the one characteristic that the robber baron era in the United States shares with contemporary Russia is that, in both, the central government was weak and largely unable to enforce its commands in outlying areas. In the late nineteenth century, the federal government in the United States was almost powerless to control private business entities; no centralized body, such as the Securities and Exchange Commission (SEC) had jurisdiction over investor protection, and business rivals could establish strong political fiefdoms in one state and largely ignore the commands of judges in a different state. In contemporary Russia, the central government appears similarly unable to control local provincial administrators, who may confiscate or extort assets from corporations operating in their area of effective control.[19]

If we focus on enforcement, however, it immediately becomes clear that the differences between the United States and the United Kingdom are probably as great as between the United States and France (a nation generally thought to enforce its investor-protection laws only weakly). In the United States, class and derivative actions are permitted, and plaintiffs' attorneys may charge contingent fees, which are usually awarded by the court based on a percentage of the recovery that the attorney obtains for the class. Under the standard "American Rule," each side bears its own legal fees (which means that the plaintiff's attorney faces only the loss of time and expenses invested in the action if the action is unsuccessful and is not generally liable for the winner's legal expenses).[20] In the United Kingdom, the reverse is generally true. Class actions and contingent fees are not authorized, and the losing side must normally compensate the winning side for its expenses. When the individual plaintiff sues the large corporate defendant, the latter will likely incur the larger legal fees, and this disproportion logically turns the prospect of fee-shifting under the English rule into a prohibitive deterrent to litigation. As a result, while in the United States a highly entrepreneurial system of private enforcement has evolved that largely overcomes the collective action problems that dissuade individual investors from suing,[21] nothing comparable exists in the United Kingdom.

Another sharp contrast involves the level of judicial activism in the two countries. For common-law systems to behave similarly, it would seem logically necessary for them to accord a similar role to the judge. But it is not clear that they do. Although the United States and the United Kingdom share a common-law tradition, judges in these two systems appear to behave quite differently. Comparative-law scholars rate U.S. courts near the top of the scale in terms of "judicial daring"—that is, the willingness of judges to create new legal rules in the absence of legislation—but place the United Kingdom near the bottom of this same scale.[22] In short, the more that one looks at the supposedly obvious differences between common-law and civil-law countries, the more that those differences begin to blur.

On the other hand, the United Kingdom has other institutions—most notably, its Takeover Panel—that appear to be highly effective and that lack any close parallel in the United States. In general, takeover defensive tactics are much more restricted in the United Kingdom than in the United States. Finally, given the more concentrated character of the British financial community (in terms of both institutional ownership and physical location in the city of London), reputational effects may matter more in the United Kingdom than in the United States. These differences may be important, but they have little to do with the line between the common law and the civil law.

The point here is not to compare the enforcement mechanisms of the United States and of the United Kingdom, but only to indicate that they may be very different. In turn, this implies a conceptual problem with the new academic research that broadly and boldly contrasts common-law countries with civil-law countries. Although real differences are clearly observable in terms of ownership concentration, the depth of markets, and the value of control, the presumed legal homogeneity of either common-law or civil-law countries may be more illusory than real. For example, many of those substantive legal rules that the United States and the United Kingdom share may have only trivial significance (or may have importance in one legal system and not the other).[23] Thus, to return to a distinction that I have made in earlier work, formal legal convergence may be less important than functional convergence.[24] Although the United States and the United Kingdom (and other common-law countries) have similar legal systems that share a common origin, their common history may be less important than the fact that they have developed quite different mechanisms for dealing with the same "agency cost" problems that in the end achieve functionally similar results. For example, the issuance of a materially false financial statement may cause a significant drop in the company's stock price upon its discovery in both nations. In the United States, it may elicit a class action; in the United Kingdom, institutional investors may protest to the board and demand corrective action. However, in both countries, responsible senior management may lose their jobs in consequence over about the same period. Similarly, in both countries, a chief executive officer whose company's stock price and earnings underperform the industry averages for a given number of successive quarters will likely be removed from office—although the mechanism of removal (a board coup d'état or a hostile takeover) may differ.[25]

In short, the danger in focusing on legal commonality is that it may obscure very different functional mechanisms that are in fact more responsible for the similar ownership structure and market characteristics of two economies. Also, the recent research on comparative corporate governance has largely focused on the firm level, examining specific characteristics of corporate and bankruptcy law that were thought to generate higher levels of investor protection in "common law" legal systems. Although important, this focus slights the importance of securities markets themselves. The one feature that the United States and the United Kingdom clearly share is strong securities markets, with high disclosure and transparency standards. Rather than attribute the strength of these markets to the alleged commonality of U.S. and U.K. corporate law, it may make more sense to look at the even clearer commonality of U.S. and U.K. securities law.[26] Their similar listing, disclosure, and corporate governance standards may be more important in producing functional convergence (at least for larger companies) than the legal remedies available to individual shareholders. Nonetheless, the indicators used by LLS&V[27] in their provocative comparisons of common-law and civil-law systems have largely focused on the corporate level and ignored the differences in securities market regulation.[28] Not only have the differences between nations in securities regulation been material, but equally important, international convergence is today proceeding more rapidly at the securities market level than at the corporate level.[29] Indeed, functional convergence among securities markets seems more attainable than formal legal convergence at the corporate-law level, both because large firms can migrate between markets and because securities markets themselves face global competitive pressures that may lead them to change and adapt, even when their national governments are resistant to change.

Much recent comparative corporate governance research has been focused on reform. In particular, the recent comparative studies seem to have come as a natural progression from the earlier efforts (and frustrations) of many of these same scholars in attempting to implement viable corporate governance systems in transitional economies that were just emerging from their socialist cocoons. That experience quickly showed two strong tendencies: first, securities markets are fragile and could collapse; and second, expropriation by managers and controlling shareholders could (and did) occur on a massive scale. The response of some scholars to this experience has largely been to call for legislative reform to implement the principal features of the "common law" systems. Such reform may be desirable, but calls for legislative reform or formal legal change often go unheeded. In a path-dependent world, it may simply be politically impossible to get from here to there, even when it is clear to most that such a transition would be efficient and would yield significant economic growth.

III. Fallacies and Blunders: A Short History of Mass Privatization

In 1995, the Prague Stock Exchange had 1,716 listings.[30] Blessed with relatively low inflation and nearly full employment, the Czech Republic's strong macroeconomic position made it seem the country in central or Eastern Europe most likely to make a smooth transition into a market-oriented economy. Yet by early 1999, the number of listings on the Prague Stock Exchange had fallen by more than 80 percent to 301, and observers estimated that fewer than a dozen of these enjoyed any liquidity.[31] Correspondingly, over the same period, the value of an investment in an index of the leading fifty stocks on the Prague Stock Exchange fell by more than 60 percent.[32] Trading dried up, and the viability of the Prague Stock Exchange was itself threatened. Where there had been 1,486 brokers in 1997, there were only 358 in mid-1999.[33]

What happened? The fundamental fallacy in Czech privatization was that securities markets would develop spontaneously, simply because voucher privatization would create an initially dispersed ownership structure. By widely distributing the stock in privatized companies to a broad segment of the Czech adult population, Czech planners expected that an active secondary market would develop naturally. The militantly laissez-faire attitude of the initial Czech government also made it highly resistant to any regulation of this market.

In fact, for an initial period of high optimism, which lasted into 1995, share prices did rise. But then, after a series of scandals, the Czech bubble began to burst. First, foreign portfolio investors began to flee the Czech market. Foreign direct and portfolio investment dropped from $103 million in 1995 to $57 million in 1996 and then turned negative in 1997.[34] By 1998, the Czech economy had entered a general recession.[35] In its wake, momentum gathered to reform the Czech securities market, and reform legislation was adopted in 1998 that established a Czech SEC and curbed some of the more egregious abuses.

Behind this massive disinvestment in the Czech market lay a pervasive loss of investor confidence, as small, dispersed owners witnessed widespread looting of Czech investment funds and the systematic exploitation of the remaining minority shareholders in Czech firms once any faction acquired a controlling position. In consequence, small shareholders systematically divested their shares and moved savings to other forms of investment. At the outset of mass privatization in the Czech Republic, more than 7 million Czech citizens purchased shares through voucher privatization, but by 1999, the number of Czech shareholders had fallen to "barely five million."[36]

If the Czech experience then seems a paradigm of a market failure caused by inadequacies in the legal system, it is still important to identify what precisely went wrong. After a period of initial optimism, investors clearly lost confidence in the Czech market, causing it to decline sharply, even though the underlying macroeconomic conditions remained relatively stable on a regional basis. Moreover, the apparent Czech failure contrasts sharply with the experience of neighboring Poland, where the privatization process was slower and where stronger disclosure and governance standards were established as preconditions. This section will therefore move from a brief review of this seemingly natural experiment to a more detailed assessment of what differentiated these two efforts and then to a broader look at other privatization programs.

A. Poland versus the Czech Republic: Divergent Approaches to Privatization

In geopolitical terms, Poland and the Czech Republic have much in common, as similar central European countries with a shared Slavic culture and historical experience, both nations being former members of the Soviet bloc. But their approaches to privatization could not have been more divergent. The Czech Republic rushed into privatization in the early 1990s, with regulatory controls being developed on an ex post basis in response to a series of crises and scandals.[37] Determined to move assets into the private sector as quickly as possible, Czech authorities privatized some 1,491 joint stock companies in the first wave of Czech privatization, and another 861 in the second wave—thereby increasing the private-sector share of Czech gross domestic product (GDP) from 12 percent in 1990 to 74 percent by 1996.[38] In fairness, this was a considerable logistical achievement.

In contrast, Poland moved far more slowly and equivocally, privatizing only some five hundred firms and only pursuant to a procedure that assigned a state-created investment fund as the controlling shareholder of each privatized firm. Rather than assuming that a secondary market would develop spontaneously, Poland designed voucher investment funds as a mechanism to solve the perceived powerlessness of the individual shareholder in a mass-privatization program. To assure that these state-created investment funds would control the privatized firms, Poland neither permitted the creation of private investment funds (which had sprung up overnight in the Czech Republic) nor initially allowed citizens to invest directly in the stock of the newly privatized firms. Rather, Polish law mandated that citizens could invest their voucher certificates only in state-created financial intermediaries, known as national investment funds (NIFs), which were to serve as controlling shareholders of the to-be-privatized firms.[39] At the outset, only fifteen NIFs were chartered, with each being assigned a controlling $33\frac{1}{3}$ percent stake in its share of the five hundred privatized firms. The balance of the stock in each firm was held by other NIFs and by the state. Each NIF then hired a management company to advise on restructuring those companies in which the NIF held a controlling stake; in fact, a number of Western investment banking firms were hired to perform this role, sometimes in preference to Polish commercial banks.

In short, viewing continued state ownership as the greater danger, Czech authorities rushed into privatization and gave relatively little attention to problems of regulation, while in Poland state planners took the reverse view of the relative dangers, and therefore moved slowly and cautiously to implement a limited privatization program that effectively substituted state-created monitors (in which citizens could invest) for direct state ownership.

Some results of these two very different approaches were easily predictable: the Czech Republic quickly developed an active securities market, while the Polish securities market developed haltingly with only very thin trading (which actually declined between 1994 and 1996).[40] In the Czech Republic, private investment funds appeared as a spontaneous, unplanned market development, with more than six hundred funds being formed during the two Czech privatization waves. Necessarily, these funds could only be regulated on an after-the-fact basis. In contrast, in Poland, privatization was delayed repeatedly by political infighting over a variety of issues, including selection of the management companies that would run the NIFs.

Both systems encountered serious problems, but of a very different character. Three distinct problems compromised Czech privatization, and each was at bottom attributable to legal failures. First, and most noticeable, was the near-total lack of transparency in the Czech securities market. Because trading was not centralized and trading off the Prague Stock Exchange did not require contemporaneous price reporting, only the prices of those transactions that the trading participants wished to disclose (and so transacted on the exchange) were reported. In fact, it appears that the majority of all trading transactions occurred off the Prague Stock Exchange,[41] with the minority of transactions that did occur on the exchange being widely thought to have been at inflated prices. In effect, current securities prices were revealed only when the traders wanted to post a price—either to influence Western portfolio investors or to inflate the value of a privatization fund's portfolio. For this and other reasons, including the absence during this period of any SEC-like authority with power to regulate trading or require contemporaneous price disclosure, foreign investors quickly grew skeptical that the reported prices on the Prague Stock Exchange reflected real values. Moreover, in this nontransparent world, informed trading predictably flourished because it was more profitable than in an efficient market.[42]

A second problem quickly arose that further compromised restructuring efforts. During the course of the two Czech privatization waves, some six hundred investment funds were created, and they competed vigorously to convince individual investors to convert their privatization vouchers into the funds' shares. Potentially, such vehicles could have become effective corporate monitors because they aggregated large stakes in Czech corporations and thereby potentially solved the collective action problem that the dispersed ownership resulting from voucher privatization necessarily implied. However, the largest investment funds were established by the principal Czech commercial and savings banks, which had obvious reputational advantages in convincing Czech citizens to deposit their vouchers with them.[43] Owning only small stakes in their own investment funds, the banks had little incentive to undertake costly restructuring activities. Instead, many sought to use their investment fund's influence over its portfolio companies to secure banking clients for themselves. Rather than concentrating their holdings (and thus maximizing their influence), most bank-administered funds sought to diversify their holdings in order to hold stakes in as many firms as possible—in part to solicit banking clients for their parents.[44] Also, to protect their banking parents from potential hostile takeovers, the bank-run funds cross-invested heavily in the common stocks of the other major banks and in that of their own banking parent. An incestuous web of cross-ownership quickly developed to insulate the major banks from hostile takeovers. Finally, most privatization funds (both bank-related funds and nonbank funds) found it more profitable to concentrate on trading than on restructuring often-inefficient portfolio companies. The combination of a nontransparent market and their privileged position as insiders made such activities profitable, but constantly filled the media with news of recurring insider trading scandals.

If the bank-related funds were passive, the nonbank funds were far worse. A subsequent study by the Czech Ministry of Finance found a negative correlation between a privatized firm's performance and the percentage of its shares held by nonbank investment funds.[45] In the first wave of Czech privatization, 3 percent of the funds became insolvent and were placed into "forced administration,"[46] but, in the second wave, the rate of insolvency accelerated, and some ten funds accounting for more than 21 percent of market capitalization in that wave were placed in "forced administration."[47] The common cause appears not to have been excessive leverage or investment failures, but "tunneling" out—the fraudulent siphoning off of assets.

The ease with which funds could be looted is shown by the similar ease with which they could escape regulation. Although Czech law did regulate the operation of investment funds, it did not restrict the ability of an investment fund to elect to deregister and become an unregulated holding company. Symptomatic of the civil law's literal narrow-mindedness, the difference between an investment company and a holding company under Czech law was formal, not functional. Simply by surrendering one's license to operate as an investment company, an investment fund could escape virtually all regulation. Because share ownership of investment companies was extremely dispersed, a small control group, holding as little as 10 percent of the voting stock of an investment fund, could usually dominate shareholder meetings and pass a resolution to convert the fund into a holding company. Once unregulated, all forms of self-dealing were effectively made possible, and the entity might reincorporate outside the Czech Republic (as some did).

The extent of such conversions seems extraordinary. In terms of market share, fully 28 percent of the investment-privatization funds in the first wave of Czech privatization and 21 percent of the funds in the second wave were converted into unregulated holding companies.[48] Although this may sound as if the rate of conversion declined, it must be remembered that an additional 21 percent of the funds in the second wave were placed in "forced administration" by the Czech authorities.[49] On this basis, nearly half the funds in the second wave of Czech privatization either failed or escaped regulation by being converted into unregulated entities. Although major bank-run funds generally stood apart from this race to convert, the banks' intentions, while nonfraudulent, seemed to have been in part to use their funds as vehicles with which to attract banking clients and other business for themselves.

The eventual upshot of these repeated scandals was that the administration of investment funds became a contentious political issue in the Czech Republic and helped to bring about the downfall of the government of Václav Klaus (which had generally opposed market regulation) and the passage of securities-reform legislation in 1998. But by then, public confidence in the securities market had been largely eroded.[50]

The Polish experience was in many respects the reverse of that of the Czechs. Privatization was delayed and delayed again, as demanding disclosure rules and fiduciary standards for directors were drafted. Polish citizens were given only one choice: which NIF (of the fifteen originally created) to invest in, as direct investment in either portfolio firms or private investment funds was not initially permitted. Trading was centralized on the Warsaw Stock Exchange, and price transparency appears never to have been a serious issue. Polish disclosure standards also won high marks from most observers, and the European Bank for Reconstruction and Development (EBRD) Transition Report rated Poland and Hungary as the two central European countries that had most closely approximated International Organization of Securities Commissions (IOSCO) standards.[51]

Still, while the Polish authorities planned a carefully integrated program of market reforms and privatization, their success in actually developing their securities market arguably presents a closer question. Advocates of "fast" privatization might point to the fact that as of late 1998, only some 253 companies were listed on the Warsaw Stock Exchange[52] (much less than the number in the considerably smaller Czech Republic). Indeed, the Polish mass-privatization program was limited to some five hundred enterprises, representing only 10 percent of Polish GDP.[53] Similarly, while it remains debatable whether the state-created financial intermediaries in Poland (the NIFs) have functioned as effective monitors, some commentators believe that the NIFs have at least been more active than the Czech investment funds in encouraging efficient restructuring.[54]

The most impressive evidence in favor of the Polish approach has been the ability of its securities market to support cash offerings of equity securities. Between 1991 and 1998, no Czech company sold equity for cash as part of its privatization program; conversely, some fifty Polish companies did.[55] Over the same period, no Czech company effected an IPO over the Prague Stock Exchange, while some 136 Polish companies did so on the Warsaw Stock Exchange.[56] In short, only the Polish system succeeded in developing its stock exchange so that it could perform the classic role of serving as an engine of economic growth.

Another strong contrast between the Czech and Polish experiences involves market performance during conditions of adversity. When the Asian financial crisis struck in 1998, Poland had a relatively mild experience. Between the end of 1996 and August 1998, the Polish stock index fell only 13.1 percent,[57] while the Czech market had already partially collapsed and fell further.[58] Up until late 1998, the NIFs listed on the Warsaw Stock Exchange seemed to be trading at or near their net asset value, while Czech funds during this period often traded at steep 20–70 percent discounts off their net asset value.[59]

Another measure of a securities market's success is the number and percentage of firms listed on it that migrate to foreign stock exchanges. Such dual listings may imply that the listed firm cannot raise capital on its home-country exchange; alternatively, it may be a bonding mechanism by which a firm credibly pledges to comply with disclosure and corporate governance standards that are not enforced (or enforceable) in its home country.[60] In any event, companies in central Europe have recently migrated to German stock exchanges (most notably the Berlin

Stock Exchange). As of early 1999, one study finds that 117 stocks from Eastern Europe were listed on the Berlin Stock Exchange, of which 24 were from the Czech Republic but only 13 from considerably larger Poland.[61] Prior to the onset of the Russian financial crisis in late 1998, Poland had 2 percent of its listed companies traded on German stock exchanges, while the Czech Republic had 5 percent (or more than twice as many).[62] This disparity should not be surprising. Having the weaker legal protections, Czech companies had the greater need to list on a foreign exchange with "stronger" governance standards in order to attract foreign portfolio investors (most of whom had already fled the Czech market because of its lack of transparency).

This happy story contrasting the regulated and unregulated worlds encounters one serious difficulty that arose in late 1998. Beginning in approximately December 1998, the stock prices of the Polish NIFs fell sharply, and they currently trade at discounts to their net asset values as steep as ever existed in the Czech Republic.[63] Meanwhile, the surviving Czech investment funds now trade at relatively modest discounts to their net asset value (typically around 20 percent).[64]

What explains this sudden reversal? Although any answer is speculative, most NIFs experienced board control contests in 1998 that replaced their old investment managers. Until late 1998, the Polish government held the majority of the voting power in NIFs. But since then, shareholders have replaced the management company in fourteen of the original fifteen NIFs. In effect, the same fear of opportunistic control struggles that eroded investor confidence in the Czech market appears to have devastated the value of Polish NIFs. No longer the stable pawns of the state, these NIFs appear to have suffered a sharp and fairly sudden loss of investor confidence.

Still, the number of firms traded on the Warsaw Stock Exchange has continued to grow, and its overall market capitalization now exceeds that of the Prague Stock Exchange.[65] Nor has evidence yet surfaced indicating that privatized companies have been looted or tunneled in Poland. Nonetheless, the bottom-line evaluation must be a cautious one: in transitional economies, it may take little to disturb investor confidence and produce a flight for the exits. As they have been "deregulated" (or, perhaps more accurately, "privatized"), the Polish NIFs may be repeating the sorry history of the Czech funds.

B. What Really Distinguishes the Czech and Polish Experiences?

To this point, the Czech and Polish experiences have been differentiated in terms of the highly spontaneous character of Czech privatization versus the carefully planned—indeed, constrained—character of Polish privatization. But both nations have in common one fact that is troubling for the new scholarship that emphasizes the importance of differences in substantive corporate law: they each had a corporation law heavily based on the German civil-law structure. Put simply, their experiences were very different, but their corporate laws were largely the same. As a result, because the corporate laws of Poland and the Czech Republic each provide only weak protection for minority shareholders,[66] their different experiences cannot be used to corroborate the claim that differences in substantive corporate law are the key causal factors that determine the success or failure of privatization.

Yet if Poland and the Czech Republic had similar corporate laws, their approaches to securities regulation were entirely different. Not only did Poland impose high disclosure standards from the outset (including quarterly reporting), it also created an SEC-like agency to enforce its laws from the beginning of its privatization experience.[67] In addition, Poland adopted ownership disclosure provisions that resembled Section 13(d) of the United States Williams Act in order to require ownership transparency—that is, the disclosure by substantial shareholders and potential acquirers of their beneficial ownership of specified levels of a company's shares.[68] Finally, Poland (but not the Czech Republic) followed the British model of takeover regulation by requiring any shareholder who acquired more than a specified level of stock to make a mandatory bid for the remaining shares.[69] In sum, as Pistor has shown, Poland had "weak" corporate law, but "strong" securities law.[70]

To give an overview, these restrictions on the undisclosed acquisition of control and the mandatory requirement that a control acquirer offer to purchase the remaining shareholders may have been responsible for some of the differences in the Czech and Polish experiences. Seemingly, these restrictions precluded (or at least slowed) the frantic scramble for control that occurred in the Czech Republic. To the extent that this is true, the Polish experience may suggest the need for refinements in the "minority protection" model developed by those scholars of corporate governance who have focused, somewhat single-mindedly, on differences in substantive corporate law as the primary determinant of ownership structure.[71] In a comparison of systems of corporate governance, many of the most important differences may lie at the level of securities regulation. Here, rules prohibiting insider trading, requiring ownership transparency, and restricting coercive takeover bids may do more to protect minority shareholders from expropriation than would the same jurisdiction's substantive corporate law rules. Indeed, as suggested earlier, the most important common denominator between the "protective" legal regimes in the United States and the United Kingdom may be their highly similar securities laws, not their common-law origins.

Another hypothesis, however, must also be noted: more important than these legal differences may have been the creation of the Polish NIFs. By holding controlling stakes, these state-created financial intermediaries blocked the path of entrepreneurs who otherwise might have competed to seize control of newly privatized companies. A critical, if possibly unintended, role of the NIFs was to provide an assurance to smaller shareholders that they need not fear the potential expropriation of their investment in a privatized company, at least because of its vulnerability to a predatory control seeker.[72] Indeed, much of the scramble for control in the Czech Republic seems to have been defensively motivated. Each large shareholder essentially realized that if it did not acquire control, someone else would, with resulting injury to it. Each shareholder would know that the acquisition of control by some other shareholder would imply a sharp decline in the value of its minority position. As a result, the fear of loss may have provided a greater incentive to compete for control than the expectation of any synergistic or opportunistic gain.

In this light, the inefficient exposure to loss that the Czech system imposed on minority shareholders may also explain the absence, noted earlier, of equity offerings for cash in the Czech Republic as contrasted with their frequency in Poland.[73] Because an offering of equity securities inherently dilutes existing shareholders, it exposes them to an increased risk of exploitation; correspondingly, it also potentially disrupts any equilibrium that may have been achieved among large shareholders. Having acquired a majority position, a controlling shareholder might prefer to rely on high-cost bank financings rather than to make use of dilutive equity financing, because dilution of its ownership could interfere with its ability to realize the private benefits of control. This fear was not a danger in the Polish context, where the NIFs gave all shareholders greater assurance of continuity for at least an interim period. Thus, one implication of the Czech experience may be that unregulated control contests and the rapid transition from dispersed to concentrated ownership can give rise to externalities—both political and economic.

Correspondingly, the sharp decline in the stock prices of Polish NIFs, once shareholders were permitted to take control of them from the government, also reinforces the interpretation that unregulated control contests expose minority investors to the risk of expropriation and result in reduced share prices.[74] Had the Polish government provided for a more phased transition (such as through transitional ownership ceilings or use of staggered boards), the severity of this decline might have been reduced.

C. Other Privatization Experiences: Do Securities Markets Develop Naturally?

Although the Czech and Polish experiences probably supply the closest approximation to a natural experiment that can be found in this area, their experiences are not unique. A brief review of earlier privatization efforts finds similar cases in which emerging securities markets collapsed after a loss of investor confidence, including cases in the United States. Although in the public mind the term "*privatization*" probably first came into popular usage with the decision of the government of Margaret Thatcher in Great Britain in 1979 to sell off government-owned enterprises, important earlier instances can be identified. The first large-scale privatization offering to public investors seems to have occurred in 1961, when the Konrad Adenauer government in the Federal Republic of Germany sold a majority stake in Volkswagen in a public offering that was aimed at small investors in Germany.[75] This was followed by an even larger offering in 1965 of the government-owned shares of VEBA A.G., a German heavy-mining company. Both offerings were initially successful, but share prices fell dramatically thereafter, forcing the Adenauer government to develop "a rescue operation . . . aimed at protecting small shareholders."[76] The experience appears to have dissuaded both Germany and other European governments from embarking on similar programs until the Thatcher administration initiated its ideologically motivated wave of privatizations in 1979.

During the early 1970s, the government of Augusto Pinochet in Chile sought to reprivatize industries that had earlier been nationalized by the Salvador Allende administration. Sales were made at extremely discounted prices, and when the Chilean economy later entered a debt-and-payment crisis in the early 1980s, it renationalized many of these same industries. Not until the late 1980s (at roughly the same time as the Thatcher government) did Chile effect a more successful privatization program through the public sale of shares in state-owned enterprises.[77] However, the key event in this later, successful privatization was the 1990 privatization of Telefonos de Chile, which was largely targeted at U.S. investors through the use of American depositary receipts. Mexico's very large and successful privatization program in the 1990s has similarly been effected through privatizations of large, state-owned companies that were directly listed on the New York Stock Exchange.[78]

Mass-privatization efforts that have not been implemented through established exchanges have fared less well. The most notable example is, of course, that in Russia. By virtually all accounts, Russian privatization has involved a spectacular series of blunders and been thwarted by pervasive corruption. As a result, most recent discussions of privatization have been largely preoccupied with the Russian experience.[79] But the lessons from the Russian failure are more difficult to draw because the Russian privatization effort was flawed from the outset by critical design failures and macroeconomic conditions that were not present in either Poland or the Czech Republic. First, Russian privatization had a significantly different design than did Czech privatization in that substantial blocks of stock were allocated to the incumbent managers as a political accommodation that was essential to the implementation of privatization. The result was probably easily predicted: within two to three years after mass privatization, most minority shareholders had sold their shares to the insiders, thereby producing the same highly concentrated ownership structures that are the norm elsewhere.[80] Second, in contrast to circumstances in other recent privatization experiences, the Russian government lacked control over its outlying regions. In these regions, privatized companies have been at least as subject to expropriation by the local government (or coalitions led by, or affiliated with, it) as by controlling shareholders.[81] Third, the legal system in Russia was almost uniquely primitive, indeed to the point that few contractual obligations could be routinely enforced and resort to extralegal means (most notably, violence) was the norm, not the exception. Finally, the macroeconomic condition in Russia proved to be particularly perverse.[82] As a result, in 1998, the Russian government defaulted on its domestic and international debt, and the RTS stock market index fell almost 90 percent from its level of eleven months earlier.[83] When an experiment fails from multiple causes, it is difficult to attribute primary responsibility to any one of them.

In contrast, what makes the Czech story more interesting than the Russian is that the same transition from dispersed to concentrated ownership occurred even without the built-in bias for insider ownership or the poor macroeconomic conditions that characterized the Russian context. Nor is the Czech experience unique. To the extent that Czech privatization malfunctioned, lack of regulation would appear to play a greater causal role, because other explanations are simply not as available. More generally, except when companies have been privatized through offerings listed on international stock exchanges, the Czech progression to concentrated ownership seems to be the dominant pattern, with the exceptions being few in number. Poland appears to be the most notable anomoly, but its story has not yet played out fully. As discussed next, this pattern raises the question of whether this transition is an inevitable progression.

D. The Reappearance of Concentrated Ownership

Both in Russia and in the Czech Republic, mass privatization through the sale or distribution of privatization vouchers to the citizenry inevitably created a highly dispersed ownership structure—but only for a transitory period. Over time, concentrated ownership reemerged. Because numerous studies have concluded that privatized firms become more efficient,[84] it is not surprising that some studies attribute this increased efficiency to the emergence of concentrated ownership. For example, one detailed study that examined the performance over the period from 1992 to 1995 of a sample of 706 Czech firms that were privatized in 1991–92 concluded that the greater the ownership concentration, the greater the improvement in profitability and market valuation.[85] Unfortunately, this study examined a period that ended in 1995, prior to the subsequent free fall in price levels on the Prague Stock Exchange. Possibly, the higher stock market valuations at this initial stage were a transitory phenomenon that reflected the prospective control fights that were already looming.

Still, let us assume for a moment that newly privatized firms with concentrated ownership do initially outperform comparable firms with dispersed ownership. Does this then imply that an economy characterized by concentrated ownership will be more efficient than one characterized by dispersed ownership—at least in the case of transitional economies? The problem with any such conclusion is that the benefits from concentrated ownership may prove to be short lived, while the costs surface only at a delayed point. Even if concentrated ownership implies superior monitoring of management, these benefits have to be balanced against the enhanced risk of expropriation by controlling shareholders. Such expropriation risks the phenomenon of securities market collapse, which in turn may result in a variety of social costs. For example, as earlier noted, Polish securities markets have been able to support IPOs and other cash offerings of equity securities, while Czech markets have not.[86] Economic growth then may be at risk.

The extent of this risk has only recently begun to emerge in new research that documents an apparent global pattern. The Asian financial crisis of 1997–98 adversely affected economic development in most emerging markets, but to varying degrees. Although most analysts have assumed that its causes lay in macroeconomic and banking policies, one provocative new study concludes that "the weakness of legal institutions for corporate governance had an important effect on the extent of [exchange rate] depreciations and stock market declines in the Asian crisis."[87]

Essentially, the study argues that the rate of expropriation increases when the rate of return on investment falls. In short, managers and controlling shareholders tend to steal more in bad times than in good—and investors expect this. Hence, given any adverse shock to the financial system of a region (or the world generally), the relative decline will be the worst in those countries with legal systems that confer the weakest protections to minority shareholders. Using as its sample the twenty-five emerging markets that are currently open to significant capital flows (and hence are the most vulnerable to speculative attack), the study concluded that "weak enforcement of shareholder and creditor rights had first-order importance in determining the extent of exchange rate depreciation in 1997–98."[88] Indeed, three indexes of legal institutions—which the authors termed "efficiency of the judiciary," "corruption," and the "rule of law"—were found to "predict the changes in exchange rates in emerging markets better than do the standard macro measures."[89] Other measures reflecting the strength of shareholder rights also correlated closely with the severity of the financial crisis, but with the proviso that "these measures reflect how rights are actually enforced."[90] To sum up, the strength of legal protections (as measured by actual enforcement practice) appeared to be the independent variable that best predicted the dependent variable of severity of financial crisis.

At this juncture, it is useful to return to the Czech experience. As noted earlier, a number of studies have found that privatized firms became more profitable to the extent that their ownership was more concentrated.[91] But is this advantage sustainable over time? The subsequent sharp decline in prices on the Prague Stock Exchange suggests that some financial shock (from whatever source) destabilized the economy and caused a withdrawal of investor capital. Why was the market decline so extreme in the absence of any major macroeconomic change in the Czech economy? Perhaps investors were aware of their potential vulnerability, but expected that managers would constrain their rate of expropriation during boom times. At the first sign of bust, however, investors race for the exits because they expect the rate of expropriation to increase.

Whether or not one accepts this premise that the rate of expropriation rises with any decline in return on investment, the critical factor in this scenario is that investor loss of confidence will be greatest in those economies in which they believe they are least protected legally. In truth, assumptions about the relationship of the rate of expropriation to the return on investment are probably unnecessary to drive this model. All that one need hypothesize is that investors will ignore legal risks and their vulnerability to expropriation by controlling shareholders during boom times, possibly on the premise that managers and controlling shareholders will not risk disrupting the momentum that is benefiting them all. Essentially, the Czech experience seems consistent with this pattern.

Although such data can be read to mean that legal development has a decisive influence on the viability of securities markets, the true independent variable in such a model may be investor confidence, and the level of such confidence may be influenced by factors other than the strength of legal protections. Investors may learn that a particular venue (whether a country or a stock exchange) has frequently experienced scandals—and decide to avoid it.

Even within the United States, there is evidence consistent with this hypothesis. In 1992, the Amex launched the Emerging Company Marketplace (ECM) to trade the stocks of small, high-growth companies.[92] By 1995, it was forced to close this market after a series of scandals had "damaged the ECM's reputation for monitoring the quality of its listings."[93] Yet investors in the ECM had the same legal rights as investors trading on the New York Stock Exchange. Although other factors also inhibited the growth of the ECM,[94] the role of scandal seems critical. Investors are neither legal scholars nor comparativists; they learn principally from experience, not theory. Moreover, they may expect any apparent pattern that they observe to continue (even if it was in fact simply an unconnected series of random events). Hence, scandal predicts future scandals, and investors expect more expropriation. This expectation of continuity may explain the relatively high failure rate of "emerging company" or "incubator" stock exchanges.[95]

The bottom line, then, may be that anything that invites public scandal (including weak legal protections) creates a negative externality. If so, public policies intended to protect market integrity and preserve investor confidence can be easily justified, even if they may sometimes impede the ability of small and nonfraudulent firms to raise capital.

IV. The Technology of Expropriation

Although a variety of tactics were used to expropriate wealth from Czech companies and investment funds, the best-known strategy was "tunneling," referred to earlier. Essentially, this practice involved the sale or transfer of a controlled firm's products or assets at below-market prices to another company, which was controlled by the same controlling group as controlled the original firm. Gradually, through a series of transactions that might involve a number of such shell companies, the controlled corporation's assets could be hollowed out (hence the term *tunneling*); alternatively, its expected future cash flow could be transferred to the shell company by causing the controlled firm to enter into long-term production contracts under which most of its output was effectively sold at cost (or less) to one or more shell companies.

Variations on this basic pattern were numerous. For example, an entrepreneur might borrow funds to buy a controlling stake in a Czech company, using a personally owned corporation as the vehicle that borrowed the acquisition debt from a bank. Once control of the firm was acquired, the entrepreneur could merge the personally controlled firm into the privatized firm, in order to make the latter liable for the entrepreneur's personal acquisition indebtedness.[96] As a result, the entrepreneur forces the other shareholders to bear much of the cost of the entrepreneur's acquisition of control.

Such unfair self-dealing is not particularly novel or imaginative. But, precisely for that reason, the fact that it worked so effectively in the Czech Republic suggests that there must be some characteristic weakness or vulnerability in Czech law and (because Czech corporate law was largely patterned after German law) in the civil law generally. A key reason why tunneling was successful involved the availability of legal techniques through which it could be insulated from judicial scrutiny. A 1997 study by the Czech Ministry of Finance examined a variety of tactics for looting privatized companies and reported:

> *"Tunneling" into companies is a frequent phenomenon.* Current "corporate raiders" have discovered a risk-free method of removing money from companies. This method consists of holding a general meeting of shareholders in which the "raiders" have a voting majority; this meeting passes a decision on a transaction involving corporate property . . . and the Board of Directors of the company then carries out this operation, with consequent damage to the company. No (minority) shareholder can blame the Board of Directors of the company for this operation as it is bound by the decision of the general meeting.[97]

In short, if the self-dealing transaction was approved by a majority of the shareholders, the directors were effectively insulated from legal liability. Although minority shareholders could sue to challenge action taken at the shareholders' meeting, they would receive little disclosure about the terms of the transaction and hence were not in a position to raise an effective challenge.

To the extent this assessment is accurate, it reveals a sharp contrast between the constraints of Czech and those of common-law jurisdictions. For example, U.S. law, although giving considerable weight to shareholder ratification, generally does not permit a self-interested shareholder to ratify a transaction between the corporation and itself (or an affiliate).[98] Typically, only the vote of a disinterested majority of the shareholders can have this impact. Thus, the practical consequence of this difference is to accord the majority shareholder (or shareholder group) far greater power to impose self-dealing transactions on the minority and hence to create a far-stronger incentive for a shareholder or group seeking control to obtain a majority interest. Although German corporate law (and hence Czech law, as a legal system substantially based on that model) permits the shareholder to attack the results of a shareholder meeting, this is an uphill battle, because it asks the court to overrule the majority of the shareholders, not simply the board of directors.

Majority ratification was not, however, the only technique through which tunneling could be effected. Well before achieving an absolute majority, a shareholder or a shareholder group might achieve de facto control of the board and thus be in a position to approve the same self-dealing transactions without shareholder ratification, based rather on board approval. Directors who approved a clearly unfair self-dealing transaction might face some risk of legal liability, but this risk is mitigated by two key factors that characterize many civil-law systems. First, shareholders will not necessarily learn of the self-dealing transaction. Under German corporate law, an elaborate body of legal strictures regulates the relationship between the companies that belong to a holding structure, or "Konzern." This body of law permits a majority shareholder to dominate its subsidiary, but expects the majority to compensate the minority for any detriment that the latter suffers.[99] Although the firm's auditors must report on such intercompany dealings, they do so only to the controlled firm's supervisory board, not to its minority shareholders. German commentators have candidly acknowledged that this nontransparent approach to the regulation of self-dealing leaves at least a potential loophole in the civil law's system of corporate governance: shareholders cannot challenge transactions of which they are unaware.[100]

More generally, German corporate law views the shareholders' meeting as the appropriate forum at which different issues are to be debated and resolved. This may work adequately in a system of concentrated ownership, in which large shareholders can be expected to attend the meetings. But privatization inherently creates dispersed shareholders with small stakes, and they are less likely to be informed or to attend such a meeting. In addition, management can schedule the meeting for a remote site at little notice, a tactic that will work to discourage at least small shareholders. Moreover, Czech law exacerbated this problem by establishing a particularly low quorum requirement (30 percent), which effectively resulted in as few as two large funds being able to satisfy this requirement and vote through action at a hastily convened meeting.[101]

In transitional economies, these dangers are further aggravated by the greater likelihood that the supervisory board may not be independent or may simply be too inexperienced or passive to evaluate the transaction's fairness. In addition, the judicial systems in transitional economies have not been able to develop remedies or standards on their own to reduce the risk of expropriation. Moreover, even if shareholders do learn of the transaction, they may lack the incentive to take action or sue. Here, the standard collective action problem surfaces: small shareholders will seldom have sufficient economic reason to undertake costly litigation. In addition, once a control block is formed, it is rare to find any other substantial shareholder group;[102] instead, other potential competitors for control appear to exit quickly once de facto control has been achieved by a rival. Thus, few individual shareholders will face a sufficiently substantial loss to justify the cost of litigation on an individual basis. In the United States, this collective action problem is at least partially solved by (1) the existence of the contingent fee agreement (which is essentially a risk-shifting device by which the small shareholder transfers the risks of the litigation to an entrepreneurial plaintiff's attorney), and (2) the prevailing legal rule in the United States that a successful plaintiff in a derivative action is entitled to have the corporation pay its reasonable attorney's fees. Absent similar enforcement mechanisms, minority shareholders in transitional economies will predictably remain passive, even if they learn that they have been defrauded.

V. Policy Lessons from the Privatization Experience

Several common denominators are discernible in the early efforts to privatize state-owned enterprises and to develop securities markets in transitional economies. First, most recent studies of the privatization process have reported that the most obvious corporate monitors (namely, institutional investors and, in particular, privatization investment funds) have shown little interest in monitoring. Either they have been clearly ill equipped for such a role or, more typically, they have used their "insider" positions to engage in informed trading in thin and nontransparent markets or to pursue other self-interested ends. While the circumstances vary, the underlying cause seems to be the same: restructuring is a costly undertaking in which the gains are necessarily shared with other shareholders. In contrast, as long as markets are nontransparent and minority protections largely nonexistent, it may be easier and more profitable to expropriate wealth than to create it. Second, to the extent that large shareholders are active, their primary focus seems to be on obtaining a controlling position—either as a means to exploit the private benefits of control or as a defensive measure to protect themselves from expropriation, or both. Once this scramble for control produces a victor, tunneling begins. Third, emerging securities markets seem vulnerable to sudden collapses. Once a market becomes stigmatized, the decline is fast, not slow, because a sudden exogenous shock can cause both foreign and domestic investors to race for the exits—if they lose confidence.

To remedy these problems, some have called for the wholesale reform of corporate and securities laws in order to introduce the more protective features of Anglo-American law into the typically civil-law codes of most transitional countries. This sounds desirable, but closer analysis reveals a problem in this approach: little consensus exists about precisely what the most important and protective features of Anglo-American law are. For example, preemptive rights play an important role in the United Kingdom, but virtually no role in the United States.[103] In contrast, class actions may generate a desirable level of deterrence in the United States, but are unknown in the United Kingdom. Although some research seems to show that common-law systems outperform civil-law systems in protecting minority shareholders,[104] a satisfactory explanation for why the common law's apparent superiority remains elusive. Other commentators have stressed that the development of strong securities markets requires high disclosure standards and protection for minority shareholders from expropriation (both of information and property) by insiders.[105] This seems clearly valid, but it still leaves open the considerable problem of how to get to such an ideal state from the existing starting points.

In sum, possible reforms can be grouped under three headings: (1) judicial reforms, which respond either to the underdeveloped state of the judiciary in transitional economies or to special problems relating to the alleged rigidity of the civil law; (2) structural reforms, which may require legislation but do not involve legal rules; and (3) legislative reforms, which might relate to either substantive corporate law or securities regulation. This section will begin with judicial reforms because it seems necessary to assess frankly what can and cannot be expected of the judiciary in developing countries. Thereafter, I will consider both structural reforms and possible legislative revisions.

A. Judicial Reforms

Although it is conclusory to simply assume that common-law systems necessarily offer greater protection to minority shareholders than do civil-law systems, the evidence is strong that dispersed ownership persists primarily in common-law legal regimes.[106] Potentially, this could be the result of statutory provisions that are generally found in common-law systems. However, to date, proponents of the common law's superiority have not been able to provide a convincing explanation of the critical statutory deficiencies of the civil law or the common law's features that better protect minority shareholders. Alternative hypotheses therefore need to be considered.

1. A HYPOTHESIS OF THE COMMON LAW'S ADVANTAGES

One plausible hypothesis is that the real superiority of common-law systems lies in the distinctive role of the common-law judge. A considerable law-and-economics literature views the corporate charter as a highly incomplete contract.[107] Necessarily, there are gaps in this contract that must be filled. Law-and-economics theorists have disagreed over the years about what principle or formula the court should use in seeking to fill these gaps,[108] but consensus exists that the common-law judge can and should fill these gaps. In contrast, the civil-law judge may not have the same authority or the same expansive understanding of the judicial role. To the extent that the civil law distrusts judicial activism or views it as a usurpation of the legislature's role, the civil-law judge is confined to the narrower role of interpreting what comprehensive civil codes have actually specified. Thus, at least at the margin, the common law encourages gap filling, while the civil law tends to impede it.

Any summary description of the differences between the civil law and the common law will necessarily omit much and risks stereotyping legal systems that have considerable subtlety and variation. Nonetheless, the role of the judge does appear to be significantly different under the two systems.[109] If it overstates the case to say that the civil-law judge is simply a bureaucrat whose job it is to interpret and apply a written body of statutes, it is still true that the civil-law jurist lacks the same freedom and discretion as the common-law judge to search through a vast storehouse of legal precedents to find the rule best suited for the case before the court.[110] By definition, the inventory of potentially applicable precedents that the common law creates confers greater discretion upon the legal decision maker.

This distinction has even greater force in the area of private law. On the one hand, civil-law codes tend to be especially comprehensive in this area and thus arguably leave less room for gap filling. Conversely, the common law (and particularly corporate law) does not view statutes as the only (or even principal) source of law. Under the common law, legal duties can arise that are independent of any statutory source. The most important example for corporate law is the concept of fiduciary duty. Fiduciary duties can develop out of a course of dealing or a relationship involving trust and confidence where neither side has contractually assumed any duty to the other.[111] In corporate law, the best example of how the concept of fiduciary duty invites common-law judges to fill gaps involves the duty of loyalty. Although some American states do define the duty of care by statute, the broader duty of loyalty is generally left to the common-law process of judicial interpretation. There, it rests on a common-law foundation consisting of several centuries of judicial precedent. Even before the modern corporation arose, the law of agency and the law of trusts held the servant accountable to the master for secret profits obtained from the use of the master's property. These decisions were later applied to hold corporate officials—including officers, directors, and controlling shareholders—to similar standards. In Delaware, the foundational decision defining the contours of this duty is *Guth v. Loft*,[112] which in broad and somewhat rhetorical prose instructs corporate fiduciaries that they are held to an "uncompromising duty of loyalty."[113] Equally famous decisions in New York and elsewhere have used similarly broad language, including, of course, Justice (then Judge) Benjamin Cardozo's famous phrase that a fiduciary must observe not merely the "morals of the marketplace . . . but the punctilio of an honor the most sensitive."[114] Sophisticated judges today recognize that such broad norms must be applied in a context-specific fashion, and this may lead them to deemphasize the rhetorical flourishes of an earlier generation and instead consider the hypothetical bargain into which shareholders and corporate fiduciaries have entered. But attempts to "contract out" from the duty of loyalty through broad exculpatory charter provisions have generally failed.[115]

The immediately relevant point is that the common law's concept of fiduciary duty both enables and instructs the common-law judge to fill in the gaps in an incomplete contract. Indeed, the fiduciary concept both tells the court that implied and noncancelable conditions must be read into the corporate contract and provides a rich repository of illustrations in the form of cases to guide the court. No similar deep inventory of legal precedents existing apart from the statutory law of the corporations code arms the civil-law judge. To be sure, some modest steps toward recognizing a fiduciary duty to minority shareholders have been taken in some civil-law jurisdictions (most notably, Germany),[116] but the concept has been stated only in the abstract and lacks any effective enforcement mechanism. As a result, although the differences between the civil law and the common law can easily be overstated, the civil law essentially views the corporations code as the law and confines the judge to, more or less, mechanically applying it, while for the common-law judge, corporate law is a complex amalgam of statutes and judicial decisions. Rather than replacing or superseding earlier judicial precedents, the statutory corporations code can be seen as attempting to codify those precedents.

This hypothesis that the common law tends to encourage gap filling, while the civil law discourages it, certainly remains open to challenge.

Some empirical evidence finds British judges, for example, to be less "daring" than their civil-law counterparts in France or Germany.[117] But whatever the overall level of caution of British judges, the context of corporate law may be distinctive. There, the concept of fiduciary duty—with its clear statement that there exists a legal duty, independent of statute or contract, to be fair to minority shareholders—invites and prods courts to fill in apparent gaps in the corporate contract.

Still, even if the common law does better arm the judge to resist opportunism, what relevance does this contrast have for transitional economies? That is, even if common-law judges have greater discretion and can fashion novel remedies, it does not follow that their style of judicial behavior can be imposed on civil-law judiciaries. It is simply not a feasible reform to attempt to convert civil-law judges into common-law judges (it would be easier to convert financial economists into law professors, or vice versa). But such pervasive reform may not be needed, because only a small portion of the workload of most judges in either system will deal with corporate or securities law matters. The simpler course may be simply to transfer this portion of their caseload to a specialized tribunal, as discussed next.

2. SPECIALIZED COURTS

The inflexibility of civil-law courts has already led in some countries to the creation of specialized courts, which have exclusive jurisdiction over some subject matters.[118] One example is the German experience with labor-law courts, which were created because labor law inherently requires a difficult style of decision making.[119] Indeed, even common-law countries have made substantial use of specialized tribunals to hear securities law disputes. For example, the federal securities laws now also contemplate their enforcement before administrative law judges.[120]

Thus, a practical approach to effective enforcement may lie in creating a cadre of administrative judges within an SEC-like agency, authorized to broadly enforce both disclosure obligations and certain rules against self-dealing (such as the insider-trading prohibition). Such judges would be trained within the agency and empowered to impose substantial civil penalties. Their jurisdiction could be limited to enforcement cases brought by the agency, or it could be expanded to include suits by investors for restitution.[121] Although these judges would presumably lack criminal-law jurisdiction, they could be authorized to grant bar orders that could effectively suspend or disbar an individual or entity from the functional activity of being a broker, investment adviser, accountant, or attorney, or from having any association with any entity that engaged in these activities. As a further backstop, persons who knowingly engaged in such specified activities with such a defendant after the time of the entry of the bar or suspension order might also face similar penalties. Further, appeal of such orders or decisions might only be made to the jurisdiction's court, which would be authorized to reverse it only on a finding that it was without any factual or legal support.

At this point, the agency acquires an in-house enforcement arm that lacks only the traditional judge's power to issue injunctions. Indeed, cease-and-desist orders could be authorized that partly fill even this gap. The remaining problem may be how to enforce bar or suspension orders. In transitional economies, a broker or investment adviser barred from that activity may persist in soliciting customers, effecting transactions, and giving investment advice. One answer may lie in centralizing trading on a more easily monitored exchange and penalizing persons who work with or for the suspended person. Another answer may be to allow customers and counter parties to rescind transactions (or refuse to pay for losing transactions) with any barred, suspended, or unauthorized person. Whatever the means used, enforcement problems can be solved, so long as the agency does not depend on (and cannot be nullified by) the traditional judiciary.

To sum up, civil-law judges may frustrate a regulatory scheme for any of a variety of reasons, including (1) because they are inflexible and literalistic, (2) because they are overworked and consider regulatory enforcement a nonessential task, or (3) because (in some countries) they are susceptible to corruption and bribery. Moving the enforcement mechanism at least partially "in house" into the administrative process is a practical answer to all of these problems. In-house administrative judges can be socialized to view securities regulation through the same lens as that of the agency; they will not have other priorities to distract them; and they should be less corruptible (or, at least, more easily monitored and removed).

B. Structural Reforms

Even if legal rules cannot be predictably or evenly enforced in transitional economies, other structural mechanisms might be used to prevent the kind of systematic expropriation that characterized the Czech experience.

1. PHASED PRIVATIZATION

The Polish experience with NIFs—in effect, state-created, controlling shareholders—may supply a useful model for a more gradual form of privatization. Such controlling shareholders could serve several distinct functions: (1) they prevent (or at least delay) the scramble for control that characterized the Czech experience—at least until the legal and regulatory structure has gained some experience with privatization; (2) they may constitute more active monitors than private investment funds—at a minimum, they can at least be charged with the mission of developing a restructuring plan for their portfolio companies; and (3) they serve as a means of aggregating individual shareholders and thus partially solving collective action problems.

Ultimately, however, true privatization requires that the NIF wither away—or else firms would still remain under indirect state control. Thus, a strategy for a phased downsizing of the NIF is necessary. Here, the Polish model was incomplete because it gave the NIFs a ten-year life, but did not provide for the gradual shrinkage of their controlling blocks. A subtler approach might have been to reduce the NIF's stakes from the 33 percent starting point on an annual basis, that is, down to 30 percent after year 1, 25 percent after year 2, 20 percent after year 3, and so on. In addition, it might be wise to stagger this schedule so that some NIFs downsized and disappeared faster than others—thereby creating a natural experiment and permitting legislative or regulatory reforms if the first generation of NIFs to disappear gave rise to a series of scandals. Such a phased reduction makes more sense than simply turning the NIFs over to private owners at a single stroke, because that approach invites the same rent-seeking struggle for control as occurred with the Czech funds.

Another attraction of this approach is that it should encourage foreign portfolio investors (who will not seek control and know they cannot actually manage portfolio companies) to remain active in the equity market and possibly become a monitoring substitute that over time could collectively replace the state-created NIFs. In contrast, a scramble for control in which the winner acquires a significant control premium may cause foreign portfolio investors to flee the market because they cannot compete. Still, the overriding attraction of this approach is that it is "self-enforcing" and does not require judicial implementation in order to discourage rent-seeking control contests.[122]

2. STOCK EXCHANGE LISTING STANDARDS

Long before there was an SEC in the United States, the New York Stock Exchange and the London Stock Exchange had succeeded in winning investor confidence. They did so by imposing relatively rigorous disclosure and listing standards and transparency requirements that exceeded those prevailing in other markets. Exchanges do not have ideal incentives, however, for the task of enforcement. Because they profit on trading volume, and they compete to list companies, they will not wish to delist an actively traded company, even when it misbehaves badly.

Similarly, their incentives to take enforcement action against powerful broker-dealers may also be suboptimal. For these reasons, at least in a transitional economy, the control over listing standards may better belong with a government agency.

Here, the contrast between the Czech and Polish experiences is particularly instructive. As of late 1998, only 253 companies traded on the Warsaw Stock Exchange, while some 1,716 firms traded in the Czech market in 1995—a nearly 7:1 ratio, despite the fact that the Polish economy dwarfs that of the considerably smaller Czech Republic.[123] Eventually, the Prague Stock Exchange was forced to delist more than 75 percent of its companies, both to maintain its credibility and to satisfy Czech regulators.[124]

Of course, if exchange trading is restricted, substitutes will develop, including formalized over-the-counter markets. Such markets may be risky and characterized by dubious offerings and market practices. So be it. Their potential failure should not jeopardize the higher-quality market. Indeed, markets may naturally self-segregate into high-quality and lesser-quality markets. In times of economic stress, the lower-quality market should incur the greater decline.

Such a pattern would permit significant privatization without exposing the principal securities market to the same risk of a Czech-style collapse. Enforcement resources might also be concentrated on the higher-quality market to maintain its reputational integrity. One goal of this effort would be to convince foreign portfolio investors that the higher-quality market could be trusted and to encourage their investment in it.

3. THE OPTIMAL MONITOR

The Polish and Czech experiences represent polar extremes. Essentially, the Czech privatization process relied on highly entrepreneurial, but legally unconstrained, monitors in the form of investment funds that more or less spontaneously arose. In contrast, the Polish approach was to rely upon highly constrained, state-created NIFs, whose entrepreneurial skills and incentives remain unproven. Neither choice seems optimal (at least by itself). There is, however, a third, obvious candidate: the existing foreign portfolio investor. Not only do foreign institutional investors have relatively scandal-free histories (and reputations that they wish to preserve), but there is evidence that they make superior monitors. In one recent study, two Harvard Business School researchers examined data from India during the 1990s and concluded that foreign institutional investors significantly outperformed domestic financial institutions as corporate monitors.[125] Domestic financial institutions, they found, had insufficient incentives or skills to monitor management or play any effective role in corporate governance. In contrast, foreign institutional ownership proved to be positively correlated with positive changes in Tobin's Q (while domestic financial ownership was actually negatively correlated with such changes).[126] Such a finding that domestic financial institutions play only a modest monitoring role (and may have conflicted motives) is essentially consistent with the Czech experience and with similar findings about Russian privatization.[127]

Equally important, the authors found that foreign institutional investment only occurs under circumstances of high transparency (for example, institutions tend to avoid investment in affiliated business groups). Hence, a stock exchange with rigorous listing requirements and high transparency seems likely to attract the most effective and experienced corporate monitors. In turn, as stock exchange listing is seen to attract foreign equity capital, the willingness of other companies to list and accept meaningful listing conditions may increase. To be sure, this strategy has its limitations: small capitalization corporations and small market countries tend to be ignored by institutional investors. But that is no reason to reject a partial answer.

More can, of course, be done to attract foreign investors. While the use of voucher privatization was politically necessary at the outset of privatization for a variety of reasons, contemporary sales of the remaining state-owned shares in partially privatized enterprises might be made through auction sales to which foreign institutional investors were specifically invited.

C. Legislative Reform

The Czech experience with tunneling does suggest that at least the German civil-law system of corporate governance unnecessarily exposes minority shareholders to risks of expropriation. The key problems center around disclosure and enforcement.

1. OVERVIEW

Because concentrated ownership systems of corporate governance have few companies in which a majority of the shares are held by public (i.e., noncontrolling) shareholders, their legal rules have understandably focused on protecting the minority shareholder from the controlling shareholder, not from management. Management, it is assumed, can be controlled by the supervisory board or by powerful shareholders. Hence, German law does not authorize an American-style derivative action in which a small shareholder can cause the company to sue management. This role is instead given to the supervisory board.

But privatization inherently creates publicly held companies with dispersed ownership, and hence it gives rise to the danger of managerial expropriation because there are not necessarily any large shareholders to monitor management at the outset. In short, there is a fundamental mismatch: a system of legal rules designed to deal with concentrated ownership works less well when confronted with the new phenomenon of dispersed ownership.

2. DISCLOSURE

German law does provide that a managing director is liable if the director intentionally or negligently fails to prevent the corporation from doing business to its disadvantage with a company affiliated with the director.[128] But German law does not obligate the director to disclose to the shareholders any personal financial interest that the director has in a proposed transaction.[129] Even when disclosure is required (as it is in the case of transactions between parent corporations and their majority-owned subsidiaries within a Konzern, or affiliated group), disclosure must only be given to the supervisory board, not the shareholders. This makes any right to sue largely academic if shareholders lack the knowledge that will cause them to raise objections. This critique is by no means new and has long been raised by German academics themselves.[130] Yet even if disclosure were required (as surely it should be), and even if a derivative action were permitted, it might have little impact unless American-style contingent fees were permitted. This seems unlikely, given the shock that civil lawyers express at such a system. As discussed below, disclosure to shareholders should be required, and might be enforced through listing standards.

3. SELF-DEALING: LISTING STANDARDS VERSUS PROPHYLACTIC RULES

A consensus seems to exist that it is unrealistic to place high expectations on either the judiciary or independent directors in transitional economies.[131] Judges are likely to enforce satisfactorily only bright-line rules. Thus, it seems ill advised to make proof of intent or purpose or bad faith necessary elements of any cause of action because this increases the unpredictability of results. But this premise leads to two immediate problems: (1) U.S. and U.K. law do not bar self-dealing transactions, but rather subject them to a variety of highly nuanced standards, and (2) in many transitional economies, affiliated business groups are the norm, meaning that intracorporate transactions within such affiliated groups will be common. Yet such transactions can often be used to expropriate wealth from minority investors.

This dilemma could be addressed in a number of ways. Corporate law could simply preclude self-dealing (or make it so legally uncertain as to place a prohibitive penalty on it). This was essentially what U.S. law did as of the late nineteenth century, when the United States was itself a transitional economy.[132] Potentially, such a prophylactic rule would last only for the time it took the transitional economy to mature (which is again the U.S. experience). But this approach might require dismantling of all affiliated groups, and this could be economically disruptive and politically impractical.

The other, more feasible alternative would be state-imposed listing standards that kept members of affiliated business groups off the "high quality" exchange, at least if their intercompany transactions reduced transparency. This would place a considerable cost on self-dealing (by denying members of affiliated groups easy access to the equity markets), but the cost is probably not prohibitive. Those firms that truly found membership in an affiliated group to be efficient could probably still obtain equity capital from the over-the-counter market. More important, this option forces a firm to choose between a "dispersed ownership" versus a "concentrated ownership" governance system, and it signals to institutional investors that a high-quality equity market is intended to accommodate only firms that elect to comply with the rules of the former system.

Supplementing this prohibition on listing members of an affiliated business group (other than the sole parent) would be listing rules precluding defined self-dealing transactions by management, controlling shareholders, or other insiders. Such rules would, of course, focus only on (1) transactions that were material to shareholders (excluding, for example, ordinary compensation), and (2) transactions that could be easily monitored (for example, purchases and sales of corporate divisions or significant corporate assets by persons affiliated with management). Some low-visibility transactions would escape the scope of these rules, and some violations would inevitably escape detection. But if the enforcement of such rules were delegated to the jurisdiction's securities commission (rather than the exchange itself), this system could be implemented with respect to the largest and most important corporations in the jurisdiction—without relying on costly and uncertain litigation. Over time, such a system could create its own culture of compliance, with smaller firms seeking to elect in as they matured. In effect, entry into the high-quality market would constitute a bonding device by which firms could assure investors of fair treatment and thereby lower their cost of equity capital.

4. CONTROL ACQUISITION

Following repeated scandals in the Czech securities market, reform legislation was adopted in 1996 that essentially introduced a key element of the British corporate governance system, namely, no person could cross a defined ownership threshold, except by making a tender offer for all the firm's shares. Polish law interestingly already had such a limitation from its outset.[133] Under the Czech legislation, once any person crossed any of the 50 percent, $66\frac{2}{3}$ percent, or 75 percent ownership thresholds, such a person is required to make a public tender offer for the remaining shares within sixty days thereafter at a price equal to the weighted price on the market over the prior six months.[134] Conceptually, this protects the minority, but there would seem to be serious flaws in the particular design of this system. For example, control can easily be obtained well short of the 50 percent level, at which point the controlling shareholder can begin to exploit the minority (by withholding dividends, engaging in self-dealing transactions, etc.). Once such conduct occurs or is signaled, the company's stock price should predictably decline. Thus, when the controlling shareholder elects to cross the 50 percent threshold, the stock price should already be deflated below its true "going concern" value. As a result, for this remedy to work, an earlier threshold (say, 20 percent) seems necessary.

Under a legal regime that allowed shareholders to aggregate shares up to 25 percent, but required a public tender offer for the remainder, many would stop at the 25 percent level. This does not seem undesirable. Some evidence suggests that such large, but noncontrolling, shareholders enhance the value of the firm by partially solving the collective action problem inherent in dispersed ownership.[135] In a world where legal controls are weak, drawing such a line may be the most practical reform that can be easily monitored and enforced.

Yet for these reforms to work, more must be required than simply mandating that a tender offer be made at the average price over a recent period. Such a rule allows the large shareholder to profit from undisclosed material information and may be spurned by suspicious minority shareholders who suspect that the firm has hidden value. Although full disclosure should, of course, be required in connection with this offer, full disclosure in this context can have a counterproductive, even perverse effect. If shareholders learn that the firm has greater value than the market previously had recognized, they will spurn the offer—and thereafter be exposed to exploitation by the new controlling shareholders if they are successful in obtaining a controlling interest. Accordingly, some minimum tender premium should be mandated. For example, a 20 percent premium over the prior average market price might be the best practical compromise, and it can be justified in part based on the reduced disclosure and regulatory costs that the company will incur once it becomes private after the tender offer. Any rule requiring a mandated premium may deter some shareholders from crossing the 25 percent ownership level that triggers a mandatory bid, shareholders who conceivably might have been more efficient corporate monitors had they been able to obtain a controlling interest. Still, it protects the public minority from rent-seeking contests in which the participants are principally seeking to realize the private benefits of control.

Predictably, some will object that this approach is inefficient because it chills the market for corporate control and precludes some potentially efficient acquisitions. This cost seems highly speculative, but it must, in any event, be balanced against the economic and political externalities caused by rent-seeking control fights between contenders who are primarily seeking to realize the private benefits of control. The Czech experience suggests that the dispersed ownership created by voucher privatization encourages a winner-take-all control fight in which the ultimate victor obtains a de facto right to expropriate wealth from other shareholders. Under such circumstances, there is every reason to expect that the contestants will use every weapon at their disposal, including bribery and corruption. Given these risks, the prudent course is to require the control seeker to offer to acquire 100 percent of the stock and permit others to contest for control by offering a higher bid. Such "high visibility" contests are preferable to "low visibility," "creeping control" contests in which the participants are likely to cut secret deals and seek to use political influence.

VI. Conclusion

Why do common-law systems outperform civil-law systems in encouraging dispersed ownership? To be assessed intelligently, this question must be broken down into its components. Although the premise that different legal systems encourage different patterns of ownership and different systems of governance seems valid, the truth is that we do not yet fully comprehend the manner in which common-law systems provide superior protection for minority shareholders. Indeed, the answers may differ widely among common-law systems. Nonetheless, although no simple formula seems likely to be discovered soon, a major part of the answer seems to lie not in the corporate law of common-law countries, but in their shared system of securities regulation. Although the laws of the United States and the United Kingdom are far from identical, and each regulates control contests quite differently, they each seek to discourage this type of rent-seeking control contests that became endemic in the Czech Republic. The common elements of the joint U.S.-U.K. system of securities regulation—that is, ownership transparency, high-disclosure standards, restrictions on "creeping control" acquisitions that preclude a shareholder from assembling a controlling block without tendering for all shares, and high listing standards—were at least partially present in Poland, but were originally absent from the Czech Republic.

More generally, privatization has produced a conceptual mismatch. Inherently, it produces an initially dispersed ownership, but under a legal regime intended to accommodate concentrated ownership. The result is necessarily short-lived. In this light, the critique advanced by new students of comparative corporate governance that civil-law systems fail to provide adequate minority protection needs to be reformulated.[136] Civil-law systems may well protect minority shareholders against the forms of abuse long known in systems of concentrated ownership (most typically, domination by a controlling shareholder). But civil-law systems do not address abuses that they have not witnessed (such as the theft of the control premium in an exploitative partial takeover). Hence, they leave public shareholders in a system of dispersed ownership exposed to a winner-take-all scramble for control, in which the losers can expect future expropriation by the winner. Privatization, of course, creates just such a system of dispersed ownership vulnerable to this form of abuse. More generally, the voting, proxy, and disclosure systems under the German civil-law approach do not contemplate that small shareholders will play any active role. This premise may be valid in their environment, but when this system is applied to privatized companies, it leaves small shareholders powerless and thus helps to compel a transition to concentrated ownership. Rather than seeing this transition as inevitable, policy planners must recognize that it is a contextual product of the dominant forces in the legal and market environment. Phrased more generally, because civil-law systems of corporate governance implicitly contemplate concentrated ownership, they have disdained disclosure to the market in favor of disclosure to the supervisory board. In consequence, the civil law tends to inhibit the development of securities markets, whose growth depends upon the breaking down of informational asymmetries.

Whether differences in judicial style and performance between common-law and civil-law systems matter significantly in the success of privatization and the stability of dispersed ownership seems more debatable. One problem with any such comparison is that the presumed homogeneity of common-law systems also seems suspect. The United States and the United Kingdom have achieved functional convergence, but not formal convergence. The effective absence in the United Kingdom of litigation remedies that are available to minority shareholders suggests that the combination of high-disclosure standards and an active, unconstrained takeover market may constitute an effective functional substitute for litigation (or other remedies that are more available in the United States). Legally, as much may separate the United States and the United Kingdom as unites them.

To the extent that one is skeptical of the ability of the judiciary in transitional economies to restrain opportunism, the natural policy response may be to recommend reliance on "self-enforcing" remedies.[137] Indeed, the Polish NIFs may supply the best feasible example of such a structural reform. Nonetheless, the idea that "self-enforcing" remedies would prove sufficient by themselves has been shown to be overconfident. The primary problem is that viable securities markets will not develop or persist in the absence of some workable mechanism of regulatory enforcement. Fraud, manipulation, insider trading—these practices became endemic in the Czech Republic (for at least a period of time) under a legal system that was as laissez-faire oriented as has existed anywhere in recent times. To develop liquid markets, regulation must overcome those practices that will otherwise drive portfolio investors from the market. This does not necessarily mean that U.S.-style class actions are necessary or that common-law judges must be imported into civil-law jurisdictions (nor do such reforms seem feasible), but it does suggest that other enforcement techniques, such as specialized courts and administrative enforcement proceedings, need to be seriously explored.

Academic attitudes are changing. Whereas not long ago concentrated ownership was seen as efficient and dispersed ownership was taken by some to imply overregulation of institutional investors,[138] concentrated ownership is now being viewed by others as a measure of weak protection for minority shareholders. Predictably, academic fashions will change again, but the critical issue is an applied one: how to establish strong securities markets? Here the data from the aftermath of the Asian financial crisis suggests that minority protection appears to be a necessary, but not a sufficient, condition to the emergence of viable securities markets.[139]

The bottom line, as usual, is that those ignorant of history are destined to repeat it. "Fast" privatization unaccompanied by minority protection and adequate disclosure standards will produce expropriation and rent-seeking. To call this outcome inevitable, however, is only to claim that ignorance is inevitable.

NOTES

This chapter was initially a paper presented at a conference sponsored by the University of Michigan Law School and the William Davidson Institute on September 23 and 24, 1999. The author would like to acknowledge the helpful comments of Bernard Black, Melvin Eisenberg, Katharina Pistor, Andrei Shleifer, and the participants at the Michigan conference, including in particular his commentators, Professors Andrew Weiss of Boston University and Ken Lehn of the University of Pittsburgh. None bears any necessary responsibility, however, for the views expressed herein.

1. This reference is to a quotation from a now obscure nineteenth-century economist, Karl Marx, who coined the phrase in 1848. *See* Karl Marx & Friedrich Engels, Manifesto of the Communist Party (1948) (observing that the specter of communism was haunting Europe). Younger scholars are not expected to be familiar with this material.

2. The principal efforts have been by four financial economists, writing jointly, called by some the "Gang of Four," but hereafter referred to more neutrally as "LLS&V." *See, e.g.*, Rafael La Porta, Florencio Lopez-de-Silanes, and Andrei Shleifer, *Corporate Ownership around the World*, 54 J. Fin. 471 (1999); La Porta, Lopez-de-Silanos, Shleifer, & Robert Vishny, *Law and Finance*, 106 J. Pol. Econ. 1113 (1998); La Porta, Lopez-de-Silanos, Shleifer, & Vishny, *Legal Determinants of External Finance*, 52 J. Fin. 1131 (1997). For another provocative effort in this same vein, see Simon Johnson et al., Corporate Governance in the Asian Financial Crisis, 1997–1998 (Jan. 1999) (working paper, on file with author).

3. For the latest commentary by LLS&V on this theme, see La Porta, Lopez-de-Silanos, Shleifer, & Vishny, Investor Protection and Corporate Governance (June 1999) (working paper, on file with author).

4. *See* sources cited *supra* notes 2 and 3.

5. Although these systems may seem static, individual firms can migrate from one to the other, principally by listing on a stock exchange in a "dispersed ownership" nation. I have suggested elsewhere that such migration and the need for global scale is destabilizing the traditional concentrated ownership system. *See* John C. Coffee, Jr., *The Future as History: The Prospects for Global Convergence in Corporate Governance and Its Implications*, 93 Nw. U.L. Rev. 641 (1999).

6. Financial economics, as a field, has long been skeptical of regulation. For an indication that this attitude is changing, *see, e.g.*, Simon Johnson & Andrei Shleifer, Coase v. The Coasians: The Regulation and Development of Securities Markets in Poland and the Czech Republic (Sept. 1999) (working paper, on file with author).

7. This possibility was first implicitly noted in Coffee, *supra* note 5, and has been explicitly advanced in convincing detail by Katharina Pistor. *See* Katharina Pistor, Law as a Determinant for Equity Market Development: The Experience of Transition Economies (Mar. 1999) (working paper, on file with author).

8. Essentially, the sentence in the text is a very short summary of the arguments advanced by Judge Frank Easterbrook and Dean Fischel for why much corporate and securities regulation is unnecessary. *See* Frank Easterbrook & Daniel Fischel, The Economic Structure of Corporate Law (1991). For an earlier statement of this view, see George J. Stigler, *Public Regulation of the Securities Market*, 37 J. Bus. 117 (1964).

9. *See* Michael Jensen & William Meckling, *Theory of the Firm: Managerial Behavior, Agency Costs, and Ownership Structure*, 3 J. Fin. Econ. 305 (1976).

10. *Id.*

11. For such well-known efforts, see Jonathan Macey & Geoffrey Miller, *Toward An Interest-Group Theory of Delaware Corporate Law*, 65 Tex. L. Rev. 469 (1987);

Roberta Romano, *The Political Economy of State of Takeover Statutes*, 73 Va. L. Rev. 111 (1987); Jonathan Macey, *Administrative Agency Obsolescence and Interest Group Formation: A Case Study of the SEC at Sixty*, 15 Cardozo L. Rev. 909 (1994).

12. Neoclassical economic theory views the firm as a "nexus of contracts." *See* Jensen & Meckling, *supra* note 9, at 310–11. Yet privatization often short-circuits this contracting process by simply creating a dispersed shareholder base. A stable equilibrium is thus not reached. The result is that the shareholders have less well defined legal rights and are more vulnerable to opportunistic actions by those in control.

13. For examples of this new critique of "fast" privatization, see John Nellis, *Time to Rethink Privatization in Transitional Economies?* Fin. & Dev., June 1999, at 16, 16–19; Bernard Black et al. Russian Privatization and Corporate Governance: What Went Wrong? (Stanford Law School Working Paper No. 178, 1999).

14. *See* sources cited *supra* notes 2 and 3. LLS&V run regression analyses that rank the minority protections given shareholders in different countries in terms of the presence (or absence) of certain specified statutory protections and then relate these rankings to the size of each country's securities market. While they find a strong relationship between weak protections and weak markets, such studies remain vulnerable to the problem of multicollinearity (that is, the true predictive variable may escape detection because it was not tested in the sample but overlapped with the independent variable that seems to show predictive power). For example, a statutory provision that seems to show predictive power may overlap with a softer and untested factor (such as a strong and independent judiciary). Necessarily, empiricists measure the data that is available, and in the case of "softer" variables (such as judicial style and judicial independence), little data is available. Hence, these softer variables may be ignored.

15. Gould, Fisk, and Drew engaged in a famous battle with Commodore Vanderbilt for control of the Erie Railroad. When Vanderbilt sought to buy control by acquiring Erie's shares in the open market, his three antagonists used their control over the Erie board to dump an endless stream of watered stock on the market. Both sides bribed judges and state legislators. *See* Maury Klein, The Life and Legend of Jay Gould 80–86 (1986); *cf.* Lawrence Friedman, A History of American Law 447–48 (1973).

16. *See* Klein, *supra* note 15, at 80–86.

17. Russian company law has borrowed heavily from U.S. and U.K. sources and, in its current version, was heavily influenced by a model developed by two American law professors. *See* Bernard Black & Reinier Kraakman, *A Self-Enforcing Model of Corporate Law*, 109 Harv. L. Rev. 1911 (1996).

18. There is already some empirical support for this modest revision of the LLS&V thesis. *See infra* notes 87–90 and accompanying text.

19. For example, the foreign (and largely institutional) shareholders of Far Eastern Shipping Company, Russia's largest commercial shipping line, have protested that the provincial governor of Vladivostok objected to their large ownership stake (42 percent) in Far Eastern and demanded that they surrender 7 percent of their shares to him. Otherwise, he allegedly threatened to reduce their voting rights by provincial decree. *See* Neela Banerjee, *Shareholders Charge Extortion in Russian Far East*, N.Y. Times, June 16, 1999, at C3. For a discussion of other instances in which

regional barons and local political groups have extorted value from foreign investors in privatized Russian firms, *see* Merritt B. Fox & Michael A. Heller, Lessons from Fiascos in Russian Corporate Governance (Sept. 1999) (unpublished manuscript, on file with author).

20. *See* Alyeska Pipeline Serv. Co. v. Wilderness Soc'y, 421 U.S. 240, 247 (1975) ("In the United States, the prevailing litigant is ordinarily not entitled to collect a reasonable attorneys' fee from the loser").

21. This is not to claim that the U.S. system is optimal. Class actions could in principle result in overdeterrence; conversely, the availability of liability insurance could nullify the legal threat. But at least one can understand why such legal remedies might create socially desirable deterrence.

22. For a survey of comparative law scholars who rated U.S. courts as second in "judicial daring" (after Israel) and U.K. courts as third from last (out of fourteen industrialized countries), see Robert Cooter & Tom Ginsburg, *Comparative Judicial Discretion: An Empirical Test of Economic Models*, 16 Int'l Rev. L. & Econ. 295, 300 (1996). Professors Cooter and Ginsburg suggest that differences in political structure and the role of dominant political parties best explain these national differences. *See id.* at 296–300.

23. Preemptive rights, for example, play an important role in constraining managements in the United Kingdom, but almost no role in the United States. *See* Bernard Black & John Coffee, *Hail Britannia? Institutional Investor Behavior under Limited Regulation*, 92 Mich. L. Rev. 1997, 2079 (1994).

24. *See* Coffee, *supra* note 5, at 679–80.

25. Indeed, this is what several empirical studies seem to show about practices across the leading industrial nations. *See* Steven Kaplan, *Top Executive Rewards and Firm Performance: A Comparison of Japan and the U.S.*, 102 J. Pol. Econ. 510 (1994); Steven Kaplan, *Top Executive Turnover and Firm Performance in Germany*, 10 J.L. Econ. & Org. 142 (1994).

26. It is noteworthy, for example, that the Securities Act of 1933 was modeled after the earlier English Companies Act of 1900, which, ironically, was itself intended to reverse the common law's tolerance for fraud. For a discussion of the different philosophies underlying the Securities Act of 1933 and the eventual triumph of a disclosure philosophy over a more regulatory philosophy, *see* Joel Seligman, The Transformation of Wall Street: A History of the Securities and Exchange Commission and Modern Corporate Finance 39–42 (1982).

27. *See* La Porta *et al.*, *Corporate Ownership around the World*, *supra* note 2.

28. This point has been earlier emphasized by Pistor. *See* Pistor, *supra* note 7.

29. *See* Coffee, *supra* note 5, at 663–76.

30. *See* Peter S. Green, *Prague Exchange's Failed Reform Efforts Leaves Some Predicting Its Demise*, Int'l Herald Trib., Mar. 17, 1999, at 16.

31. *Id.* It must be acknowledged that the Prague Stock Exchange itself delisted many of these companies and imposed higher listing standards during this period as part of its struggle to survive. *See* Pistor, *supra* note 7. At the outset of Czech privatization, there were no real listing standards, and the vast majority of privatized companies were listed. Still, the decision to delist these stocks was not truly voluntary. Their continued trading on the exchange would likely have left that market without any credibility.

32. Green, *supra* note 30, at 16. Specifically, the PX-50 index fell from 1,000 to 371.

33. *Id.*

34. *See* Czech Ministry of Finance, *Current Aspects of the Czech Capital Market*, (internal report dated 1997).

35. Czech GDP contracted by more than 2.5 percent in 1998 (whereas neighboring countries experienced a 4–5 percent annual growth). *See* Nellis, *supra* note 13, at 16–19.

36. Green, *supra* note 30.

37. I have discussed the contrasting experiences of these two nations at greater length elsewhere. *See* John C. Coffee, Jr., *Inventing a Corporate Monitor for Transitional Economies: The Uncertain Lessons from the Czech and Polish Experiences*, *in* Comparative Corporate Governance: The State of the Art and Emerging Research 67, 122–25 (Klaus J. Hopt et al. eds., 1998).

38. *See* Saul Estrin *et al.*, *The Impact of Privatization Funds on Corporate Governance in Mass Privatization Schemes: The Czech Republic, Poland and Slovenia*, *in* The Governance of Privatization Funds: Experiences of the Czech Republic, Poland, and Slovenia 137, 142 (Marko Simoneti et al. eds., 1999).

39. For a detailed description of the NIF, which essentially resembled closed-end mutual funds and were created by the Polish Ministry of State Treasury to hold controlling stakes in privatized firms, *see* Jannsa Lewandowski & Roman Szyszko, *The Governance of Privatization Funds in Poland*, *in* The Governance of Privatization Funds, *supra* note 38.

40. *See* Eva Thiel, *The Development of Securities Markets in Transitional Economies: Policy Issues and Country Experience*, 70 Fin. Market Trends 111 (June 1998), *available in* Lexis, News Library, Curnws file.

41. According to Thiel, only 3 percent of actual trades were executed on the Prague Stock Exchange. *See* Thiel, *supra* note 40, at 111. In part, this was attributable to the existence of a Nasdaq-like alternative system, which also disclosed prices contemporaneously. Still, investment funds could trade on a face-to-face basis off the exchange and use the exchange only for transactions at inflated prices.

42. Emerging markets appear in general to have very different characteristics from mature, efficient markets. In particular, stocks in emerging markets exhibit strong "momentum," meaning that one period's performance tends to predict the next period's performance; also, high beta stocks do not outperform low beta stocks. *See* K. Geert Rouwenhorst, *Local Return Factors and Turnover in Emerging Markets*, 54 J. Fin. 1439, 1441 (1999).

43. Of the thirteen largest investment funds in the first wave of Czech privatization, eleven were created by financial institutions. *See* Estrin et al., *supra* note 38, at 151. This was probably predictable, because citizens were already familiar with the local savings, commercial, or postal banks that sponsored these funds.

44. Other motivations can also explain this failure to concentrate holdings (which continued in secondary market trading as well as in the original privatization auctions). For example, in nontransparent markets, trading in the stocks of newly privatized firms may be highly profitable for informed traders with seats on the boards of their portfolio company.

45. *See* Czech Ministry of Finance, *supra* note 34.

46. *See* Jozef Koterba et al., *The Governance of Privatization Funds in the Czech Republic*, *in* The Governance of Privatization Funds, *supra* note 38, at 7, 29–30.

47. *Id.*

48. *Id.* at 30.

49. *Id.*

50. For a similar assessment that emphasizes the "very visible exploitation of opportunities for wealth creation by collusion and arbitrage," *see* Thiel, *supra* note 40, at 111.

51. *See* EBRD, Transition Report, Nov. 1998, *available in* Lexis, News Library, Curnws file. The EBRD Transition Report evaluates the progress of transitional economies toward a free market system in a variety of different areas (e.g., banking, bankruptcy, and securities market reforms) using a common five-point index rating system. In 1998, it awarded Poland a rating of 3+ (and the Czech Republic a rating of 3) for their efforts at securities market reform.

52. *See Securities Commission Head Displeased with 1998*, PAP News Wire (Poland), Dec. 28, 1998, *available in* Lexis, News Library, Curnws file.

53. *See* Marko Simoneti & Paul Estrin, *Introduction*, *in* The Governance of Privatization Funds, *supra* note 38, at 1, 5; *see also* EBRD, Transition Report, *supra* note 51. However, the Polish securities markets have been able to support at least some initial public offerings (IPOs). In 1997, Polish IPOs issued stock having a value equal to 1 percent of Polish GDP. *Id.*

54. These commentators have argued that only in Poland did the investment privatization funds acquire sufficiently large stakes to attempt active management and restructuring. *See* Marko Simoneti & Andreja Böhm, *The Governance of Privatization Funds: Open Issues and Policy Recommendations*, *in* The Governance of Privatization Funds, *supra* note 38, at 163, 166.

55. *See* Johnson & Shleifer, *supra* note 6, at 26.

56. *Id.*

57. *See* Johnson et al., *supra* note 2, at 48. This paper groups countries by severity of stock market decline between the end of 1996 and August 1998 and places Poland in the "relatively moderate" category of decline. *See id.*

58. The Czech market collapse worsened after the time of the Asian financial crisis and hit bottom following the 1998 Russian financial crisis. Between August 1998 and March 1999, the Czech market decline was 30.5 percent, which far exceeded the 17.5 percent decline on the Polish market or the very mild 5.7 percent decline on the Hungarian market. *See* Pistor, *supra* note 7, at 46. Pistor also finds that Czech market capitalization declined 35 percent following the 1998 Russian financial crisis, while Polish market capitalization actually increased 17.8 percent over this same period. *See id.*, at 47. The Prague Stock Exchange has since recovered, although this may be partly attributable to stock market reforms enacted largely in 1998.

59. *See* Simoneti & Böhm, *supra* note 54, at 163, 174. In addition, roughly 25 percent of the first five hundred privatized firms are now also publicly traded. This contrast between the steep discounts in the Czech market and the absence of discounts in the Polish market is, however, subject to an important qualification: because of the absence of transparency in the Czech market, reported prices on the Prague Stock Exchange were often inflated, thereby overstating the discount. The subsequent history of the NIFs after 1998 is discussed in the text accompanying notes 63–65.

60. *See* Coffee, *supra* note 5, at 673–76 (discussing foreign listings as a bonding mechanism).

61. *See* Pistor, *supra* note 7, at 45.

62. *Id.* at 46.

63. Data showing these discounts as of the fall of 1999 has been provided to me by Professor Andrew Weiss, an economist at Boston University. He informs me that, as of late September, 1999, the average discount on the Polish NIFs relative to their net asset value had grown to 60 percent, which was as great or greater than the standard discount on Czech funds earlier in the decade.

64. Professor Weiss points to the example of the Restitution Fund, which is the largest Czech fund and which now trades at 1,300 (as of late September 1999) and has a net asset value of 1,550 (or less than a 20 percent discount). In 1994, it traded for between 500 and 600. Another example is SPIF Cesky, which now trades at 1,346 and was trading at 400 in December, 1994. One possible reason for this resurgence may have been reform legislation, which was adopted in 1998. Pursuant to this legislation, many Czech funds converted to a basically open-end status. Open-end funds do not, of course, have the same discount as a closed-end fund because their shares can be redeemed.

65. *See* Pistor, *supra* note 7, at 48.

66. For a closer assessment of the similarities and differences in Czech and Polish corporate law during the period, see Pistor, *supra* note 7, at 35–44. Pistor notes that the Czech Republic did have a considerably lower quorum requirement (30 percent), which may have facilitated some fraud, and a higher (and hence less protective) mandatory bid requirement, but overall she finds that both countries provided only weak protections in their corporate law for minority shareholders.

67. *See id.* at 37–38.

68. *Id.* at 37 (noting that Polish law has required ownership disclosure at the 10 percent and 25 percent levels). Section 13(d) of the Securities Exchange Act of 1934 requires shareholders of a "reporting company" to disclose to both the issuer and the SEC their identity, sources of financing, plans and intentions, and certain other information when—either alone or as a part of a group—they acquire more than 5 percent of any class of equity security of such an issuer. Securities and Exchange Act of 1934 § 13(d), 15 U.S.C.§ 78m(d) (1994).

69. Poland adopted a 33 percent threshold (originally, it was 50 percent), while the Czech Republic introduced this reform (but only at the 50 percent level) only more recently. Pistor, *supra* note 7, at 37–38.

70. *Id.*

71. *See* sources cited *supra* notes 2 and 3.

72. Lucian Bebchuk has theorized that these competitive struggles for a controlling position are predictable whenever the private benefits of control are large and control is not locked up by special charter provisions. *See* Lucian A. Bebchuk, A Rent-Protection Theory of Corporate Ownership and Control (Nat'l Bureau of Econ. Research, Working Paper No. 7203, 1999). These conditions would seem usually to be satisfied when voucher privatization is used in a transitional economy, because it exposes control to acquisition and the private benefits of control are necessarily high when judicial controls are undeveloped.

73. *See supra* notes 55–56 and accompanying text.

74. *See supra* notes 63–65 and accompanying text.

75. For a fuller description of these offerings, *see* William Megginson et al., *The Financial and Operating Performance of Newly Privatized Firms: An International Empirical Analysis*, 49 J. Fin. 403, 406 (1994). An arguably controlling stake in Volkswagen continues to be held by one German state (Lower Saxony).

76. *Id.* at 407.

77. *See* Pan A. Yotopoulos, *The (Rip) Tide of Privatization: Lessons from Chile*, 17 World Dev. 683, 684–87, 697–99 (1989).

78. For an overview of Mexican privatization, see Rafael La Porta & Florence Lopez-de-Silanos, *Benefits of Privatization: Evidence from Mexico, Private Sector*, at 21–24 (World Bank, June 1997).

79. For recent detailed accounts, see Fox & Heller, *supra* note 19; Bernard Black et al., Russian Privatization and Corporate Governance: What Went Wrong? (Sept. 1999) (unpublished manuscript, on file with author).

80. *See* Joseph Blasi & Andrei Shleifer, *Corporate Governance in Russia: An Initial Look*, *in* Corporate Governance in Central Europe and Russia (Roman Frydman et al. eds., 1996).

81. *See supra* note 19 and accompanying text.

82. *See* Black et al., *supra* note 79.

83. William Megginson & Jeffry Netter, From State to Market: A Survey of Empirical Studies on Privatization 16 (New York Stock Exch. Working Paper No. 98–05, 1998).

84. *See, e.g.*, Juliet D'Souza & William Megginson, *The Financial and Operating Performance of Privatized Firms during the 1990s*, 54 J. Fin. 1397, 1408–09 (1999) (finding significance increases in profitability and efficiency); Nicholas Barberis et al., *How Does Privatization Work? Evidence from the Russian Shops*, 104 J. Pol. Econ. 764 (1996) (study of 452 retail stores); Roman Frydman et al., Why Ownership Matters: Politicization and Entrepreneurship in the Restructuring of Enterprises in Central Europe (C. V. Starr Center Working Paper No. 98–14, 1998) (summarizing other studies); Megginson & Netter, *supra* note 83.

85. Stign Claessens et al., Ownership and Corporate Governance: Evidence from the Czech Republic (World Bank Policy Research Paper No. 1737, 1997).

86. *See supra* notes 55–56 and accompanying text.

87. Johnson et al., *supra* note 2, at 3.

88. *Id.* at 4.

89. *Id.* at 6.

90. *Id.*

91. *See supra* notes 84–85 and accompanying text.

92. For a detailed discussion of the ECM, *see* Reena Aggarwal & James J. Angel, *The Rise and Fall of the Amex Emerging Company Marketplace*, 52 J. Fin. Econ. 257 (1999).

93. *Id.* at 283.

94. Aggarwal and Angel in fact give greater weight in their account to an adverse selection problem: "good" firms matured from the ECM to the Amex, while "bad" firms remained behind. *Id.* at 263.

95. Aggarwal and Angel observe: "During the 1980s, virtually every stock market in Europe established a special section for companies that were too small to meet

the normal listing requirements. . . . Many of these markets appeared to prosper for a short time, but ultimately they all suffered from severe illiquidity and attracted few companies or investors." *Id.* at 281. Amsterdam closed its Official Parallel Market in 1993, and London closed its Unlisted Securities Market in 1996. *Id.*

96. For these and other examples, see Coffee, *supra* note 37, at 113–14.

97. *See* Czech Ministry of Finance, *supra* note 34.

98. Some U.S. statutes specifically sterilize the votes of interested shareholders in establishing the procedures by which a conflict of interest transaction may be approved by the board or shareholders so as to overcome the presumption against fiduciary self-dealing. *See, e.g.*, Cal. Corp. Code § 310 (West 1990). Others, including Delaware, have reached a similar result by judicial decision. *See* Fleigler v. Lawrence, 361 A.2d 218, 222 (Del. 1976) (shareholder approval merely removes "cloud" and does not sanction unfairness).

99. For a brief overview, relating the application of this law to transitional economies, see Pistor, *supra* note 7, at 17–18.

100. *See, e.g.*, Herbert Wiedemann, *The German Experience with the Law of Affiliated Enterprises*, *in* Groups of Companies in European Law: Legal and Economic Analysis on Multinational Enterprises (Klaus J. Hopt ed., 1982); Ulrich Immenga, *The Law of Groups in the Federal Republic of Germany*, *in* Groups of Companies in the EEC 85 (Eddy Wymeersch ed., 1993).

101. *See* Pistor, *supra* note 7, at 35–44. These techniques were in fact used in practice by one notorious Czech entrepreneur. *See* Charles Wallace, *The Pirates of Prague*, Fortune, Dec. 23, 1996, at 78 (discussing the career of Victor Kozeny); Coffee, *supra* note 37, at 115.

102. *See* La Porta et al., *Corporate Ownership around the World*, *supra* note 2, at 505 (in 75 percent of cases, no other large shareholder exists when there is a controlling shareholder).

103. *See* Black & Coffee, *supra* note 23 at 2079.

104. *See* sources cited *supra* notes 2 and 3.

105. *See* Bernard Black, The Legal and Institutional Preconditions for Strong Stock Markets: The Nontriviality of Securities Law (July 1999) (working paper, on file with author).

106. Japan is the marginal case because it has dispersed ownership (along with a unique control structure). It is primarily a civil-law country, but with American securities laws imposed in the aftermath of World War II. This pattern may suggest that securities laws are more important than common-law remedies, or it may just be that Japan has developed unique institutions by which to preserve investor confidence.

107. For standard statements of this perspective, see Easterbrook & Fischel, *supra* note 8, at 1–39; *see also* Jonathan R. Macey, *Corporate Law and Corporate Governance: A Contractual Perspective*, 18 J. Corp. L. 185 (1993).

108. *Compare* Ian Ayres & Robert Gertner, *Filling Gaps in Incomplete Contracts: An Economic Theory of Default Rules*, 99 Yale L.J. 87 (1989) (recommending "information forcing" rule), *with* Easterbrook & Fischel, *supra* note 8 (preferring wealth maximizing rule).

109. *See, e.g.*, Rene David & John E. C. Brierley, Major Legal Systems in the World Today 339 (2d ed. 1978).

110. *See* Mirjan R. Damaska, The Faces of Justice and State Authority (1986) (emphasizing the technocratic role of common-law judges); *see also* Martin Shapiro, Courts: A Comparative and Political Analysis 136 (1981).

111. The law of insider trading has shown how complex this issue can be when a fiduciary duty arises, but the key criteria are (1) the possession of discretion to act for the beneficiary by the party to be charged with the duty, and (2) dependence by the beneficiary. *See, e.g.*, United States v. Chestman, 947 F.2d 551, 569 (2d Cir. 1991).

112. 23 Del. Ch. 255, 5 A.2d 503, 510 (Del. 1939).

113. *Id.* at 510–11.

114. Meinhard v. Salmon, 164 N.E. 545, 546 (N.Y. 1928).

115. *See, e.g.*, Irwin v. West End Dev. Co., 342 F. Supp. 687, 701 (D. Colo. 1972) ("Exculpatory provisions of corporate articles create no license to steal"), *modified on other grounds*, 481 F.2d 34 (10th Cir. 1973).

116. The German Federal Supreme Court recognized that controlling shareholders owe a fiduciary duty of loyalty to minority shareholders in the much-discussed "Linotype Case" in early 1988. *See* Entscheidungen des Bundesgerichtshofs in Zivilsachen [BGHZ] [Supreme Court] 103, 184 (F.R.G.). *See generally*, Hwa-Jin Kim, *Markets, Financial Institutions, and Corporate Perspectives from Germany*, 26 Law & Pol'y Int'l Bus. 371, 392–94 (1995). In addition, Germany has a separate body of law called "Konzern law" which is intended to protect both minority shareholders in, and creditors of, companies that belong to a group of companies. *See also* Immenga, *supra* note 100. *See generally*, J. Bantz Bonano, *The Protection of Minority Shareholders in a Konzern under German and United States Law*, 18 Harv. Int'l L.J. 151 (1977).

Whatever the situation in Germany, far fewer rights (or remedies) that can be exercised by minority shareholder seem to be recognized elsewhere on the Continent. *See* Jonathan R. Macey, *Italian Corporate Governance: One American's Perspective*, 1998 Colum. Bus. L. Rev. 121, 129–35.

117. *See* Cooter & Ginsburg, *supra* note 22, at 300–301.

118. Russia has experimented with an "economic court" system, but with mixed results at best. *See* Karen Halverson, *Resolving Economic Disputes in Russia's Market Economy*, 18 Mich. J. Int'l L. 59 (1996). In contrast to an independent economic court, the proposal here is made for a specialized court that is located within the agency in whose law the court is to specialize.

119. German labor courts date back to the Weimar Republic and were designed "to force labor-management disputes into a procedural framework similar to the political process of party competition and parliamentary decision making." *See* Erhard Blankenburg, *Patterns of Legal Culture: The Netherlands Compared to Neighboring Germany*, 46 Am. J. Comp. L. 1, 26 (1998). The German labor courts now have ten divisions at the federal level and twenty-seven judges at this level alone. *Id.* at 27.

120. As a result of recent legislative revisions, Section 21B of the Securities Exchange Act of 1934 now authorizes civil penalties in administrative proceedings in amounts up to $500,000 (in egregious cases). Similarly, Section 21C of the same statute authorizes the SEC to impose administrative "cease and desist" orders—in effect, a type of civil injunction. Thus, even in the United States where judicial remedies are probably most available and most flexible, securities regulators be-

lieved it important to bring at least some remedies "in house" where they would be litigated before administrative law judges trained at the agency and exclusively involved with the securities law enforcement.

121. In civil-law countries, there is no right to a jury trial, which is the factor probably most responsible for limiting the jurisdiction of administrative-law judges in civil cases in the United States.

122. I use *self-enforcing* here in the same sense as that term was originally used by Professors Black and Kraakman to mean a remedy or protection that did not require judicial enforcement to be effective. *See* Black & Kraakman, *supra* note 17.

123. *See supra* notes 30, 52, and accompanying text.

124. *See* Pistor, *supra* note 7, at 39 (1301 of 1716 Czech firms delisted under pressure from regulators).

125. *See* Tarun Khanna & Krishna Palepu, Emerging Market Business, Foreign Investors, and Corporate Governance (Nat'l Bureau of Econ. Research Working Paper No. 6955, 1999).

126. *Id.* at 19. *Tobin's Q* is a well-recognized financial measure that consists of the ratio of the firm's market value to the replacement cost of its assets. A low Tobin's Q (which arises if the replacement cost exceeds or approaches the firm's market value) is seen as indicating poor managerial performance. *See, e.g.*, Henri Servaes, *Tobin's Q and the Gains from Takeovers*, 46 J. Fin. 409 (1991).

127. *See generally*, Roman Frydman et al., *Needed Mechanisms of Corporate Governance and Finance in Eastern Europe*, *in* Economics of Transition 171 (1993).

128. I rely here on the advice of Professor Theodor Baums of the University of Osnabruck for this proposition, who cites me to Section 93 of the German Stock Corporation Act.

129. I again rely on Professor Baums for this statement. *See also* Ekkehard Wenger & Christogh Kaserer, The German System of Corporate Governance—a Model That Should Not Be Imitated 27–29 (working paper, on file with author) (discussing the absence of disclosure obligations under German corporate law and weakness of German proxy system).

130. *See supra* notes 100, 116, and accompanying text.

131. For a strong and sensible statement of this view, *see* Black & Kraakman, *supra* note 17, at 1925–27.

132. The shifting attitude of U.S. law and the progression from flat prohibition of fiduciary self-dealing to greater tolerance is described in Harold Marsh, Jr., *Are Directors Trustees? Conflicts of Interest and Corporate Morality*, 22 Bus. Law. 35 (1966).

133. Poland uses a $33\frac{1}{3}$ percent ceiling, which is a more meaningful definition of actual de facto control; also, this level corresponded to the amount assigned to the lead NIF in each privatized company. *See* Pistor, *supra* note 7, at 37–38.

134. Ironically, the Czech law already limited any investment privatization fund to a 20 percent ownership of the equity securities of any firm. *See* Coffee, *supra* note 37, at 121–22. But these rules were easily evaded, either by using multiple funds run by the same investment manager or, ultimately, by deregistering as a fund and becoming an unregulated holding company.

135. *See* Andrei Shleifer & Robert Vishny, *Large Shareholders and Corporate Control*, 94 J. Pol. Econ. 461 (1988) (finding firm value in U.S. firms to be maximized when there is a large but noncontrolling shareholder).

136. *See* sources cited *supra* notes 2 and 3.

137. For precisely this reason, Professors Black and Kraakman recommended use of "self-enforcing" remedies. *See* Black and Kraakman, *supra* note 17, at 1925–27.

138. *See* Mark Roe, Strong Managers, Weak Owners: The Political Roots of American Corporate Finance 233–34, 243–44 (1994).

139. *See supra* notes 87–91 and accompanying text.

CHAPTER EIGHT

The Information Content of Stock Markets: Why Do Emerging Markets Have Synchronous Stock Price Movements?

Randall Morck, Bernard Yeung, and Wayne Yu

STOCK PRICES move together more in poor economies than in rich ones. This is not a result of market size and is only partially explained by higher fundamentals correlation in low-income economies. However, measures of property rights do explain this difference. The systematic component of returns variation is large in emerging markets and appears unrelated to fundamentals comovement, consistent with noise trader risk. Among developed economy stock markets, higher firm-specific returns variation is associated with stronger public-investor property rights. We propose that strong property rights promote informed risk arbitrage, which capitalizes detailed firm-specific information.

I. INTRODUCTION

Stock returns reflect new market-level and firm-level information. As Richard Roll makes clear, the extent to which stocks move together depends on the relative amounts of firm-level and market-level information capitalized into stock prices.[1] We find that stock prices in economies with high per capita gross domestic product (GDP) move in a relatively unsynchronized manner. In contrast, stock prices in low per capita GDP economies tend to move up or down together. A time series of stock price synchronicity for the U.S. market also shows that the degree of comovement in U.S. stock prices has declined, more or less steadily, during the twentieth century. These findings are not the result of differences in market size or economy size.[2]

We consider three plausible explanations for our finding. First, firms in low-income countries might have more correlated fundamentals, and this correlation might make their stock prices move more synchronously. For example, if low-income economies tend to be undiversified, firm-level earnings may be highly correlated because industry events are essentially marketwide events. Second, low-income economies often provide poor and uncertain protection of private-property rights. Political events and rumors in such countries could, by themselves, cause marketwide stock price swings. Moreover, inadequate protection for property rights could make informed risk arbitrage in their stock markets unattractive. According to Bradford De Long and coauthors, a reduction in informed trading can increase marketwide noise trader risk, which we would observe as increased marketwide stock price variation unrelated to fundamentals.[3] Third, in countries that provide poorer protection for public investors from corporate insiders, problems such as intercorporate income shifting could make firm-specific information less useful to risk arbitrageurs and therefore impede the capitalization of firm-specific information into stock prices. This effect would reduce firm-specific stock price variation, again increasing stock return synchronicity.

We reject the first hypothesis and find some evidence consistent with the second and third hypotheses previously stated. Our formal statistical analysis shows that economies with more correlated fundamentals do have stock markets with more synchronous returns, but our best efforts to control for fundamentals correlation and volatility do not render per capita GDP insignificant. Adding a variable that measures government respect for private property, however, does render per capita GDP insignificant in explaining stock price synchronicity. Finally, among developed economies, more protection of public shareholders' property rights against corporate insiders is correlated with more firm-specific information being capitalized into stock prices.

We conjecture that the degree to which a country protects private property rights affects both the extent to which information is capitalized into stock prices and the sort of information that is capitalized. While our econometric evidence is consistent with this conjecture, we recognize that our explanation is incomplete. We invite alternative explanations of our empirical finding that stock returns are synchronous in low-income economies and asynchronous in high-income economies. Any such explanations must be consistent with our findings that market size, economy size, and many aspects of fundamentals volatility do not affect the relation between per capita GDP and synchronicity, but that measures of property rights protection render per capita GDP insignificant in explaining stock price synchronicity.

In the following section, we review the empirical regularities that motivate this research. In section III, we develop our basic synchronicity measures and show their negative relationship with per capita GDP. In Section IV, we discuss our empirical framework and the dependent variables we adopt. In sections V, VI, and VII, we present our hypotheses and empirical specifications, report our results, and conduct various robustness checks. Section VIII concludes.

II. Emerging Markets and Developed Economies

Table 8.1 compares the synchronicity of stock returns in some representative stock markets during the first twenty-six weeks of 1995. Data from other periods in the 1990s display similar patterns. In emerging markets such as China, Malaysia, and Poland, more than 80 percent of stocks often move in the same direction in a given week. In Poland, 100 percent of traded stocks move in the same direction during four of the twenty-six weeks. In contrast, Denmark, Ireland, and the United States lack any instances of more than 57 percent of the stocks moving in the same direction during any week, despite a rising market in the United States. Figure 8.1 contrasts Chinese, Malaysian, and Polish stocks with U.S. stocks. For clarity, the data for Denmark and Ireland is omitted. As table 8.1 shows, the stocks data for Denmark and Ireland closely resemble the returns in the U.S. market.

We can easily reject the trivial explanation, based on the law of large numbers, that markets with many stocks should show less dispersion around the mean. First, the stock markets of Denmark and Ireland resemble the U.S. market, despite listing substantially fewer securities than China or Malaysia. Below we shall show that stock price co-movement is negatively correlated with per capita income, regardless of market or economy size. Second, the contrast between the U.S. market and emerging markets is too stark to be based solely on a statistical artifact. To test these differences, we calculate

$$f_{jt} = \frac{\max[n_{jt}^{\text{up}}, n_{jt}^{\text{down}}]}{n_{jt}^{\text{up}} + n_{jt}^{\text{down}}}, \tag{1}$$

where n^{up}_{jt} is the number of stocks in country j whose prices rise in week t and n^{down}_{jt} is the number of stocks whose prices fall. For each country j we calculate $f_{\text{US}} - f_j$. The variance of the estimate is approximately

$$\frac{f_{\text{US}}(1-f_{\text{US}})}{n_{\text{US}}} + \frac{f_j(1-f_j)}{n_j}, \tag{2}$$

assuming that f_{US} and f_j are uncorrelated. By the central limit theorem, the statistic

$$\frac{(f_{\text{US}} - f_j)}{\sqrt{f_{\text{US}}(1-f_{\text{US}})/n_{\text{US}} + f_j(1-f_j)/n_j}} \tag{3}$$

is approximately normal for sufficiently large sample sizes such as n_{US} and n_j. The null hypothesis that the fraction of stocks moving together

Table 8.1
Stock Price Comovement in Selected Emerging and Developed Stock Markets, First 26 Weeks, 1995

	China			*Malaysia*			*Poland*			*Denmark*			*Ireland*			*United States*		
Week	*% up*	*% down*	*% same*	*% up*	*% down*	*% same*	*% up*	*% down*	*% same*	*% up*	*% down*	*% same*	*% up*	*% down*	*% same*	*% up*	*% down*	*% same*
	32	61	7	18	73	9	97	3	0	50	29	21	39	46	16	47	29	24
2	4	89	6	8	86	6	5	95	0	45	25	30	33	32	35	47	38	15
3	6	88	7	22	69	9	59	31	10	36	33	31	32	40	28	49	37	13
4	7	88	5	1	95	3	3	92	5	27	36	37	33	32	35	54	32	14
5	84	8	7	80	11	9	3	97	0	48	33	18	44	26	30	33	53	15
6	7	50	42	92	2	6	100	0	0	41	30	29	42	39	19	44	43	14
7	59	31	10	77	14	10	15	77	8	41	30	28	42	40	18	57	30	13
8	18	73	9	47	39	13	10	90	0	29	35	36	28	35	37	48	38	14
9	71	22	7	28	60	12	82	13	5	40	33	27	37	42	21	42	43	15
10	93	4	4	13	77	11	95	5	0	23	36	41	25	30	46	44	42	14
11	9	88	3	12	78	9	3	95	3	31	38	31	26	39	35	33	52	15
12	41	51	7	66	23	11	0	92	8	30	37	33	28	39	33	50	37	13
13	89	7	4	53	34	13	15	67	18	21	36	42	35	39	26	41	44	15
14	84	9	6	41	50	8	100	0	0	28	37	35	32	44	25	50	35	15
15	21	73	5	15	73	12	100	0	0	27	43	30	33	39	28	47	37	15
16	18	75	7	23	66	11	56	38	5	30	52	18	28	46	26	45	40	15
17	29	63	8	56	25	19	90	10	0	34	40	26	42	37	21	41	44	15
18	5	92	3	6	87	6	8	92	0	48	33	18	47	37	16	50	35	15
19	35	56	9	33	57	10	41	49	10	39	36	26	35	44	21	46	40	14
20	29	60	11	94	3	3	87	10	3	41	36	22	40	35	25	49	37	14
21	89	8	3	21	72	7	0	100	0	39	35	26	46	37	18	42	44	14
22	21	76	4	51	42	7	92	5	3	38	33	29	40	44	16	46	39	15
23	16	79	5	78	17	5	74	23	3	34	40	26	49	44	07	47	39	14
24	55	37	8	16	77	7	36	51	13	24	40	36	40	33	26	44	41	15
25	4	84	12	72	18	9	41	49	10	22	41	37	49	33	18	52	34	14
26	73	20	7	30	60	9	82	5	13	26	40	34	39	49	12	47	39	14
Sample	308 stocks			349 stocks			38 stocks			233 stocks			57 stocks			6,889 stocks		

Source: Price changes from Datastream, adjusted for dividends.

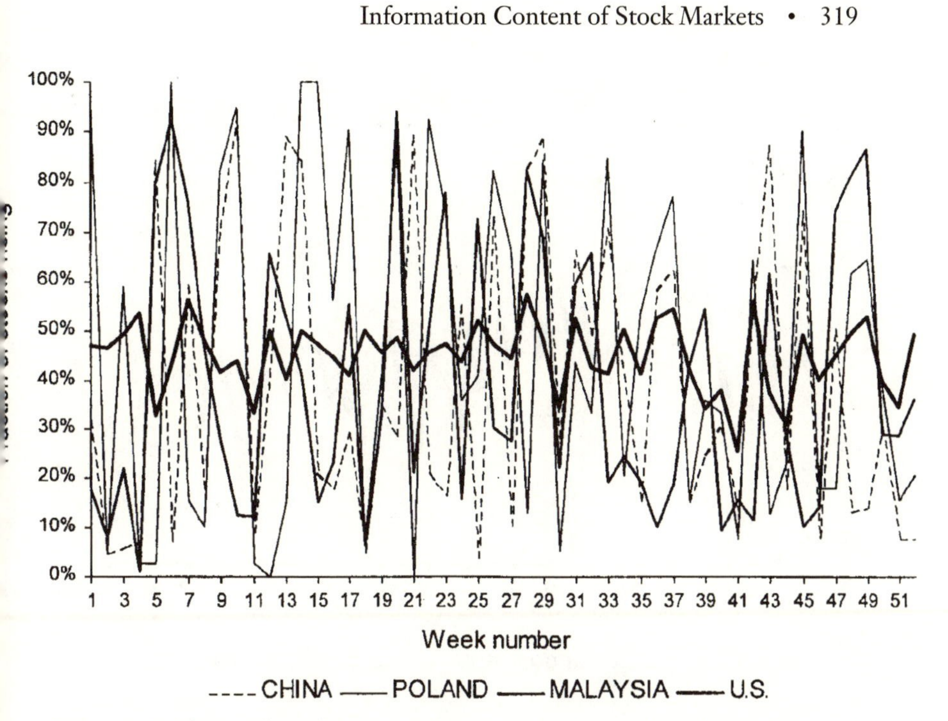

Figure 8.1 Observed stock price synchronicity in the stock markets of selected countries. The fraction of stocks whose prices rise each week of 1995 in the stock markets of China, Malaysia, Poland, and the United States based on returns including dividend income from Datastream.

in the United States is the same as that in the emerging markets can be rejected in forty-three out of fifty-two weeks for China, thirty-seven weeks for Poland, and forty-five weeks for Malaysia. In contrast, the null hypothesis can be rejected in only eighteen weeks for Denmark and New Zealand, and in only two weeks for Ireland.

The differences are economically as well as statistically significant. Using the weekly data for the whole of 1995, equation (1) shows that 79 percent of the stocks in China move together in an average week. The same calculation indicates that 77 percent of the stocks in Malaysia move together in an average week of 1995, as do 81 percent of the stocks in Poland. In contrast, in the United States, Denmark, and Ireland, the fraction of stocks gaining value in a given week typically barely exceeds the fraction of stocks losing value.

A. The United States as an Emerging Economy?

Figure 8.2 plots the fraction of U.S. stocks that move together in a given month, excluding stocks whose prices do not move, over the period

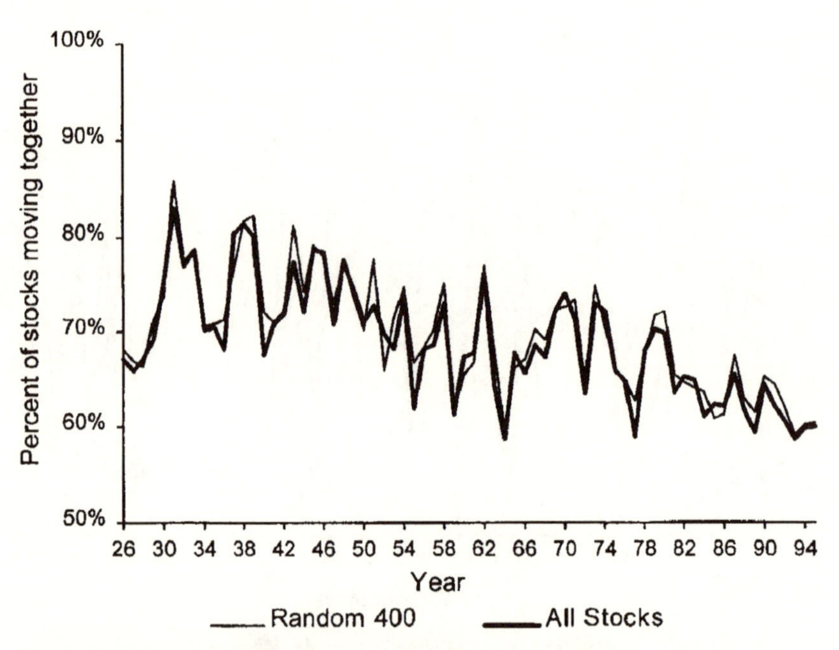

Figure 8.2 The declining synchronicity of U.S. stock prices. The fraction of stocks moving together each month from 1926 to 1995 using all available U.S. stocks and using a portfolio of 400 stocks randomly chosen each month. Returns include dividend income and are from the Center for Research in Securities Prices.

1926–95. In the earlier half of this period, the fraction of stocks that move together is comparable to the fractions for emerging markets displayed in table 8.1. Figure 8.2 demonstrates that price synchronicity decreased as the U.S. economy developed.

The number of stocks traded in the United States has increased over time, so the fraction moving together should fall toward the theoretical mean of approximately 50 percent that would prevail were monthly returns approximately zero and independent. Figure 8.2 addresses this problem by graphing the fraction of four hundred stocks, randomly selected each period, that move together each month. The same decline remains apparent. The decline in synchronicity in U.S. stock prices is not caused by the increase in the number of traded stocks.

As a robustness check, we develop an alternative measure of stock price synchronicity using the linear regression

$$r_{it} = \alpha_i + \beta_i r_{mt} + \varepsilon_{it}, \tag{4}$$

where r_{it} is stock i's return in week t, and r_{mt} is a market index return. A high R^2 in such a regression indicates a high degree of stock price syn-

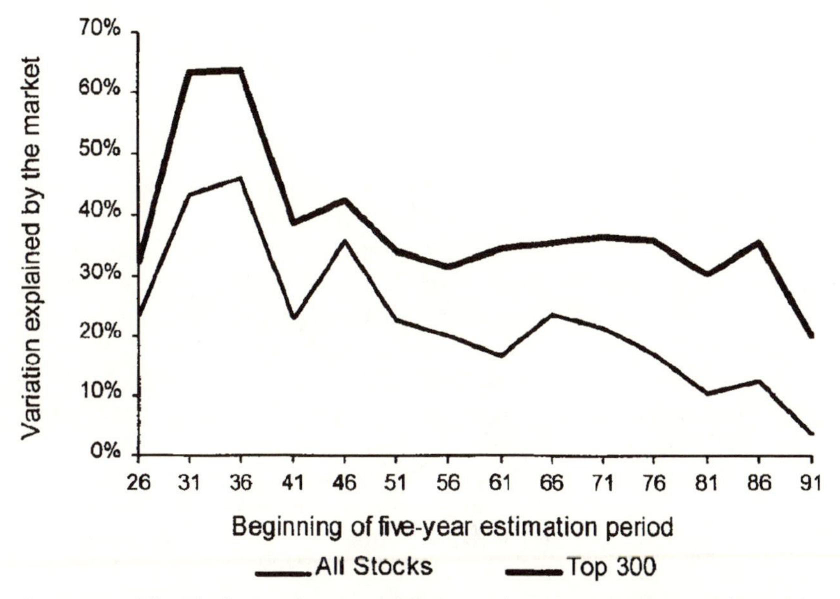

Figure 8.3 The declining fraction of U.S. stock return variation explained by the market. The fraction of U.S. stock return variation explained by the value-weighted market index is estimated by running a simple market model regression of using monthly returns including dividend income for sequential disjoint four-year periods from 1926 to 1995, using all available U.S. stocks and a portfolio of 400 stocks randomly chosen each period. Returns and indexes include dividend income and are from the Center for Research in Securities Prices.

chronicity.[4] We expand on this point when we introduce our formal measures of stock price synchronicity, below. Figure 8.3 graphs the average R^2 for equation (4) across stocks, based on monthly returns, for each nonoverlapping five-year period from 1926 to 1995. Figure 8.3 was constructed first using data for all available stocks, and then using only the largest three hundred stocks. The latter is based on rankings at the beginning of each five-year period and uses an equally weighted market index based on those stocks only. A decline in both R^2s from the 1930s to the present is apparent, demonstrating again that the behavior of U.S. stock prices earlier in the twentieth century was similar to that of emerging market stock prices now.

III. Two Stock Price Synchronicity Measures

A simple and direct measure of synchronicity in stock price movements is a formalization of the discussion surrounding table 8.1. We therefore calculate the fraction of stocks that move in the same direction in country j,

$$f_j = \frac{1}{T}\sum_t \frac{\max\left[n_{jt}^{\text{up}}, n_{jt}^{\text{down}}\right]}{n_{jt}^{\text{up}} + n_{jt}^{\text{down}}} = \frac{1}{T}\sum_t f_{jt}. \tag{5}$$

In equation (5), $n^{\text{up}}{}_{jt}$ is the number of stocks in country j whose prices rise in period t, $n^{\text{down}}{}_{jt}$ is the number of stocks whose prices fall, and T is the number of periods used. We drop stocks whose prices do not move to avoid bias caused by nontrading. Thus, we define f_j as the average value of f_{jt}, as defined in equation (1), across periods. Values of f_j must lie between 0.5 and 1.0.

Table 8.2 juxtaposes the ranking of countries by per capita GDP in panel A with their ranking by stock price synchronicity, as measured by f_j, in panel B. Generally, high-income countries have asynchronous stock prices, and the United States has the lowest fraction of stocks moving together, f_j. In contrast, low-income economies have the highest f_js. The five highest f_js are for Poland, China, Taiwan, Malaysia, and Turkey. Our calculation of f_j, the fraction of stocks in each country that move together, are based on 1995 data. Our GDP per capita variable is averaged over 1992–94 to mitigate any transitory noise. Using a three-year average of f_{jt} gives similar results to those shown in table 8.2.

An alternative way to distinguish firm-specific stock price movements from marketwide price movements, following Kenneth French and Roll and Roll, both of which works use U.S. data only,[5] is to calculate the R^2s of regressions of the form

$$r_{it} = \alpha_i + \beta_{1,i} r_{m,jt} + \beta_{2,i}[r_{\text{US},t} + e_{jt}] + \varepsilon_{it}, \tag{6}$$

where i is a firm index, j a country market index, t a two-week-period time index, $r_{m,jt}$ a domestic market index, and $r_{\text{US},t}$ the U.S. market return. The rate of change in the exchange rate per U.S. dollar is e_{jt}.

The regression specified in equation (6) is similar to classical asset-pricing equations. We do not pursue this asset-pricing interpretation of equation (6) because we view the present chapter as an application of Sanford Grossman's and Roll's approach to information capitalization, and not as a refinement or critique of any asset-pricing model.[6] Our emphasis is on the type of information that enters stocks prices, not on any trade-off between risk and return.

We include the U.S. stock market return in equation (6) because most economies are at least partially open to foreign capital. The expression $r_{\text{US},t} + e_{jt}$ translates U.S. stock market returns into local-currency units. We use biweekly returns to overcome thin trading problems, which arise when securities are traded infrequently. These returns are compounded from daily total returns. For stock markets in the Far East, we

ABLE 8.2
er Capital Gross Domestic Product and Stock Return Synchronicity

Panel A			*Panel B*		*Panel C*	
untry	*Number of listed stocks*	*log of 1995 per capita US$ GDP*	*Country*	*% stocks moving in step* (f_j)	*Country*	R_j^2
pan	2276	10.41	United States	57.9	United States	0.021
enmark	264	10.21	Canada	58.3	Ireland	0.058
orway	138	10.14	France	59.2	Canada	0.062
ermany	1232	10.10	Germany	61.1	United Kingdom	0.062
nited States	7241	10.10	Portugal	61.2	Australia	0.064
ustria	139	10.08	Australia	61.4	New Zealand	0.064
veden	264	10.08	United Kingdom	63.1	Portugal	0.068
rance	982	10.05	Denmark	63.1	France	0.075
elgium	283	9.98	New Zealand	64.6	Denmark	0.075
olland	100	9.95	Brazil	64.7	Austria	0.093
ngapore	381	9.91	Holland	64.7	Holland	0.103
ong Kong	502	9.90	Belgium	65.0	Germany	0.114
anada	815	9.86	Ireland	65.7	Norway	0.119
inland	104	9.84	Pakistan	66.1	Indonesia	0.140
aly	312	9.84	Sweden	66.1	Sweden	0.142
ustralia	654	9.76	Austria	66.2	Finland	0.142
nited Kingdom	1628	9.75	Italy	66.6	Belgium	0.146
eland	70	9.56	Norway	66.6	Hong Kong	0.150
ew Zealand	137	9.47	Japan	66.6	Brazil	0.161
pain	144	9.47	Chile	66.9	Philippines	0.164
aiwan	353	9.28	Spain	67.0	Korea	0.172
ortugal	90	9.11	Indonesia	67.1	Pakistan	0.175
orea	461	8.93	South Africa	67.2	Italy	0.183
reece	248	8.90	Thailand	67.4	Czech	0.185
exico	187	8.28	Hong Kong	67.8	India	0.189
hile	190	8.12	Philippines	68.8	Singapore	0.191
alaysia	362	8.11	Finland	68.9	Greece	0.192
razil	398	8.05	Czech Republic	69.1	Spain	0.192
zech Republic	87	8.03	India	69.5	South Africa	0.197
outh Africa	93	7.96	Singapore	69.7	Columbia	0.209
urkey	188	7.87	Greece	69.7	Chile	0.209
oland	45	7.75	Korea	70.3	Japan	0.234
hailand	368	7.69	Peru	70.5	Thailand	0.271
eru	81	7.56	Mexico	71.2	Peru	0.288
olumbia	48	7.32	Columbia	72.3	Mexico	0.290
hilippines	171	6.78	Turkey	74.4	Turkey	0.393
donesia	218	6.60	Malaysia	75.4	Taiwan	0.412

(*continued*)

TABLE 8.2 (*continued*)

Panel A			*Panel B*		*Panel C*	
Country	*Number of listed stocks*	*log of 1995 per capita US$ GDP*	*Country*	*% stocks moving in step (f_j)*	*Country*	*R*
China	323	6.12	Taiwan	76.3	Malaysia	0.4
Pakistan	120	6.05	China	80.0	China	0.4
India	467	5.71	Poland	82.9	Poland	0.5

Note: Countries are ranked by log of 1995 per capita GDP in Panel A. In panel B, countries are ranked stock return synchronicity, measured by the fraction of stocks moving together in the average week of 19 In panel C, countries are ranked by stock market synchronicity, measured as the average R2 of firm-level gressions of biweekly stock returns on local and U.S. market indexes in each country in 1995. Returns clude dividends and are trimmed at ±25%.

lag U.S. market returns by one day to account for time zone differences. Thus, if the biweekly stock return in Japan used data from May 7, 1995, to May 21, 1995, the contemporaneous U.S. market return uses data from May 6, 1995, to May 20, 1995. When we calculate equation (6) using U.S. data, we set $\beta_{2,i}$ to zero.

Our daily with-dividend stock returns data begin with all companies covered by the Datastream information service as of January 1997. Datastream also allowed us access to data for companies no longer traded, but whose stock prices were formerly covered by their service. Our total cross-section for 1995 thus contains 15,920 firms spanning forty countries. Newly listed or recently delisted stocks are included in our sample only if more than thirty weeks of data is available for the year in question. This requirement yields sufficient observations to reliably assess the explanatory power of the market returns on each stock. Thus, we omit newly traded stocks that have been traded for roughly less than five months in a year, as well as stocks that are about to be delisted. When trading of a stock is suspended, the returns data during the suspension period are coded as missing and also excluded from our regressions. In addition, for most countries, Datastream returns are either unavailable or seriously incomplete until the mid-1990s. For this reason, we focus on 1993 through 1995, and use only 1995 data in our international cross-sectional analysis. As a robustness check, we reproduce our results using 1993 and 1994 data.

Datastream claims that its total returns are adjusted for splits and other unusual events, but our data do contain some very large stock returns. If these very large returns reflect coding errors, they could add noise to our data or create bias in our results. On the assumption that coding errors are overrepresented in extreme observations, we trim our data by dropping biweekly observations for which the stock's return exceeds 0.25 in absolute value.

The regression statistic for equation (6), R^2_{ij}, measures the percentage of the variation in the biweekly returns of stock i in country j explained by variations in country j's market return and the U.S. market return. Given this statistic for each firm i in country j, we define

$$R_j^2 = \frac{\sum_i R_{ij}^2 \times SST_{i,j}}{\sum_i SST_{i,j}} \tag{7}$$

as an alternative stock price synchronicity measure, where $SST_{i,j}$ is the sum of squared total variations. We use this weighting rather than a simple average to facilitate the decomposition of returns variation in (16) and (17) (see section VI). A higher R^2_j indicates that stock prices frequently move together.[7]

Panel C of table 8.2 juxtaposes the ranking of countries by stock price synchronicity, as measured by R^2_j, against their ranking by per capita GDP in panel A. Only four relatively wealthy countries have notably high R^2s. These countries are Japan, Italy, Greece, and Spain. Note that the stock market in Japan is regarded by many practitioners as notoriously bubble-prone, and that Italy has a demonstrably poorly functioning stock market.[8] With these exceptions, low-income economies account for the high R^2s. The five-highest R^2_js are for Poland, China, Malaysia, Taiwan, and Turkey. The five-lowest R^2s are for developed high-income countries—the United States, Ireland, Canada, the United Kingdom, and Australia. Overall, the R^2_j estimates for high-income countries tend to be below the median.[9]

Figure 8.4 graphically highlights the large differences across countries in the f_j and R^2_j measures of stock market synchronicity. Panel A of figure 8.5 plots the f_j of each country against the logarithm of its per capita GDP, illustrating a clear and statistically significant negative correlation equal to -0.571 and significant at the 0.1 percent level. Panel B of figure 8.5 plots each country's R^2_j against the logarithm of its per capita GDP, again making evident a clear and significant negative correlation of -0.394, significant at the 2 percent level. A closer look at figure 8.5 suggests two data clusters: high-income countries with low synchronicity and low-income countries with high synchronicity. This clustering suggests that per capita GDP might be proxying for another measure of economic development that also exhibits such clustering.

In summary, the R^2_j and f_j measures of synchronicity behave similarly. Both measures show a clearly negative relation between stock price synchronicity and per capita income, with some evidence of clustering.

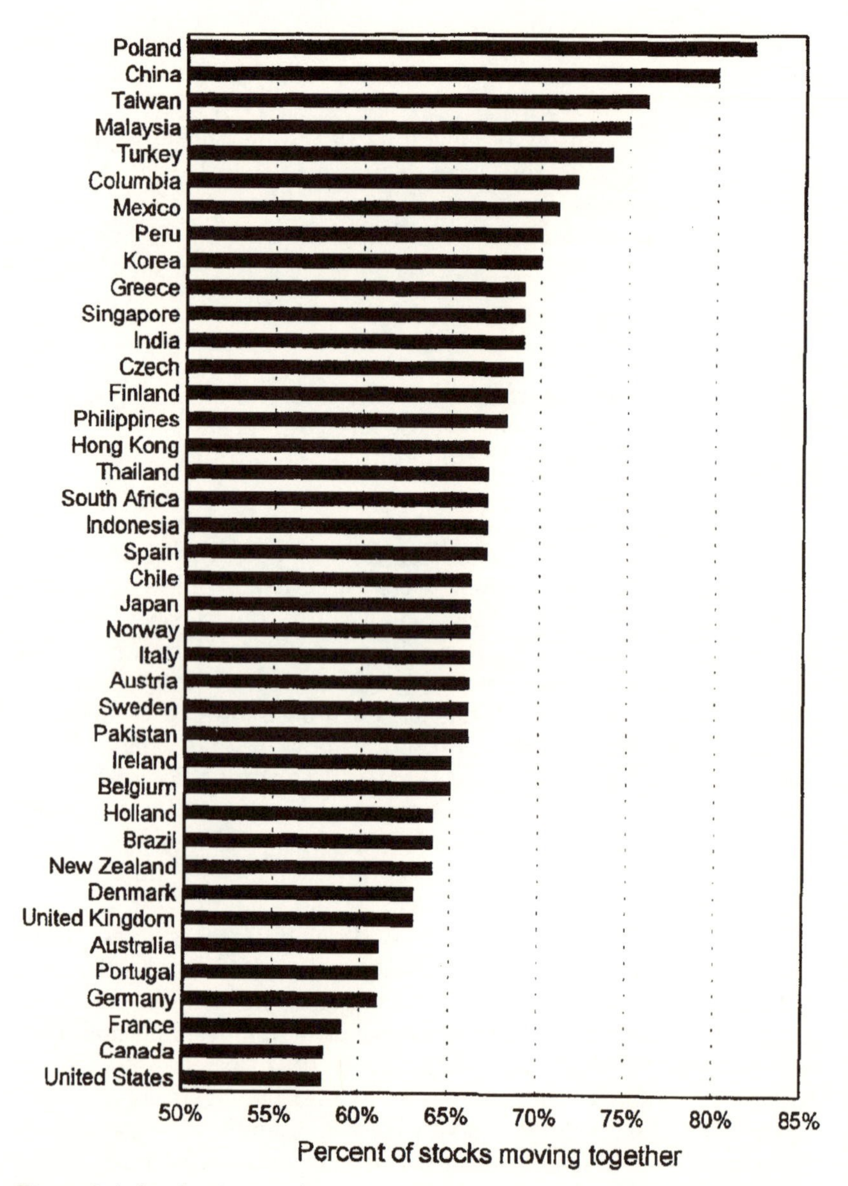

Figure 8.4 Stock price synchronicity in various countries. Panel A. Stock price synchronicity measured by the average fraction of stock prices moving in the same direction during an average week in 1995. Stock prices that do not move during a week are excluded from the average for that week. Price movements are adjusted for dividend payments, and are based on Datastream total returns.

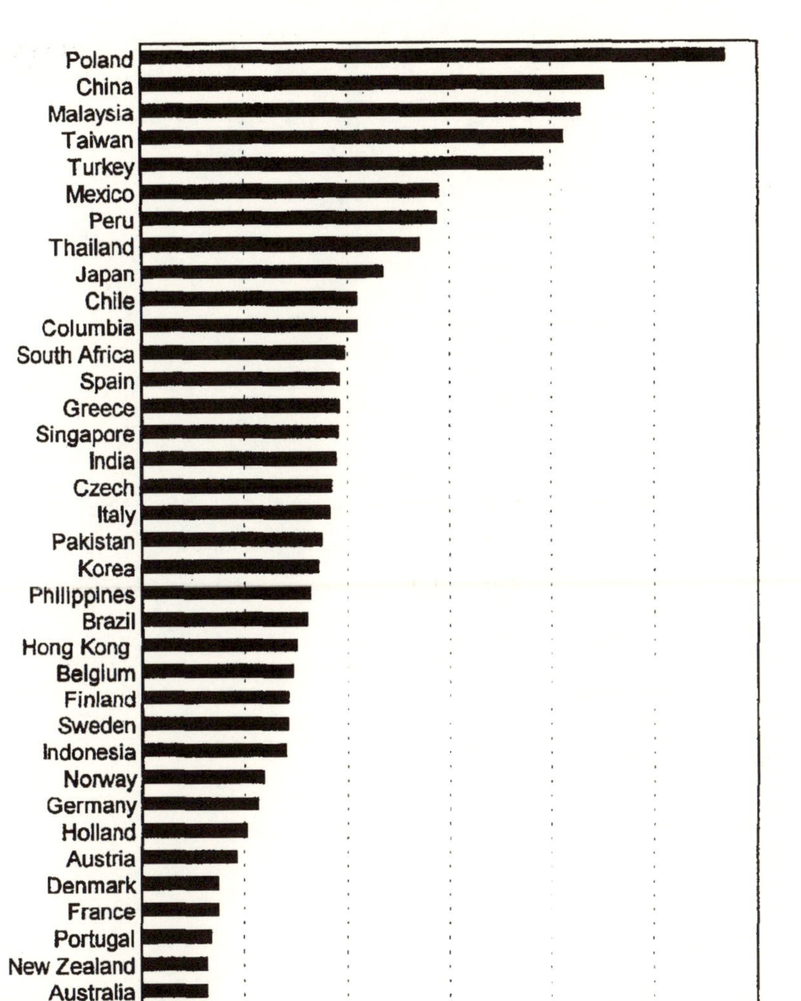

Figure 8.4 (*continued*) Panel B. Stock price synchronicity measured by the average percentage of total biweekly firm-level return variation in 1995 explained by local and U.S. value-weighted market indexes. Stock returns and indexes include dividend payments and are obtained from Datastream.

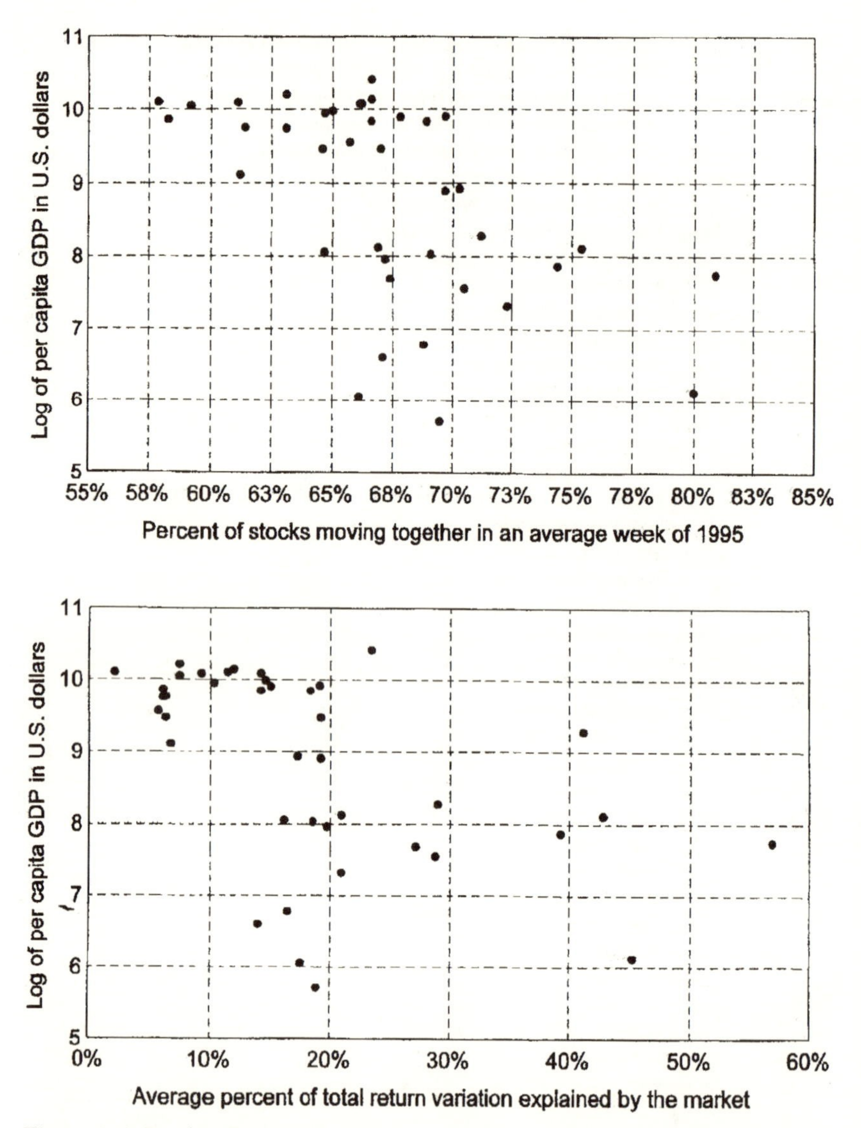

Figure 8.5 Stock price synchronicity and GDP. Panel A. The logarithm of per capita GDP plotted against stock return synchronicity measured by the average percentage of stock returns moving in the same direction each week. Each observation is for one country. Data are for 1995. Panel B. The logarithm of per capita GDP plotted against stock return synchronicity measured by the percentage of total return variation explained by local and U.S. value-weighted market indexes in ordinary least squares regressions. Each observation is for one country. Returns and indexes include dividends. Data are for 1995.

IV. Empirical Framework

What explains the highly significant negative correlation between stock price synchronicity and per capita GDP? Per capita GDP is a general measure of economic development. In this section, we hypothesize that particular economy characteristics, or dimensions of economic development, might plausibly be related to stock price synchronicity and that per capita GDP might serve as a proxy for these characteristics. Our strategy is to see which development measures are most correlated with stock price synchronicity and to ask whether they render per capita GDP insignificant in multivariate regressions. From this exercise, we hope to learn what economic linkages might underlie the correlation between stock price synchronicity and per capita income.

A. Stock Price Synchronicity Dependent Variables

Our two stock price synchronicity measures, f and R^2, are unsuitable as dependent variables in regressions because they are bounded within the intervals [0.5, 1] and [0, 1], respectively. We therefore adopt a standard econometric remedy and apply logistic transformations to these variables. Our left-hand side variables are thus

$$\Psi_j = \log\left(\frac{f_j - 0.5}{1 - f_i}\right), \tag{8}$$

$$\Upsilon_j = \log\left(\frac{R_j^2}{1 - R_j^2}\right). \tag{9}$$

In equation (8), Ψ_j maps f_j from the interval [0.5, 1] to $\mathbb{R}$, the set of real numbers from negative to positive infinity. Similarly, in equation (9), Υ_j maps $R^2{}_j$ from the unit interval to $\mathbb{R}$. The construction of $R^2{}_j$ and f_j are as described in section III. Both variables are based on 1995 data, though our results are similar if we use 1993 or 1994 data. Scatter plots (not shown) reveal that these transformations preserve the clustering effect noted above.

B. Controlling for Stock Market Size

By construction, the comovement measures, R^2 and f, decrease with the number of securities in a country's stock market. If the sign of the stock return is random, the law of large numbers pushes f_j to approximately 0.5 as the number of stocks grows large. That is,

$$E[F_{Jt}] = E\left[\frac{\max[n_{jt}^{\text{up}}, n_{jt}^{\text{down}}]}{n_{jt}^{\text{up}} + n_{jt}^{\text{down}}}\right] \cong \frac{1}{2}. \tag{10}$$

for a short window in which the expected return is close to zero. Also, the market index on the right-hand side of equation (6), which forms the basis for the construction of our $R^2{}_f$ price synchronicity variable, is a weighted average of the individual stock returns used as dependent variables. This construction produces a similar spurious correlation between number of securities listed and this price synchronicity variable. Intuitively, in a market with few securities, each individual security is a more important part of the market index. Thus, higher synchronicity might simply reflect fewer traded stocks.

To control for these effects, we use the logarithm of the number of listed stocks in 1995 in each stock market, taken from Datastream. However, a correlation between synchronicity and market size may also reflect better-functioning stock markets having more listings. By controlling for number of listings, we may be introducing downward bias in the significance of variables that measure stock market quality.

C. Regression Framework

In the following analysis, we propose hypotheses for why certain economy characteristics might be related to stock price synchronicity. We construct a vector $\boldsymbol{x}_j$ measuring these characteristics and include it in regressions of the form

$$\Upsilon_j \text{ or } \Psi_j = c_0 + c_1 \log y_j + c_2 \log n_j + \boldsymbol{c} \cdot \boldsymbol{x}_j + u_j, \tag{11}$$

where Υ_j and Ψ_j are our logistically transformed price synchronicity variables, y_j is per capita GDP, n_j is the number of listed stocks, and u_j is a random error term. Our objective is to see which characteristics x_j significantly explain stock price synchronicity and render the logarithm of per capita GDP insignificant.

V. Structural Explanations

In this section, we consider the hypothesis that the negative correlation between stock price comovement and per capita income is caused by firms in low-income economies having more correlated economic fundamentals. To test this hypothesis, we include specific structural variables in the vector $\boldsymbol{x}_j$ that might provide separate proxies for such an effect. These variables are macroeconomic volatility, country size, and economy diversification. Since these variables may not encompass all sources of marketwide price movement, we also include a direct measure of earnings comovement for firms in each economy using standardized firm-level accounting data. If including these variables in the vector $\boldsymbol{x}_j$ renders per capita income insignificant in regression (11), we can conclude that per capita income provides a proxy for these structural effects.

A description of each structural independent variables follows.

A. Macroeconomic Instability

Some economies could have unstable market fundamentals because of macroeconomic instability. In these economies, volatile market fundamentals may overwhelm variations resulting from firm-specific factors, so that stock prices tend to move together. If so, our finding of greater stock price synchronicity could be attributed to macroeconomic instability.

To measure macroeconomic instability, we use the variance of per capita GDP growth for each country, with per capita GDP measured in nominal U.S. dollars, estimated from 1990 to 1994. We use the variance of the domestic inflation rate across the same period as a robustness check.

B. Country Size

Country size per se could matter in at least two ways.[10] First, economic activity in a small country could be geographically localized, so that nearby geopolitical instability or localized environmental catastrophes such as earthquakes or monsoons might have marketwide effects that would not be as evident in a larger country. For example, Finland's economy shrank by 15 percent in the early 1990s as the neighboring Soviet Union disintegrated amid severe structural changes and Finland's role as a gateway to Russia temporarily lost value. Hong Kong's economy is similarly dependent on events in mainland China.

Second, Jeffrey Bernstein and David Weinstein observe the economic specialization predicted by standard international-trade theory across geographical units of similar size, but not across countries.[11] This finding is consistent with larger countries having factor endowments that exhibit less uniformity, and this relation in turn suggests that the stocks of firms in large countries might move more independently than those in small countries. For example, if oil prices fall, the prospects of Ohio manufacturing firms brighten, while those of Texas oil companies dim, resulting in observable asynchronous stock price movements in the U.S. markets. In contrast, stocks in a smaller oil-producing country, such as Venezuela, might move more synchronously as oil prices change, given that a larger position of Venezuelan economic activity is devoted to providing goods and services for oil companies and their employees. Similar stories might be told about the dependence of smaller countries on particular agricultural crops, mining operations, or industries.

To capture any relation between country size and synchronicity in stock returns, we use the logarithm of geographical size, in square kilometers, for each country. We use the logarithm of population in a robustness check.

C. Economic and Managerial Diversification

The second point above is closely related to economic specialization. In some economies, listed firms could be concentrated in a few industries. Consequently, the fundamentals of these firms could be highly correlated, and their stock prices highly synchronous. Undiversified economies should therefore exhibit more stock price synchronicity than diversified ones. If poor countries are relatively undiversified, this characteristic might explain our finding.

Alternatively, some economies may be dominated by a few very large firms. If most other listed firms are suppliers or customers of these dominant firms, a high degree of stock price synchronicity might ensue. Problems that would be firm specific in a larger economy, such as leadership succession within a controlling family, can potentially affect the entire economy. If economies of poor countries depend disproportionately on a few large firms, our finding could follow.

To capture these effects, we construct an industry Herfindahl index and a firm Herfindahl index for each country. We define the industry Herfindahl index of country j as $H_j = \Sigma_k h^2_{k,j}$ where $h_{k,j}$ is the combined value of the sales of all country j firms in industry k as a percentage of those of all country j firms. Analogously, we define the firm Herfindahl index of country j to be $\hat{H}_j = \Sigma_i \hat{h}^2_{i \in j}$ where $\hat{h}_{i,j}$ is the sales of firm i as a percentage of the total sales of all country j firms. These indexes are constructed using 1995 data and industry classifications from Datastream. The classifications are roughly equivalent to using two-digit Standard Industrial Classification (SIC) codes to define industry categories. High values of the industry and firm Herfindahl indexes indicate, respectively, a lack of industry diversity and the dominance of a few large firms.[12]

D. Synchronous Fundamentals

Firm fundamentals might move together more in low-income countries for the above reasons, or for other reasons. For example, if highly diversified conglomerates account for a larger fraction of listed firms, their returns should all resemble the market return. Widespread intercorporate ownership might also cause firm fundamentals to move together, as intercorporate ownership implicitly causes the performance of some firms to depend on that of other firms. This effect is exacerbated if related firms use intercorporate transactions to assist one another in bad times or to share the bounty in good times. All such explanations posit a greater correlation across firms in economic fundamentals. A general measure of comovement of firm fundamentals can therefore act as a comprehensive structural independent variable, capturing all these various explanations.

To capture the general synchronicity of firm-level fundamentals, we construct an earnings comovement index by running the regression

$$ROA_{i,j,} = a_i + b_i \times ROA_{m,j}, \tag{12}$$

for each firm i in each country j. $ROA_{i,j}$ is a firm's returns on assets, calculated as annual after-tax profit plus depreciation over total assets. $ROA_{m,j}$ is the value-weighted average of the return on assets for all firms in the country.

Our firm-level earnings data contain isolated irregularities, appearing as single spikes in the data. These irregularities generally reflect extraordinary items in the calculation of firm earnings and are treated as statistical noise for our purposes. To mitigate these data problems, we exclude $ROA_{i,j}$ in period t if $(ROA_{i,j,t} - ROA_{i,j,t-1})$ and $(ROA_{i,j,t} - ROA_{i,j,t+1})$ are opposite in sign and are both greater than 0.75 in absolute value.

Firm-level accounting data are sparse for some countries and are completely unavailable in a few, especially prior to the mid-1990s. Using more years of data arguably allows better regression estimates, but also worsens the problem of obtaining comparable data for a statistically meaningful number of countries. We use five years of data from 1993 to 1997. Because of missing data, we can run such firm-level *ROA* regressions in only twenty-four countries. These are Australia, Austria, Belgium, Brazil, Chile, Denmark, Finland, France, Germany, Greece, Holland, India, Italy, Japan, Mexico, Norway, Portugal, South Korea, Spain, Sweden, Taiwan, Turkey, the United Kingdom and the United States. For three of these countries, Austria, Chile, and Taiwan, earnings data are available for very few firms. Dropping these three countries does not qualitatively affect our basic findings. To mitigate problems associated with the loss in sample size, we conduct our empirical investigation both with and without the earnings comovement index.

After running these regressions on firm-level return on assets data for these countries, we then average the R^2s of these regressions to construct a weighted average earnings R^2 for each country. This calculation yields our earnings comovement measure,

$$\textit{Earnings comovement index}_j = \frac{\sum_i R^2_{i,j}(ROA) \times SST_{i,j}(ROA)}{\sum_i SST_{i,j}(ROA)}. \tag{13}$$

Our earnings comovement index is analogous to using the R^2 from equation (6) as a stock price synchronicity measure, but it measures the synchronicity of firm fundamentals instead. We expect fundamentals synchronicity to be positively related to stock return synchronicity.

E. Stock Price Synchronicity and Structural Variables

Table 8.3 displays univariate statistics and simple correlation coefficients for our stock price synchronicity variables, the logarithm of per capita GDP and the number of listed stocks, and the structural variables listed above. The logarithm of the number of listed stocks is negatively correlated with price synchronicity, as anticipated.

The signs of the correlations of stock price synchronicity with the structural variables are largely as expected. Price synchronicity is negatively correlated with a country's geographical size and positively correlated with both GDP growth variance and earnings comovement, although these correlations are all statistically insignificant. More diversification is not consistently correlated with less stock price synchronicity. Overall, these correlations suggest that no one structural variable is likely to explain the link between per capita GDP and stock price synchronicity.

Panel B of table 8.3 also shows that per capita GDP is significantly negatively correlated with a country's geographical size and is essentially uncorrelated with diversification. Clearly, our basic result cannot be the result of low-income countries being small and undiversified.

Table 8.4 displays multivariate regressions of the form of regression (11), to see if the structural variables, acting in concert, might explain the link between per capita GDP and stock price synchronicity. First, note that a small-country effect appears in this multivariate setting. Stock prices do move together more in smaller countries. However, this effect does not explain the correlation between price synchronicity and per capita GDP, as that variable remains highly significant. This result suggests that per capita GDP does not serve as a proxy for our structural variables, taken either separately or all together, and that factors beyond our structural explanations underlie the negative relation between per capita GDP and stock price synchronicity.

TABLE 8.3
Description of Main Variables

Panel A. Univariate statistics and simple correlation coefficients between stock price synchronicity indices, stock return variance decomposition variables $log(\sigma_\varepsilon^2)$ and $log(\sigma_m^2)$, and structural and institutional variables

Variables	*Mean*	*Standard deviation*	*Minimum*	*Maximum*	*Simple correlation with* Ψ_i	Υ_j	$log(\sigma_\varepsilon^2)$	$log(\sigma_m^2)$
Stock comovement indices								
Average fraction of stocks moving in same direction (f_j)	0.659	0.052	0.570	0.772	0.993 (0.00)	0.900 (0.00)	0.162 (0.34)	0.855 (0.01)
R square of market model based on weekly data for country j	0.169	0.099	0.020	0.429	0.888 (0.00)	0.949 (0.00)	0.146 (0.39)	0.891 (0.00)
Logistic transformation of f_j for country $j(\Psi_i)$	−0.808	0.501	−1.84	0.180	—			
Logistic transformation of R^2 for country $j(\Upsilon_j)$	−1.76	0.758	−3.84	−0.284	0.909 (0.00)	—		
Logarithm of firm-specific variation ($\log(\sigma_\varepsilon^2)$)	−2.30	0.360	−3.05	−1.52	0.115 (0.50)	0.073 (0.67)	—	
Logarithm of marketwide variation ($\log(\sigma_m^2)$)	−3.97	0.930	−5.60	−1.86	0.843 (0.00)	0.904 (0.00)	0.449 (0.00)	—
Logarithm of per capita GDP	8.94	1.30	5.71	10.4	−0.512 (0.00)	−0.457 (0.00)	−0.406 (0.01)	−0.573 (0.00)
Logarithm of number-listed stocks	5.61	1.06	3.81	8.89	−0.381 (0.02)	−0.307 (0.06)	0.200 (0.23)	−0.183 (0.28)

(continued)

TABLE 8.3 (*continued*)

Panel A. Univariate statistics and simple correlation coefficients between stock price synchronicity indices, stock return variance decomposition variables $log(\sigma_\varepsilon^2)$ and $log(\sigma_m^2)$, and structural and institutional variables

Variables	*Mean*	*Standard deviation*	*Minimum*	*Maximum*	*Simple correlation with*			
					Ψ_i	Υ_j	$log(\sigma_\varepsilon^2)$	$log(\sigma_m^2)$
Structural variables								
Logarithm of geographical size	12.7	2.11	6.46	16.1	−0.160	−0.0105	0.372	0.084
					(0.34)	(0.54)	(0.02)	(0.62)
Variance in GDP growth	0.0001	0.0002	0.0007	0.001	0.0703	0.0999	−0.190	0.010
					(0.68)	(0.56)	(0.26)	(0.97)
Industry Herfindahl index	0.113	0.0559	0.030	0.281	0.0116	−0.035	−0.0175	−0.020
					(0.94)	(0.84)	(0.28)	(0.00)
Firm Herfindahl index	0.0482	0.0505	0.0001	0.219	−0.001	−0.126	−0.142	−0.148
					(0.99)	(0.46)	(0.38)	(0.36)
Earnings comovement index	0.383	0.164	0.055	0.777	0.0555	0.201	0.100	0.250
					(0.80)	(0.35)	(0.63)	(0.23)
Institutional variables								
Good-government index	23.9	4.98	12.9	29.6	−0.552	−0.527	0.477	0.664
					(0.00)	(0.00)	(0.00)	(0.00)
Accounting-standards index	63.7	10.9	0.36	83	−0.237	−0.230	−0.034	−0.218
					(0.18)	(0.19)	(0.85)	(0.22)
Antidirector rights index	1.78	1.93	0	5	−0.586	−0.595	0.271	−0.077
					(0.00)	(0.00)	(0.10)	(0.65)

Panel B. Simple correlation coefficients of structural and institutional variables with one another

	a	*b*	*c*	*d*	*e*	*f*	*g*	*h*	*i*
a. Logarithm of per capita GDP	—								
b. Logarithm of number of stocks listed	0.364	—							
	(0.03)								
Structural variables									
c. Logarithm of geographical size	−0.371	0.111	—						
	(0.02)	(0.51)							
d. Variance in GDP growth	−0.020	−0.196	0.010	—					
	(0.91)	(0.24)	(0.97)						
e. Industry Herfindahl index	0.025	−0.674	−0.214	0.115	—				
	(0.88)	(0.00)	(0.20)	(0.97)					
f. Firm Herfindahl index	−0.020	−0.573	−0.040	0.091	0.710	—			
	(0.91)	(0.00)	(0.82)	(0.59)	(0.00)				
g. Earnings comovement index	−0.03	0.105	0.109	−0.100	−0.168	−0.325	—		
	(0.88)	(0.63)	(0.61)	(0.64)	(0.43)	(0.12)			
Institutional variables									
h. Good-government index	0.919	0.335	−0.298	−0.010	−0.040	0.011	−0.126	—	
	(0.00)	(0.04)	(0.07)	(0.96)	(0.82)	(0.95)	(0.56)		
i. Anti-director rights	0.706	0.403	−0.259	−0.292	−0.060	−0.070	−0.108	0.729	—
	(0.00)	(0.01)	(0.12)	(0.08)	(0.73)	(0.65)	(0.61)	(0.00)	
j. Accounting standards index	0.442	0.427	−0.090	−0.265	−0.552	−0.267	0.035	0.554	0.531
	(0.01)	(0.01)	(0.60)	(0.13)	(0.00)	(0.13)	(0.87)	(0.00)	(0.00)

Note: Univariate statistics and simple correlation coefficients between main variables. Sample is 37 countries, except for the accounting standards index, which is available for 34 countries and the earnings comovement index, which is available for only 25 countries. Numbers in parentheses are probability levels at which the null hypothesis of zero correlation can be rejected in two-tailed tests.

TABLE 8.4
Regressions of Stock Price Synchronicity on Economy Structural Variables

Dependent variable	*Ψ_j is a logistic transformation of the average fraction of stocks moving together*		*Υ_j is a logistic transformation of the R_j^2s of regressions of stock returns on market indices*	
	4.1	4.2	4.3	4.4
Intercept	4.36	8.11	4.66	8.04
	(0.00)	(0.00)	(0.04)	(0.04)
Logarithm of per capita GDP	−0.189	−0.288	−0.238	−0.324
	(0.01)	(0.01)	(0.04)	(0.04)
Logarithm of number of stocks listed	−0.180	−0.200	−0.270	−0.367
	(0.11)	(0.14)	(0.13)	(0.09)
Logarithm of geographical size	−0.867	−1.89	−0.948	−1.78
	(0.04)	(0.02)	(0.16)	(0.15)
Variance in GDP growth	68.6	−253	228	−106
	(0.84)	(0.48)	(0.67)	(0.85)
Industry Herfindahl index	−2.37	−4.30	−2.08	−5.70
	(0.27)	(0.09)	(0.54)	(0.15)
Firm Herfindahl index	−0.446	1.49	−3.71	1.04
	(0.83)	(0.55)	(0.26)	(0.80)
Earning comovement index	—	0.375	—	1.09
		(0.49)		(0.22)
F statistic for the regression	3.88	3.51	2.87	2.50
	(0.01)	(0.02)	(0.03)	(0.06)
Sample size	37	25	37	25
R^2	0.44	0.59	0.36	0.51

Note: Estimated coefficients from ordinary least squares regressions of stock price synchronicity variables, Υ_j and Ψ_j, on the logarithm of per capita GDP and structural variables. A control for market size, log(number of stocks), is included in all regressions. The structural variables are log(geographical size), variance of GDP growth, industry Herfindahl index, and the firm Herfindahl index. Regressions 4.2 and 4.4 include, as an additional structural variable, the earnings comovement index. Sample is 37 countries, except for regressions on the earnings comovement index, which is available for only 25 countries. Numbers in parentheses are probability levels at which the null hypothesis of zero correlation can be rejected in two-tailed t-tests.

F. Robustness Checks

Some clarifications are in order. First, we can never categorically reject the structural hypothesis using regressions such as the alternative specifications defined above. Additional structural variables can always be found, and some combination of these variables may explain price synchronicity, rendering per capita GDP insignificant. Second, our structural variables may be noisy. Third, earnings comovement is not necessarily successful in capturing the comovement of fundamentals, as stock prices are thought to be based on expected future cash flow, not current earnings. The relationship of price fundamentals to variables based on accounting numbers, as well as to historical macroeconomic variables, can be complicated.

Since we run country-level cross-sectional regressions, our sample size is limited. As we add variables to our model, the available degrees of freedom are exhausted quickly. Our robustness tests therefore consist of statistical fit tests, replacing structural variables with alternatives or adding only a small number of additional variables at a time.

1. OUTLIERS

Our regression results are not driven by outliers. We conduct diagnostic checks on the residuals obtained in table 8.4. We find no outliers using Student R and Cook's D measures.

2. TIME-PERIOD EFFECTS

One way to check whether our results are caused by transitory time effects is to repeat our regressions using data taken from other years. Because of missing-data problems in Datastream for earlier years, we can only repeat the regressions using 1993 and 1994 data. We obtain identical conclusions using the two earlier years.

The major transitory event in 1995 was the aftermath of the depreciation of the Mexican peso. This major macroeconomic event could have driven up the synchronicity of stock prices in Latin American countries. We repeated our regressions, dropping all Latin American countries in our sample. Our results are not qualitatively affected.

3. ALTERNATE STOCK RETURN SYNCHRONICITY MEASURES

Our stock return synchronicity indexes are necessarily arbitrary. However, our stock price synchronicity measures, both Υ_j and Ψ_j, give qualitatively similar results, despite substantial differences in their construction. In estimating $R^2{}_j$ statistics for stock return regressions, we incorporate the possibility that stock prices in other economies are influenced by the U.S. market. If some stock markets are isolated, adding the U.S. market return should not affect their $R^2{}_j$ regression statistics. The $R^2{}_j$ statistic for the United States is constructed without allowing for the influence of foreign markets on U.S. stock prices. This construction could create a downward bias in the estimated U.S. R^2. However, our results are qualitatively unchanged if we drop the United States from our sample.

As further robustness checks, we consider several alternative measures of stock return synchronicity. The first is the average simple correlation across pairs of stocks,

$$\frac{1}{2(n-1)^2 \sum_{i=1}^{n} \sum_{k \neq i} \rho_{ik}}.$$

The second is the average squared simple correlation,

$$\frac{1}{2(n-1)^2 \sum_{i=1}^{n} \sum_{k \neq i} \rho_{ik}^2}.$$

The number of pairwise combinations rises with the square of the number of listed stocks, n. Computation becomes difficult for $n > 150$. We therefore randomly choose fifty stocks from each country and calculate the average of the 2,450, or $n^2 - n$, resulting pairwise simple correlation coefficients. Another alternative measure is the fraction of pairs in which the average simple correlation coefficient is above a certain threshold, as given by

$$\frac{1}{2(n-1)^2 \sum_{i=1}^{n} \sum_{k \neq i} \delta_{ik}}, \tag{14}$$

where δ_{ik} is one if ρ_{ik} is above $\hat{\rho}$, and is zero otherwise. We consider $\hat{\rho}$ equal to 50 percent, 40 percent, 30 percent, and 20 percent.

All these alternative synchronicity measures generate results that are qualitatively similar to the measures used in the text, but at generally lower levels of statistical significance. Average correlation coefficients generate less significant results than both average squared correlation coefficients and the fraction of correlations above threshold values of $\hat{\rho}$. For the last calculation, a 50 percent cutoff generates results with statistical significance similar to the reported results.

4. ALTERNATIVE METHODS OF CONTROLLING FOR MARKET-SIZE EFFECTS

By construction, the synchronicity indexes are affected by the number of stocks in a market. We control for this market-size effect by explicitly introducing the logarithm of the number of listed stocks as an independent variable. Another way to overcome this effect is to constrain the number of stocks we use to construct our synchronicity indexes. The alternative synchronicity measures discussed in the previous section are based on fifty stocks from each country, and so are unaffected by such problems. Yet they generate results that are qualitatively similar to those shown. We can also reproduce our results using a restricted number of stocks in each country to construct our stock price synchronicity variables, Υ_j and Ψ_j. The median number of listings in the stock markets in our sample is three hundred. For countries with fewer than three hundred stocks, we use all stocks to construct the information content measures. For countries with more than three hundred stocks, we randomly select three hundred stocks. We then reestimate the test shown in table 8.4 twenty times, using three hundred different randomly drawn firms each time and indexes based only on those firms. In every run, the results are qualitatively identical to those reported.

5. UNSTABLE MONETARY POLICIES

If the stock markets in low-income countries are volatile because of swings in monetary policy, the variance in the inflation rate might be a better variable than the variance of GDP growth for explaining stock price synchronicity. This variable, like GDP growth variance, enters our equation with the predicted sign, but is even more insignificant than the variable it replaces.

6. ALTERNATIVE MEASURE OF COUNTRY SIZE

In table 8.4, we measure country size by the logarithm of the area of each country in square kilometers. This metric makes sense if extreme weather or other localized natural phenomena cause synchronicity in stock prices. However, geographical area is only one measure of country size, and population is an obvious alternative country-size metric. Substituting the logarithm of population does not change our findings.

7. COMMODITY-BASED ECONOMIES

If poor countries are disproportionately dependent on raw-materials production, and these industries are more procyclical than others, our basic finding might follow. Including a dummy variable that equals one if raw materials are the country's most important sector, and zero otherwise, also changes nothing in our reported results. This structural hypothesis is also apparently not responsible for our basic finding.

Because our focus is on the stock market data, our sample excludes very small and very poor countries, as such countries generally have no stock markets. We thus are neither proving nor disproving the idea that dependence on undiversified raw-materials production might cause economy-wide fluctuations in such economies.

8. ALTERNATIVE MEASURES OF FUNDAMENTALS COMOVEMENT

Our earnings comovement variable could be a noisy measure of fundamentals comovement. Using many years of historical data makes the variable too dependent on the past, which is likely inappropriate for fast-changing economies. However, using too few years of data makes it difficult to estimate the variable precisely. The earnings comovement measure is estimated using five years of annual data. We experimented with six and seven years of data instead. Both alternatives generate results that are qualitatively similar to those reported. We use return on assets (ROA) market indexes that are weighted by asset values. Using equally weighted indexes also leads to similar findings. Applying a logistic transformation also generates qualitatively similar results.

As another measure of disparity in firm fundamentals, we use the cross-sectional variance of firm ROA in each country. We average these cross-sectional variances over 1992, 1993, and 1994. Using this variable does not change our results.

In conclusion, after treating an exhaustive list of robustness concerns, we find that our results remain intact.

VI. An Institutional Development Explanation

In the previous section, we showed that including structural variables in the vector $\boldsymbol{x}_j$ does not render per capita income insignificant in the regression in equation (11) and argued that per capita income is not proxying for structural effects. In this section, we consider a second general hypothesis, that the negative correlation between stock price comovement and per capita income is caused by low-income economies providing poor protection of private-property rights.

We construct a "good-government index" to measure how well country j protects private-property rights. We denote this index g_j and include it in regressions of the form

$$\Upsilon_j \text{ or } \Psi_j = c_0 + c_1 \log y_j + c_2 \log n_j + \boldsymbol{c} \cdot \boldsymbol{x}_j + c_3 g_j + u_j, \quad (15)$$

where Υ_j and Ψ_j are our logistically transformed price synchronicity variables, y_j is per capita GDP, n_j is the number of listed stocks, $\boldsymbol{x}_j$ is a vector of economy structural characteristics, and u_j is a random error term. If the good-government index is significant, and including it renders per capita GDP insignificant, we have evidence that a lack of property-rights protection underlies the high degree of stock price synchronicity.

A. *Why Property-Rights Protection Might Affect Stock Price Movements*

In many countries, governments and courts are mercantilist devices for diverting wealth to an entrenched elite. Politicians can "shut down [a] business, kick it out of its premises, or even refuse to allow it to start"[13] by using a variety of tactics, including open legislation, licensing requirements, repudiation of commitments, and nationalization. Asset values are predominantly affected by political connections and events.

For example, based on stock price movements in response to rumors about the health of Indonesia's President Suharto, Raymond Fisman estimates that as much as 25 percent of the market value of many Indonesian firms is related to political connections.[14] In countries such as Indonesia, political events, or even rumors about political events, can cause large marketwide stock price swings and generate high levels of stock price synchronicity.

Thus, stock price synchronicity might reflect higher political risk. However, it is important to recall that stock price synchronicity is not explained above by macroeconomic volatility or synchronous economic fundamentals.

If our structural variables are adequate, political risk must affect share prices through some other channel. Admittedly, our structural measures could be flawed. For example, investors might expect systematic fluctuations in future fundamentals to arise from current political events. Such politically sensitive growth options in low-income countries might explain how their highly synchronous stock returns can be unrelated to synchronicity in past earnings. We invite further work to explore these possibilities.

However, bad government might increase stock price synchronicity through channels that are not directly associated with economic fundamentals. Finance theory posits that risk arbitrageurs expend resources uncovering proprietary information about stocks and earn an acceptable return by using that information to trade against less-informed investors. Risk arbitrageurs accumulate information until the marginal cost of gathering an additional unit of information exceeds its risk-adjusted marginal return. Such trading by many risk arbitrageurs, each with unique proprietary information, is thought to capitalize information into share prices.[15] Risk arbitrage of this sort may be less economically attractive in countries that protect private-property rights more poorly for several reasons.

First, economic fundamentals may be obscured by political factors in many low-income countries. Second, political events may be hard to forecast in low-income countries, whose governments are often relatively opaque and erratic. Third, risk arbitrageurs who do make correct predictions may not be allowed to keep their earnings in countries that protect private-property rights poorly, especially if the risk arbitrageurs are political outsiders. Because of these factors, firm-specific risk arbitrage could be relatively unattractive in countries that protect private-property rights poorly, and informed trading could be correspondingly thin.

If weak property rights discourage informed risk arbitrage, they might also create systematic stock price fluctuations. De Long and coauthors argue that insufficient informed trading can "create space" for noise trading.[16] Indeed, what De Long and coauthors call a "create space" effect is central to their model of systematic noise trader risk. They define this effect as follows: "As the variability of noise traders' beliefs increases, the price of risk increases. To take advantage of noise traders' misperceptions, sophisticated investors must bear this greater risk. Since sophisticated investors are risk averse, they reduce the extent to which they bet against noise traders in response to this increased risk."[17] If the proportion of noise traders in the market is above a critical level, this effect causes noise trading to grow in importance relative to informed trading and eventually to "dominate the market."[18]

Thus, DeLong and coauthors argue that stock markets without a sufficient amount of informed trading could be characterized by large systematic price swings caused by noise trading. If the governments of low-income countries do not respect property rights and thereby discourage informed trading in their stock markets, share prices in those markets should exhibit intensified marketwide variation and high synchronicity.

B. Measuring Good Government

To capture the extent to which a country's politicians respect private-property rights, we construct a good-government index as the sum of three indexes from Rafael La Porta and coauthors, each ranging from zero to ten. These indexes measure (1) government corruption, (2) the risk of expropriation of private property by the government, and (3) the risk of the government repudiating contracts.[19] Low values for each index indicate less respect for private property.

La Porta and coauthors describe these three indexes as follows: The "corruption index" is an assessment of corruption in government by the International Country Risk Guide (ICR). Low scores of this index indicate that "high government officials are likely to demand special payments" and that "illegal payments are generally expected throughout lower levels of government" in the form of "bribes connected with import and export licences, exchange controls, tax assessment, policy protection, or loans." The "risk of expropriation index" is the ICR's assessment of the risk of "outright confiscation" or "forced nationalization." The "repudiation of contracts by government index" is ICR's assessment of the risk of a "modification in a contract taking the form of a repudiation, postponement, or scaling down" caused by "budget cutbacks, indigenization pressure, a change in government, or a change in government economic and social priorities." All three ICR indexes are averages of the monthly indexes for April and October from 1982 to 1995.[20] The good-government index, like our synchronicity measures, tends to be quite high for developed countries and quite low for emerging economies.

C. The Relation of Stock Price Synchronicity to Good Government

The good-government index is available for all countries except China, the Czech Republic, and Poland. Table 8.3 reports univariate statistics for our good-government index, as well as its simple correlations with the stock price synchronicity indices, Υ_j and Ψ_j, per capita income, market size, and the structural variables.

The pattern of the simple correlation coefficients in panel A of table 8.3 is consistent with the view that better protection of private-property rights reduces stock price synchronicity. In addition, panel B shows that countries with higher per capita income have higher good-government indexes. It also shows that the good-government index is significantly correlated with market size, measured as the logarithm of the number of stock in the country's stock market, a finding that is consistent with more institutionally advanced economies having markets on which more stocks trade. This result confirms our premise that including market size as a control variable biases our tests against finding that institutional development matters.

The regressions in table 8.5 show that the good-government index remains significantly negatively correlated with stock price synchronicity after controlling for market size and the structural variables. More important, the logarithm of per capita GDP becomes insignificant in regressions containing the good-government index.

In summary, our results in this section are consistent with the view that a greater respect for private-property rights by governments in developed economies underlies our finding that stock prices in high-income countries are less synchronous than in low-income countries.

D. More Marketwide Variation or Less Firm-Specific Variation?

Our stock return synchronicity measure Υ_j can be decomposed into marketwide variation and firm-specific variation. Υ_j is the logistic transformation of the R^2_j in equation (7), which can be written as

$$R_j^2 = \frac{\sum_{i\in j} R_{i,j}^2 SST_{i,j}}{\sum_{i\in j} SST_{i,j}} = \frac{\sum_{i\in j} \frac{\sigma^2_{m,i,j}}{\sigma^2_{m,i,j}+\sigma^2_{m,i,j}}(\sigma^2_{m,i,j}+\sigma^2_{\varepsilon,i,j}}{\sum_{i\in j}(\sigma^2_{m,i,j}+\sigma^2_{\varepsilon,i,j})}, \tag{16}$$

where $\sigma^2_{m,i,j}$ is the variation in the return of firm i in country j explained by market factors and $\sigma^2_{\varepsilon,i,j}$ is the residual variation in firm i's return. Substituting equation (16) into the definition of Υ_j yields

TABLE 8.5
Regressions of Stock Price Synchronicity on Economy Structural Variables and a Good Government Index

Dependent variable	*Ψ_j is a logistic transformation of the average fraction of stocks moving together*		*Υ_j is a logistic transformation of the R_j^2s of regressions of stock returns on market indices*	
	5.1	5.2	5.3	5.4
Log(GDP per capita)	0.033	0.025	0.170	0.188
	(0.83)	(0.87)	(0.48)	(0.46)
Logarithm of number of stocks listed	−0.204	−0.197	−0.315	−0.331
	(0.06)	(0.10)	(0.07)	(0.07)
Good-government index	−0.059	−0.098	−0.110	−0.161
	(0.11)	(0.03)	(0.07)	(0.03)
Structural variables				
Log. of geographical size	−0.811	−1.98	−0.846	−1.92
	(0.05)	(0.01)	(0.19)	(0.09)
Variance in GDP growth	72.1	2216	235	247.2
	(0.82)	(0.49)	(0.65)	(0.93)
Industry Herfindahl index	−3.44[a]	−4.97	−4.07	−6.79
	(0.12)	(0.03)	(0.24)	(0.06)
Firm Herfindahl index	0.282	1.83	−2.38	1.59
	(0.89)	(0.41)	(0.46)	(0.65)
Earning comovement index	—	0.117	—	0.671
		(0.81)		(0.40)
F-test for the structural variables	1.91	2.93	1.67	1.78
	(0.14)	(0.05)	(0.19)	(0.17)
F statistics for the regression	3.89	4.63	3.19	3.55
	(0.00)	(0.00)	(0.02)	(0.01)
Sample size	37	25	37	25
R^2	0.48	0.70	0.44	0.64

Note: Estimated coefficients from ordinary least squares regressions of stock price synchronicity variables, Υ_j and Ψ_j, on the logarithm of per capita GDP, and structural variables and a good government index. A control for market size, log(number of stocks), is included in all regressions. The structural variables are log(geographical size), variance of GDP growth, industry Herfindahl index, and the firm Herfindahl index. Regressions 5.2 and 5.4 include, as an additional structural variable, the earnings comovement index. Sample is 37 countries, except for regressions on the earnings comovement index, which is available for only 25 countries. Numbers in parentheses are probability levels at which the null hypothesis of zero correlation can be rejected in two-tailed *t*-tests.

$$\Upsilon_j = \log\left(\frac{\sigma^2_{m,j}}{\sigma^2_{\varepsilon,j}}\right) = \log(\sigma_{m,j}) - \log(\sigma_{\varepsilon,j}), \tag{17}$$

where the average variation in country j stock returns that is explained by market factors is $\sigma^2_{mj} = (1/n)\Sigma_i \sigma_{i,j,m}$, and $\sigma^2 \varepsilon_j = (1/n)\Sigma_i \sigma^2_{i,j,e}$, is the average firm-specific variation in country j stock returns.

If noise trader risk makes stock prices more synchronous in countries with weak private-property rights, we should find Υ_j to be high in those countries because of high marketwide stock price variation, $\sigma^2_{m,j}$. If higher synchronicity in emerging markets is caused by less firm-specific variation, $\sigma^2_{\varepsilon,j}$, other explanations must be sought.

In figure 8.6 we explore this issue by displaying the average firm-specific variation, $\sigma^2\varepsilon$, and marketwide variation, σ^2_m, in U.S. stock returns from 1926 to 1995. Each bar represents a three-year average. The decreases in R^2s in the postwar period appear to be associated both with the capitalization of more firm-specific information into stock prices and with a decline in the influence of marketwide factors. J. Campbell and coauthors replicate this result and elaborate on its statistical properties.[21]

Since a high R^2 can reflect low levels of firm-specific variation, $\sigma^2_{\varepsilon,j}$, or high levels of marketwide variation, $\sigma^2_{m,j}$, or both, it is useful to relate these measures. Table 8.6 reveals $\sigma^2_{\varepsilon,j}$ to be greater than $\sigma^2_{m,j}$ in all countries except Poland. Figure 8.7 shows that the greater synchronicity exhibited across countries is associated with greater systematic stock return variation, $\sigma^2_{m,j}$, and with no clear pattern of higher or lower firm-specific return variation, $\sigma^2_{\varepsilon,j}$. In contrast, table 8.6 shows lower synchronicity within developed economies associated with lower $\sigma^2_{\varepsilon,j}$, and with $\sigma^2_{m,j}$ at a relatively uniform low level.

Panel A of table 8.3 shows the simple correlations of $\log(\sigma^2_{\varepsilon,j})$ and $\log(\sigma^2_{m,j})$ with our other country-level cross-sectional variables. Stock price synchronicity is positively correlated with high market risk, but not with low firm-specific risk. Both per capita GDP and the good-government index are negatively correlated with $\log(\sigma^2_{\varepsilon,j})$ and $\log(\sigma^2_{m,j})$, and in both cases, the correlations with systematic risk are stronger and more significant.

To test the hypothesis that increased synchronicity is primarily caused by increased marketwide price variation, in table 8.7 we consider regressions of the forms

$$\log(\sigma^2_{\varepsilon,j}) = c_0 + c_1 \log y_j + c_2 \log n_j + \mathbf{c} \cdot \mathbf{x}_j + c_3 g_j + u_j, \tag{18}$$

$$\log(\sigma^2_{m,j}) = c_0 + c_1 \log y_j + c_2 \log n_j + \mathbf{c} \cdot \mathbf{x}_j + c_3 g_j + u_j, \tag{19}$$

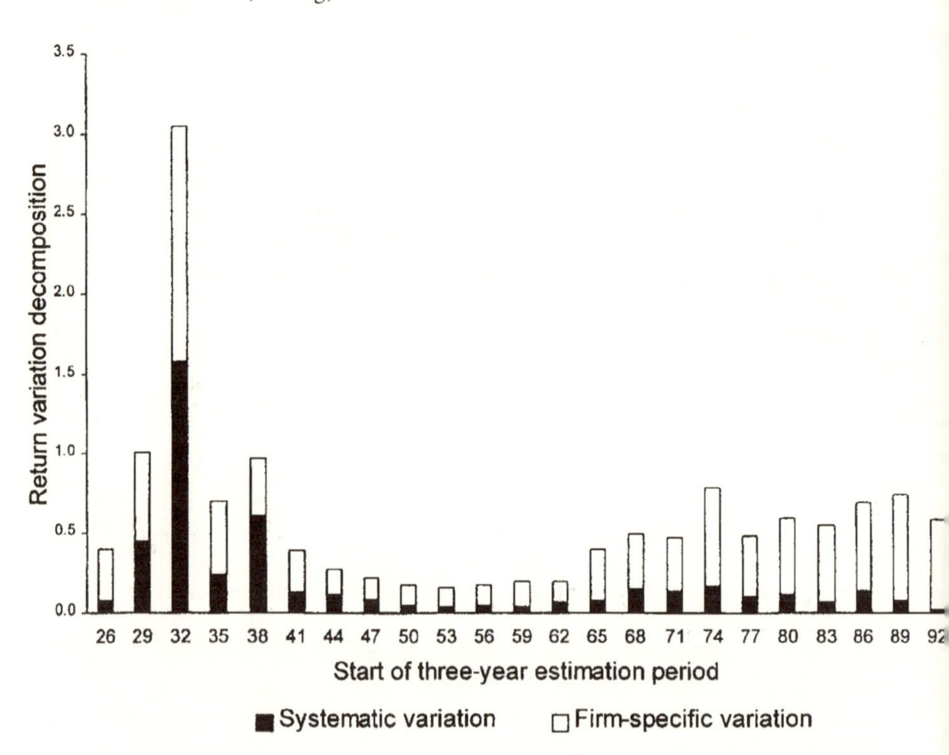

Figure 8.6 The changing structure of U.S. stock return variation from 1926 to 1995. Total returns variation is decomposed into a systematic component, which is related to the value-weighted market index, and a firm-specific component, which is not. Each bar represents an estimate over a three-year period based on monthly dividend-adjusted returns. Returns and indexes include dividends. Data are from the Center for Research in Securities Prices.

where $\boldsymbol{x}_j$ is a vector of structural and institutional development variables, y_j is per capita GDP, n_j is the number of listed stocks, g_j is the good-government index, and u_j is a random error term.

Table 8.7 shows the good-government index to be negatively and significantly related to marketwide stock price variation. The good-government index is also negatively related to firm-specific stock price variation, but this effect is smaller in magnitude and, at best, significant only in a one-tailed test, as seen in column 3 of table 8.7. Although figures 8.6 and 8.7 are more ambiguous, tables 8.3 and 8.7 are broadly consistent with the conjecture that noise trading generates marketwide stock price fluctuations unrelated to fundamentals movements in economies with uncertain private-property rights.

TABLE 8.6
The Components of Stock Return Variation

Country	R_j^2	σ_ε^2	σ_m^2	*Country*	R_j^2	σ_ε^2	σ_m^2
United States	0.021	0.174	0.004	Korea	0.172	0.174	0.036
Ireland	0.058	0.073	0.005	Pakistan	0.175	0.140	0.030
Canada	0.062	0.190	0.013	Italy	0.183	0.073	0.016
United Kingdom	0.062	0.068	0.005	Czech Republic	0.185	0.125	0.028
Australia	0.064	0.149	0.010	India	0.189	0.132	0.031
New Zealand	0.064	0.111	0.008	Singapore	0.191	0.102	0.024
Portugal	0.068	0.084	0.006	Greece	0.192	0.103	0.024
France	0.075	0.087	0.007	Spain	0.192	0.067	0.016
Denmark	0.075	0.087	0.005	South Africa	0.197	0.074	0.018
Austria	0.093	0.061	0.006	Columbia	0.209	0.086	0.023
Holland	0.103	0.051	0.006	Chile	0.209	0.086	0.023
Germany	0.114	0.067	0.009	Japan	0.234	0.111	0.034
Norway	0.119	0.086	0.012	Thailand	0.271	0.109	0.041
Indonesia	0.140	0.127	0.021	Peru	0.288	0.128	0.052
Sweden	0.142	0.084	0.014	Mexico	0.290	0.129	0.052
Finland	0.142	0.113	0.019	Turkey	0.393	0.218	0.141
Belgium	0.146	0.047	0.008	Taiwan	0.412	0.084	0.058
Hong Kong	0.150	0.118	0.021	Malaysia	0.429	0.079	0.059
Brazil	0.161	0.143	0.027	China	0.453	0.079	0.066
Philippines	0.164	0.145	0.029	Poland	0.569	0.118	0.156

Note: Countries are ranked by stock market synchronicity, measured as the average R^2 of firm-level regressions of biweekly stock returns on local and U.S. market indexes in each country in 1995. This is decomposed into a firm-specific stock return variation, σ_ε^2, and a marketwide stock return variation, σ_m^2. Returns include dividends and are trimmed at $\pm 25\%$. Because of rounding errors, R_j^2 does not exactly match $\sigma_m^2/(\sigma_m^2 + \sigma_\varepsilon^2)$.

E. More Robustness Checks

The results in tables 8.5 and 8.7 survive all the same robustness checks discussed above in connection with table 8.4. The results are not attributable outliers, transitory effects, particular synchronicity measures, different-sized markets, monetary instability, commodity dependence, fundamentals comovement, or fundamentals volatility.

In principle, it would be desirable to add more institutional variables. However, this exercise is impractical given our limited sample size, and because other measures of institutional development tend to be highly correlated with the good-government index. We therefore replace the good-government index with other measures of property rights protection, testing each alternative measure in turn.

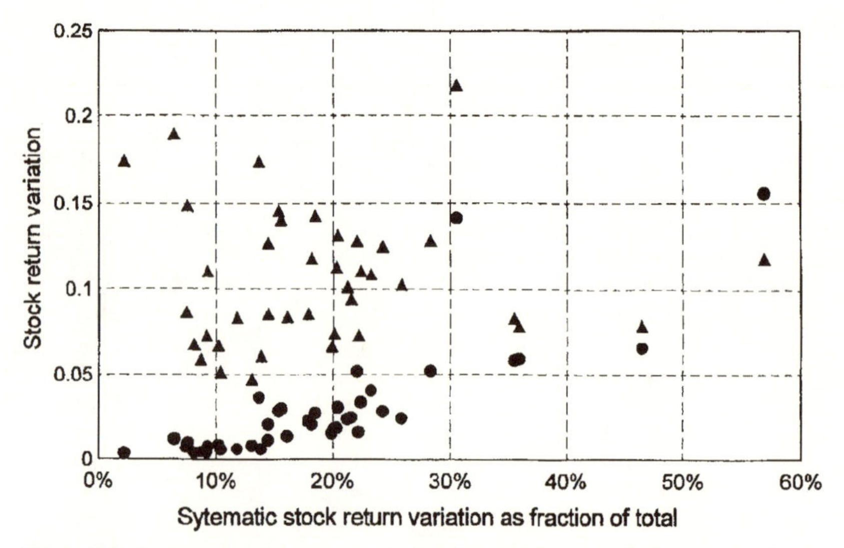

Figure 8.7 Average stock return variation for each country is decomposed into a systematic component, σ2m, denoted by circles, and a firm-specific stock component, σ2e, denoted by triangles, and these are plotted against stock return synchronicity, as measured by systematic variation as a percentage of total variation. Biweekly 1995 firm-level returns are regressed on local and U.S. value-weighted indexes to construct this data. Returns and indexes are adjusted for dividends and are from Datastream.

The alternative property rights measures we use are a "rule of law index" and a "judicial efficiency index," both described in detail by La Porta and coauthors.[22] Both measures generate results that are qualitatively similar to those shown for the good-government index.

The size of a country's stock market may be a function of its institutional maturity. We already include the logarithm of the number of listed stocks. Adding stock market capitalization or its logarithm as an additional variable does not qualitatively change our results.

F. Two Stock Market Regimes?

We remarked above that figure 8.5, which displays scatter plots of stock price synchronicity versus income, shows two clusters: high-income countries with low stock price synchronicity and low-income countries with high synchronicity.[23] The regressions in table 8.5 show that the good-government index captures this dichotomy better than per capita income does. Indeed, replacing the logarithm of per capita GDP in figure 8.5 with the good-government index again clearly reveals two clusters.

TABLE 8.7
Regressions of Systematic or Firm-Specific Stock Price Variation on Economy Structural Variables and a Good-Government Index

Dependent variable	*log (σ_m^2) is the logarithm of average systematic returns variation*		*log (σ_ε^2) is the logarithm of average firm-specific returns variation*	
	7.1	7.2	7.3	7.4
Log(GDP per capital)	0.228	0.248	0.057	0.059
	(0.38)	(0.42)	(0.63)	(0.67)
Logarithm of number of stocks listed	−0.176	−0.313	0.140	0.0500
	(0.34)	(0.17)	(0.10)	(0.63)
Good-government index	−0.164	−0.213	−0.0540	−0.0520
	(0.01)	(0.02)	(0.06)	(0.17)
Structural variables				
Log. of geographical size	−0.418	−0.128	0.430	1.79
	(0.54)	(0.92)	(0.17)	(0.01)
Variance in GDP growth	9.59	−211	228	−167
	(0.99)	(0.73)	(0.37)	(0.55)
Industry Herfindahl index	−3.81	−6.59	0.256	0.213
	(0.30)	(0.12)	(0.88)	(0.91)
Firm Herfindahl index	−1.89	1.26	0.481	−0.317
	(0.58)	(0.77)	(0.76)	(0.87)
Earning co-movement index	—	0.621	—	−0.051
		(0.51)		(0.91)
F statistics for the regression	4.29	3.26	3.18	3.42
	(0.00)	(0.02)	(0.01)	(0.02)
Sample size	37	25	37	25
R^2	0.51	0.62	0.43	0.63

Note: Ordinary least-squares regressions of the logarithm of systematic stock return variation, $\log(\sigma_m^2)$, and the logarithm of firm-specific stock return variation, $\log(\sigma_\varepsilon^2)$, on the logarithm of per capita GDP, structural variables and a good-government index. A control for market size, log(number of stocks), is included in all regressions. The structural variables are log(geographical size), variance of GDP growth, industry Herfindahl index, and the firm Herfindahl index. Regressions 7.2 and 7.4 include, as an additional structural variable, the earnings comovement index. Sample is 37 countries, except for regressions on the earnings comovement index, which is available for only 25 countries. Numbers in parenthesis are probability levels at which the null hypothesis of zero correlation can be rejected in two-tailed *t*-tests.

This clustering suggests the possibility of a threshold effect. If institutional development, as measured by our good-government index, is below a critical level, a different regime governs stock prices, and a high degree of synchronicity is observed. Marginal changes that do not cross this threshold might have little effect.

To test whether our results hold within both subsamples or mainly describe differences between the two subsamples, we repeat the correlations and regressions in our tables separately on subsamples of high and low good-government-index countries. We use the mean of the good-government index (23.92) as the dividing line in creating these subsamples, yielding a developed economy subsample of twenty-two countries and an emerging economy subsample containing fifteen countries. Minor changes in the dividing line do not affect our results. Note that dividing the sample into the two clusters shown in figure 8.5, countries with a logarithm of per capita GDP above and below 9, generates precisely the same partition. Dividing the sample according to whether the rule of law index, introduced in the previous subsection, is above and below its average also generates precisely the same partition.

Across emerging economies, analogues of table 8.3 and table 8.5 (not shown) reveal stock market synchronicity to be correlated with neither the logarithm of per capita GDP nor good government. Indeed, in the analogue of table 8.5, both variables remain uncorrelated with synchronicity. Overall, synchronicity in the emerging markets appears unrelated to marginal changes in the protection accorded private property. This result is consistent with the existence of a threshold level of institutional development associated with relatively asynchronous stock pricing.

In the developed-country subsample, the situation is more complex. As in emerging markets, synchronicity is unrelated to per capita GDP. But across developed countries, synchronicity is higher when the good-government index is lower in the analogues of tables 8.3 and 8.5, though this effect is significant only in one-tailed tests. Moreover, high synchronicity in developed countries is associated both with low levels of firm-specific variation, $\sigma^2\varepsilon$, and high levels of marketwide variation, σ^2_m. This result is consistent with the U.S. data shown in figure 8.6. This finding motivates a closer look at the developed countries to clarify the determinants of stock price synchronicity there.

VII. More Capitalization of Firm-Specific Information in High-Income Countries?

In this section, we consider two variants of the hypothesis that a country's institutions might affect the relative amounts of firm-specific versus marketwide information that are capitalized into stock prices set by rationally informed risk arbitrageurs. First, we test the hypothesis that firm-specific risk arbitrage is more attractive in economies that force firms to provide better accounting data. Second, we test the hypothesis that firm-specific risk arbitrage is more attractive in economies that provide better protection for public investors from corporate insiders. We motivate both hypotheses in more detail below.

We conduct our tests on the emerging-economy subsample of countries with below-average good-government indexes, on the developed-economy subsample of countries with above-average good-government indexes, and on the full sample. We repeat the tests for these three groups because accounting rules and investor rights laws might be dead letters in countries with weak institutions. Since accounting rules and public-investor protection require the rule of law, the two hypotheses introduced above might be relevant primarily in the developed-country subsample.

A. The Importance of Proprietary Firm-Specific Information in the United States

Recall from equation (17) that high stock return synchronicity can result from high systematic variation, low firm-specific variation, or both. Figure 8.7 reveals that both systematic and firm-specific return variation differ substantially across countries. In emerging economies, higher stock price synchronicity is mainly associated with greater systematic variation, $\sigma^2_{m,j}$; but in developed economies, lower synchronicity is also associated with greater firm-specific variation, $\sigma^2_{\varepsilon,j}$.

Roll and French and Roll stress the importance of proprietary firm-specific information, which they propose is reflected by $\sigma^2\varepsilon$, in U.S. stock prices.[24] Roll considers cross-sectional average R^2 measures comparable to equation (7) as measures of the explanatory power of asset-pricing models.[25] Using 1982–87 data, he finds low R^2s of about 35 percent with monthly data and about 20 percent with daily data and concludes that asset-pricing models have very limited explanatory power. Pointing out that stock price changes reflect unpredictable industry and firm-specific factors as well as systematic factors, he drops observations for dates when news about a firm, or its industry, is reported in the financial press. This refinement improves his R^2s only slightly. French and Roll find U.S. stock returns to be more volatile during exchange trading hours than during nontrading hours, and they argue that private information is the principle factor behind high trading-time variance.[26]

French and Roll and Roll conclude that most of the variation in U.S. stock prices reflects the capitalization of proprietary firm-specific information.[27] These results raise the possibility that low levels of synchronicity in the stock prices of some countries might reflect the incorporation of more firm-specific information into prices in their stock markets.

B. Firm-Level Accounting Data and Stock Price Synchronicity in Developed Economies

If accounting data are more useful, more firm-specific public information is available to all investors. This plausibly lets risk arbitrageurs make more precise predictions regarding firm-specific stock price movements. Thus, we might observe more firm-specific price variation in countries with better accounting standards.

To test this hypothesis, we rerun the correlations and regressions in tables 8.5 and 8.7, for both the full sample and the emerging- and developed-economy subsamples separately, using a direct measure of the sophistication of each country's accounting standards in place of our good-government index. We take this variable from La Porta and coauthors, who construct the measure using 1990 data from the Center for International Financial Analysis and Research's *International Accounting and Auditing Trends*.[28] La Porta and coauthors describe the construction of the accounting standards index as follows: "This index was created by examining and rating companies' 1990 annual reports on their inclusion or omission of 90 items. These fall into seven categories (general information, income statements, balance sheets, funds flow statement, accounting standards, stock data and special items). A minimum of 3 companies in each country were studied. The companies represent a cross section of various industry groups where industrial companies numbered 70 percent while financial companies represented the remaining 30 percent." They obtain annual reports from Moody's International, CIFAR, EXTEL, WorldScope, 20-Fs, Price Waterhouse, and various country sources.[29] The accounting-standards index ranges from 36 to 83, with a high value indicating more detailed and useful disclosure requirements.

Univariate statistics for the accounting-standards variable and its simple correlation coefficients with our other variables are shown in table 8.3. Accounting standards are negatively correlated with synchronicity, but the significance levels are in the neighborhood of 20 percent indicating only a marginal relation between the variables, even in one-tailed tests. In regressions analogous to those in tables 8.5 and 8.7 for both the full sample and the emerging- and developed-economy subsamples, substituting the accounting standards variable for the good-government index produces results similar to those in table 8.4. The accounting-standards index itself is uniformly statistically insignificant. Adding the accounting-standards measure as an additional explanatory variable also leaves it statistically insignificant and does not affect the magnitude or significance of the good-government index in the whole sample or either subsample. We conclude that either this effect is unimportant in explaining our findings or our measure of accounting standards is flawed.

C. Differential Capitalization of Firm-Specific and Marketwide Information?

A lack of respect for the property rights of public investors by corporate insiders might impede the capitalization of firm-level information in stock prices in some developed countries. This hypothesis is motivated by the observation, noted above, that greater stock price synchronicity is associated with lower firm-specific returns variation among developed-country stock markets.

This observation requires explanation. We conjecture that firm-specific risk arbitrage could be less cost effective in economies that more poorly protect public investors from insiders. If less firm-specific risk arbitrage therefore occurs, and Roll and French and Roll are correct in arguing that such risk arbitrage is the primary cause of firm-specific share price movements, we should observe lower firm-specific share price variation in such economies.[30]

At this point we can only speculate about the underlying mechanism that might discourage firm-specific risk arbitrage in economies that fail to protect public investors from insiders. One possibility follows from the finding of La Porta and coauthors, that control pyramids are the most common device that insiders use to control public firms outside the United States.[31] In a control pyramid, a family controls one firm, which holds controlling blocks of other firms, each of which holds controlling blocks in yet more firms, and so on. Such pyramids can have a dozen or more layers. Minority shares in some or all of these firms are traded publicly. Ron Daniels and Randall Morck stress that in Canada, where many publicly traded stocks are minority shares in firms in such control pyramids, the most important corporate governance laws are "oppression remedies," which stop controlling shareholders from shifting income between controlled firms through non-arm's-length transactions for goods, services, or capital at artificial prices. The problem is a type of insider trading, but it is also akin to transfer pricing in multinational firms.[32] In economies with control pyramids, weaker protection for public investors might render such income shifting more routine.

If income shifting involved strong firms subsidizing weak firms, firm fundamentals would become more correlated. If other criteria, such as each firm's relevance to the wealth, pet projects, status, or political influence of insiders, governed income-shifting decisions, fundamentals correlation need not rise. Although the former sort of income shifting may happen in situations of financial distress, we postulate that the latter sort is more commonplace.

Shifting away abnormal profits that arise from marketwide factors attracts attention unless all other firms do likewise. In contrast, shifting firm-specific abnormal profits away requires no such concurrent action. Rational risk arbitrageurs, knowing that they cannot predict where firm-specific abnormal profits will come to rest, should thus invest fewer resources in predicting firm-specific abnormal profits and instead focus on marketwide plays. Such a focus implies that less firm-specific information should enter stock prices in economies where income shifting is easier. Stock return synchronicity should rise as firm-specific return variation falls in economies with poorer investor protection.

At least partly consistent with this mechanism, Utpal Bhattacharya and coauthors find that Mexican stock prices, return volatilities, trading volumes, and spreads simply do not respond to many types of firm-specific news that are known to affect U.S. stock prices.[33] Although Bhattacharya and coauthors present evidence of insider trading to explain their finding, this evidence does not exclude the possibility that insiders appropriating firm-specific profits might limit firm-specific stock price movements.[34] However, we acknowledge the conjectural nature of this mechanism, and welcome alternative explanations of why low firm-specific returns variation is associated with higher synchronicity in developed economies.

To test the more basic hypothesis that poor investor protection is associated with a reduced capitalization of firm-specific information, we rerun the regressions in table 8.5 using a direct measure of the extent to which public shareholders' property is protected from appropriation by corporate insiders, an "anti–director rights index." This index is a score card of shareholders' rights against directors in various countries compiled by La Porta and coauthors.[35] The measure can range from 0 to 6 according to whether or not shareholders (1) can vote by mail, (2) are barred from selling stock a few days prior to a shareholder meeting, (3) can use cumulative voting for directors, (4) have legal standing to sue directors or to force the company to buy back their shares, (5) have preemptive rights to new issues, and (6) call extraordinary shareholder meetings relatively easily. Higher scores indicate that corporate insiders are more accountable to shareholders. Univariate statistics of the anti–director rights index and its simple correlation coefficients to our other variables are shown in table 8.3.

La Porta and coauthors emphasize that, for such rights to provide effective protection, a country must have functional political and legal systems. It is therefore plausible that the anti–director rights index might be most relevant in countries with good government, where the rule of law prevails.[36] La Porta and coauthors show that many countries, including some with strong property rights protection in general, poorly protect the property rights of public investors. This finding suggests that there might be enough variation in anti–director rights within our developed country subsample for statistical tests.[37]

We therefore ran regressions like those in table 8.5, but substituting the anti–director rights index for the good-government index. We ran these regressions for the whole sample and the developed- and emerging-economy subsamples. The anti–director rights index is insignificant in the whole sample and emerging-economy subsample, but negative and highly statistically significant in the developed-economy subsample. Recall that the good-government index is also significant in the developed-economy subsample. However, if both the anti–director rights and good-government indexes are included in regressions using the developed-country subsample, the good-government index is insignificant.

If more firm-specific information is capitalized into stock prices in developed economies, decreased synchronicity in that subsample should be related to higher levels of firm-specific variation. In table 8.8 we test this hypothesis by running regressions analogous to those in table 8.7, but either replacing the good-government index with the anti–director rights index or including both. These regressions are run using only the developed-economy subsample. Table 8.8 shows significantly more firm-specific price variation in stocks in developed countries that provide better protection of public shareholders against corporate insiders.

D. Additional Robustness Tests

We replicated the regressions in table 8.8, replacing the anti–director rights interaction variable with a dummy variable for the origin of the country's legal system. La Porta and coauthors show that countries with legal systems derived from those of France or Germany give public shareholders little protection against insiders.[38] Thus, we set our legal-origin dummy to 0 if a country's legal system is modeled on that of France or Germany, and to 1 if it is modeled on those of Britain or Scandinavia. The results are qualitatively similar, and significance levels are similar to those for the anti–director rights variable. Regressions including the fundamentals correlation measure yield qualitatively similar results. In summary, we cannot reject the hypothesis that less firm-specific information is capitalized into stock prices in developed economies that

Table 8.8

Regressions of Systematic or Firm-Specific Stock Price Variation on Economy Structural and Institutional Development Variables across Countries with Good Government

Dependent variable	*$log(\sigma_{\varepsilon}^2)$ is the logarithm of average firm-specific returns variation*				*$log(\sigma_m^2)$ is thelogarithm of average systematic returns variation*			
	8.1	8.2	8.3	8.4	8.5	8.6	8.7	8.8
Log (per capital GDP)	−0.279	0.058	0.119	0.172	0.350	−0.156	0.546	0.450
	(0.45)	(0.82)	(0.73)	(0.63)	(0.64)	(0.83)	(0.53)	(0.63)
Log of number of stocks listed	0.140	0.040	0.027	0.026	−0.294	−0.188	−0.350	−0.349
	(0.25)	(0.67)	(0.80)	(0.81)	(0.24)	(0.46)	(0.22)	(0.23)
Good-government index	0.036	—	−0.022	−0.024	−0.226	—	−0.254	−0.251
	(0.68)		(0.77)	(0.76)	(0.21)		(0.19)	(0.22)
Anti–director rights index	—	0.168	0.173	0.173	—	0.022	0.085	0.085
		(0.01)	(0.02)	(0.02)		(0.89)	(0.60)	(0.62)
Structural variables								
Logarithm of geographical size	0.289	0.383	0.421	0.431	−0.439	−0.818	−0.374	−0.391
	(0.47	(0.21)	(0.22)	(0.22)	(0.59)	(0.32)	(0.66)	(0.66)

Variance in GDP growth	−500	−20.3	−3.29	−16.4	−446	−399	−201	−177
	(0.13)	(0.95)	(0.99)	(0.96)	(0.50)	(0.63)	(0.81)	(0.84)
Industry Herfindahl index	1.37	0.918	0.541	0.803	−4.93	−0.969	−5.34	−5.80
	(0.62)	(0.62)	(0.81)	(0.74)	(0.39)	(0.85)	(0.37)	(0.36)
Firm Herfindahl index	−1.70	−1.67	−1.34	−1.60	−2.22	−5.97	−2.04	−1.56
	(0.50)	−(0.33)	(0.53)	(0.47)	(0.67)	(0.21)	(0.70)	(0.78)
Earning comovement index	—	—	—	−0.319	—	—	—	0.569
	(0.56)	(0.68)						
Joint significance F test for the regression	1.41	3.37	2.77	2.38	1.00	0.680	0.870	0.740
	(0.28)	(0.03)	(0.05)	(0.08)	(0.47)	(0.68)	(0.57)	(0.67)
Sample size	22	22	22	22	22	22	22	22
R^2	0.41	0.63	0.63	0.64	0.33	0.25	0.35	0.36

Note: Ordinary least squares regressions of the logarithm of systematic stock return variation, $\log(\sigma_m^2)$, and the logarithm of firm-specific stock return variation, $\log(\sigma_\varepsilon^2)$, on the logarithm of per capita GDP, structural variables and either a good-government index, an index of investor rights against corporate insiders, or both. A control for market size, log(number of stocks), is included in all regressions. The structural variables are log(geographical size), variance of GDP growth, industry Herfindahl index, and the firm Herfindahl index. Regressions 8.4 and 8.8 include, as an additional structural variable, the earnings comovement index. The sample consists of the 22 countries whose good-government index is above the average for the full sample of 37 countries. Numbers in parentheses are probability levels at which the null hypothesis of zero correlation can be rejected in two-tailed t-tests.

provide less protection of public shareholders' property rights from corporate insiders.

VIII. Conclusions

We present empirical evidence that stock returns are more synchronous in emerging economies than in developed economies. We show that this result is not an artifact of structural characteristics of economies, such as market size, fundamentals volatility, country size, economy diversification, or the comovement of firm-level fundamentals. Although some of these factors contribute to stock return synchronicity, a large residual effect remains, and this effect is correlated with measures of institutional development.

In particular, less respect for private property by government is associated with more marketwide stock price variation and therefore also with more synchronous stock price movements. Since these marketwide price fluctuations are uncorrelated with fundamentals, we conjecture that poor property rights protection might deter risk arbitrage and, in the words of De Long and coauthors, "create space" for noise traders.[39] However, since we may be controlling for fundamentals volatility imperfectly, we cannot rule out other explanations.

We also show that, in developed economies, providing public shareholders with stronger legal protection against corporate insiders is associated with greater firm-specific returns varition, and so with lower synchronicity. We conjecture that economies that protect public investors' property rights might discourage intercorporate income-shifting by controlling shareholders. Better property rights protection thus might render firm-specific risk-arbitrage more attractive in the stock markets of such economies.

Overall, our results suggest that stock markets in emerging economies may be less useful as processors of economic information than stock markets in advanced economies. The function of an efficient stock market is to process information and thereby guide capital toward its best economic use. If stock price movements in emerging economies are mainly caused by either politically driven shifts in property rights or noise trading, numb invisible hands in their stock markets may allocate capital poorly, thereby retarding economic growth. Consistent with this interpretation, J. Wurgler finds a higher elasticity of capital expenditure with respect to value added in countries whose stock returns are less synchronous, as measured in this study.[40]

Finally, we recognize that these interpretations, though supported to some extent by our findings, remain conjectures. We invite alternative explanations of our econometric findings.

Notes

Reprinted from Journal of Financial Economics, vol. 59, R. Morck et al., *The Information Content of Stock Markets: Why Do Emerging Markets Have Synchronous Stock Price Movements?* pp. 215–69, copyright 2000, with permission from Elsevier.

This research was supported by the NTT Fellowship program at the University of Michigan Business School and by the Center for International Business Studies at the University of Alberta. We are grateful for superb computer work by Rade Mladenov, and for helpful assistance from Datastream. We also thank Yehning Chen, Alan Deardorff, Merritt Fox, Ken Froot, Roger Gordon, Larry Merville, Philip Shively, Mark Huson, Ken Lehn, Li Huaizu, Vikas Mehrotra, Ted Neave, Gerard Roland, Alan Schwartz, G. William Schwert, Andrei Shleifer, Jan Svejnar, Katherine Terrell, Rob Vishny, David Weinstein, Michael Weisbach and two anonymous referees. We also thank seminar participants at the 2000 APFME Conference, the 1st CAFR Conference, the European International Business Association 1997 Meetings, George Mason University, Harvard Business School, the Behavioural Finance course at the Harvard Economics Department, Hong Kong Polytechnic University, the Hong Kong University of Science and Technology, M.I.T., the National Bureau of Economic Research Behavioral Finance Seminar, New York University, the 1998 joint NFA/APFA conference, Texas A&M University, Queen's University, Tulane University, the University of Arizona, the University of British Columbia, the University of Maryland, the Western Economic Association 1998 Meetings, the William Davidson Institute Law and Economics conference at the University of Michigan, the William Davidson Institute Research conference at the University of Michigan, and Xi'an Jiaotong University. This research was completed while Randall Morck was a visiting professor at Harvard and Bernard Yeung relocating from the University of Michigan to the Stern School of Business at New York University.

1. Richard Roll, "R^2", 43 J. Fin. 541–66 (1988).

2. At present, we only have a long panel of returns for the United States. We are beginning our exploration of historical patterns of other advanced economies.

3. Bradford J. De Long, Andrei Shleifer, Lawrence H. Summers, & Robert J. Waldmann, *The Size and Incidence of the Losses from Noise Trading*, 44 J. Fin. 681–96 (1989); De Long et al., *Noise Trader Risk in Financial Markets*, 98 J. Pol. Econ. 703–38 (1990).

4. Roll, *supra* note 1. Our thinking is akin to Roll, who examines this regression statistic for individual stocks in the United States.

5. Following work by Kenneth R. French & Richard Roll, *Stock Return Variances: The Arrival of Information and the Reaction of Traders*, 17 J. Fin. Econ. 5–26 (1986); Roll, *supra* note 1, at 541.

6. Sanford Grossman, *On the Efficiency of Competitive Stock Markets Where Traders Have Diverse Information*, 31 J. Fin. 573–85 (1976); Roll, *supra* note 1.

7. Roll, *supra* note 1; French & Roll, *supra* note 5. This measure of stock price synchronicity follows Roll and French and Roll.

8. *See* L. Zingales, *The Value of the Voting Right: A Study of the Milan Stock Exchange Experience*, 7 Rev. Fin. Stud. 125–48 (1994).

9. Roll, *supra* note 1. Although the R^2_j for the U.S. stock markets is lower than that reported by Roll, note that we use 1995 biweekly data while he uses monthly

data from September 1982 to August 1987. Our R^2 estimate for the U.S. market in the early 1980s ranges between 12 percent and 13 percent (see figure 8.3), and so is much closer to the average R^2 of 0.179 he reports.

10. We are grateful to Alan Deardorf and seminar participants at the University of Arizona, the University of British Columbia, George Mason University, Texas A&M University, and Tulane University for stressing the need to include a "country size" effect.

11. Jeffrey Bernstein & David Weinstein, Do Endowments Predict the Location of Production? Evidence from National and International Data (Nat'l Bureau of Econ. Research, Cambridge, MA, unpublished working paper no. 6815, 1998).

12. Richard Roll, *Industrial Structure and the Comparative Behavior of International Stock Market Indices*, 47 J. Fin. 3–41 (1992). Roll finds that high industry or high-firm concentration, as captured by such Herfindahl indices, partly explains the high volatility of some stock market indices.

13. Andrei Shleifer, *Establishing Property Rights*, World Bank Research Observer, 93–117 (Ann. Conf. Supp. 1994).

14. Raymond Fisman, It's Not What You Know . . . Estimating the Value of Political Connections (1999) (unpublished manuscript).

15. Andrei Shleifer & Rob Vishny, *The Limits of Arbitrage*, 52 J. Fin. 35–55; Grossman, *supra* note 6, at 573.

16. De Long, et al., *supra* note 3.

17. De Long, et al., *supra* note 3, at 715.

18. De Long, et al., *supra* note 3, at 720.

19. Rafael La Porta, Florencia Lopez de-Silanes, Andrei Shleifer, & Robert W. Vishny, The Quality of Government (1998) (Nat'l Bureau of Econ. Research, Cambridge, MA, unpublished working paper no. 6727).

20. La Porta, et al., *supra* note 19.

21. J. Campbell, M. Lettau, B. Malkiel, & Y. Xu, *Have Individual Stocks Become More Volatile? An Empirical Exploration of Idiosyncratic Risk*, J. Fin. (forthcoming, 2000).

22. Rafael La Porta, Florencia Lopez de-Silanes, Andrei Shleifer, & Robert W. Vishny, *Law and Finance*, 106 J. Pol. Econ. 1112–55 (1998).

23. We are grateful to Michael Weisbach and an anonymous referee for stressing this clustering effect and suggesting that we consider it more thoroughly.

24. Roll, *supra* note 1; French & Roll, *supra* note 5.

25. Roll, *supra* note 1.

26. French & Roll, *supra* note 5.

27. French & Roll, *supra* note 5; Roll, *supra* note 1.

28. La Porta, et al., *supra* note 22.

29. La Porta, et al., *supra* note 22.

30. Roll, *supra* note 1; French & Roll, *supra* note 5.

31. Rafael La Porta, Florencio Lopez-de-Silanes, & Andre Shleifer, *Corporate Ownership around The World*, 54 J. Fin. 471–517 (1999).

32. Ron Daniels & Randall Morck, Corporate Decision Making in Canada (1994).

33. Utpal Bhattacharya, Hazem Daouk, Brian Jorgenson, & Carl Kehr, *When an Event Is Not an Event: The Curious Case of an Emerging Market*, 55 J. Fin. Econ. 69–101.

34. Bhattacharya et al., *supra* note 33, at 69.
35. La Porta et al., *supra* note 22.
36. *Id.*
37. *Id.*
38. *Id.*
39. De Long, et al., *supra* note 3.
40. J. Wurgler, *Financial Markets and the Allocation of Capital*, 58 J. Fin. Econ. 187–214 (2000).

PART V

What Does Transition Contribute to Theory?

CHAPTER NINE

Conclusion: The Unexplored Role of Initial Conditions

Merritt B. Fox and Michael A. Heller

We have focused so far on how the transition experience suggests broader lessons for corporate governance theory. In part I, we saw how Russian privatization suggests a framework for giving precision to our definition of good corporate governance and its relationship to the real economy. Part II showed how transition teaches lessons about the corporate governance role of law, owners and managers, and institutions. Finally, in this conclusion, we move from lessons for theory derived from postsocialist transition generally to lessons that derive from the particular experience of a given country. As each country creates its distinctive corporate governance system, much emerges that is held in common. But each country begins that process from a unique starting point. The role of initial conditions is itself an important overlooked aspect of the diversity of corporate governance, an argument suggested by Mahoney in chapter 3 and Miwa and Ramseyer in chapter 6.

Again, we look at Russia to identify those initial conditions that may account for the economy's particular performance, but also that may offer new directions for theory more generally. By *initial conditions* we mean to look beyond factors that are common to all postsocialist corporate economies and beyond the standard causal explanations of poor corporate governance, such as the low level of corporate transparency, the lack of effective adjudication of corporate law violations, the weak enforcement of judgments, and the absence of a network of trust.[1] While these explanations are important, they are common to all transition economies to one extent or another.[2]

Without discounting these other explanations, we believe that to understand why Russian corporate governance problems were so severe,[3] it is helpful to include consideration of the initial conditions of Russian privatization—in particular, the often untenable boundaries of newly privatized firms and the insider-dominated ownership and control structures—and the bargaining dynamics that have followed from these conditions. These initial conditions were unique to Russia and most of the other former Soviet republics.[4] Focusing on these two conditions identifies previously overlooked factors that help explain why Russian corporate performance in the early post-socialist period was so much worse than that of other transition countries. The goal in this part, then, is to expand the inquiry by using a country's distinct starting point both to help explain performance and as a lever for theorizing more generally.

As noted by Black, Kraakman, and Tarassova in chapter 4, Russia's unusual starting point results from a privatization program that followed the course of least resistance.[5] The domestic Russian architects of privatization and their foreign advisers believed it politically necessary to move quickly. As with real estate privatization,[6] the initial path in corporate privatization represents not only political expediency, but also the primacy of pure economists over those more sensitive to the bargaining implications of packaging rights. The reformers hoped, naively as it turned out, that regardless of whoever initially received resources, these resources would flow naturally to their highest-value users after markets were established. This experience shows how these reformers underestimated not just the impediments to such resource allocation resulting from weak corporate and financial regulation,[7] as noted by Professor Coffee in chapter 7,[8] but also the roadblocks that these initial conditions would continue to impose.

In the first three sections of this last chapter we describe the initial conditions of Russian privatization and show how they continue to cause corporate governance failures. The last section then concludes the volume with our suggesting how the analytic tools we create here may inform pressing debates in contemporary corporate law. We rely heavily on the framework we developed in part I to define what counts as bad corporate governance. Bad corporate governance means either the non-maximization of residuals or non–pro rata distributions, or both. In turn, each of those categories can be further subdivided into discrete governance pathologies. Our hope in using the framework in this chapter is to bring the volume full circle—the framework helps explain why the initial conditions of Russian privatization have had such devastating effects on corporate performance. Because we will refer extensively to our framework of corporate governance pathologies, we reprint on page 375 the summary table from part I.

I. Initial Conditions in Russia

A. Untenable Firm Boundaries

The first unique feature of Russian privatization is the bizarrely tangled and complex pattern of firm boundaries. To crystallize the problem, we compare the way in which firm boundaries are defined in developed competitive economies with how they were determined during privatization in Russia.

1. FIRM BOUNDARIES IN DEVELOPED COMPETITIVE ECONOMIES

Transaction cost economics provides an easy way to understand the nature of firm boundaries in a developed competitive economy. As transaction cost economists envision the world, a country's productive economic activities consist of a set of transactions—potentially value-enhancing reallocations of goods and services—that occur between two or more parties. Every transaction that is not simultaneous and unambiguous in its implications for each party requires some kind of mechanism to govern the actions of the parties over time. In the simplest model, there are only two possible mechanisms, either an easily enforceable contract that specifies for each possible future state of nature what each party must do (referred to as a *well-specified contract*), or a firm. With a firm, one party owns all the assets related to making the transaction value-enhancing. The owner enters into an agreement with another party in which the owner promises compensation and the other party promises in return to do whatever, within a specified range of activities, the firm owner commands it to do.[9] In this simple model, every transaction in the economy occurs in one of two places: either within a firm, (i.e., it occurs under this command arrangement) or between a firm (or other individual) and another firm (or individual) pursuant to a well-specified contract. A firm's boundary is defined, on the one hand, by the transactions that occur within it and, on the other, by the transactions that occur between it and others. Thus, for example, an auto manufacturer might produce its own seats or it might purchase them from outside suppliers. In the first instance, the reallocations of resources within the firm necessary for seats to be available to install in the cars would involve transactions within the firm. In the second instance, the transaction necessary to make the seats available would be governed by a contract and would involve a transaction between the auto firm and another firm.

The least cost approach to governing some transactions is by command within a firm; for other transactions, by well-specified contracts with outsiders. The central tenet of transaction cost economics is that, in a competitive economy, market forces push transactions toward the mechanism that minimizes governance costs, referred to as *transaction costs*,[10] a process that in turn determines firm boundaries. The work of transaction cost economists suggests plausible, and in some instances empirically verifiable, reasons why in developed competitive economies we see the existing pattern of firm boundaries.[11]

2. FIRM BOUNDARIES IN RUSSIA

In Russia, the privatization process created an initial set of firms that divided up national economic activity in ways largely unrelated to the concerns of transaction cost minimization. Each privatized firm had a management team, workers, assets, and product mix that roughly corresponded to an administrative unit in the old Soviet economy. Often this unit was largely geographically based, so that a firm might encompass all the economic activity occurring within a given town or district, perhaps including a major enterprise such as an auto manufacturer, activities constituting any locally produced inputs for that enterprise, and other activities that met consumption needs of local residents, such as a dairy or a bakery. The firm was also often highly integrated horizontally, being the only such firm in the country, or one of only a few, that produced its main product, even though in many cases scale economies did not require such a high level of concentration.[12] The boundaries of such a firm may (or may not) have made sense within a centrally planned and managed economy, but they in no way correspond to the boundaries that would minimize transaction costs in a competitive market economy.

Severstal, one of Russia's largest steel companies, illustrates the plight of large employers in one-factory towns. The company's forty-eight thousand employees make up the dominant wage base of Cherepovets, a city of three hundred thousand; and the firm alone contributes more than one-third of the regional government's budget.[13] Even though the company is headed by an "energetic 31-year-old general director, who was elected by shareholders,"[14] the firm faces numerous difficulties raising capital, shedding labor, and spinning off apartments and other social services. The general director notes that "the economy of Cherepovets largely depends on Severstal. Employment is an important issue, especially in this time of political uncertainty."[15]

A firm such as Severstal, with poor firm boundaries, massive overemployment, and increasingly obsolete equipment, cannot drum up much outside-investor interest even with a relatively benign corporate governance reputation.[16] "Outside bidders for the stake would be taking a risk by buying into a company with a closed management style."[17] When the regional office of the State Property Committee decided to sell its 10 percent share in the company, the only likely bidder was the insider management, whose current share is a "well guarded secret."[18] Most likely, acquiring the 10 percent would boost management from its current majority-control position to more than 75 percent, at which point it would have "absolute control"[19] of the company, free of many protections for minority shareholders.[20] Thus, we get a preview of how poor firm boundaries can lead to potential corporate governance problems and inflict more economic damage than simply the increased transaction costs they cause.

B. Dominance by Insider Groups

The second unique feature of Russian privatization is the initial pattern of share ownership initially resulting from privitization.

1. INSIDER CONTROL BEFORE PRIVATIZATION

Russia has a long history of control by a combination of management, labor representatives, and local-government insiders. During the Soviet era, central planning and ministry supervision disciplined insiders' decision making to some extent. Beginning with Mikhail Gorbachev's reforms in the late 1980s and Boris Yeltsin's reforms in the early 1990s, central ministry control was loosened without any outside monitor being installed as a replacement. Managers quickly came up with the idea that enterprises needed owners, and that they indeed were those owners.[21]

Before firms were privatized, they went through an intermediate step, "*corporatization*," in which the enterprise was formally created as an incorporated business unit with a separate legal identity, a board of directors, senior management, and a notional economic value ascribed to its assets.[22] When a firm was corporatized, the state owned 100 percent of its stock but central ministries lost day-to-day control. During this preprivatization stage, boards of directors explicitly divided control between the general director, who received two votes; rank-and-file workers, who received one vote; and the local and federal governments, which each received a vote.[23] The employees elected the senior management during this period,[24] but employees rarely exercised their power in anything but the most nominal sense.[25] By cooperating with or intimidating the workers, managers positioned themselves to keep control of the firm at privatization.[26]

2. MANAGEMENT-EMPLOYEE BUYOUT DISGUISED AS STOCK OWNERSHIP

Russia's mass-privatization program from 1992 to 1994 transferred more than fifteen thousand medium and large state-owned firms to private ownership[27] with "a speed that is quite unprecedented in the post-Communist world."[28] These firms employed more than seventeen million workers and managers and included the bulk of the Russian industrial core,[29] except for a few key categories of firms, including energy, defense, and infrastructure.[30] By 1996, when the big wave of privatization was over, 77.2 percent of medium and large state enterprises were privatized, accounting for 88.3 percent of industrial output.[31] At the time of privatization, most issuers chose an option whereby a majority of their shares went to three groups of insiders: issuer management, the issuer labor force, and regional governmental agencies. The government's decision to give firms this option involved following the path of least political resistance by granting a continuing stake to each group that had had significant power running the firm prior to privatization. Although the mass privatization used vouchers and formally created open stock ownership, the program "was basically a management-employee buyout program because of its preferential treatment of managers and workers."[32] After insiders bought shares, each citizen could bid, using vouchers they were given, for some of the remaining shares at auctions. Immediately after privatization, insiders undertook additional share purchases on the open market and typically ended up owning about two-thirds of the shares of firms. On average, managers owned 9 percent and workers about 56 percent.[33] Outsiders used vouchers to buy about 20 to 30 percent, split between investment funds and individual investors. The government retained the remainder of shares, and, even more important, it often retained control of the land on which enterprises were located.[34]

Postprivatization, senior managers used numerous mechanisms to thwart the power of employees and outsiders and to maintain control. To start, as Professor Coffee has pointed out in chapter 7 with regard to the the Czech Republic, the absence of an established exchange in Russia with good securities regulation meant that initially dispersed shares quickly found their way into the hands of concentrated owners.[35] Other, even more extreme methods of enhancing managerial power included, for example, keeping share registries locked up in their offices and refusing to acknowledge ownership by people they disfavored, threatening to fire workers who sold shares to outsiders, and reducing the power (as well as the financial claims noted earlier) of outsider shareholders by means of stock dilutions.[36] Managers also provided little or no disclosure about the business operations or finances of their firms. Even voucher investment funds, which are the most aggressive and informed outside shareholders, often cannot get rudimentary information about the firms in which they hold shares[37] and instead "resort to spying on their own companies."[38] Thus, managers did not acquire a majority of shares during the initial privatization, but they locked up nearly unshakable control.[39] Workers, who did acquire majority shareownership, did not achieve anything like a "workers' democracy."[40] Rather, they remained locked in an uneasy arrangement with management, often able to block restructuring but not able to seize control.[41] Among the many reasons for continued employment of redundant labor, managers sometimes kept employees to prevent them from selling shares to outsiders.[42] If managers fired workers, they could no longer use the threat of job loss to deter share sales.

3. THE PERSISTENT PATTERN OF INITIAL PRIVATIZATION

The effects of the initial privatization are persistent. Insider ownership is declining slightly (dropping from 65 percent in 1993 to about 56 percent in 1995),[43] but the problems of majority insider ownership remain pervasive. By 1996, the typical board contained four managers, one state representative, and two outside shareholders.[44] Because five directors were required to make decisions, the insiders and the state representative always could prevail, if they cooperated.[45]

The 1996 corporate law, analyzed by Black, Kraakman, and Tarassova in chapter 4, includes measures that respond precisely to the problem of insider domination that emerged from the initial privatization scheme and from the immediate postprivatization enterprise behavior.[46] For example, the new corporate law improves the position of minority outside shareholders by mandating cumulative voting.[47] As a result, outside owners of share blocks are increasingly able to get themselves elected to the board of directors, despite resistance by insiders to the cumulative voting rule.[48] In turn, Roman Frydman and Andrzej Rapaczynski show that outsider representation on the board has had some positive effect on firm performance.[49] Also, significant transactions in which insiders are interested are supposed to be approved by the outside shareholders. Nevertheless, insiders have found numerous mechanisms to circumvent the protections offered by the 1996 reforms and to continue effecting non–pro rata distributions.[50] Rapaczynski's work in chapter 5 suggests the hidden costs imposed on the Russian economy by a privatization scheme that left insider managers in place.

4. THE ENDURING COST OF INSIDER OWNERSHIP

To summarize, we observe three interrelated failures in Russia that are associated with the initial structure of insider ownership and control. First, the three groups of insiders have been unable to work together to operate their firms in a way that would maximize even their own joint benefit. They have tended to view their shares more as control rights than as financial instruments. Each group has, despite privatization, continued to focus primarily on how the firm could be run in a way that would most benefit that group directly.[51] Managers extract extensive perquisites and sweetheart business deals for themselves and associates. Labor ensures continued employment of redundant workers. Regional government entities continue receiving public services for the community.[52] Each group goes along to get along; it agrees to meet the other groups' minimal demands in exchange for getting its direct benefit. But these insider deals ignore the cumulative effects on the value of the firm for themselves and for outsider shareholders.[53] One Russian fund manager notes that "the majority of directors still fear loss of control to an outside investor and have not yet recognized that a smaller piece of a growing pie is more valuable than ownership of a dead enterprise."[54]

Second, the three groups run the firm in a way that is particularly disadvantageous to outsider shareholders.[55] Consistent with Pistor's findings in chapter 2, the low level of enforcement in the Russian legal system and the general lack of corporate transparency mean that outside shareholders gain no real protection from the fiduciary duties nominally placed on managers and only weak protection from procedural rules designed to police interested transactions.[56] Majority insiders usually can crush what otherwise would be the only meaningful constraints on their behavior: the ability of outsiders to vote out the board and the threat of a hostile takeover.[57]

Third, the occurrence of the failures noted above inside existing firms in turn limits capital market development and result, as Morck, Yeung, and Yu have shown in chapter 8, in shares prices that are poor predictors of the firms' future cash flows.[58] These securities market problems have collateral consequences for both existing and new firms. Established firms cannot raise new capital through the public sale of new equity, a particularly grave problem given the primitive state of banking in Russia.[59] Further, the resulting lack of vibrancy in the secondary market for insider shares means that primary and secondary markets do not develop for the shares of new, postprivatization firms.[60] This lack of stock market vibrancy also slows outsider purchases of employee shares and delays the resulting conversion of firms with majority insider ownership to majority outsider ownership. The result of these three failures has been an overall lack of much-needed restructuring.[61]

II. How Initial Conditions Cause Corporate Governance Failures

A. Peculiar Firm Boundaries and the Failure to Maximize Residuals

In this section we establish the causal links between the initial conditions just described, the corporate governance failures detailed in table 9.1, and the resulting harms to the Russian economy.

TABLE 9.1
Framework of Corporate Governance Pathologies

	I. Nonmaximization of residuals
Pathology 1: Unreformable value-destroying firms fail to close	Arises when an unreformable value-destroying firm can dissipate cash reserves or salvageable assets. Corporate governance is not the key issue when firm has no reserves or salvageable assets, or when subsidies or unsuitable credits are present.
Pathology 2: Viable firms fail to use existing capacity efficiently	Arises when continued firm operation, if undertaken as efficiently as possible and without new investment, would be a positive net present value (NPV) decision, but costs are not minimized, the best price is not obtained for given output, or a non-profit-maximizing output level is chosen.
Pathology 3: Firms misinvest internally generated cash flows	Arises when a firm uses internally generated cash flow to invest in new negative NPV projects instead of paying out this cash flow to shareholders who could invest the funds better elsewhere in the economy.
Pathology 4: Firms fail to implement positive NPV projects	Arises when a firm identifies but then fails to act on positive NPV projects. Managers tend to be risk averse because they can't diversify away unsystematic risk of a firm's project. If others do not pick up the opportunity, the firm's failure also reduces social welfare.
Pathology 5: Firms fail to identify positive NPV projects	Arises when a firm's managers fail to identify positive NPV projects that the firm is particularly well positioned to find. The possibility of venture financnancing and spinoffs can reduce the prevalence and social costs of this pathology.
	II. Non–pro rata distributions
Pathology 6: Firms fail to prevent diversion of claims	Arises when some residual owners of a firm manipulate corporate, bankruptcy, and other laws to shift ownership away from other residual owners—often by diluting shares held by outside minority shareholders.
Pathology 7: Firms fail to prevent diversion of assets	Arises when some residual owners privately appropriate assets and opportunities belonging to the firm, but leave the firm's formal ownership structure intact.

Poorly defined boundaries render firms with weakly constrained and weakly incentivized management particularly susceptible to several of the five residual nonmaximization pathologies. To start, consider Pathology 1, continued operation of a value-destroying firm. From the moment of privatization, Russia had many such firms that should have been shut down instantly.[62] Because of their peculiar boundaries, these stillborn firms made little sense as a way to match location, assets, workers, and product mix, but they often had assets with significant salvage value, urban land in particular. Despite the damage they cause to social welfare, managers of such firms indulge their personal preferences by continuing firm operations. When land is the salvageable asset, managers can easily avoid taking the residual-maximizing decision because Russia does not have a well-developed land market. There is, therefore, no effective way to make salient the opportunity costs of using the land for continued firm operation.[63]

A similar story can be told with respect to Pathology 2, in which potentially viable firms fail to use existing capacity efficiently. Most Russian firms not displaying Pathology 1 are likely to display Pathology 2. Cost minimization is a necessary condition for residual maximization. By definition, what made these firms' borders peculiar was the fact that they were not transaction cost minimizing, so by definition, firms in this second category require major restructuring.[64] Unlike the case of managers of firms in the first category, it is not self-evident why loosely constrained managers of these firms would avoid restructuring and operate their firm in a residual nonmaximizing way.[65] However, the story told below of bargaining failures among the insider groups suggests that, in a large number of cases, managers may have reason to avoid restructuring, thus dooming their firms to the long-term display of Pathology 2.

The peculiar borders of Russian firms also have made them more prone to Pathology 3. This pathology is more likely to occur in an enterprise encompassing an unnecessarily large number of different activities: if the cash flow from one activity exceeds the positive net present value projects arising out of that activity, then the managers are likely to invest the surplus in negative net present value projects associated with other firm activities.[66] If the two activities were split into different firms, the cash flow more likely would be paid out as dividends, and investors would have the chance to fund projects with more promising returns.

Finally, compared with outside investors facing a fragmented set of single purpose firms, the management of an enterprise encompassing an unnecessarily large number of activities will—because of its distance from idea sources and the rigidity of internal communications channels—likely have more difficulty finding positive net present value projects. Thus, the peculiar boundaries of Russian firms also aggravate the effects of Pathology 5.

B. Insider Dominance and the Failure to Maximize Residuals

1. THE NATURE OF THE FAILURE AND THE NEED FOR A CREDIBLE PROMISE

As discussed earlier, after privatization, most Russian firms were majority owned by three groups of insiders: management, employees, and regional governmental authorities.[67] At first glance, this ownership pattern appears to offer many advantages and to solve several firm-level problems. Management's large stake, typically more than 20 percent of what are often very large enterprises, should have led to a substantial identification with the interests of shareholders, while not being so large as to provide an insuperable barrier to takeover. The employees' stake substantially should have helped some of the contracting problems associated with long-term employment relationships—such as encouraging asset-specific human capital investments by employees—and should have significantly reduced resistance to needed downsizing, by offering implicit compensation through increased share value.[68] More important, when the stakes of the three groups were taken together, the groups typically had a right to receive 70 percent or more of the residuals. Thus, they had huge incentives to agree that the firm itself should be operated in a fashion that maximizes these residuals. Yet the structure of ownership and control actually has worked in the opposite direction, contributing to the failure to maximize residuals.[69] Strikingly, modern Russia, like the nineteenth-century Japanese example that Miwa and Ramseyer discuss in chapter 6, belies the standard corporate-theory predictions regarding the role of concentrated ownership.

Traditionally, the choice between public and private ownership has been seen as involving a trade-off. Public ownership leads to a lower cost of capital because the firm's shares can be sold for a higher price as a result of both their liquidity and their capacity to be part of a diversified portfolio.[70] Public ownership also permits a degree of outside monitoring.[71] Private ownership, however, greatly reduces the substantial residual-reducing agency costs of management that are associated with public firms.

At first glance, Russian firms have an ownership structure that would appear to come close to that of a private firm, suggesting that they should do well at maximizing their residuals. A large portion of the shares not owned by management are owned by just two other entities—the workers and government. This, one should expect, would radically reduce the transaction costs and collective action problems associated with shareholder monitoring and action that plague the public firm. But Russian firms are falling far short of maximizing their residuals, suggesting that they are suffering instead from the worst of both worlds. They do not seem to be getting the benefits of a private ownership structure; yet the existence of insider control combined with weak corporate law makes raising capital by public sale of equity impractical and so they are not receiving the traditional benefits of public ownership either.

The three groups of insiders have been unable to work together to operate their firms in a way that would come close to maximizing their own joint benefit. Their actions suggest that they continue to view their shares more as control rights than as financial instruments. Therefore, each group has, despite privatization, continued to focus primarily on how each firm could be run in a way that would most benefit the group directly.[72] For example, managers cut side deals, labor ensures that redundant workers stay on, and regional government extracts public services. These behaviors are major deviations from the decisions that would maximize the firm's residuals. By failing to cooperate through good corporate governance, the insiders fail to capture the potentially large financial value of their shares. The aggregate benefit to these three groups from these deviations is less than the resulting diminution in the residuals. Management's gain from the sweetheart contracts is less than the price improvement or other advantages of using the suppliers and purchasers chosen on an arm's-length basis.[73] Labor's gain from receiving wages and benefits beyond what they could in alternative employment is less than the reduced residuals enjoyed by the firm as a result of their continued employment.[74] And government savings from not having to pay other suppliers of services is less than the cost to the firm of providing these services, which would be outside the boundaries of the firm if it were operated in a transaction cost–minimizing fashion.

Explaining why insiders do not agree to maximize the firm's residuals as part of an obvious Coasian bargain starts with the following observation: Under existing arrangements, the insiders receive their benefits immediately, as they are generated by the firm's ongoing operation. Under any kind of bargain to run the firm to maximize its residuals, they would not receive them until later, in the form of shareholder distributions.[75] This delay is significant, as a deal is not possible unless management is able to make a credible promise that it will live up to its end of the bargain. Otherwise, labor and local government would be put in a position of having to give up their benefits now without an assurance that management, which runs the corporation from day to day, would live up to its end of the bargain (i.e., giving up its special benefits and subsequently distributing the gains from the overall deal as dividends).

2. THE DIFFICULTY IN MAKING THE PROMISE CREDIBLE

Under current conditions in Russia, management would find it almost impossible to make credible promises to live up to its end of the bargain.

a. Legal Enforcement. One way that a promise can be credible is if the promisee can use the courts easily and economically either to gain the promisor's compliance or to obtain damages.[76] For a number of reasons, labor and local government are unlikely to be able to do so. For a promise's credibility to be based on the availability of court enforcement, there must be a legal obligation on the part of the promisor. As a formal matter, Russian managers may be bound to maximize residuals and distribute them pro rata even without an explicit deal with other insiders, but this is not clear as a matter of law. The Russian corporate code nominally imposes on the management of joint stock companies the obligation to act in the interests of the company reasonably and in good faith.[77] The language of this obligation is similar to that of the statutory provisions for fiduciary duties under U.S. corporate law,[78] which are interpreted as banning extensive perquisites[79] and prohibiting transactions between the corporation and management or its associates, unless the transactions offer the firm terms as good as can be obtained in an arm's-length deal.[80] There is essentially no judicial gloss, however, to affirm that this language would be interpreted in the same way in Russia, an important factor, as Mahoney demonstrated in chapter 3.

The second step, discussed by Pistor in chapter 2, is the actual availability of court enforcement. Russian law again nominally provides for a form of derivative suit for damages in the event of a breach of management's statutory obligations.[81] Even if we assume that as a formal matter management is obliged to behave in the fashion contemplated by the Coasian bargain hypothesized here, labor and local government are unlikely to be able to use the courts to stop violations of that obligation.[82] Bernard Black and Reinier Kraakman note that "in Russia . . . courts function slowly if at all, some judges are corrupt, and many are Soviet-era holdovers who neither understand business nor care to learn. Better judges and courts will emerge only over several decades, as the old judges die or retire."[83]

Another possible way of gaining managerial compliance while relying less on the court system is through legal regulation of the corporation's own process of transaction authorization.[84] Russian law has procedural rules designed to make less likely the authorization of transactions in which management or a major shareholder is interested and that are disadvantageous to the corporation. These rules require that such transactions be approved by the vote of a majority of those directors who are not interested in the transaction or, in certain cases, by a disinterested majority-share vote.[85] Special procedural rules apply also to the approval of very large transactions.[86] The theory is that these rules require much less court intervention to be effective because the factual determination of whether or not there has been compliance is sufficiently simple and clear as to make the rules nearly "self-enforcing."[87]

In the end, however, these rules may not be much help either.[88] To show that management or a major shareholder is interested in a transaction requires proving that it is associated in some specified way with the other party to the transaction. A general lack of transparency concerning who owns the shares of, or has managerial positions in, the corporations involved makes this proof difficult.[89] Even when owners or managers are identified, it is hard to know whether the voting results in fact conform with the procedural requirements, in part because of similar transparency problems and in part because of difficulties in determining who voted which way.[90]

b. Reputation. Another way that a promise can be credible is where the promisor has a prior reputation for keeping its promises in situations in which legal enforcement is difficult and the nonlegal consequences—other than damage to reputation—would not have been expected to be great.[91] Such a promisor is unlikely to breach the promise in question, because doing so debases its reputation, which is costly.[92] The problem in Russia is that in the few years since privatization, the management of the typical corporation has not had the time to develop such a reputation, either through informal networks or formal verification institutions,[93] at least with respect to promises of this magnitude.

While the same management team may have been in place for a significant time prior to privatization, the team, and all those with whom it dealt, had been subject to strict ministerial supervision. Because of this supervision, the need for credible promises was lesser and the non-reputation-related negative consequences of breaching the promises that were made were greater. Also, most promises were made with persons within the context of an ongoing course of dealing, but those networks have been disrupted in the new postsocialist economy.

An additional problem here is that the promise that management needs to make is contrary to the norm for managerial behavior in Russia. A person who makes a particular promise that he or she has not made before, but the promised behavior is the norm, is likely to be credible if he or she has fulfilled other promises that conform to the norm with respect to other kinds of behavior over time. Such a person may be viewed as a "regular fellow" or a "straight shooter." Where the behavior promised runs contrary to the norm, such a reputation is of no help.

c. Hostages. A third way a promise can be made credible is where the promisor gives the promisee a "hostage" that can be taken by the promisee if the promisee feels that there has been a breach.[94] The ideal hostage is something that is worth much less to the promisee than the promisor. A firm's plant might serve this kind of hostage function if it were vulnerable to certain kinds of labor actions, such as sit-ins. Labor is poorly organized in Russia, however, and so collective action problems make it unlikely that it would be able to use the plant in this fashion.[95] Such actions also likely would be repressed by governmental authorities. Any promise by management to waive its rights to such governmental assistance would have its own credibility problems.

d. The Need for Ex Post Verification. None of these ways of making a promise credible will work unless there is some method of ascertaining whether or not the promise has been kept. This is another serious obstacle to the parties' making a Coasian bargain requiring management to use its control to maximize residuals and then distribute them pro rata.[96] In terms of ex post verification, management is in the same position making this promise to labor and government as it would be making this promise to any noncontrolling outside shareholder. The whole apparatus of modern auditing and accounts is designed to provide a reasonable assessment of the amount of residuals that have been generated, to identify the amount of spending for management compensation and perquisites, to ferret out corporate transactions in which management is interested, to identify which investors receive how much in distributions, and to highlight outright theft. Application of this apparatus to Russian corporations is in its infancy and so most transactions remain far from transparent.[97]

3. THE LACK OF STRONG CAPITAL MARKETS

Along with the inability of management to make credible promises, the absence of strong capital markets (itself a result of widespread corporate governance failures) frustrates the parties' intentions to make a Coasian deal to maximize residuals. Even if workers were able to obtain what they believe to be a credible promise from management, they would have great difficulty selling for cash today their rights to receive in the future the benefits of the deal. This is an important additional complication because the desperate living conditions of many Russian workers, combined with a belief that the future could not be worse and might be better, may give them a strong positive time preference—an illustration of the difficulty of making social welfare evaluations of decisions involving the allocation of resources over time when capital markets fail. If discounting to present value is done at the interest rate implied by the strong positive time preference of highly credit-constrained workers, managers may be running firms in ways that suddenly appear far more efficient.

4. APPLICABILITY TO DIFFERENT PATHOLOGIES

Understanding the bargaining dynamics among competing inside owners of privatized Russian firms helps explain the widespread incidence in Russia of Pathologies 2 and 3, the failure to use existing capacity efficiently and the misinvestment of internally generated cash flows.[98] The preference of labor shareholders to retain redundant workers rather than maximize residuals leads directly to Pathology 2. There are two ways that the firm can keep employment high in the short run. One is to produce more output than would be called for if the firm set marginal cost equal to marginal revenue. The other is to produce this level of output using a combination of inputs that includes more labor than would the cost-minimizing input combination. Both decisions involve failures to use existing capacity as efficiently as possible, and both reduce residuals as a consequence. The labor shareholders' desire to retain redundant workers also leads to Pathology 3.[99] While firm investment in negative net present value projects is not necessary for employment to be maximized in the current period, it is necessary for employment to be maximized in the future, assuming that the new investment does not embody a radically labor-saving new technology. This is true whether the investment replaces worn-out existing capacity or represents an actual expansion of capacity. Labor's interest here parallels managers' personal interest in running as large an enterprise as possible, everything else being equal.

The bargaining-dynamics story is not as helpful in explaining Pathology 1. The residual-maximizing change necessary for firms displaying Pathology 1 is to close them immediately. As we have seen in part I, to the extent that an unreformable, value-destroying firm continues operating because of corporate governance problems, it is because the firm has cash reserves (unlikely in Russia) or salvageable assets.[100] The Coasian deal here would be to close the firm as soon as these assets could be sold. There is no time delay requiring a credible promise on the part of management, and hence none of the problems discussed above should block the deal.

How, then, can the existence of firms displaying Pathology 1 be explained? One possibility is that such firms do not exist (i.e., that Pathology 1 is an empty set). The anecdotal evidence presented here, however, suggests that this is not the case.[101] Another possibility is that title to these salvageable assets, at least in the case of land, is not as clear as we have portrayed it; in particular, it might be that local authorities have the power to block land sales independent of the powers they have as shareholders.[102] If so, the needed reform is in property law and public law, not improved corporate governance. Yet another possibility is that the market for such salvageable assets is extremely illiquid because of severe limitations in capital markets in Russia generally. Thus, existing Pathology 1 firms gradually will be shut down as buyers are found who will pay full value for the assets, but this process will take considerable time.[103] If that is the case, the initial conditions explain the problem not by their direct effects on the Pathology 1 firms, but by their contribution to the failure of corporate governance in Russia generally, with that failure's attendant deadening of Russian capital markets. Finally, Coasian deals may not be made in Pathology 1 firms because of the perception of bias among firm employees. Labor may believe that the redundant jobs it wishes to save are worth more to it than is really the case. The shareholder distribution that labor would receive upon sale of the salvageable asset then would not seem to labor to be worth the loss of these jobs. If this is the case, however, it would form an additional (or alternative) explanation for the failure of the Coasian bargain in the cases of firms displaying Pathologies 2 and 3 as well.

The failed Coasian bargain story also does not explain Pathologies 4 and 5 very well. These pathologies involve failures of suitability and capability, not conscious decisions by managers to put their personal interests above that of firm residual maximization. In essence, as Rapaczynski explores in depth in chapter 5, managers of firms displaying these pathologies are doing as well as they can, but a firm with less risk-averse or more imaginative managers could do better.[104] The problem is thus not the result of competing insiders unable to make a Coasian bargain. The social welfare effects of these failures would be corrected either by replacing the incumbent managers or by assuring that there are other venues for implementing the positive net present value projects being rejected or unrecognized by these managers. The failings here are in the market for corporate control and the market to provide capital for new firms. Thus, again, the initial conditions help explain Pathologies 4 and 5 not directly but by their contribution to the failure of corporate governance in Russia generally and the attendant deadening of Russian capital markets.

C. Insider Dominance and Non–Pro Rata Distributions

Initial conditions in the form of insider dominance also can help explain the massive failure of Russian firms to distribute their residuals pro rata to their investor owners. The primitive state of the Russian legal system and the general lack of corporate transparency mean that outside shareholders gain no real protection from the fiduciary duties nominally placed on managers and only weak protection from procedural rules designed to police interested transactions. Privatization, as we have seen, resulted in most firms' having the insiders in the majority. This crushes what would otherwise be the only remaining meaningful constraints on these insiders' behavior: the ability of outsiders to vote out the board and the threat of hostile takeover.[105]

Initial conditions also play a role, though more indirectly, in the non–pro rata distributions by firms in which the insiders have less than a majority of shares but managers still control the firm. In theory, these managers would at least be subject to being thrown out by the vote of the majority outsiders or as a result of a hostile tender offer. Shareholder votes have significant collective action problems associated with them, however,[106] and as for hostile tender offers, the same story applies here as discussed just above. The initial conditions and their effect on corporate governance among Russian firms have done severe damage to the creation of vital capital markets generally. Thus, no effective market for corporate control has developed, and the hostile-takeover check against non–pro rata distributions by majority outsider-owned firms is a chimera.

It is worth considering the other causal factors of non–pro rata distributions as well, and here the governance-failure typology is quite useful. For example, of all the pathologies, Pathology 6, diversion of claims, is perhaps most amenable to traditional law-reform efforts, at least in some of the pathology's forms. Perhaps registering transfers of shares could be centralized in a public or quasi-public institution rather than being left to the whims of individual firm managers. Particular loopholes in corporate law, such as those regarding convertible bonds, can be tightened; standards of review in bankruptcies can be adjusted. But even here, when so much is at stake, insiders may be able to invent ever more subtle diversion mechanisms, as Pistor has emphasized in chapter 2. For example, many of the procedural protections available to shareholders depend on identifying outside disinterested owners and require a majority of their votes for important changes in corporate structure. Recent proposals attempt to strengthen these key protections.[107] But insiders have proved adept at obscuring the identity of owners and evading these procedural protections with ostensibly outside owners actually controlled by insiders.

Pathology 7, diversion of assets, is not as amenable to simple law-reform efforts, even assuming that it became easier for shareholders to obtain judgments and enforce them. Even the Delaware Chancery Court, presumably the most sophisticated court in the world for detecting breaches of the duty of loyalty, has a difficult time separating out management decisions that are legitimately taken to increase residuals, but have the incidental effect of disproportionately benefiting insiders from management decisions primarily motivated by a management desire to effect a non–pro rata distribution.[108] It will be a long time before Russian courts are likely to achieve Delaware's level of competence.[109] As for the more blatant examples of non–pro rata distributions, they are usually criminal and implicate a broad array of institutional and legal deficiencies in Russia. These deficiencies include the refusal of local officials to recognize, in their role as enforcers of property rights, decisions of legitimate corporate processes when these decisions run contrary to the desires of incumbent managers.[110]

III. Trends in Corporate Control

A. Dynamics of Initial Ownership Patterns

The original allocation of shares at the time of privatization is not a sustainable ownership pattern over time. Many firms already have been taken over completely by one group of insiders, usually the managers, who purchase the shares of the other insiders. This is a predictable result because the multiple groups of insiders are unable to make joint wealth-maximizing agreements. When managers take complete control, they can operate the corporate assets more as if the assets were their sole private property. This is a more stable ownership pattern, and it represents a social gain because the managers are more motivated to put assets to their first best uses.

The management-control equilibrium is still far from ideal, however, and its shortcomings represent large continued failings in the Russian system of corporate governance. First, the deals necessary to buy out the other insiders are not easy to make because management itself has no ready access to capital. As emphasized by Black, Kraakman, and Tarassova in chapter 4, often, their aims are achieved by extralegal means.[111] Thus, the new equilibrium will take considerable time to reach and often does not put assets, at least immediately after the ownership restructuring, in the hands of the persons most capable of using them.[112] The stakes are especially large because these assets include control over cash flows that the managers often cannot invest sensibly within their own firms, but capital market failures mean cash flows are denied to other entrepreneurs who could make better use of them. These failures, as we have seen, stem from the continued ability of insiders to divert wealth from the remaining outside shareholders, which makes raising capital through public sales of equity by any firm virtually impossible.

Given the paucity of other sources of capital, many promising investment opportunities go unfunded. Moreover, the absence of outside-investor voice in the affairs of the firm may mean that it is not run efficiently even to the extent that doing so is now in the best interests of the management insiders. These managers are often still holdovers from the communist era and would be able to act more in their own and society's best interests if prodded by more market-oriented outsiders, but their continued desire to engage in non–pro rata distribution makes such consciousness-raising advice inadvisable to obtain.

Early empirical work, consistent with Rapaczynski's argument in chapter 5, suggests that the greatest improvement in corporate performance in Russia comes when firms have substantial outside ownership and those owners place outside directors on the board.[113] This observation may be causally backward, in that outsiders tend to invest in the best firms, particularly those that are generating sufficient positive cash flow that payment of dividends becomes possible.[114] The question is whether the privatized enterprises can move systematically in the direction of increasing outsider ownership and control. The analysis in the sections above suggests cause for concern. When multiple insiders block one another, there is little commitment by insiders to the financial aspects of share ownership. Similarly, when manager insiders take control and divert assets illegally, outside investors have little incentive to purchase minority interests.[115]

Privatization is intended to create wealth that is available for reinvestment in Russia, but the insider structure of corporate ownership may stimulate capital flight instead. Diversifying risk through portfolio investment in domestic firms is impossible.[116] Domestic equity investments, to be worthwhile, must be in controlled amounts under the current system. A system that started with fragmented insider ownership has led to one in which public offerings are impossible, and capital leaves Russia in part because of the unavailability of viable domestic portfolio investment opportunities to reduce risk through diversification.

B. Evolution of Financial Industrial Groups

For a short period, Russia seemed to be moving to a system of corporate control concentrated in huge, sprawling conglomerates that came to be known as financial-industrial groups (FIGs), organized around one of seven chief oligarchs, each with a captive bank, a holding company, and multiple privatized companies as subsidiaries.[117] The most significant boon for the FIGs occurred in 1995 with the infamous "shares-for-loans" scheme in which the oligarchs' banks gave relatively small loans to the government to plug the budget deficit and in exchange received the rights to run some of the most valuable Russian resource-extracting firms: oil, minerals, timber, and so on.[118] When the government, predictably, did not pay back the loans, the oligarchs conducted rigged auctions through which the collateral on the loans became controlling share ownership in these firms.[119] One oligarch, Vladimir Potanin, in discussing the shares-for-loans program, noted, "'It was bad. . . . The prices were cheap. We can stop discussing this. It was bad. But it did solve the problem of having more efficient owners.'"[120]

According to one estimate, the chief oligarchs, through their FIGs, were said to control 40 percent of Russia's economy.[121] These seven "gray cardinals,"[122] however, rather than each working to improve the operations already under his particular control, fought one another to extend control to additional assets. This led George Soros to compare Russia to "'a canoe in which seven men are fighting over a horde of gold [and] are too absorbed by this to recognize they are heading toward a waterfall.'"[123] The 1998 financial collapse set the FIGs back, bankrupting several of them, and so it is too early to see if they really put assets in the hands of more efficient owners. Initial indications, however, are not promising.[124]

Early in the transition, optimistic commentators argued that the FIGs would roughly parallel the *keiretsu* in Japan and the *chaebol* in Korea.[125] Another analogy would be Oliver Williamson's M-form corporation, in which the head office substitutes for the capital market's capital allocation and managerial monitoring functions.[126] Given the extreme weakness of Russian capital markets, this substitution seemed a step forward. FIG oligarchs argued that they were relatively more productive than other sectors of the economy because their captive banks gave them access to funds at rates much lower than what was generally available, presumably because of reduced information asymmetries. And, echoing Williamson, they argued that "subsidiaries are overseen by group executives at the center, forcing local managers to pay attention to shareholder value, something that few other firms in Russia ever consider."[127] According to Mikhail Khodorkovsky, one of the oligarchs, the FIGs "'are an excellent way of distributing scarce managerial resources throughout the economy. . . . Surely, you can see that.'"[128]

In practice, the *keiretsu* and *chaebol* were not the right analogy; rather, the FIGs more closely resemble the old Soviet nomenklatura networks of former Communists and Komsomol members,[129] and "'are to some extent a revival of the old [Soviet] branch ministries.'"[130] They have not managed the enterprises under their control any better than firms generally have in the economy. Instead, oligarchs focused on non–pro rata distributions and generally continued to ignore problems of residual nonmaximization within the firms they controlled. According to one commentator, "'The oligarchs were qualified to run banks only because of their familiarity with the corridors of power. . . . Uneximbank [one of the FIG banks] never had any interest in improving manufacturing at any of its companies. It just wanted to channel money through the bank.'"[131] So far, FIGs seem to have exhibited all the corporate governance pathologies we already have noted; they do not appear to be a step forward.

C. Some Reform "Thought Experiments"

The critical problems we identify for Russian corporate governance lie at the intersection of uneconomic firm boundaries and control by competing groups of insiders. Poorly drawn firm boundaries exacerbate the corporate governance problems that arise when, as in Russia, managers are loosely constrained and poorly incentivized. Control by competing groups of insiders confounds the usual prediction that insider-dominated firms should be good at residual maximization and robs outsiders of their only mechanism for limiting non–pro rata distributions of residuals. For Russia, at least, the firm borders at the time of initial privatization are water over the dam, and all that can be hoped for now is greater development of a market for corporate assets. Voting rights, however, are something that can be altered by legal fiat, at least in theory. The Russian situation represents a case in which the usual rationales for one-share-one-vote do not hold. It would be preferable if the voting rights of the competing corporate insiders could be sterilized in return, perhaps, for an even greater share of equity.[132] Unless Russia undertakes such a reform, the best it can hope for is a slow and costly transition to a low-value equilibrium in which outsiders are not available to provide public capital.

A primarily procedural approach to reform, which does not rely heavily on court enforcement, goes some way toward creating a viable corporate governance regime.[133] However, we are skeptical that such reforms alone would sufficiently protect outsiders in a way that would make public equity finance possible—even after firms made the transition to management control. Instead, as just suggested, we believe that the problems associated with insider blocks require a more substantive approach that effectively disenfranchises the initial groups of insiders. For example, Bernard Black and Reinier Kraakman sensibly have suggested neutralizing the voting rights of local governments, which make up one of the competing blocks of insiders and which are unlikely to use their rights to maximize shareholder wealth.[134] But the suggestion to sterilize shares of local-government owners applies with equal force to management and labor blocks. Rules allowing only outside shareholders to vote also could be used to take control of the board away from the initial group of insiders, thereby increasing the value of being an outside shareholder. Insiders with a reduced capacity to engage in non–pro rata distributions could focus more on the gains to be made from increased share value if residuals were maximized. Under such a reform, the shares would regain their vote when transferred to genuinely outside hands.

A grand political deal of insider vote sterilization in return for an even greater share of equity is obviously impractical in the environment of today's Russia, in part because, again, no one would trust the results. Policing the independence of outsider shareholders and setting up effective institutions to aggregate their votes is beyond Russian capabilities today.[135] Nonetheless, over time, with the evolution of a somewhat more effective legal system and somewhat greater corporate transparency, insider vote sterilization might represent one mechanism by which Russia could move toward a modern capitalist economy, a mechanism that involves less reliance on these institutions than the bright-line procedural approach that informs the current Russian code. Such a reform basically would involve taking the logic of those reforms one step further. Instead of insiders being partially disenfranchised through disinterested and supermajority votes being required for a wide range of corporate actions, insiders would be disenfranchised entirely. The entire focus of the corporate law system then could be on policing the single question of which supposedly outside shareholders are genuinely independent from management. The incentive for a party to enter the grand political deal would be the potentially large gains that better-governed corporations could produce.

Another possibility along these lines—equally implausible now but perhaps conceivable in the future—would be to create a mechanism that requires payments of dividends when certain benchmarks are met by a firm. Proposals for minimum dividend payments have been floated in the American context but could prove even more useful in the Russian one.[136] Most important, minimum dividend payments by firms with a certain level of assets or revenues could help people come to view shares as financial instruments rather than just as levers for control.[137]

IV. Conclusion

A typology of Russian corporate governance can offer useful lessons for corporate governance theory. The rich array of deviant behavior we canvass in Russia helps flesh out a framework of pathologies that, in a comprehensive way and for the first time, links corporate governance failures to real economic effects. How is this analytic tool useful? It helps give more precision to the often vague notion of corporate governance failures. Scholars write about the costs of poor corporate governance without telling us the mechanisms by which loosely constrained and poorly incentivized managers cause social welfare losses. We suggest that these losses may be inflicted in differing degrees through one of seven distinct pathologies—five types of nonmaximization of residuals and two versions of non–pro rata distributions. Losses that are not inflicted through one of these seven mechanisms cannot be attributed properly to something called "poor corporate governance." More positively, identifying which pathology predominates may help point to more appropriate corporate governance reforms.

The focus of this chapter—explaining what has caused the flowering of Russian corporate pathologies—also may prove useful for corporate governance theory. Not surprisingly, the existing scholarly literature on comparative corporate governance mostly reflects a sliver of experience in the United States, Western Europe, and modern Japan. (Several of the authors in this volume, particularly Mahoney, in chapter 3, and Miwa and Ramseyer, in chapter 6, caution us about universalizing this experience.) In the United States, it is unusual for a corporation to maintain a share ownership pattern over the long term that involves a majority of shares owned by insiders and a minority owned by outsiders who trade their shares publicly. Our understanding of the mechanisms that constrain management to act in relatively share value–maximizing ways—one-share-one-vote; the hostile-takeover threat; share price–based management compensation schemes; board elections; shareholder approval of certain interested and extraordinary transactions; ex post court review; the managerial labor market; and other reputational incentives—is built primarily against the U.S. backdrop because the typical American public corporation forms the paradigm for theorizing.

We suggest that looking at Russia introduces an analytic focus not immediately obvious from studying such long-established systems. Among other things, we see concretely how initial conditions matter for subsequent corporate governance development. The Russian experience suggests two salient initial conditions, uneconomic firm boundaries and competing groups of insider owners, that offer avenues for further research. At a minimum, the bargaining failures that followed privatization provide evidence that counsels skepticism toward the periodic claims of some scholars and activists for including "stakeholders"—such as labor, the local community, and the local government itself—in corporate governance. The Russian experience reminds us, also quite starkly, of the trade-off between the agency costs of management in a publicly held corporation and the disadvantages of lack of access to public equity finance. This trade-off appears in the leveraged buyouts of the late 1980s and the "going private" trend of the early 1970s: firms involved in both movements have tended to go public again at some later point.

More generally, the Russian experience suggests that we rethink how close corporations operate. While there is a well-developed jurisprudence of close corporations in the United States, there is only a modest literature on the economics of such legal relations. Governance of the close corporation traditionally has been viewed by lawyer-economists as a contracting problem among well-informed, well-represented, motivated individuals in which the best policy advice that can be given is to have the law not obstruct the deals these individuals reach with one another.

The bargaining failures that followed privatization in Russia could shed light on our own system by focusing attention on the understudied area of losses from fragmented ownership in close corporations and other special corporate governance arrangements such as those associated with start-up companies backed by venture capital. When competing blocks of insiders exercise their rights so that each blocks the others, corporate assets may be wasted in a "tragedy of the anticommons."[138] If competing blocks of insiders each have incentives to veto share value–maximizing decisions, or if the costs of aggregating and negotiating insider interests to reach such decisions are sufficiently high, then corporate assets may be wasted in low-value uses. In short, the Russian experience counters recent theoretical and empirical research that argues that control by multiple large shareholders may improve firm performance.[139]

The Russian experience of corporate governance is unique. No other place in the world offers such ample and creative corporate governance pathologies, and nowhere else do firms have such strange boundaries and competing insiders so much control. But the lessons that Russia teaches are not parochial at all. Russian enterprise fiascoes improve our basic understanding of how corporate governance works.

Notes

1. *See supra* ch. 4 for a discussion by Black, Kraakman, and Tarassova concerning these factors.

2. *See, e.g.*, Bernard Black & Reinier Kraakman, *A Self-Enforcing Model of Corporate Law*, 109 Harv. L. Rev. 1911, 1915 (1996) (emphasizing similarities among different emerging capitalist economies but characterizing Russia as extreme).

3. *See, e.g., id.*; Melissa Akin, *Stalled Transition*, Moscow Times, Nov. 16, 1999, at 15, 1999 WL 6809815 (discussing release of 1999 European Bank for Reconstruction and Development (EBRD) Transition Report criticizing Russia's economic reforms).

4. *See, e.g.*, Black & Kraakman, *supra* note 2, at 1915; Martin Wolf, *Transition Proves Long and Hard*, Fin. Times (London), Nov.10, 1999, at II (contrasting transition in republics of former Soviet Union with smoother transitions made in Eastern and central Europe and Baltics).

5. *See supra* ch. 4, sec. II.A.

6. Michael A. Heller, *The Tragedy of the Anticommons: Property in the Transition from Marx to Markets*, 111 Harv. L. Rev. 621, 633–59 (1998) (showing how poorly conceived real estate privatization can lead to "tragedy of the anticommons").

7. Interestingly, Black, Kraakman, and Tarassova observe in ch. 4 that in the Czech Republic, minimal corporate and securities regulation was by design: the fervent free-marketeers who dominated the government wanted it that way because they believed the actors could largely govern themselves. *See supra* ch. 4, sec. IV.D.1.

8. *See supra* ch. 7, sec. I.

9. This is the simple model that underlies Coase's seminal 1937 article. *See* Ronald H. Coase, *The Nature of the Firm*, 4 Economica 386 (1937), *reprinted in* R. H. Coase, The Firm, the Market, and the Law 33 (1988). Modern work in transaction cost economics identifies a wide range of governance mechanisms between the two extremes described in the simple model, *see infra* note 114, but the simple model is sufficient to illustrate the important points in the discussion here.

10. *See* Oliver Williamson, *Corporate Governance*, 93 Yale L.J. 1197, 1200 (1984).

11. For representative work, *see* Oliver E. Williamson, The Economic Institutions of Capitalism (1985) (applying transaction cost economics to various economic institutions); Benjamin Klein et al., *Vertical Integration, Appropriable Rents, and the Competitive Contracting Process*, 21 J.L. & Econ. 297 (1978) (discussing postcontractual opportunistic behavior as impetus for intrafirm contracting). Oliver Hart's "property rights" approach further explains the forces that define firm boundaries in a competitive economy. Hart builds on the transaction costs approach by exploring in more detail exactly what changes when the same transaction occurs within a firm instead of between firms. *See* Oliver Hart, Firms, Contracts, and Financial Structure 13–91 (1995).

12. Putting issues of market power aside, there is in any given industry an optimal firm size that involves a trade-off between scale economies (to the extent that they exist) and the managerial incentive problems that tend to grow with firm size. *See* Hart, *supra* note 11, at 51.

13. *See* Stephanie Baker-Said, *Steel Mill Begins Crawl to Productivity*, Moscow Times, July 2, 1997, in Lexis, News Library, Mostms file; *see also* Neela Banerjee, *Russian Firm Controls Elections, Profits by Buying City's Media*, Dallas Morning News, June 15, 1997, at 16A ("Almost everyone works for the steelmaker or has a relative who does").

14. Baker-Said, *supra* note 13.

15. Patrick Ninneman, *Growth in China and India; Turmoil in Russia*, New Steel, Aug. 1997, at 76, 77 (reporting on discussion of vast employment rolls of Russian steel company at 1997 Steel Survival Strategies conference).

16. According to one firm analyst, "'Severstal does not have a track record of either cheating investors or treating them fairly. . . . They are not interested in the capital markets, but at the same time they don't engage in share issues or transfer pricing to the extent that other companies do.'" Brian Humphreys, *State to Sell 10% Stake in Northern Steel Giant*, Moscow Times, May 12, 1999, at 11, 1999 WL 6807252 (quoting metals analyst Kakha Kiknavelidze).

17. *Id.*

18. *Id.*

19. *Id.*

20. The insiders may secure absolute control, not just of the firm, but also of the surrounding governments. The firm's odd boundaries make it particularly vulnerable to political depredations by local and regional governments. Rather than restructure, Severstal has defended itself by buying all of the newspapers and radio and television stations in the region, even though they are for the most part unprofitable. *See* Banerjee, *supra* note 13, at 16A. These captive media then backed company-sponsored candidates who captured all of the city's elected positions and then "voted to cut Severstal's property taxes retroactively for all of 1996, despite budget shortfalls. The decision saved the company several million dollars in taxes." *Id.*

21. As Blasi, Kroumova, and Kruse recount: "The Russian general director is similar in authority to the chief executive officer (CEO) of a capitalist company. . . . In the past, a Soviet ministry could hire and fire him. Once Gorbachev removed cabinet supervision from the top managers of [the general director's] plant, the only formal authority over his enterprise was a distant state bureaucracy that was spinning out of control, and the now independent, authoritarian [general director] could do what he pleased. [The general director] was probably tempted to treat the company as his personal property. This process has been called spontaneous privatization." Joseph R. Blasi, Kroumova, & Kruse, Kremlin Capitalism: The Privatization of the Russian Economy 33 (1997).

22. *See id.* at 40.

23. *See id.*

24. *See id.*

25. *See id.* at 91.

26. *See, e.g., id.* (stating that trade union officials were sometimes kept on board of directors for "window dressing," and describing instance of silent intimidation by managers); *see also* Natasha Mileusnic, *The Great Boardroom Revolution*, Moscow Times, July 16, 1996, at I (describing how Russian company directors "intimidate employees who side with" foreign investors).

27. *See* Blasi, Kroumova, & Kruse, *supra* note 21, at 192 table 3 (discussing slight discrepancies in number of firms privatized and citing sources); World Bank, World Development Report 1996: From Plan to Market 55 (1996) (estimating that insiders acquired around two-thirds of shares in fifteen thousand privatized firms).

28. Roman Frydman et al., *Investing in Insider-Dominated Firms: A Study of Russian Voucher Privatization Funds*, in 1 Corporate Governance in Central Europe and Russia 187, 189 (Roman Frydman et al., eds., 1996).

29. In 1988, medium (more than two hundred employees) and large (more than one thousand employees) enterprises accounted for about 95 percent of employees and production in Russia. *See* Blasi, Kroumova, & Kruse, *supra* note 21, at 25.

30. In 1995, a few large, rich firms, such as oil and gas companies, were privatized through a controversial "shares for loans" program that handed shares over to a number of financial-industrial groups controlled by new private tycoons. *See infra* text accompanying notes 118–20 (discussing "shares-for-loans" scheme).

31. *See* Blasi, Kroumova, & Kruse, *supra* note 21, at 25–26. The totals now are higher: 4600 mainly small and medium enterprises underwent some form of privatization in 1996. *See* EBRD, Transition Report 1997, at 195 (1997).

32. World Bank, *supra* note 27, at 55. Insiders had several privatization options. About one-quarter of enterprises chose option 1, which gave minority employee ownership for free. About three-quarters of firms chose option 2, which allowed managers and workers to acquire 51 percent of the firm for extremely low prices (and therefore to take formal control of the firm). A third option attracted only 2 percent. This option allowed a management buyout on the promise of reaching particular restructuring targets. *See* Blasi, Kroumova, & Kruse, *supra* note 21, at 41 (describing three plans for transfer of shares at privatization, each of which transferred "40 to 51 percent of ownership to managers and employees").

33. *See* Frydman et al., *supra* note 28, at 189; World Bank, *supra* note 27, at 55.

34. *See* Poul Funder Larsen, *Buying Land Is Next Hurdle for Private Firms*, Moscow Times, Nov. 26, 1996, at III ("Many companies seeking to get a clearer title to their land still face stiff resistance from regional authorities who see land ownership as a source of power in dealing with local enterprises"). This is reported to be a declining problem in the big cities but is still serious in the rest of the country.

35. *See supra* ch. 7, sec. III.D.

36. Peter Galuszka & Patricia Kranz, *Look Who's Making a Revolution: Shareholders*, Bus. Wk., Feb. 20, 1995, at 60 ("New tricks . . . range from diluting the ownership stake of investors to such simple ploys as erasing the names of outside investors from computerized shareholder lists"); Carole Landry, *Russia's Communist Bosses Are On the Way Out*, Agence France-Presse, Dec. 15, 1994, 1994 WL 9647596 ("Old-guard managers, who supported privatisation in exchange for assurances they would keep their jobs and full array of perks, are desperately fighting back. Some managers physically threaten challengers at shareholder meetings, rig shareholder votes or illegally change corporate charters" (citing Prof. Andrei Shleifer and Dmitry Vasilyev)).

37. *See* Elizabeth V. Mooney, *Russia Must Implement Tax, Corporate Governance Reforms*, RCR Radio Comm. Rep., Feb. 28, 2000, at 26, 2000 WL 9540310 (noting that, according to one analysis, "'there is a need for transparency and disclosure because accurate information is hard to come by. Companies frequently hold their shareholder meetings in remote places like Siberia'" (quoting Lee Wolosky)).

38. Roman Frydman, et al., *supra* note 28, at 187.

39. A reporter notes: "Most Russian enterprises are still run by red directors—former communists who stack their boards with old-regime subordinates or cronies, bully workers into selling their shares back to management, and deny outside shareholders access to their books, boardrooms, and shop floors. Many consolidate control of their companies by issuing large blocks of new shares to company insiders,

often at bargain-basement prices." Patricia Kranz, *Shareholders at the Gate*, Bus. Wk. (Int'l ed.), June 2, 1997, at 60, 1997 WL 8270209.

40. A reporter notes:

> If [directors] see outside shareholders trying to get hold of their company, these managers often shout down their proposals at meetings, intimidate employees who side with them and hold tight to the board—which is often still considered a Soviet-era workers' council.
>
> Most employee shareholders, . . . are still passive and exert little influence over corporate governance because they are underrepresented on company boards. (Natasha Mileusnic, *The Great Boardroom Revolution*, Moscow Times, July 16, 1996, at I)

41. *See, e.g.*, Blasi, Kroumova, & Kruse, *supra* note 21, at 147 (describing stockholders' meeting where workers used their votes to prevent holding company from gaining influence in Lebedinsk Ore Processing Company).

42. *See id.* at 135, 147.

43. *See* World Bank, *supra* note 27, at 55.

44. *See* Blasi, Kroumova, & Kruse, *supra* note 21, at 99.

45. *See id.*

46. *See id.* at 98 (describing provisions of 1996 corporate law); Black & Kraakman, *supra* note 2, at 1924 (describing problem of entrenched insider control).

47. *See* Blasi, Kroumova, & Kruse, *supra* note 21, at 99 (describing details of cumulative voting law).

48. *See id.* at 99. But *see id.* at 148 ("Most of the companies do not . . . use cumulative voting, and the number of blockholders' seats on the board does not reflect the size of their ownership stakes"); *id.* at 201 table 9 (indicating that 39 percent of companies used cumulative voting in 1996).

49. *See* Frydman et. al., *supra* note 28, at 214–18.

50. While new bills keep being introduced to close loopholes, they do not appear to be effective. Thus, "[c]ritics said the legislation fails to attack the real problem—insider dealing—and doubt anything but better information disclosure requirements and an understanding of basic ethics will help the situation. In Russia, company directors and managers are routinely accused of insider dealing, which includes everything from accepting bribes to act against their company's interests to selling assets or shares to relatives or friends." Katy Daigle, *Bill Improves Shareholder Rights in Russia*, Moscow Times, July 14, 1998, Lexis, World Library, Mostms file. Insider dealing is not limited to management, but also includes deals in favor of local governments and labor. *See, e.g.*, Stephanie Baker-Said, *Watchdog Gives Nod to MGTS Floatation*, Moscow Times, Apr. 22, 1998, available in Lexis, News Library, Mostms file ("Moscow City Telephone Network, or MGTS, is planning to increase its authorized capital by 50 percent, handing the shares over to a single shareholder linked to the Moscow city government for next to nothing").

51. Professor Coffee, in chap. 7, finds this view to be be prevalent wherever privatization occurs in the absence of established, well-regulated securities markets. *See supra* ch. 7, sec. I. Russia, however, has the additional dysfunction that arises from the mutual blocking by multiple groups each possessing concentrated power.

52. In Moscow, "this cozy relationship is multiplied a thousand times. According to many business people, [Moscow mayor] Luzhkov used property as leverage. The

property was leased for a nominal sum, but the city also made unwritten demands not in the lease: to plant trees, rebuild a hospital, pave a highway." David Hoffman, *The Man Who Rebuilt Moscow: Capitalist Style Could Propel Mayor to National Power*, Wash. Post, Feb. 24, 1997, at A1.

53. One reporter notes: "The reluctance of many directors to use the stock market to their benefit is a paradox: After all, an overwhelming majority of directors managed to grab sizable portions of equity in their companies during the wild privatization years of 1993 to 1994, usually by buying out swathes of shares with the help of cheap bank loans through a highly abused process known as closed subscription. Were directors to understand the virtue of shareholder value, they could help make themselves even richer." See Gary Peach, *1997 an Outstanding Year Despite Market Narrowness*, Moscow Times, Jan. 13, 1998, Lexis, World Library, Mostms File.

54. *Neither CEOs nor Red Directors: The Managers of Russia's Privatized Industrial Firms*, Russia Express Briefing, Dec. 9, 1996, 1996 WL 8619171.

55. Commenting on the aluminum smelting industry, one reporter suggests: "Since they aren't now looking to attract capital through share issues, the companies' directors are not concerned about plummeting stock prices, and don't really care what the market thinks about them. Aluminum shares last traded actively in 1994 and 1995, when various insiders were trying to establish control of smelters during the privatization process." *See* Elizabeth V. Mooney, *Russia Must Implement Tax, Corporate Governance Reforms*, RCR Radio Comm. Rep., Feb. 28, 2000, 1t 26, 2000 WL 9540310.

56. *Cf.* Stefan Wagstyl, *Region's Financial Transparency Uneven: Corporate Governance*, Fin. Times (London), Sept. 24, 1999, World Economy & Finance, at 28 (stating: "A critical role is played in the economy by laws affecting pledges, bankruptcy and company formation because these protect the position of creditors and outside shareholders vis-a-vis majority shareholders and/or managers. In virtually every country in the region, there are complaints about securing redress under pledge, mortgage and bankruptcy laws. A common concern is about the effectiveness of courts to produce rapid judgments. Justice delayed is often justice denied").

57. According to the 1997 EBRD Transition Report: "In over 65% of Russia's 18,000 privatised medium-sized and large firms management and employees have majority ownership, whereas non-state outsiders control only 20% of these companies. While in the top 100 largest companies outsiders have an ownership stake well above the average, the wide dispersion of these shareholdings often ensures a controlling position for the management. Insiders typically focus more on maintaining control over their firms than on restructuring." EBRD, *supra* note 31, at 195.

58. *See supra* ch. 8, secs. I, II.

59. *See, e.g.*, World Bank, *supra* note 27, at 100 box 6.1 (describing Russian banking reform in the 1980s and 1990s). Professor Coffee points out in chap. 7 the importance of good securities law in this regard: better-regulated Polish securities markets have been able to support IPOs but the poorly regulated Czech ones have not. *See supra* ch. 7, sec. III.C.

60. *See* EBRD, *supra* note 31, at 195 ("The main source of the expansion of the private sector remains the privatisation process and the contraction of the state sector. . . . The creation of de novo businesses continues to lag far behind the pace typ-

ical for the central European countries and many newly established businesses continue to operate in the informal economy").

61. According to the 1997 EBRD *Transition Report*:

> Enterprise restructuring has hitherto been achieved mainly through changes in the product mix, shedding of labour through attrition, expanded use of unpaid leave or reduced hours. Deeper restructuring in the form of factory shutdowns, changes in management, major reorganisations and modernisation is at a very early stage and is constrained by, among other factors, limited access to investment resources. Recent evidence suggests that roughly 25% of the medium-sized and large companies are engaged in serious restructuring, many of them being members of Financial and Industrial Groups (FIGs). About half of the medium-sized and large companies have not as yet undertaken any meaningful restructuring. (*Id*).

62. *See, e.g.*, Maura Reynolds, *A Russian Company Town's Miracle*, L.A. Times, Mar. 5, 1999, at A1. (describing a company that continues to operate despite consistent net losses, and noting that such businesses are not considered bankrupt in Russia); see also *supra* sec. I.B.1 (giving examples of value-destroying firms).

63. *See* Roman Frydman et al., The Privatization Process in Russia, Ukraine, and the Baltic States 71–74 (1993) (describing slow development of land markets in Russia, which has resulted in part from a ten-year moratorium on alienation of land, established in 1991).

64. *See supra* ch. 1, sec. I.B.2 (giving examples of firms exhibiting Pathology 2).

65. *See, e.g.*, Simon Clarke & Veronika Kabalina, *Privatisation and the Struggle for Control of the Enterprise*, *in* Russia in Transition: Politics, Privatisation, and Inequality 142, 151–52 (David Lane ed., 1995) (suggesting that managers' own stake should motivate them to maximize company prosperity but identifying rent-seeking and short-term goals as factors that may temper incentive to maximize company profits).

66. *See supra* ch. 1, sec. I.B.3 (giving examples).

67. *See supra* note 32 and accompanying text.

68. *See, e.g.*, Milica Uvalic & Daniel Vaughan-Whitehead, *Introduction: Creating Employee Capitalism in Central and Eastern Europe*, *in* Privatization Surprises in Transition Economies 1, 23 (Milica Uvalic & Daniel Vaughan-Whitehead eds., 1997) (offering reasons why employees' stakes do not solve problems of control and inefficiency).

69. Irrationality may be a problem here too. In one odd report, "'one company director who owned over 51 percent of a company . . . took personal bribes of about $10,000 to push through decisions that robbed the company of millions. Obviously, this man doesn't understand what he's doing.'" Daigle, *supra* note 50 (quoting Konstantin Kontor).

70. *See* Frank H. Easterbrook & Daniel R. Fischel, The Economic Structure of Corporate Law 230–31 (1991) (explaining how illiquid market in shares provides investors with less information and with less ability to sell quickly without sacrificing price, both of which decrease their willingness to invest).

71. *See* Bengt Holmström & Jean Tirole, *Market Liquidity and Performance Monitoring*, 101 J. Pol. Econ. 678, 679 (1993) (explaining that "a firm's ownership structure influences the value of market monitoring").

72. Black, Kraakman, & Tarassova, in ch. 4, attempt to explain the failure of Rus-

sian firms to maximize residuals without reference to, or explanation of, this bargaining failure by the three control groups. *See supra* ch. 4, sec. III.A. One explanation they suggest is confiscatory corporate tax rates. This appears to be an application of the more general principle that income taxes create inefficiency-inducing distortions and, at very high rates, can lead to large losses in efficiency. We agree that residual maximization will be deterred if, to avoid taxes, cash flows must be extracted from the firm before they are counted as earnings. Their other two primary explanations are less persuasive to us, however. One explanation starts with the assumption that there is some kind of trade-off between engaging in non–pro rata distributions and maximizing residuals. They contend that, if firm profitability would be low even if the firm were run optimally, as with most Russian firms, then the opportunity cost of engaging in non–pro rata distributions is lower and more will occur. This proposition, however, ignores the likelihood that in such a situation, the value of the assets to be stripped will be correspondingly less as well. The second explanation relates to the separation between control and cash flow. They suggest when less of a firm's stock is owned by a control party, the control party can externalize more of the failure to maximize residuals. Also, the less the control part's shareownership the less non–pro rata distributions are just taking money from one pocket of the control parts and putting it into another. The problem with this explanation is that in Russia when the three control groups are put together (which, absent a bargaining failure, they would be) their shares constitute claims for a large portion of the firm's total cash flow and so there is in fact not much separation of control from cash flow.

73. *See* Mark Whitehouse, Slow Death, Moscow Times, June 16, 1998, *in* Lexis, Work Library, Mostms file. (noting adverse effect of insider deals on financial health of AvtoVAZ).

74. *See* Bogdan Lissovolik, *Rapid Spread of Employee Ownership in the Privatized Russia*, *in* Privatization Surprises in Transition Economies, *supra* note 68, at 204, 223–24 (suggesting that managers maintain overemployment levels so they will receive government subsidies).

75. The reader may raise two questions here. The first is that the failure of insiders to come to these deals may be related intimately to the delay because the insiders may have very high rates of time discount, and hence receiving benefits now is preferred to receiving larger benefits later. The answer to this, however, is that the Coasian bargain that we are contemplating already takes such discounts into account. Efficient operation of the firm contemplates that the residuals be discounted to present value.

The second question concerns whether an insider could avoid the delay problem by selling her shares to others. But this does not make the problems associated with delay go away; the buyer instead must suffer them. If delay also implies uncertainty about whether the gain will ever in fact be received, the buyer will pay commensurately less for the shares, and so in this regard, the insider is just as badly off as he or she would be had he or she held on to the shares.

76. *See* Chong Ju Choi et al., *A Note on Countertrade: Contractual Uncertainty and Transaction Governance in Emerging Economies*, 30 J. Int'l Bus. Stud. 189, 195 (1999) (describing most effective enforcement mechanism for promises with different ex ante conditions).

77. *See* Federal Law on Joint Stock Companies, Federal Law No. 208-FZ, art.

71(1) (Russ.) (Bernard S. Black & Anna S. Tarrassova trans., 1997), *reprinted in* Bernard S. Black et al., Guide to the Russian Law on Joint Stock Companies III-1, III-59 (1998).

78. *See, e.g.*, Model Bus. Corp. Act Ann. 8.30(a) (Supp. 1998–99) (offering model statute that imposes obligations on directors to act "in good faith, and . . . in a manner the director reasonably believes to be in the best interests of the corporation"); *see also id.* commentary at 8–178 (noting that majority of jurisdictions have adopted version of model statute).

79. *See* William L. Cary & Melvin Aron Eisenberg, Cases and Materials on Corporations 689–700 (7th ed. 1995) (collecting cases in which executive compensation was challenged but noting difficulties of prevailing in such challenges).

80. *See id.* at 673 (noting that self-interested transactions in which corporations deal with management must be "on fair terms" and "in the corporation's interest").

81. *See* Federal Law No. 208-FZ, art. 71(1), (5), *reprinted in* Black et al., supra note 77, at III-59 to III-60 (providing for suits by company or shareholders against directors and management for negligent actions). The Russian joint stock company law makes no provision for shareholders to receive injunctive relief against management. *See id.*

82. *See, e.g.*, Elizabeth V. Mooney, *Russia Must Implement Tax, Corporate Governance Reforms*, RCR Radio Comm. Rep., Feb. 28, 2000, at 26 2000 WL 9540310 (stating that "'transfer pricing already is against the law in Russia. However, it is an example of a larger problem. The body of law is not that bad, but it lacks reliable means of enforcement, legal systems, regulatory regimes'" [quoting Lee Wolosky]).

83. Black & Kraakman, *supra* note 2, at 1914.

84. *See id.* at 1915–16.

85. *See* Federal Law No. 208-FZ, art. 83, *reprinted in* Black et al., *supra* note 77, at III-69 to III-70 (requiring that some transactions by interested directors be approved by majority of noninterested directors or by shareholders).

86. *See id.* arts. 78–79, *reprinted in* Black et al., *supra* note 77, at III-66 to III-67 (requiring approval by all directors or by three-fourths majority of shareholders to conduct certain "major transactions").

87. *See, e.g.*, Black & Kraakman, *supra* note 2, at 1916 (describing model corporate governance rules that incorporate "bright-line rules" easily enforced by judges).

88. *See id.* at 1918 (noting that "there are limits to what a self-enforcing corporate law can accomplish").

89. In theory, interested persons are required to disclose this information to the company's board, inspector, and auditors. *See* Federal Law No. 208-FZ, art. 82, *reprinted in* Black et al., *supra* note 77, at III-68 to III-69. However, there is no obvious incentive for such persons to comply with this provision. Even if they do, it is not clear that the information would become available to anyone who, possessing it, might act to challenge the transaction for lack of compliance with the approval procedures. It was the experience of the authors, in connection with an interested transaction involving one of Russia's largest oil companies, that this information was not available, either because the insiders did not comply with Article 82 or because the company did not make the information public. See supra notes 85–88 and accompanying text (discussing Sidanko).

Also, as Professor Coffee points out in chapter 7, shareholder approval requirements cannot stop self-dealing if outside shareholders do not know of the existence of the self-dealing transaction in the first place. *See supra* ch. 7, sec. V.C.2.

90. It was also the experience of the authors in connection with a Sidanko transaction that the public records of the directors' meeting and the shareholders' meeting at which an interested transaction was approved did not reveal who voted for and against the transaction.

91. *See* Choi et al., *supra* note 76, at 192 ("The value of a reputation for fair trading, not restricted by any legal requirement other than sanctions of social nature, provides the basis for confidence in future performance, promotes cooperation, and thus creates networks and clusters of relational or implicit contracts"); Ronald Dore, *Goodwill and the Spirit of Market Capitalism*, 34 Brit. J. Soc. 459, 463–64 (1983) (discussing obligated relational contracting in Japan).

92. *See* Roger C. Vergin & M. W. Qoronfleh, *Corporate Reputation and the Stock Market*, Bus. Horizons, Jan.–Feb. 1998, at 19, 25 (noting that positive corporate reputation increases corporations ability to "obtain[ ] capital more easily and at better rates"). Vergin and Qoronfleh also note that prior financial performance, including ten-year annual return to shareholders, is a critical determinant of corporate reputation. *See id.* at 22.

93. *See generally* Ronald J. Mann, *Verification Institutions in Financing Transactions*, 87 Geo. L.J. 2225 (1999).

94. *See* Choi et al., *supra* note 76, at 199 ("Where neither contracts nor trust provide a viable institutional force of enforcement, hostages can impose mutual commitment in an interlinked or reciprocal fashion. We have argued that trust, contracts and hostages are seen as alternative mechanisms of exchange"); *see also id.* at 194 (describing countertrade, buyback, and production sharing agreements as hostage-taking approaches, in which one party pays for asset that remains in control of other party); Dalia Marin & Monika Schnitzer, *Tying Trade Flows: A Theory of Countertrade with Evidence*, 85 Am. Econ. Rev. 1047, 1049 (1995) (describing countertrade agreements with assets as hostages).

95. *See* John Thornhill, *Russian Unions Struggling for Their Workers' Trust*, Fin. Post (Toronto), Oct. 26, 1995, *available in* Lexis, World Library, Natpst file, noting:

> A recent nationwide survey of 2,000 Russians by the University of Strathclyde in Scotland revealed widespread distrust of trade union representatives. Only 16% of the respondents who were trade union members said they trusted their national leaders to look after their interests. . . .
>
> On paper, at least, the official trade union movement has a strong base from which to begin the reconstruction. . . .
>
> But the report concluded this strength was largely illusory, given the official unions' compromised past and the slowness of its leaders to adapt to new circumstances).

96. *See* Choi et al., *supra* note 76, at 191 (noting that enforcement costs, including measurement costs, are principal barriers to Coasian bargaining, especially in international context where "the level of complexity and uncertainty tends to be particularly severe").

97. For example, consider the following account:

> [A] barrier to action by outsiders is the information vacuum that prevails

in many insider-held companies. They all try to look poor. The only real books are in the director's safe, or his head. It's hard even to know which firms are worth taking over. Once a successful bid is made, one Russian consultant described the takeover itself in virtually military terms: Advance spies must learn which safes and computers hold the key files. On takeover day, armed guards must secure all of these within minutes or the data, and the cash behind them, will simply vanish. All physical assets must be nailed down or nothing will be left but an empty shell. These are little details foreign investors don't always understand, noted the consultant. (Edwin Dolan, *Resisting Shock of New*, Moscow Times, Apr. 8, 1997, at 10)

98. *See supra* ch. 1, secs. I.B.2, I.B.3.

99. *See supra* ch. 1, sec. I.B.3.

100. *See supra* ch. 1, sec. I.B.1.

101. *See, e.g.*, Reynolds, *supra* note 62, at A1 (describing Russian engine factory with large losses and quoting analyst stating that continued operation of factory "makes no sense" in "economic terms" (quoting factory director Boris N. Peshkov)); James Surowiecki, *Why Won't Anyone Pull the Plug on UPN?* New Yorker, Apr. 3, 2000, at 32 (providing examples of firms exhibiting Pathology 1).

102. *See* Poul Funder Larsen, *Buying Land Is Next Hurdle for Private Firms*, Moscow Times, Nov. 26, 1996, at III ("Most of Russia's . . . privatized firms . . . do not even have a clear lease agreement. Instead . . . city officials [have] a big say in how the land is used and . . . companies [have] few rights to sublet, sell or redevelop").

103. *See supra* ch. 1, sec. I.B.1.a (discussing relationship of corporate governance and other factors to when value-destroying firms close).

104. *See supra* ch. 1, secs. I.B.4, I.B.5. Outside shareholder pressure is no help here. *See* Andrew Jack, *Pouring Oil on Troubled Waters*, Fin. Times (London), Jan. 19, 2000, at 21 ("Profitable companies do exist within the country, even if they prefer to keep a low profile to avoid unnecessary attention from the tax authorities or extortion gangs. But with less than a 51 per cent stake in a business, an investor has no influence in how it is run").

105. Where insiders did not start out with unassailable majority control, they still had working control, which they often later used to attain majority status. This was frequently accomplished through discounted sales to affiliates. *See* Mooney, *supra* note 82 ("Lack of evenhanded treatment in the private sales of corporate securities is another roadblock to outside investment. . . . 'Companies often sell securities in private placements at below-market prices to participants in subsidiaries of the issuer'" (quoting Lee Wolosky)).

106. *See* Bernard S. Black, *Shareholder Passivity Reexamined*, 89 Mich. L. Rev. 520, 526–28 (1990) (noting that rarity of successful proxy contests, difficulty for shareholders to become informed, and relatively small gains to be derived from action lead most shareholders to choose "rational apathy" in voting); Dale A. Oesterle & Alan R. Palmiter, *Judicial Schizophrenia in Shareholder Voting Cases*, 79 Iowa L. Rev. 485, 486–87 (1994) (highlighting "ineffectiveness of shareholder voting as a control device").

107. *See* Jeanne Whalen, *FSC's Vasiliyev Soldiers On Amid Dismissal Rumors*, Moscow Times, Dec. 5, 1998, 1998 WL 11691750 (noting proposed "amendments to close loopholes in the Law on Joint Stock Companies and a draft Law on Affiliated Persons that would closely regulate the actions of majority shareholders").

108. *See, e.g.*, Lewis D. Solomon et al., Corporations Law and Policy 748 (4th ed. 1998).

109. Professor Coffee suggests in ch. 7 that, at least in theory, the inability of transition country courts to sort out which self-dealing transactions are and are not beneficial to the corporation could be solved by simply prohibiting all self-dealing transactions—the way U.S. law did in the late 19th century at a similar point in our development. *See supra* ch. 7, sec. V.A.1. Coffee acknowledges, however, that this solution would pose serious problems given the important role played in transition economies by affiliated groups and suggests instead that members of affiliated groups be kept off the high quality exchange.

110. *See, e.g., supra* text accompanying notes 60–64 (discussing Segezhabumprom).

111. *See supra* ch. 4, sec. I.

112. *Id. See also* ch. 4.

113. For example, consider Baltika Brewing. "Business has boomed thanks to a steady stream of foreign investment, effective marketing and a good management team." John Varoli, *Baltika Plans to Boost Output 250%*, Moscow Times, Apr. 22, 1999, 1999 WL 6807006. The firm has been implementing a large capital investment program using its own reserves as financing, has secured outside credit, and has been one of the few firms in Russia to pay dividends. One element in the firm's success and credibility on international financial markets has been firm oversight by a Scandinavian brewing group that holds 70 percent of Baltika's shares. See *id.*

114. *See* Vladimir Popov, *The Financial System in Russia Compared to Other Transition Economies: The Anglo-American versus the German-Japanese Model*, 49 Comp. Econ. Study 1, 27 (1999), stating: "In the largest and most attractive Russian companies with high market liquidity, outside investors by now own more shares than workers and managers, and this pattern is likely to emerge in other companies, whose shares are not yet traded in the market and which are still controlled by work collectives. While in the large, but not the largest, privatised Russian companies outsiders owned in 1996 only 31% of shares, with 59% of shares belonging to insiders and 9% to the state, in the 100 largest Russian companies outsiders owned on average 57% of all shares (insiders—22%, the state—21%").

Popov's data highlight this problem. He notes that most successful Russian firms are also majority owned by outsiders. *See id.* at 23. It is unclear, however, which way the causation runs.

115. *See* Jack, *supra* note 104, at 21 ("From now on, . . . new investment will require the strengthening of the rights of minority shareholders, enhancements to international auditing and accounting standards, and a better tax regime").

116. A "portfolio investment" in an issuer is an investment in an amount constituting a sufficiently small percentage of the issuer that it is easily liquidated and causes no control significance.

117. *See* Timothy O'Brien, *The Shrinking Oligarchs of Russia*, N.Y. Times, Sept. 27, 1998, 3, at 1; *see also* Patricia Kranz, *Fall of an Oligarch*, Bus. Wk., Mar. 1, 1999, at 44, 45 (listing all seven oligarchs).

118. *See* David Fairlamb, *Reining in the Oligarchs*, Institutional Investor, Nov. 1998, at 146, 148 (explaining shares-for-loans scheme).

119. *See* Daniel Treisman, *Blaming Russia First: Three Books Examine Russia's Woes*, Foreign Aff., Nov.–Dec. 2000, at 146, 151 (book review).

120. O'Brien, *supra* note 117, 3, at 1.

121. *See* Fairlamb, *supra* note 118, at 147.

122. *Id.*

123. *Id.* at 150 (alteration in original).

124. *See id.* at 154 (noting lack of evidence that new investors would manage oligarchs' former assets any better).

125. *See generally* Ronald J. Gilson & Mark J. Roe, *Understanding the Japanese Keiretsu: Overlaps between Corporate Governance and Industrial Organization*, 102 Yale L.J. 871, 872 (1993) (asserting that Japanese system, featuring investment overlaps between banks and industry, harmonizes corporate relationships and "facilitates productive efficiency"); Mark D. West, *Information, Institutions, and Extortion in Japan and the United States: Making Sense of Sokaiya Racketeers*, 93 Nw. U.L. Rev. 767, 797 (1999) (noting similarity between Korean chaebol and Japanese keiretsu).

126. *See* Oliver Williamson, *Corporate Governance*, 93 Yale L.J. 1197, 1225–26 (1984) (describing beneficial effects of M-form enterprise on monitoring and capital allocation).

127. Fairlamb, *supra* note 118, at 150 (summarizing oligarchs' arguments).

128. *Id.*

129. *See* Poul Funder Larsen, *1996: The Year Big Business Became the State*, Moscow Times, Jan. 5, 1997, at 1.

130. *Id.* (quoting Anders Aslund) (alteration in original).

131. O'Brien, *supra* note 117, 3, at 1 (quoting Andrei Piontkovsky, director, Center for Strategic Studies, Moscow). The usual routine was for the FIG banks to make loans to captive borrowers, and once those loans were disbursed, secretly to channel the funds directly into the bankers' private offshore accounts. *See id.* "It would have been O.K. if these loans were made on an arms-length basis. But they weren't. . . . When some banks made loans they didn't specify interest rates or even when the loans had to be paid back." *Id.* (quoting financial analyst requesting anonymity). In short, "the oligarchs' idea of shareholder value is to asset-strip the companies they control and shunt the money offshore." Fairlamb, *supra* note 118, at 150–52. Boris Nemtsov, a former deputy prime minister and key reform politician, attributes the failure of reform generally to the role of the FIGs. He says: "'The reason for this crisis is that after seven years of trying to build a market economy, we've ended up with oligarchic capitalism. . . . It is characterized by the fact that a few FIGs, which, incidentally, work very inefficiently and are managed by greedy managers whose main aim is to pump money out of their enterprises and stockpile it abroad, produce the lion's share of GDP.'" (*Id.* at 152)

132. This recommendation seems consistent with Professor Coffee's recommendation in ch. 7 that there needs to be more emphasis on protection of dispersed shareholders from exploitation by management, rather than assuming that management can be controlled by the board. *See supra* ch. 7, sec. V.A.2.

133. *See* Black & Kraakman, *supra* note 2, at 1932–37 (describing essential features and advantages of "self-enforcing" model).

134. *See id.* at 1971. Black and Kraakman write: "Because we are skeptical about

whether local officials will behave as responsible shareholders, we favor neutralizing government shares in the election of boards of directors: state bodies should neither nominate nor vote for candidates for the board of directors, although they should retain authority to vote on potentially company-transforming actions such as mergers and charter amendments." (*Id.*)

135. *See, e.g.*, *id.* at 1914.

136. *See* Merritt B. Fox, Finance and Industrial Performance in a Dynamic Economy: Theory, Practice, and Policy 375–402 (1986) (describing advantages and drawbacks of rule requiring dividend payments). Other markets experiencing corporate governance problems are contemplating minimum dividend payments. *See, e.g.*, Long Hui Ching, *Private Firms Should Also Practise Good Governance*, New Straits Times (Malaysia), June 7, 1999, 1999 WL 7466714 (reporting suggestion that Malaysian government study possibility of adopting minimum dividend payments).

137. *See* Fox, *supra* note 136, at 375–402 (explaining that minimum dividend payments may encourage shareholders to see shares as long-term investment opportunities).

138. *See* Heller, *supra* note 6, at 622–26 (describing such tragedy in allocation of property rights in postcommunist Russia).

139. *See* Armando Gomes & Walter Novaes, *Multiple Large Shareholders in Corporate Governance* (1999) (draft), available at ⟨http://finance.wharton.upenn.edu/gomes/MLS.pdf⟩ (arguing that maximally efficient corporate structure consists of multiple large controlling shareholders together with some noncontrolling shareholders); David Kang, *The Internal Control of Organizations: How Large-Block Ownership by Insiders Leads to Increased Firm Performance* (1998) (unpublished manuscript on file with authors) (abstract available at ⟨http://papers.ssrn.com/paper.taf?ABSTRACTID=10576⟩) (presenting evidence for superior performance of insider-owned firms in textile industry).

List of Contributors

Bernard S. Black is the Hayden W. Head Regents Chair for Faculty Excellence and Professor of Law at University of Texas Law School and Professor of Finance at University of Texas's McCombs School of Business.

John C. Coffee, Jr., is the Adolf A. Berle Professor of Law at Columbia Law School.

Merritt B. Fox is the Michael E. Patterson Professor of Law at Columbia Law School and Codirector of the school's Center for Law and Economic Studies.

Roman Frydman is Professor of Economics at New York University.

Michael A. Heller is Vice Dean and Lawrence A. Wien Professor of Real Estate Law at Columbia Law School.

Marek Hessel was Associate Professor of Management at Fordham University's Graduate School of Business.

Reinier H. Kraakman is the Ezra Ripley Thayer Professor of Law at Harvard Law School.

Paul G. Mahoney is the Brokaw Professor of Corporate Law and the Albert C. BeVier Research Professor at University of Virginia School of Law.

Yoshiro Miwa is Professor of Economics at the University of Tokyo.

Randall Morck is the Stephen A. Jarislowsky Distinguished Chair in Finance at the University of Alberta.

Katharina Pistor is Professor of Law at Columbia Law School.

J. Mark Ramseyer is the Mitsubishi Professor of Japanese Legal Studies at Harvard Law School.

Andrzej Rapaczynski is the Daniel G. Ross Professor of Law at Columbia Law School.

Anna S. Tarassova is a Russian lawyer who from 1993 to 1994 was a senior legal advisor to the Russian Privatization Ministry.

Bernard Yeung is the Abraham Krasnoff Professor in Global Business, Professor in Economics, and Professor in Management at New York University Stern School of Business.

Wayne W. Yu is Associate Professor of Accounting and Finance at Hong Kong Polytechnic University.

Index